From Rebellion to Riots

From Rebellion to Riots

Collective Violence on Indonesian Borneo

Jamie S. Davidson

THE UNIVERSITY OF WISCONSIN PRESS

This book was published with the support of
the Center for Southeast Asian Studies at
the University of Wisconsin–Madison and a grant from
the Association for Asian Studies, Inc.

The University of Wisconsin Press
1930 Monroe Street, 3rd Floor
Madison, Wisconsin 53711-2059

www.wisc.edu/wisconsinpress/

3 Henrietta Street
London WC2E 8LU, England

1   3   5   4   2

Printed in the United States of America

Library of Congress Cataloging-in-Publication Data
Davidson, Jamie Seth, 1971–
From rebellion to riots : collective violence
on Indonesian Borneo / Jamie S. Davidson.
p.   cm.—(New perspectives in Southeast Asian studies)
Includes bibliographical references and index.
ISBN 0-299-22580-1 (cloth: alk. paper)
ISBN 0-299-22584-4 (pbk.: alk. paper)
1. Riots—Indonesia—Kalimantan Barat.
2. Ethnic conflict—Indonesia—Kalimantan Barat.
3. Ethnic relations—Indonesia—Kalimantan Barat.
4. Madurese (Indonesian people)—Indonesia—Kalimantan Barat.
5. Dayak (Indonesian people)—Indonesia—Kalimantan Barat.
6. Kalimantan Barat (Indonesia)—Politics and government.
I. Title.   II. Series.
DS646.34.K34D38   2008
305.89009598´3—dc22   2007039161

To

Mom, Dad, and Portia

And in memory of Dan

There comes a point in the unfurling of communal violence in which it becomes irrelevant to ask, "Who started it?"

Salman Rushdie, The Moor's Last Sigh

Contents

Illustrations

Figures

Maps

Tables

Acknowledgments

Thanking the number of people behind this book is a daunting task. This book's origins date back to the summer of 1996 when I was finishing an internship at Human Rights Watch/Asia under the stewardship of the indefatigable Sidney Jones. As I was headed to study with Dan Lev at the University of Washington, Sidney and I discussed possible dissertation topics. Having just returned from West Kalimantan herself, she mentioned exploring research possibilities there. Little did she know that some six months later horrendous ethnic violence would buffet the province.

A graduate student could not have dreamed of a better adviser than Dan. His unflinching support kept me afloat. The respect he afforded me from day one pushed me to prove that his decision was not misguided. His professional integrity and honesty has been an invaluable guide. I also benefited intellectually from the stimulating tension (one that I likely exacerbated in my head) between other dissertation committee members: Laurie Sears, who forced me to explore the unquestioned assumptions of disciplinal knowledge; and Steve Hanson, who enthusiastically kept me grounded in political science as a discipline. Laurie read the dissertation and its manuscript form in their entirety and for this I owe her a special debt of gratitude.

The following people over the years have read different parts of this work in its various manifestations and offered insightful comments: Barbara Andaya, Ben Anderson, Ed Aspinall, Mary Callahan, Freek Colombijn, Howard Dick, Maribeth Erb, Michael Feener, Diego Fossati, Mark Frost, Jeremy Gross, Kikue Hamayotsu, Eva-Lotta Hedman, Mary Somers Heidhues, Deborah Homsher, Noboru Ishikawa, Doug Kammen, Gerry van Klinken, Rodolphe de Koninck, Didi Kwartanada, Peter Li, R. William Liddle, Michael Malley, Daniel Miller, Erik Mobrand, Michael Montesano, Billy Nessen, Yoshinori Nishizaki, Remco Raben, Tony Reid, Portia Reyes, Jim Schiller, Henk Schulte Nordholt, Dan Slater, Mary Steedly, Reed Wadley, and Brad Williams.

A trio of (academically) junior scholars, fellow West Kalimantan travelers—Iqbal Djajadi, Taufiq Tanasaldy, and Hui Yew-Foong—have shared their encyclopedic knowledge of the region with me and in doing so have rescued me from sophomoric errors. I anticipate their own innovative research, some of which will challenge the conclusions I have reached. In this regard, Mary Somers Heidhues also deserves mention.

John Sidel, with whom I studied at SOAS, read the dissertation in its entirety and his shrewd comments put me on the right track as I began revisions. In large part revisions were carried out at two renowned institutes whose directors deserve a special word of thanks: Tony Reid of the Asia Research Institute (ARI) at the National University of Singapore and Jan-Michiel Otto of the Van Vollenhoven Institute (VVI) of Law, Governance, and Development at Leiden University. ARI was an ideal setting for a freshly minted Ph.D. to write, to explore new literatures, and to interact with a corpus of young, exciting post-docs and established scholars (and to meet one's future lifelong partner, of course). At the VVI, Jan-Michiel displayed uncommon patience as I completed the first round of revisions. Everyone at the VVI was cordial, professional, and intellectually acute. They made my and Portia's time in Leiden a memorable one.

Two coauthors have lent me their wisdom on writing and researching about Indonesia: David Henley and Doug Kammen. I have benefited more from these experiences than they have. Paul Hutchcroft, during an evening drunk with delight over Portia's *adobo*, convinced me to submit a proposal to the University of Wisconsin Press. He subsequently provided incisive comments on that proposal.

Papers on the material contained within this book were delivered in various seminars and conferences from the United States, Canada, and the Netherlands to Singapore, Malaysia, Indonesia, and Australia. I thank all the organizers of these events for the opportunity to present my research and to receive priceless feedback from participants. Norman Naimark graciously invited me to a series of seminars on mass violence at the Center for Advanced Studies in Behavioral Sciences at Stanford University, where I gained immensely from interacting with today's leading lights writing on the subject. Emily Greble Balic did a fantastic job organizing the seminars.

Readers for the University of Wisconsin Press, Hans Antlöv and Michael Leigh, read the manuscript with exquisite care and expertise. I have striven to pay their constructive criticisms heed and offer my apologies if I have failed to meet their lofty expectations. Kris Olds boldly guided the project through the Siberian tundra that can be the academic publication business, but I am ever grateful that he stuck with me (and that I stuck with him). Gwen Walker lent a professional and reassuring hand at the project's final yet critical stages, while Matt Levin, Adam Mehring, and Carla Aspelmeier expertly aided in the preparation of the manuscript for publication. Jan Opdyke edited the manuscript with incredible attention to detail, smoothing its style and sharpening its argumentation along the way. I acknowledge Lee Li Keng's skill in drawing the maps.

Sections of this book have appeared elsewhere. Parts of chapters 2 and 3 were first published in Cornell University's journal *Indonesia*. See Jamie Davidson and Douglas Kammen, "Indonesia's Unknown War and the Lineages of Violence in West Kalimantan," *Indonesia* 73 (April 2002): 53–87. Part of chapters 3 and 4 are found in Jamie S. Davidson, "The Politics of Violence on an Indonesian Periphery," *South East Asia Research* 11, no. 1 (2003): 59–89. I thank Deborah Homsher of Cornell University's Southeast Asia Program Publications and Ian Brown for granting me permission to use this material here. Some of chapter 5 appeared in "Decentralization and Regional Violence in the Post-Suharto State," in *Regionalism in Post-Suharto Indonesia*, ed. Maribeth Erb, Priyambudi Sulistiyanto, and Carole Faucher (London: Routeldge Curzon, 2005), 170–90 (copyright Jamie S. Davidson). A small grant from the Southeast Asia Center at the University of Washington funded my first trip to West Kalimantan, while a Fulbright-IIE (1999) award allowed me to spend ample time to conduct dissertation field-work. Subsequent trips were liberally funded by ARI, the VVI, and the Leiden University Alumni Funds.

In Jakarta, the Indonesian Institute of Sciences (LIPI) sponsored my research. At LIPI, I have been blessed to know Dr. Riwanto Tirto-sudarmo, perhaps Jakarta's most modest intellectual. AMINEF also provided much needed institutional support. Like my predecessors, I remain eternally indebted to Cornelia Polhaupessy.

In West Kalimantan, countless people welcomed me into their homes and willingly discussed sensitive and uncomfortable subjects. Where requested, I have respected their wishes to remain anonymous. Professor Tangdililing of Tanjungpura University in Pontianak was the initial sponsor of my research. The dedicated activists at the many Pancur Kasih institutes possess a treasure trove of knowledge about the region. My criticism of some of their work, while I believe fair and proportionate, should ultimately be taken as a sign of respect and admiration for what they accomplished.

Rather than stress over the awesome task of mentioning all the individuals who made life in West Kalimantan so enjoyable—I would invariably forget some names anyway—below are some places and institutions whose people gave more than they received: Hotel Merpati, Bali Agung III, UNTAN Social-Political Department, Mimbar/KIPP/(now defunct) Warung Demokrasi, HIMMA, Mandanika, Dian Tama, the library staff at the Governor's Office, Fotocopi MM, *Pontianak Post,* and *Equator*. And were it not for the four special people described below, this book would have been dedicated to all the young, fearless, energetic, and tireless activists, researchers, and other folks who are working to make West Kalimantan a place where human rights, the rule of law, and local forms of democracy are respected and enjoyed by all.

This book is dedicated to four beautiful people. Dan Lev—my mentor, my adviser, my friend, and in some respects my savior—sadly passed away before this manuscript reached its publication stage but not before he provided me with a lifetime of inspiration. The standard he set as a scholar and intellectual is unattainable. My respect for him remains boundless. This is not the first book to be dedicated in Dan's memory. Nor will it be the last.

It borders on cliché to say that without the love, support, understanding of my parents this book would not have been possible. This does not make it any less true. To be sure, they would have preferred if I had spent the last decade or more closer to home. But I hope this book will begin to show them why I have not.

Portia Reyes was not around when this project began (so don't blame her). She came on board while I was at ARI and, luckily, it appears that she will be around long, long past the time I will remember writing this book. I continue to be awed by her intellectual prowess, her kindness, her sense of humor, and her willing ability to adapt and thrive in a multitude of trying circumstances. Anyone should be so fortunate to share each and every day with someone like her. I'm especially privileged.

Gillman Heights, Singapore
January 2008

Abbreviations

ABRI	Armed Forces of the Republic of Indonesia (Angkatan Bersenjata Republik Indonesia)
AMA	Alliance of Indigenous Peoples (Alliansi Masyarakat Adat)
AMAN	Alliance of the Indigenous Peoples of the Archipelago (Alliansi Masyarakat Adat Nusantara)
Baperki	Indonesian Citizenship Consultative Body (Badan Permusyawaratan Kewarganegaraan Indonesia)
Bappeda	Regional Planning and Development Agency (Badan Perencanaan dan Pembangunan Daerah)
BPI	Central Intelligence Bureau (Badan Pusat Intelijens)
BPS	Central Statistics Bureau (Badan Pusat Statistik)
Brimob	Police Mobile Brigade (Brigade Mobil)
BTI	Indonesian Peasants Front (Barisan Tani Indonesia)
CAN	Christian Association of Nigeria
Danrem	Subregional Military Commander (Komandan Resort Militer)
DDII	Indonesian Council for Islamic Predication (Dewan Dakwah Islamiyah Indonesia)
DIA	Daya in Action
DIKB	West Kalimantan Special Region (Daerah Istimewa Kalimantan Barat)
DPR	People's Representative Council (Dewan Perwakilan Rakyat)
DPRD	Provincial/District/City People's Representative Council (Dewan Perwakilan Rakyat Daearah)
FKPM	Communication Forum of Malay Youth (Forum Komunikasi Pemuda Melayu)
FKPPI	Communication Forum of Sons and Daughters of Indonesian Veterans (Forum Komunikasi Putra-Putri Purnawirawan Indonesia)
GAM	Free Aceh Movement (Gerakan Aceh Merdeka)

Golkar	Functional Group (Golongan Karya)
GOR	sports complex (Gedung/Gelanggang Olahraga)
HMI	Islamic Students Association (Himpunan Mahasiwa Islam)
HPH	forest concession rights (Hak Pengusahaan Hutan)
HRW	Human Rights Watch
ICG	International Crisis Group
ICMI	Association of Muslim Intellectuals of Indonesia (Ikatan Cendekiawan Muslim se-Indonesia)
IDRD	Institute of Dayakology Research and Development
IKAMRA	Madurese Family Association (Ikatan Keluarga Madura)
IMF	International Monetary Fund
IPKI	League of the Supporters of Indonesia's Independence (Ikatan Pendukung Kemerdekaan Indonesia)
ISAI	Institute for the Study and Flow of Information (Institut Studi Arus Informasi)
Kalbar	West Kalimantan (Kalimantan Barat)
KAMI	Joint-Action Front of Indonesian University Students (Kesatuan Aksi Mahasiswa Indonesia)
KAPPI	Joint-Action Front of Indonesian Youth and Students (Kesatuan Aksi Pelajar Pemuda Indonesia)
KKN	collusion, corruption, and nepotism (korupsi, kolusi, nepotisme)
KNIL	Royal Netherlands Indies Army (Koninklijk Nederlands Indisch Leger)
Koga	Alert Command (Komando Siaga)
Kodam	Regional Military Command (Komando Daerah Militer)
Kodam XII	West Kalimantan's Regional Military Command
Kodim	District Military Command (Komando Distrik Militer)
Kolaga	Mandala Alert Command (Komando Siaga Mandala)
Komnas-HAM	National Human Rights Commission (Komisi Nasional Hak Asasi Manusia)
Korem	Subregional Military Command (Komando Resort Militer)
KR	*Kalimantan Review*
LBBT	Institute for the Defense of the Talino Homeland (Lembaga Bela Benua Talino)

Lembayu	Malay Brotherhood and Customary Institute (Lembaga Adat dan Kekerabatan Melayu)
LMMDD-KT	Central Kalimantan Dayak and Regional Consultative Institute (Lembaga Musyawarah Masayarakat Dayak dan Daerah-Kalimantan Tengah)
MABM	Malay Cultural and Customary Council (Majelis Adat Budaya Melayu)
MPR	People's Consultative Council (Majelis Permusyawaratan Rakyat)
MPRS	Provisional People's Consultative Council (Majelis Permusyawaratan Rakyat Sementara)
MRLA	Malayan Races Liberation Army
MQM	Muhajir Ethnic Movement (Muhajir Quami Movement)
MSF	Doctors without Borders (Médecins sans Frontières)
NGO	nongovernmental organization
NICA	Netherlands Indies Civil Administration
NIT	State of East Indonesia (Negara Indonesia Timur)
NPC	Northern Peoples Congress (Nigeria)
NU	Council of Islamic Scholars (Nahdlatul Ulama)
PAB	Union of Borneo Natives (Persatuan Anak Borneo)
PAN	National Mandate Party (Partai Amanat Rakyat)
Paraku	North Kalimantan People's Force (Pasukan Rakyat Kalimantan Utara)
Parindra	Greater Indonesia Party (Partai Indonesia Raya)
PBI	Unity in Diversity Party (Partai Bhinneka Tunggal Ika)
PBR	Reform Star Party (Partai Bintang Reformasi)
PD	Daya[k] Unity Party (Partai Persatuan Daya)
PDI	Indonesian Democratic Party (Partai Demokrasi Indonesia)
PDI-P	Indonesian Democratic Party of Struggle (Partai Demokrasi Indonesia-Perjuangan)
PDKB	Love Thy Nation Democratic Party (Partai Demokrasi Kasih Bangsa)
PFKPM	Union of Malay Youth Communication Forums (Persatuan Forum Kommunikasi Pemuda Melayu)
PGRS	Sarawak People's Guerilla Force (Pasukan Gerilya Rakyat Sarawak)
PHH	anti-riot police unit (Pasukan Anti Huru-Hara)

PKI	Indonesian Communist Party (Partai Komunis Indonesia)
PKS	Justice and Prosperity Party (Partai Keadilan Sejahtera)
PMKB	Malay Youth of West Kalimantan (Pemuda Melayu Kalimantan Barat)
PPP	Development Unity Party (Partai Persatuan Pembangunan)
PRB	People's Party of Brunei (Partai Rakyat Brunei)
PRC	People's Republic of China
RMS	Republic of the South Moluccas (Republik Maluku Selatan)
RPKAD	Army Para-Commando Regiment (Resimen Para Komando Angkatan Darat)
RUSI	Republic of the United States of Indonesia
SARA	ethnic, religious, race, and intergroup relations (Suku, Agama, Ras, dan Antar-golongan)
SCO	Sarawak Communist Organization(s)
SHK	People's Forestry System (Sistem Hutan Kerakyatan)
SOBSI	All-Indonesia Central Labor Organization (Sentral Organisasi Buruh Seluruh Indonesia)
SR	People's Association (Sarekat Raykat)
SUPP	Sarawak United People's Party
TKKB	West Kalimantan Communist Army (Tentara Komunis Kalimantan Barat)
TNI	Indonesian National Army (Tentara Nasional Indonesia)
TNKU	North Kalimantan National Army (Tentara Nasional Kalimantan Utara)
UN	United Nations
UNTAN	Tanjungpura University

From Rebellion to Riots

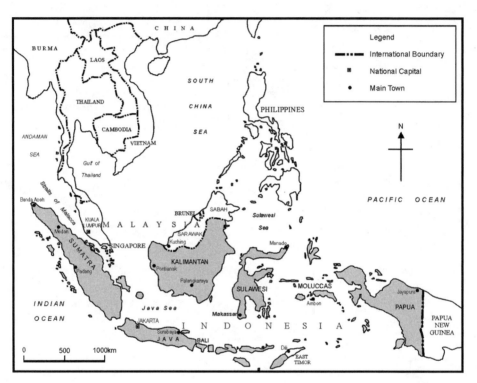

Map 1. Indonesia

Introduction

This book is at its core a diachronic study of the genesis of a series of ethnic riots that took place in the province of West Kalimantan, Indonesia, from 1967 to 2001. Its primary purpose is to explain the origins of these riots, their persistence, the particular forms the violence assumed, and how and why these modalities changed over time. This is done with an eye on the wider context of coercive state-building in the country's outer islands as pursued by the New Order regime (1966–98) headed by President Soeharto, its military, authoritarian ruler. West Kalimantan, a province rich in ethnic diversity and natural resources located on the westernmost part of the island of Borneo, has witnessed outbreaks of killings so extreme that they are considered by one leading scholar, Donald Horowitz, to be among the world's most recurrent examples of deadly ethnic riots (2001, 1, 411). Yet, unlike such prominent cases as those of Sri Lanka, Assam, Karachi, and northern Nigeria, even Horowitz's superb study lacks an adequate historical contextualization for the killings in West Kalimantan. Using ethnographic methods and tapping previously unused sources, including military documents, this book is a richly contextual political analysis that aims to fill this gap.

Research methodology of this type begs a host of questions. How much value do we gain from examining a single case of ethnic violence even if it is studied over time? What can studying ethnic riots in this peripheral province tell us about other violent conflicts elsewhere in Indonesia? Finally, how does this kind of research advance the study of group violence more generally? By demystifying the violence in this vast and rugged province, I hope to provide answers to these questions by embedding the ethnic clashes in the parameters of grounded historical and political interpretation and by situating them in a larger pattern of riots in Indonesia and beyond.

Competing Explanations of Regional Violence in Indonesia

Often overlooked in the broader literature, Indonesia constitutes an excellent test case for the growing study of two forms of collective violence. One is civil war, for which the focus of fruitful theorizing has been sub-Saharan Africa. Using econometric models predicated on rational rent-seeking behavior, scholars have pointed to greed, the looting and smuggling of contraband, and natural resource dependence as the chief causes of the outbreak and protraction of these wars (Collier 2001; Collier and Sambanis 2002; Sambanis 2002).

Riots are the second type of collective violence that has received much scholarly scrutiny. In fact, they occur far more frequently than civil war. Contemporary riot studies trace their lineages to the great corpus of literature on the 1960s "race riots" in urban America. Since then, the geographical focus has shifted to the Indian subcontinent. The theoretical focus has moved from broad behaviorist assumptions that linked objective sociological conditions to civil violence to a mix of agent-oriented, structural, and discursive factors that feed ethnic fighting.[1] Notable among these are riots' routinization as a distinct form of normal political action (Tambiah 1996); the institutionalization of riot systems and the discursive formation of mutually hostile ethnic identities (Brass 1997, 2003); the dearth of urban, interethnic civic associations (Varshney 2002); and electoral incentives (Wilkinson 2004).

In Indonesia in May 1998, under the mounting pressure of student demonstrations in the national capital, Jakarta, of civilian elite defections and of army leadership unease, Soeharto resigned from the presidency after some thirty-two years of rule and handed authority over to his vice president, B. J. Habibie. Under Habibie, this transitional period, commonly called *era reformasi* (the reform era), marked a horrific upsurge in regional mass violence. Three locations in which separatist-inspired violence erupted were home to longstanding rebellions against Indonesian rule. The province of Aceh, the last territory subdued by the Dutch colonial army and home to a long-term, albeit low-intensity, independence movement, became the site of arson attacks and intense armed clashes between the Indonesian military and the Gerakan Aceh Merdeka (Free Aceh Movement, or GAM). The conflict seemed intractable until a tsunami slammed into Aceh's north and west coasts on

December 26, 2004, killing more than two hundred thousand people. The calamity brought GAM rebels and Indonesian authorities to the negotiating table in Helsinki, where they concluded what appears to be a sustainable peace accord. Another location, East Timor, which was brutally invaded and annexed by the Indonesian military in late 1975, was a site of massive violence both before and after an August 1999 referendum, through which it achieved independence. A third site of violence, Papua,[2] was invaded by the Indonesian military in 1962 and integrated into the republic via a sham "act of free choice" sponsored by the United Nations in 1969. Like Aceh, home to a long-term, low-intensity separatist movement, it has witnessed ceremonial raisings of the movement's Morning Star flag, demonstrations, and riots.

More surprising to observers was the fact that incidents of civilian-on-civilian violence erupted in areas that were not home to longstanding resistance movements. While the Moluccas have a history of separatism that predates the Soeharto era, separatism did not lie at the core of Muslim-Christian fighting that began in January 1999 and drew Islamic militias from Java to the islands. These clashes, which ebbed and flowed for three years, left more than five thousand people dead and thousands more displaced. West of the Moluccas, a second site of religiously ascribed violence beset Poso in Central Sulawesi. Though less extensive than the killings in the Moluccas, the bloodshed here also featured the mobilization of militant groups from beyond the conflict area.

Two other sites of nonseparatist, mass violence were found in Kalimantan. In February 1999 in the district of Sambas, West Kalimantan, a widespread riot between Muslim Malay and Muslim migrant communities from the island of Madura broke out. Later, indigenous Dayak joined in against the Madurese. These clashes, which lasted several weeks and led to the forcible expulsion of some fifty thousand Madurese from Sambas, followed closely on the heels of a similarly massive Dayak-Madurese clash in early 1997 that claimed at least four hundred Madurese lives. Finally, horrific Madurese-Dayak killings erupted in early 2001 in Central Kalimantan province, which resulted in the expulsion of tens of thousands Madurese from the afflicted area. This surge in regional unrest that followed Soeharto's resignation left scholars grappling for answers. Broadly speaking, three competing explanations have come to the fore. They differ on a single question: at what point do we seek purchase in explaining the post-Soeharto mass strife?

One view focuses on the political dynamics of the early post-Soeharto state. This perspective highlights the significant inequities generated by the New Order's institutional makeup. In the post-Soeharto state, taking advantage of the uncertainties and insecurities characteristic of political transitions, formerly marginalized or excluded groups mobilized to make bolder claims for inclusion, or at least greater access to resources. As such, these contests led directly to a series of violent conflicts.

There are three principal variations on this explanation. In an important new book, Jacques Bertrand (2004) puts forth a rather rigid institutional model that sees rapid political transitions such as democratization as fraught with danger. These decisive moments in the political development of a state, known as "critical junctures," are prone to group strife. "[T]he causes of ethnic violence," Bertrand observes, "can be traced to the institutional context that defines and shapes ethnic identities, the official recognition of groups, their representation in state institutions, and their access to resources. Ethnic identities become politicized and the potential for mobilization is heightened when groups feel threatened by the structure and principles embedded in political institutions" (4). The other two variations emphasize the role of elites rather than institutional imprints in the sparking of riots. What differentiates them are the positions of these elites. One variation identifies national figures as creating regional unrest to seek gain in Jakarta (Aditjondro 2001; Aditjondro 2002, 48). The other blames newly empowered regional elites for the instigation of bloodshed in their attempts to control the largess associated with two fundamental elements that compose Indonesia's post-Soeharto democratization: competitive elections and a program of deliberate administrative and fiscal decentralization (Huxley 2002, 55–56; Van Klinken 2005). Taken together, the three variations can be called "the post-Soeharto scramble."

Skeptical of this school's synchronic view of group bloodshed, a second perspective sees such violent phenomena as outcomes of longer historical processes (Colombijn 2005; Colombijn and Linblad 2002; Cribb 2005; N. Schulte Nordholt 2002). In so doing, this school of thought finds little that is novel in the country's recent unrest. Instead, to better understand the bloodshed, this thrust champions a thorough investigation of the colonial impact on Indonesia. Whereas the post-Soeharto scramble school favors discontinuity in the political development of Indonesia, the colonial thesis privileges continuity.

A third viewpoint situates itself between these two extremes. It underscores the New Order era as the most relevant time frame. This is the case because it considers the Indonesian army to be the principal factor behind the regional violence (Anderson 2001; Liem 2002). In short, this argument posits that Soeharto's military regime—born out of the slaughters of 1965–66 wherein hundreds of thousands of Indonesians associated with the Partai Komunis Indonesia (the Indonesian Communist Party, or PKI) or those accused thereof were massacred by the army's Special Forces, right-wing vigilante Muslim and Christian groups, and ordinary neighbors—reigned as long as it did through repression and the fear it induced. Accordingly, these scholars argue that much of the recent collective strife can be traced to certain elements within the army—described in one source as skilled "masters of terror" (MacDonald et al. 2002; see also O'Rourke 2002)—and their attempts to protect their political and economic interests even as Indonesia strives to consolidate its hard-won democracy.

How do these three perspectives fare in light of the existing evidence? While there is much that is insightful, no one viewpoint alone constitutes an adequate basis for generalizing about the post-Soeharto regional unrest. The great variation across time, space, and forms in which the violence has occurred confounds monocausal explanations. Put differently, each school seems to fit some cases better than others.

This notion relates to the post-Soeharto scramble approach. If applied to the ethnoreligious violence that occurred in the Moluccas, Central Kalimantan, and Poso, the perspective is cogent. Because each of these regions lacks a history of mass civilian-on-civilian bloodshed, the specific political context of the early post-Soeharto state in which violent conflict erupted becomes crucial. But in places whose violent legacies far anticipate Soeharto's downfall, that context seems less important. Of course, collective violence in the so-called reform era escalated in the places of longtime political insurgency: East Timor, Aceh, and Papua. Arguing that the group violence there stems from recent political machinations is myopic.

An unfortunate feature of the post-Soeharto scramble view, and in particular its institutional version, is an undue emphasis on the national level. Why does most of the country lack group violence most of the time? If institutional inequities resonate nationally—and conniving for power by local or national elites should also be pervasive—why have the denizens of, say, Poso suffered and not those of Bengkulu, Bima, or Bandung? Why did two to three days of riots on Lombok in 2000 (leading to the evacuation of thousands of foreign tourists) leave almost no fatalities while a short riot in Pontianak a year later claimed some forty lives? Why did killings in West and Central Kalimantan only go on for weeks, whereas the fighting in the Moluccas and Poso lasted years? The failure to address these signal variations has hampered efforts to explain Indonesia's recent unrest from a strictly national perspective.

Does the *long durée* view of the colonial impact school fare better in dealing with the particularities of the place, nature, and length of the recent violence? The basic approach is appealing. Like the New Order state, its colonial counterpart was fundamentally a violent apparatus. Despite claims to a Pax Neerlandica, late colonial state expansion under the so-called ethical policy fomented significant bloodshed (Coté 1996; Kipp 1993; Locher-Scholten 1994; N. Schulte Nordholt 2002). This viewpoint is useful for looking at how the Dutch allocated resources, created or reified ethnic groups for purposes of law and control, buttressed certain local power holders, offered differential educational opportunities, granted missionaries access to areas in which to proselytize, and established state institutions for purposes of surveillance and warmaking.

But even proponents of this approach readily warn of its pitfalls (see Colombijn and Lindblad 2002). They note their theory's implied historical determinism — in this case, the idea that past troubles necessarily stimulate strife in subsequent periods or that past structural changes inevitably produce bloodshed. Further, there is the even more problematic cultural determinism — the notion that the violence is peculiarly Indonesian or that Indonesians are inherently prone to violence.

Here I am concerned with a more immediate problem: like the post-Soeharto scramble school, the colonial impact view fails to handle the specifics. No study produced by this school satisfactorily links specific instances of contemporary group bloodletting to colonial times. Neither does there appear to be a study effectively reconciling the disjuncture between the systemic nature of colonial influence and the episodic characteristics of mass violence. The colonial thesis cannot explain why collective strife occurs or when and where it will surface.

Similar problems of place limit the army perpetrator approach. It holds for the insurgent case of East Timor and is instructive in the context of Papua and Aceh. In other cases, the military has been an ancillary or exacerbating factor. In the Moluccas, sales of army weaponry to belligerents are widely known, and strong evidence points to army-related support for the mobilization of forces external to the region; a prime example is the Muslim militia Laskar Jihad (Aditjondro 2001; Hefner 2000; ISAI 2000). But local factors were central in triggering the riots (HRW 1999; Van Klinken 2001). Members of the Laskar

Jihad, for instance, arrived in the Moluccas more than a year after the initial outbreak of clashes. Claims of army-related interference here would benefit from distinctions among instigation, escalation, and strategic indifference. The same limitations hold in the case of Poso, where accusations of military involvement are limited to the clashes' third phase, that is, the period after they became widespread (Aditjondro 2004; Sangaji 2004). Even more clearly, the post-Soeharto riots in West and Central Kalimantan were not a product of machinations by the security apparatus. Ultimately, this approach suggests an omnipotence that the army does not have. It remains open to question why cliques within it would have "selected" certain places in which to wreak havoc and not others, whether failed attempts to incite bloodshed outnumbered successful ones, or why certain local societies were more susceptible to great conflagrations than others.

From this brief survey we can draw an important conclusion: that no one thesis adequately explains the evident variation constitutive of Indonesia's collective strife. Given this conundrum, this book attempts to probe deeply into a particular case in order to shed light on the microprocesses that generate group violence. It is hoped that, in turn, this will help illuminate the causes of similar phenomena more broadly.

A Case of Ethnic Violence

There are many compelling reasons to limit our focus to West Kalimantan. Restricting analysis in this way allows us to control for many explanatory social, political, cultural, and economic variables. Moreover, the recurrence of riots in this province allows for an analytical distinction between collective violence and conflict. In this connection, I warn against the susceptibility of studies of Indonesian politics to conflate the former with the latter. As authors of a thorough literature review on mass killings have noted, "[V]iolence is not a quantitative degree of conflict but a qualitative form of conflict, with its own dynamics." Accordingly, "[T]he study of violence should be emancipated from the study of conflict and treated as an autonomous phenomenon in its own right" (Brubaker and Laitin 1998, 425, 426). In the stuff of politics, conflict is ubiquitous; collective violence is not. Accounting for this difference is critical. In particular, I am concerned, though not exclusively, with the phenomenon of ethnic violence, which Brubaker and Laitin (1998) define as "violence perpetrated across ethnic lines, in which at least one party is not a state (or a representative of a state), and in which the putative ethnic difference is coded—by perpetrators, targets, influential third parties, or analysts—as having been integral rather than incidental to the violence, that is, in which the violence is coded as having been meaningfully oriented in some way to the different ethnicity of the target" (427).

Seen as a case of collective violence, the riots in West Kalimantan also have several intrinsically interesting properties that justify in-depth, empirical study. For one thing, the number of deaths due to ethnic riots in this single province over thirty-five years (1967–2002) approximates casualty figures for Hindu-Muslim riots in India over a longer period (1950–95) (Wilkinson 2004, 12). Furthermore, not only is West Kalimantan larger than the island of Java; it is bigger than several countries and territories—for instance, Guatemala, El Salvador, Kosovo, Northern Ireland, Rwanda, Burundi, and Sri Lanka—whose violent conflicts have been chronicled in monographs. The ethnic diversity of these areas also pales in comparison to that of West Kalimantan's social tapestry. In fact, this sparsely populated province of some four million boasts three ethnic groups that are regularly, if not controversially, accorded native son (*putera daerah*) status: indigenous Dayaks, who comprise more than one hundred ethnic subgroups; Muslim Malays; and the country's largest ethnic Chinese population.[3] As a corollary to this, few provinces have experienced the politicization of ethnicity longer than West Kalimantan has.[4]

The latter point is central. This province's history stands as a check against the popular view that sees the politicization of ethnicity as a novel, post-Soeharto phenomenon that sidelines the salience of ethnicity in the political development of Indonesia more generally. Such factors as the country's nationalist movement and its bloody four-year revolution against the Dutch; the one-time existence of the largest communist party in the world save for those of Russia and China; the absence of ethnicity as a census category; and the New Order regime's coercive policing of the public sphere, which denied discussions of ethnicity, have obscured ethnicity's relevance in nation- and state-building by successive regimes. Instead, to degrees greater than has been thought, the politicization of ethnicity has shaped strategies of domination by the central government—colonial and postcolonial alike—over regional locales. This politicization has signal historical legacies that are particularly pronounced in the outlying islands. Since the advent of European colonialism, ethnically based claims to the institutions of government, especially local bureaucracies, and access to resources have been the rule rather than the exception. All in all, political ethnicity has arisen not in spite of but due to the modernity that is the very idea of "Indonesia" (H. Schulte Nordholt 2003; Van Klinken 2004).

Finally, West Kalimantan represents a crucial case of group violence, for the forms in which killings have occurred do not fit either of the two categories of massive regional upheaval: the separatist-related violence suffered under the New Order (Aceh, Papua, and East Timor) or the ethnoreligious strife that first exploded in the post-Soeharto state (the Moluccas, Poso, and Central Kalimantan).[5] Only West Kalimantan experienced sustained, nonseparatist bloodletting throughout the New Order. In this way, the temporal extent of these disturbances begins to undermine popular contentions that conditions particular to Indonesia's democratization have *caused* the country's regional, nonseparatist violence. The experience of West Kalimantan suggests that we need to reflect on the origins of Soeharto's regime and the ways in which it violently imposed its authority in the outer islands. Regional violence says as much about the regime's birth as it does about its demise.

By the same token, we must remain aware that the reasons and logic that produce novel mass violence are not necessarily the same as those that sustain it. It does not follow that, although the New Order army instigated pogroms against the Chinese in West Kalimantan in late 1967 (see below) outside provocation was central to subsequent riots. On the contrary, the Dayak-Madurese riots were generated as *unintended* consequences of the anti-Chinese massacres. And, as each clash succeeded another, local agency, notions, and actions gained currency. Here violence begot violence. Exemplary were the massive 1997 and 1999 clashes, which were devoid of effectual outside instigation. It is time we turn to these events.

Collective violence in this frontierlike region lies in the details of local history. Despite the troubled legacies of the colonial and Japanese occupation periods, including the establishment of ethnicity as the primary prism through which to view social and political action, the intermittent riots experienced under the New Order were not natural, inevitable, or historically predetermined. They were forged out of contingent events. The crucial factors explaining the pattern of ethnic clashes or cooperation in West Kalimantan date from the tumultuous mid- to late 1960s. This period was punctuated by the ideological polarization of cold war geopolitics. In West Kalimantan, it was a time when state institutions deteriorated. In a specific locale that enjoyed relatively harmonious social relations, substantial national and local elite politicization of ethnicity was necessary to spark shocking violence. These experiences fed succeeding episodes, wherein constructions of the adversarial Other and internalized notions of "us" versus "them" coalesced and solidified.

In Indonesia, cold war polarization manifested itself in the New Order army elite's rabid anticommunism and the anticommunist slaughters on Java and Bali that it orchestrated. Following these massacres, the army leadership then turned to another "problem" it faced on its periphery, where Soeharto and his officer corps, along with their Western allies, feared that the People's Republic of China was using communists based in Sarawak (in Malaysia) and West Kalimantan—Chinese and non-Chinese alike—to infiltrate Indonesia. In fact, many of these communist guerrillas had received material support from the Indonesian military during the country's Confrontation (*Konfrontasi*) campaign directed against the newly formed Malaysian Federation.

Critically, in West Kalimantan, the bloodshed was rooted in a little-known but ruthless counterinsurgency campaign launched by the army in late 1967. Soeharto's military officers, in an effort to wipe out a local communist rebellion, used "warrior" Dayaks to expunge ethnic Chinese from the region's heartland.[6] Aided by an opportunistic clique of Dayak elites, raiders killed thousands and forced tens of thousands more to relocate to coastal urban locales where they could be controlled, monitored, and governed. Landgrabs then set off the first violent Dayak-Madurese encounter, an unintended consequence of the army's atrocities yet one that adumbrated a dynamic that has ebbed and flowed up to the present. Viewed against these events, West Kalimantan's recurrent violence, though lacking in separatist aspirations, proves to be more political than observers have supposed (Alqadrie 1999; Chang 2003; Darwin 2003; Sihbudi and Murhasim 2001; Suparlan 2004; Wessel 2001, 80).

Working within a contentious politics framework (McAdam, Tarrow, and Tilly 2001) but focusing on expressive subnational processes, this study traces the subsequent ethnic violence through the prism of New Order centralization, state-building, and domination of local politics. It shows how local populations came to grips with these state-formation processes and how different individual and collective responses reflected their positions within the nation-state and region. The region's endemic bloodletting, while not the whole story or the totality of social life, does offer a unique insight into the history of the independent Indonesian state and its successive regimes. All told, this book attempts to disaggregate the nation-state into its meaningful regional constituencies, accounting for the ways in which regional societal forces impinge upon and constitute the center (Migdal 2001).

Alternative Explanations of Local Violence: Culture, Development, Institutions

Indonesian and foreign scholars and observers have submitted alternative explanations for the clashes in West Kalimantan. Some of these admittedly sound assessments, however, gloss over the specific temporal, spatial, and modular variations in these riots. One such argument, which involves the clash of cultures, is exemplary. Both local and foreign media accounts frequently reflect such primordial views, as if shedding blood is fundamental to being Dayak or Madurese.[7] In this characterization, although they are monolithically characterized as kind, innocent, and tolerant, Dayaks, if crossed, are believed to run amok spontaneously, taking heads indiscriminately. Meanwhile, the migrant Madurese are seen as fanatical Muslims, rugged, salt-of-the-earth types who, to save face, are believed to be keen to stab adversaries from behind, a cultural practice known as *carok*.[8] Thus, these disturbances are rendered as natural outcomes of two crude cultures locked in a dynamic inherently prone to brutality.

This book provides sufficient empirical evidence to undermine such thinking. Popular, primordial viewpoints cannot explain, for example, why the first serious Madurese-Dayak riot did not occur until late 1967, although Madurese migration dates to the mid- to late nineteenth century. Accounting for the riots' spatial dimensions within the province is equally confounding. Take, for example, the fact that clashes have yet to afflict Ketapang, the province's southernmost district and one with sizable Dayak and Madurese populations. Essentialist perspectives also shed little light on why the forms of violence changed over time. For instance, Chinese villagers in 1967 were targeted by Dayak bands but remained unscathed in subsequent riots.

A significant advance beyond the primordial vantage point is the critical development/natural resource conflict approach. Proffered by concerned scholars, discerning journalists, and environmental nongovernmental organizations (NGOs), this compelling and multifaceted perspective concentrates on the injurious effects New Order development had on Dayak cultures and welfare and its role in sparking unrest.[9] It proposes that New Order development put a squeeze on local resources—particularly on land through extensive logging, transmigration, and large-scale oil palm plantations—which inflamed Dayak discontent. Stigmatized as backward and primitive, Dayaks were also underrepresented in government. This depredation, it is argued, coalesced into accumulated grievances that exploded in the widespread atrocities against the Madurese in 1997.

While there is some truth in these accusations and they are somewhat relevant to the 1997 affair, this perspective has a tendency to see the Dayak-Madurese dilemma through the prism of the 1997 incident, which obscures its specific lineages. Put another way, the critical development school tends to conflate explanations of the 1997 violence with references to the origins of Dayak-Madurese clashes, although the two are incommensurable.

In essence, such riots occurred before the consequences of New Order development adversely affected local populations. For example, the first large-scale logging concessions under the New Order were granted concurrently with the initial riots, too early for the logging's social dislocations to materialize. A knottier issue is the fact that most of the original concessions were located in areas unaffected by the fighting. A comparable case can be made for transmigration. Not only did Madurese rarely participate in the state-sponsored transmigration program, but transmigration also grew apace in West Kalimantan in the mid-1970s, succeeding the critical juncture of these riots' history. Akin to the forest concession example, many transmigration sites were located far from riot sites. In all, the broad casting of the critical development argument tends to blind it to the specifics of the violence and its evident variations over time and space. Neither is it instructive in the context of Ketapang's peacefulness and the 1999 riots, which featured the instrumental participation of Sambas Malays, who from this perspective have not been cast as victims of New Order development.

A third competing hypothesis also seeks recourse in rising Dayak frustration under the New Order. Put forth by Bertrand (2004), this view emphasizes the New Order's institutional context rather than natural resource concerns to explain Dayak marginalization and hence its role in triggering riots. Bertrand finds such frustration rooted in "their status as a 'backward' group in Indonesian society" (8) and in the regime's "institutional structure, as reflected in its normative interpretation of the basis of citizenship, of the modernity of the Indonesian national identity, and of the characteristics of inclusion and exclusion" (49). For Bertrand, the horrific incidents of 1997, 1999, and 2001 (the latter referring to events in Central Kalimantan) "showed that such (an ethnic) consciousness did arise out of the New Order institutional context and its concomitant policies" (50).

This viewpoint is an accurate assessment of the Dayaks' position under the New Order. Institutional frustration as an explanatory framework for the province's intermittent riots, however, like the critical development approach, measures up inadequately against the empirical evidence. Part of a broader attempt to explain post-Soeharto unrest, this argument should hold for innumerable "backward" members of indigenous communities nationwide who were marginalized by the regime's institutional structure. They, like Dayaks, should have committed similarly massive violence. The evidence suggests otherwise. Most have avoided attacking migrants. This is most striking in East and South Kalimantan provinces where Dayaks have not participated in such clashes.[10]

Evidence from West Kalimantan also limits the explanatory range of this institutional model. Growing frustration under the New Order cannot account for the anti-Chinese pogroms that occurred at the regime's beginning. While frustration did grow, evidentiary links between an individual's level of frustration and his or her participation in the killings would need to be provided. Just as troubling is the notion that although indigenous marginalization may have been widespread, geographically the riots were circumscribed within (central) Sambas and (northern) Pontianak districts. As an overly structural argument that assumes the existence of social groups—what Brubaker calls "groupist" social ontology (1998, 274)—the institutional frustration model both strips Dayaks of individual agency and papers over their different positionings vis-à-vis the fighting. A grounded analysis requires differentiating among Dayak civil servants, members of the government party Golkar (or other political parties), small entrepreneurs, thugs, and NGO activists and their roles in either articulating indigenous grievances or sparking the riots. Such an explanation modeled on the Dayak experience also misses the mark with reference to the 1999 clashes and the instrumental participation of Sambas Malays. All told, as an explanation of collective violence, the institutional frustration argument raises more questions than it answers.

Subnational Dynamics, Critical Junctures, and Changing Forms

One of this book's basic contentions is that the communist rebellions and pogrom against the Chinese of late 1967 are crucial in explaining the genesis and most salient forms of West Kalimantan's periodic riots. This thesis relates to broader methodological issues in three important respects. First, it puts this book in agreement with those scholars who are reexamining group strife in subnational contexts. This new literature stands in contrast to the once dominant mode, in which political scientists especially sought in national, institutional arrangements explanations for the absence or presence of collective violence in multiethnic societies. Variable electoral systems, governmental structures such as unitary or federal systems, and degrees or kinds of democracy are oft-cited factors. Yet, by moving below the national level, a growing literature has shown that these institutions, no matter how influential, fail to account for the incontrovertible variation of collective violence within states. The fact is that institutional frameworks produce considerably different levels of intranational mass strife. Characteristically, such disturbances are regionally concentrated and "not evenly spread across the length and breadth of the country" in question (Varshney 2002, 23). Exemplary of this approach, scholars recently have explored the subnational dynamics of group violence across countries (Kalyvas 2006) and within countries at the town (Varshney 2002), state (Wilkinson 2004), and neighborhood levels (Brass 2003).

Second, this study follows other recent diachronic investigations of mass strife that underscore a particular series of events that decisively, irrevocably, and unpredictably alter sociopolitical relations. René Lemarchand, in his study of mass killings in Burundi, for instance, sees one 1972 anti-Hutu bloodbath as a "watershed" that fundamentally restructured state-society relations and whose irrepressible memories directly contributed to the "mass hysteria that led to the grim slaughter of 1988" (1994, 106). Writing about similarly horrific massacres, Gyanendra Pandey deems India's Partition-related tragedies a "moment of rupture" (2001, 1). While the "singularly violent character of the event stands out," Pandey notes that it "occurred with remarkable suddenness and in a manner that belied most anticipations of the immediate future. . . . [F]ew had foreseen that this division of territories and power would be accompanied by anything like the bloodbath that actually eventuated" (2). Drawing on a South American experience, Mary Roldàn (2002) superbly recounts the social and political context in which *la Violencia* (1948–53) in the Colombian department of Antioquia was waged. Skillfully examining the geographical concentrations and selective nature of the killings, Roldàn fingers *la Violencia* as the defining period in Antioquia's contemporary history. It is only through a deep exploration of these events that the central issues of state formation, citizenship, ethnicity, class, and regionalism can be understood.

Conceptually, such studies attest to what William Sewell theorizes as formative "historical events," which he defines as "that relatively rare subclass of happenings that significantly transform structures" (1996a, 262). Calling this notion "eventful temporality," Sewell contends that historical events propel history in unanticipated ways and characteristically do so in fits and starts. "Lumpiness, rather than smoothness, is the normal texture of historical temporality," he contends, observing that: "[t]hese moments of accelerated change . . . are initiated and carried forward by historical events. While the events are sometimes the culmination of processes long underway, events typically do more than carry out a rearrangement of practices made necessary by gradual and cumulative change. Historical events tend to transform social relations in ways that could not be fully predicted from the gradual changes that may have made them possible. What makes historical events so important . . . is that they reshape history, imparting an unforeseen direction to social development and altering the nature of the causal nexus" (1996b, 843).

These views link up with a renewed sensitivity on the part of qualitatively oriented political scientists (and sociologists) toward historical processes and temporal sequencing. The latter refers to the idea that the timing of events critically affects their consequences. In the words of one of this view's principal proponents, what matters is "not just what, but *when*" (Pierson 2000, emphasis in original). Here the term popularly employed is *critical junctures,* conceived as those times when new, unforeseen paths in political development are forged out of contingent events. A subsequent yet unintended path—one constrained by past trajectories—then coalesces and continues until another critical juncture materializes. While critical junctures are often discussed in relation to national developments (Bertrand 2004; Thelen 1999), they are just as analytically useful in regional theaters. Mass violence can provide such a context. Like the 1972 anti-Hutu bloodbath, Partition-related slaughters, and *la Violencia* killings, the New Order army's counterinsurgency campaign and subsequent anti-Chinese pogrom in West Kalimantan unpredictably constituted two of those "relatively abrupt and diversionary moments [that] . . . give rise to changes in overall direction or regime, and do so in determinate fashion" (Abbot 1997, 92, 93). Juxtaposed against relatively stable, prior sociopolitical relations, these atrocities generated evident violent legacies. Seen as an unintended yet distinct path, subsequent Dayak-Madurese riots gained an internal logic in

which a routinization of violence among belligerents figured prominently (Tambiah 1996). Violence became self-perpetuating.[11]

The third and final methodological issue this book raises is the theoretical implications of case study research. The limited generalizability
of this methodology, and in particular its weakness in testing hypotheses, are well documented and to rehash them would be superfluous. Yet,
as theorists and chroniclers of ethnic violence have noted, over time
within a given site riots display prominent temporal and spatial variations (Brass 2003; Brubaker and Laitin 1998). This observation makes
small-N, controlled comparison feasible and thus suggestive generalizations possible. As one scholar put it: "Placing variance at the heart of
new research is likely to provide by far the biggest advances in our
understanding of ethnicity and ethnic conflict" (Varshney 2002, 6; see
also Tilly 2003, 20).

Riots in West Kalimantan are a case in point. For one thing, by "scaling down" the analysis to lower levels of aggregation, one increases the
number of observations on the phenomenon to be explained (R. Synder
2001; see also Coppedge 1999). As such, each violent episode or discernible set of incidents within discrete time periods can be construed as an
individual case study (Gaventa 1980, ix-x; Haydu 1998; G. King, Kohane, and Verba 1994, 30-31, 219-23; Petersen 2001, 29-30). In this way,
this work, which conceptually comprises five case studies, seeks to explain five corresponding features of the intermittent riots:

1. The conditions that led to the 1967 pogrom against the
    Chinese (chapter 2)
2. The persistence and geographical containment of early
    Dayak-Madurese clashes (chapter 3)
3. The great intensity and scale of the 1997 bloodletting
    (chapter 3)
4. The large-scale 1999 Sambas riots, which featured the
    instrumental participation of Sambas Malays, who had
    hitherto remained uninvolved in the fighting (chapter 4)
5. The spatial transformation of the 2000 and 2001 unrest
    from the region's theater of violence—semirural Sambas
    and Pontianak districts—to the once quiescent provincial
    capital, Pontianak (chapter 5).

These transformations are not chance occurrences but are politically
salient. The relevant literature focuses on temporal and spatial variation, of which riots in West Kalimantan excel on both dimensions. On

occasion, however, this literature tends to keep other modalities—including participant categories, intensity, and repertoires of violent action—constant. For instance, in Varshney's celebrated book (2002), he tends to understate the analytical importance of variations in size or intensity of Hindu-Muslim bloodshed and how or when other such communal groups such as Sikhs or Christians become embroiled in riots. Similarly, in an otherwise remarkable study, Brass (2003) on occasion overlooks meaningful modular modifications other than time and space. My study demonstrates that, in an environment of recurrent clashes, other modalities of violence contain descriptive and explanatory power (Perry 1984, 428; Tilly 2003). As dynamic configurations, they have their own traceable histories and discrete lineages. Rather than changing randomly, they do so amid significantly altered political, social, and institutional contexts.

Take the intensity and scope of the 1997 riots, which far surpassed those of prior Dayak-Madurese incidents. What accounted for the change? Politicization of the countryside, especially the province's western half, bolstered by the growth of Dayak-oriented NGOs, was key. Vigorously promoting the idea of indigeneity among West Kalimantan's Dayak communities, these organizations actively participate in the national and global indigenous peoples' movement, which is predicated on the increasing internationalization of human rights, environmentalism, and identity politics and discourse (Li 2000; Niezen 2003). Although these activists neither incited nor engineered the violence, they fostered a complicated yet tangible awareness of deprivation among disparate communities. Tapping into a consciousness of Dayak grievance, they encouraged, facilitated, and provided the means by which frustration could be productively molded and articulated, which ultimately led to a confrontation with state authority.

Although now perhaps overshadowed by the Moluccan and Poso tragedies, which lasted for years and garnered significant international attention due to the specter of violent, fundamentalist Islam, this study also argues that the 1997 riots in West Kalimantan were critical in setting the stage for the unprecedented regional unrest that marred Indonesia's transition from authoritarianism. At the time the country's gravest civilian-on-civilian bloodshed in some three decades, this unrest was far more severe than the other violent incidents of 1996–97. The latter included an attack on the Indonesian Democratic Party's headquarters in Jakarta and the anti-Christian and anti-Chinese property riots in the cities of Situbondo and Tasikmalaya on Java—events that observers are retroactively identifying as the beginning of the New Order's demise (Eklöf 1999; N. Schulte Nordholt 2002). The 1997 riots in West Kalimantan demonstrated the susceptibility of regional societies to extensive bloodletting. For nearly three decades, regional, ethnoreligious fighting had been fleeting and containable. After 1997, it attained enormous dimensions. Collective violence in this vast province contributed greatly to this qualitative change. In all, extensive ethnoreligious violence in the outer islands did not begin with the country's economic crisis or with Soeharto's downfall but in early 1997 in West Kalimantan.

Changes in other modular forms of the violence reflect political processes. The 1999 riots and the sudden involvement of Malays in Sambas are illustrative of this. A consequence of indigeneity activism, "victory" in the 1997 riots, and the widening political space provided by the reform movement, a forceful Dayak ethnopolitical movement placed Malay elites on the defensive. Consequently, the latter countered with an ethnopolitical movement of their own to gain a share of the monopoly Dayaks had on indigeneity. This, in turn, would preserve their local government positions of power and patronage. In other words, the Malay identity needed to demonstrate that it would formidably compete with the Dayak identity in the heightened competitiveness of local politics caused by the country's great experiment in decentralization, which has resulted in copious amounts of resources passing through local elite hands. In West Kalimantan, violence against a vulnerable enemy—in this case, Madurese neighbors—sought to accomplish this aim. Galvanizing the movement, mobilizations against the Madurese fortified Malay identities and proved that local Malay indigeneity was on a par with that of Dayaks. The expulsion of some fifty thousand Madurese from Sambas district, the second significant change in the repertoire of violent collective action, was integral to this development.

I suggest that these modular changes stem from the broader political landscape of the post-Soeharto polity. Foremost was the impact of decentralization on local political contests and constellations. While it is correctly theorized as crucial to the democratic empowerment of regional government and local populations, democracy theorists have cast decentralization in an idealized light (Crook and Manor 1998; Diamond 1999). There is little acknowledgment of its dark side—for instance, heightened ethnocentrism and pernicious nativism. Although decentralization has been seen as the means of putting an end to the New Order's coercive and excessive centralization and defusing the separatist aspirations of resource-rich regions, it nonetheless engendered several instances of mass violence, including ethnoreligious expulsions. Events in Sambas were exemplary. Amid the frenetic rise of ethnic polarizations, only in a post-Soeharto, decentralized state would systematic cleansings, once unimaginable, become thinkable and thus possible. All told, these developments, along with the 2000 and 2001 unrest in Pontianak, juxtapose the marked disjuncture between the progress of institutional reform and the consensual politics displayed at the national level against its violently contested, zero-sum counterpart in the regions.

I next attempt a further exploration of this incongruity, one meant to put the lessons of violence in West Kalimantan in comparative perspective. I examine the three cases of regional, nonseparatist riots—Central Kalimantan, the Moluccas, and Poso—and emphasize the importance of the forms of collective violence in those events. In contrast to the mainstream ethnic violence literature, it is shown that the ascriptive framings of collective violence matter. In Indonesia's regions, the duration of the bloodshed turned on a religious-ethnic pivot. Religious clashes, due to balanced riot demographics and the drawing of militants from elsewhere, lasted significantly longer than their ethnic counterparts. I also demonstrate the usefulness of studying group strife over time in helping to explain why the ethnic framing of violence in Kalimantan persists and why religious identifications of unrest materialized in the Moluccas and Poso. Finally, I view the clashes in West Kalimantan alongside recurrent cases in Nigeria, India, and Pakistan. This is done as an effort to help surmount an evident divide in the literature: the thorny elite- versus mass-led dualism in the igniting of unrest. Rather than proposing a dichotomy between these two types of riots, the cases point to a back-and-forth, shifting balance between the two over time.

I conclude by exploring two hitherto partly addressed issues that resonate across the country's outer island societies: conflict resolution and competing conceptions of rights. In all, as Indonesians struggle to deepen their embryonic democracy and institutionalize a decentralized system of government that respects individual human rights, the extent that demands for collective rights and entitlements at the local level clash with these priorities is a defining question that will determine the quality of democratic life in Indonesia.

1

Identity Formations and Colonial Contests

This chapter provides the macrohistorical context in which to situate the postcolonial collective violence in West Kalimantan. By tracing the broad patterns of power relations in the two centuries or so preceding the New Order, I decipher the processes of class formation and ethno-religious identity making, and explore the ways in which these various entities became imbued with significant political meaning and how power asymmetries and relations of economic production constantly reconfigured these understandings.

In particular, this chapter demonstrates how ethnicity, among many markers, became dominant in politics and mobilization (Laitin 1986), as well as accounting for the geographical distribution of these groups (Posner 2003). Forms of differentiation anticipated colonialism, but the colonial politics of divide and rule solidified these differences and precipitated evident polarizations. To buttress their tenuous hold on power, the Dutch over time forged the bounded ethnic categories of "Dayak" and "Malay," terms that will be subjected to examination to guard against reification. These colonial legacies were reinforced by religious proselytizing, race-based systems of law, and processes of decolonization, including party politics and electoral competition.

Migrants and their incorporation into the regional social fabric also made their mark. Foremost were thousands of Chinese miners, whose turbulent experiences infused these communities with a militancy that would persist throughout the postcolonial era. Just as significant, I also aim to lift the apolitical myths of Dayaks in West Borneo/Kalimantan that pervade the relevant literature.[1] In so doing, I shed light on an important yet frequently overlooked story of activism, organization, and participation in formal spheres of political action. Under the influence of Dutch civilizing ideals, the vibrant Partai Persatuan Daya[2] (Daya Unity Party) was fashioned in response to competition from other ethnic groups. In the context of an embryonic democratic and modern nation-state, not until the 1950s did the ethnic identity Dayak first become historically available to the great majority of the province's non-Islamic, indigenous populations. In large part, the existence of a Dayak provincial-level elite informs the modernity that constitutes postcolonial violence in West Kalimantan.

The collective violence of the period under consideration in this chapter reflected the changes taking place as the region became enmeshed in a wider web of state formation and the rationalization of economic and social relations. Local responses to such exogenous shocks as warfare and occupation ranged from fierce resistance and substantial upheavals to quiescence and indifference. Significantly, in addition to underscoring these violent incidents' political salience, I strive to show how these episodes differ in subtle ways from their postcolonial counterparts. The impact of exogenous forces on West Borneo/Kalimantan should not be overstated, however. For most of its denizens, colonialism's effect was minimal. The Dutch never did effect a "social revolution" here as they did on Java (Onghokam 1978).

All told, the landscape explored here is too intricate to be sufficiently mapped within this chapter's confines. Relying on the work of historians and historically oriented anthropologists, this brief sketch traces the general framework within which socioethnic relations have evolved, focusing in particular on their political manifestations.

Trade and Coastal Powers

To illustrate how Dutch colonial rule forged a Dayak identity out of a heterogeneous, autochthonous population of over a hundred ethnolinguistic groups, I draw on Mahmood Mamdani's concept of political identities, deployed in his penetrating account of the Rwandan genocide (2001). In contrast to economic or cultural identities, Mamdani sees political identities as embedded in and products of the organization of power and state formation. Unlike the situation in Rwanda, the construction of Dayak and Malay as political identities in West Borneo/Kalimantan has yet to instigate massive internecine bloodshed; it has nonetheless precipitated a marked solidification and contentious bipolarization. This account will not answer definitively the question of who is Dayak and who is Malay. Instead, it will illustrate how these political identities have evolved and changed over time amid a complicated matrix of unfolding power relations.

Significantly, this Malay/non-Malay fissure, which was encouraged by the arrival of Muslim traders and proselytizers from Java, Sumatra, other parts of Kalimantan and elsewhere, anticipated Dutch colonialism (Laffan 2003). Religious conversion, however, did entail a shift in ethnic affiliation. Non-Muslim natives who adopted Islamic ways of life and settled in villages along the main rivers became Malay (*masuk Melayu*), particularly in the region's headwaters (V. King 1985, 58–61). Accordingly, the majority of Malays, especially those upriver, are converts from indigenous populations. Colonialism did not generate this differentiation, but it facilitated its hardening and fashioned a polarization by constructing a homogeneous Dayak identity (as opposed to a Malay one) out of a variegated, non-Muslim population. Thus were laid the foundations of an inexorable but slippery dichotomization.

As Islamic seafarers, traders and adventurers—Arabs, Bugis,[3] and Malays alike—settled in western Borneo in the sixteenth and seventeenth centuries, they introduced new forms of statecraft and legal institutions that altered power configurations, although in some respects these foreign modalities were integrated into autochthonous Malay notions of rule and kingship (Healey 1985; Heidhues 1998; Milner 1983). The growing regional prominence of Islam prompted the conversion of indigenous coastal rulers—such as those in Sukadana—who in turn sought to capture gains from the vibrant trading networks among such Malay world polities as Johor, Siak, Kedah, Pahang, Trengganu, Palembang, and Brunei. This meant that converts acquired a new structure of meaning that was conceived as progressive and modern. Over time, more avowedly Islamic principalities such as Sambas, Mempawah, and Pontianak—in 1771 the last major power established—were founded at strategically located river deltas. Given that these coastal powers were integrated into a broad network of Malay sultanates, which extended from southeastern Sumatra and the Malay Peninsula to the coast of Kalimantan, historians have perceived a cultural coherence among the people of this region, despite discordance and regional variations. Milner (1982) notes that by the mid-nineteenth century Malays expressed "some awareness of a cultural unity and sharing a language, a literature, and a style of life" (11). Moreover, "the ease with which peoples beyond the frontier might enter 'Malaydom' suggests that some 'form or logic' endowed this culture with intelligibility and, therefore, attractiveness, enabling it to be identified and assimilated" (12). Similarly, Drakard talks with some confidence of a Malay political culture (1990, 9), an integral part of which was the ancient prowess and prestige accorded to local rulers. The preeminence of a king, prince, or sultan gave Malaydom a human, if not magical and mythical, face (L. Andaya 2004; Kessler 1992). Importantly, it was during this period—and later when European colonialism gained ground in the region (Matheson 1979)—that the identity Malay became increasingly expressed in Islamic idioms.

In western Borneo, Islamic principalities and sultanates were not sustained by amassing standing armies or controlling large-scale agricultural production. Instead they taxed the trade of agricultural and forest products and collected obligatory deliveries from indigenous, non-Islamic populations residing in their domains (Healey 1985). Dependent on such goods as salt, iron, and tobacco, the latter were often debt-bondage slaves to the sultans or their appanage holders.[4] Some converted to avoid exploitation, for the sultans' Muslim subjects were exempt from taxation. Many more fled farther inland along the region's vast serpentine river system. In all, despite distinctions in religion, language, and customs, the region's peoples were drawn together by an economy in which Muslim coastal powers depended on their ability to offer foreign traders the produce of the interior while enjoying an ephemeral command over inland peoples. Barbara Andaya (1993, 77) refers to this condition as the inherent "ambiguity" rooted in upstream-downstream relations (see also Healey 1985 and Rousseau 1990, 287–97).

In western Borneo, communities considered to be ethnically Malay comprise the downstream part of this equation, whether downstream meant on the coast or along the banks of the Kapuas River and its tributaries. Non-Islamic, autochthonous populations residing upstream would become monolithically and popularly known by the exonym Dayak. Primarily exogenous pressures such as colonial state-building, however, instilled a coherence and political meaning in this Dayak identity. To do so, the Dutch state first required a local presence. And, given that colonial authorities first came to western Borneo not to create an indigenous political identity but to quash the "rebellious" Chinese mining communities—and seek a profit in turn—it is this latter development to which we first turn. An exploration of the colonial-inspired generation of the Dayak political identity then follows.

Kongsi and Dutch Anxiety

European interference and influence in western Borneo was minimal until the mid-nineteenth century. Prior to this, the Dutch colonial state concentrated its resources on the exploitation of agriculture on Java. Only from the 1840s onwards did the Dutch gradually adopt a more aggressive stance toward the eastern archipelago. In western Borneo, colonial anxiety was piqued by the establishment of a regime in Sarawak under James Brooke, a British adventurer.[5] To counter this development, the Dutch sought to strengthen their commitment to the region. This meant waging war against the semiautonomous Chinese *kongsi* (gold-mining cooperatives). As protocorporations in which miners received a share of the profits, *kongsi* prospered from a lively trade with Singapore and other surrounding islands (Dalton 1837). Of course, the Dutch also hoped to capture and control what for them was an "illegal" trade ("Speech of Baron Vander Capellen" 1837).[6]

Most of the miners were Chinese Hakka from the inland hills of Guangdong Province (and Fujian) in southeastern China and were renowned for their hard work, diligence, and pioneering spirit (Constable 1996; Wang 1994, 48, 53). Invited by coastal rulers to work the local mines, they first came to the region in large numbers in the mid-eighteenth century.

The geographic distribution of the *kongsi* is important, for these sites would host the region's fiercest bouts of collective violence — not only warfare against the Dutch (see below), but centuries later the 1967 anti-Chinese pogroms and the subsequent Dayak-Madurese riots. The mines were primarily concentrated in Sambas (around Montrado and east toward present-day Bengkayang) and farther south in the area surrounding Mandor (see map 2).

The mines' impressive production (Jackson 1970) stimulated an influx of migrants — as many as ten thousand by 1770 (Cator 1936, 149). To increase efficiency, small mining cooperatives were consolidated to form alliances and large federations that over time gained considerable autonomy from coastal overlords. Growing resources, populations, and feelings of sovereignty motivated these federations to institute local systems of government, establish educational and tax systems, and build roads, canals, and temples. Accordingly, as the exploited surface area rapidly expanded, port and inland towns and urbanlike services multiplied (Doty and Pohlman 1839; "Memoir of the Residency" 1837).

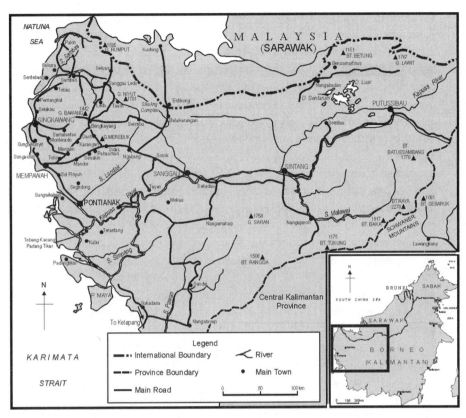

Map 2. West Kalimantan

Some accounts situate this history within a frontier milieu and underscore the violence inherent in such expansion (Cator 1936, 147; Doty and Pohlman 1839; Ismail 1994; Siahaan 1994; Yuan 2000). Intense competition over resources required the constant opening, closing, and absorbing of mines, thereby precipitating strife among the *kongsi* (Heidhues 2003, 54–65, 77–78; Wang 1994, 68). Exhausted mines forced miners to seek new opportunities, often violently. The violence was directed not only against other *kongsi* but against local populations, which were threatened with dispossession of their land. In 1841 and again in 1846, for instance, members of the large Lanfang *kongsi* federation (of Mandor) and indigenes clashed as the former, due to mine exhaustion, expanded north into the Landak area. In another recorded incident in 1843, miners expelled locals from mines farther north in the Lara area (Yuan 2000, 158).

Scholars caution against sweeping generalizations, however. They acknowledge the occasional violence but do not wish to overstate the case. In many areas little or no fighting occurred. Following the initial period of adjustment and an occasional clash, relations stabilized and evolved somewhat peacefully among miners and indigenes, perhaps aided by mutual disdain for the Malay aristocracy. Over time, Chinese merchants replaced Muslim traders as natives sought protection from appanage holders (Heidhues 2003, 53). Intermarriage also drew Chinese and natives closer. The absence of women migrants and prohibitions against marrying Malay women prompted more affluent miners and officials to take non-Islamic, local wives. Accounts agree that the children of these unions were brought up "Chinese," in terms of dress, customs, and language. The extent and meaning of Chineseness, however, was in flux as the society in which these children were reared was undergoing significant sociocultural transformations. As Heidhues aptly puts it, "These people were 'in the *Indonesian* tropics,' with limited freedom to develop a 'little China'" (2003, 13, emphasis in the original).

In 1851, with a new governor-general in Batavia, the colonial government adopted a hawkish stance toward the Chinese "problem" in West Borneo—as the region was now known. Located in Mandor, some thirty-five miles northeast of Pontianak, the Lanfang federation quickly came to terms with the Dutch. This was in part because of its dependence on Pontianak's port,[7] but also because its autocratic leadership structure made negotiations feasible (Heidhues 2003, 103-4). In contrast, centered in Montrado and characterized by a more egalitarian form of government, the great Fosjoen federation rebuffed Dutch suzerainty and intervention. Tension and mutual animosity grew. Marked Dutch belligerency resulted in a series of bloody confrontations against Thaikong, Fosjoen's largest *kongsi*. In 1854 following extensive loss of life, Thaikong capitulated and was forced to recognize Dutch suzerainty (Yuan 2000).

Migration, Economy, and State Formation

The Dutch-*kongsi* wars prompted three crucial developments in West Borneo. First they brought Madurese to the area as colonial soldiers.[8] Although we do not know what percentage settled locally, we know that others followed. "Pushed out" of increasingly overcrowded and soil-poor

Madura and fleeing the island's stifling social and political hierarchy, Madurese in large part arrived via a system of indentured servitude. To settle debts held at home, they worked on Chinese or Bugis plantations, cut and hauled wood and built roads. Along with Bugis sailors, they also participated in the steady trade between West Borneo and Java often backed by local Chinese capital (Cator 1936, 177). In the early twentieth century, some families arrived by means of Dutch migration programs, although over time more and more came on their own. After migrants returned home to their pay debts, they brought their families and other dependents back to West Borneo. Meanwhile, word spread about promising opportunities and the availability of land in this vast region, enticing news for the land-starved inhabitants of densely populated Madura. In particular, the hardship of the 1930s depression brought many Madurese (and Javanese) to West Borneo looking for work (Djawatan Penerangan Propinsi Kalimantan 1953, 164), of which Dutch road-building projects were a major draw (Sugadung 2001, 82). A source from the 1950s maintains that the area was still "in great need of manual labor [*buruh kasar*]" (Tobing ca. 1953, 132).

Madurese settlements first materialized on the southern coast near Ketapang and then spread north to Pontianak and eventually Sambas. Although migrants owned little land, some cleared forested tracts for habitation. The Madurese population grew not only due to migration, but to the fact that the children of unions between Madurese males and local Malay females were raised "Madurese" (Sudagung 2001, 78–81). While migration and land ownership grew apace after independence, during the period under consideration, there were no reports of serious collective violence against the Madurese.

A second significant development subsequent to the Dutch-*kongsi* warfare was that the Chinese driven out by the conflict soon returned and the economy recovered under more stable conditions. Importantly, the original Chinese districts were reconstituted (Heidhues 2003, 127–36), unlike what would transpire as a result of the 1967–68 expulsions (see chapter 2). By 1880 the Chinese population had reached some 28,000; by 1930, it stood at 107,998 or 13.4 percent of the regional total (Siahaan 1974, 41). Absent during the pioneering period, women migrants fueled this growth.

Changes in settlement patterns accompanied this population boom. With the demise of the *kongsi*, some miners moved inland along the Kapuas River to participate in the rubber and forest produce trade. Others inhabited coastal towns. In Pontianak, which evolved into the prime entry point for migrants, Teochiu Chinese dominated commerce.[9] Dense with Hakka, Singkawang established itself as the region's second city (Heidhues 2003, 136). Yet the majority stayed close to exhausted mines and became small-scale agriculturists. By 1930, West Borneo had the greatest percentage of Chinese in the archipelago engaged in agriculture, estimated at 19 percent. Similarly, 79 percent of the Chinese population was rural, compared to 41 percent on Java (Cator 1936, 161–62).

Energies also shifted to intensive cash crop production—notably rubber, whose production soared in step with the booming demand for automobile tires. Consistent with other outer islands (Barlow and Drabble 1990), in West Borneo smallholding with little or no Western capital fueled the growth of the rubber industry (Notowardojo with Noor 1951). Yet sharp ethnic divisions of labor found elsewhere—such as southern Sumatra (Thomas and Panglaykim 1976)—were less distinct in West Borneo. While the majority of the Chinese were middlemen who controlled most of the capital invested in rubber processing, Chinese farmers did tap trees around former mining sites, as did Dayaks farther inland (Cator 1936, 174).[10] Besides cash crops, Chinese farmers increased their production of wet rice to meet the populace's growing demand. Although nearby Dayaks relied on swidden agriculture, interest in wet-rice cultivation grew (Heidhues 2001, 140; Peluso 1996). Nevertheless, the region remained a net importer of rice.

The third and final implication of the Dutch-*kongsi* wars was colonial state formation and expansion. With the violent dismantling of the *kongsi*, the Dutch obtained the *rust en orde* (tranquility and order) necessary to develop a "state" through which governance and civilizing missions could be conducted. From the outset, colonial officials renewed treaties with coastal polities, over which, despite Dutch suzerainty, they had minimal influence (Ricklefs 2001, 179). Upriver expeditions were also conducted to conclude *overeenkomsten* (formal treaties) with smaller inland polities, whose powers were further reduced when colonial officials later replaced the formal treaties with *korte verklaring* (short contracts). Having finalized external border issues with the British—negotiated in a series of treaties—1884, 1891, and 1912—the Dutch also began a complicated process of delineating territorial rights and access to resources predicated on ethnicity and administrative units. Starting in 1886, officials executed a long-term mapping project through which they sought to "'straighten out' what they saw as messy boundaries among various ethnic groups and the native kingdoms" (Wadley 2003,

94). All told, the colonial state extended its administrative and coercive reach into West Borneo's uplands, in part driven by territorial ambitions and the desire for prestige (Locher-Scholten 1994), and in part seeking to contain the spread of Islam, which gained pace beginning in the mid-nineteenth century (Tagliacozzo 2005). In West Borneo an integral component of state expansion was also the fashioning of a bounded pan-ethnic marker, known as Dayak, to encompass the great diversity of non-Muslim autochthonous populations. The colonial strategy of divide and rule helped to generate this collective identity.

Formation of Dayak Political Identities

The category "Serer"—an agglomeration of a number of distinct peoples—thus tells us much more about colonial interests and anxieties in the late nineteenth and early twentieth centuries than it does about the politics, religion, culture, agricultural practices, or even language of the people who lived in the area that came to be known as the Serer country.

Galvan, *The State Must Be Our Master of Fire*

Like the formation of the Serer ethnic identity in Senegal by external forces, a similar process took place in West Borneo. As Dutch authorities advanced up the Kapuas River into the Borneo highlands, they brought with them colonial conceptions of race, ethnic categorization, and hierarchy. Writing on the matter, Harwell notes: "For the purposes of Dutch administration, the crucial difference to delimit was that of the non-Muslim 'Dayak' farmers eligible for tribute, corvée labor, taxation and, later, Christian salvation; Muslim 'Malay' elite for indirect rule and control of trade . . . and Chinese merchants, miners and cash crop farmers" (2000, 32).

The main brokers of colonial authority were the (Muslim) Malay coastal and riverine princes. The Dutch instituted a system of indirect rule whereby the princes produced revenue and ensured law and order on behalf of the Dutch. Two ways in which the princes subjugated their non-Muslim subjects was through excessive taxation and compulsory labor. Ironically, colonial support of these princedoms helped to facilitate the spread of Islam, which the Dutch had hoped to stymie. Buttressing inland Malay polities had solidified Islam's modern and prestigious symbolic value. The exception was in the province's easternmost district, Boven Kapoes (which today comprises Kapuas Hulu, Sintang, and Melawi districts), where the Dutch did not rely on Malay princes as proxies. Instead they governed the area directly to provide "protection" from oppressive Malays and Islam. East of Sintang town, only a handful of minor principalities was formed; there were none east of Putussibau (V. King 1979, 28-34). Here non-Muslim populations were referred to as *Dajak mardaheka* (free Dayaks) (V. King 1985, 59).

Colonial authorities—including the Brookes in Sarawak—also generated this monolithic Dayak identity through warmaking. In West Borneo, the imposition of Dutch rule and the fundamental alteration of status relations between rulers and the ruled set off a flurry of low-level incidents of violence. "The Dutch did not seem to understand that their own state-making project in fact created much of this violence," Tagliacozzo (2000, 75) remarks in his study of Indonesia's "border arc" of the late nineteenth century. "People were being asked to live under new sets of rules, and under terms and conditions set by the colonial state. It was only natural that there would be resistance to this evolving matrix of power." To quash this unrest, the Dutch (and more famously the Brookes) frequently used the services of Dayak auxiliaries (Pringle 1970, 210-46). In the process, the branding of this subject identity materialized.[11]

In 1885, for instance, the Dutch used such irregulars to quell a revolt of gold miners from the decaying Lanfang federation in Mandor (Heidhues 2003, 104-11). Yet nowhere was this dynamic more pronounced than along the Sarawak border, an infamous theater of violence whose lively yet "illegal" trade, coupled with Brooke machinations, continued to arouse Dutch anxiety. In the 1850s and 1860s, Dutch border officers increasingly intervened among strife-torn Malay principalities.[12] And in 1886, in a rare act of cooperation, the Dutch permitted Charles Brooke to cross the colonial border with a war party eleven thousand strong to stage a punitive expedition against Iban Dayak, who were "troublesome" borderland inhabitants renowned for their fearsome raids. The Dutch, though aghast at the expedition's excesses, put other Dayaks (and some Kapuas Malays) in service to fight as well (Wadley 2001).

Later, widespread violence erupted in the Chinese districts again, and this time Dayaks were found on the side opposing colonial rule. Underpinning the rebellion was a growing Chinese nationalist consciousness that was spawned by modern education, which inculcated a uniform "Mandarin Chinese" identity. The revolt was also buoyed by Sun Yat-sen's republican movement in China. Locally, changing power relations exacerbated tensions. Reflecting their increasing power, the

Dutch raised taxes and instituted a program of compulsory labor for road construction whose burdens fell hardest on the laboring classes, while the better off bought their way out. In 1914, perhaps exhorted by disgruntled local Malay nobles who resented the eclipse of their authority, some Dayaks joined Chinese rebels in the rebellion; others were called upon by the colonial authorities to put down the revolt (The 1981). In one sense, this abortive rebellion marked the end of an era in which multiethnic alliances that confronted external state intrusion were common. With nationalist chauvinism growing among the Chinese and *pribumi* (native) Indonesians and the state actively promoting ethnic divisions, interethnic disturbances soon became the norm.

In addition to warmaking, colonial peacemaking figured prominently in indigenous political identity formation. To achieve stability in the upper Kapuas area (and in the larger central Borneo region), apart from crushing unrest the Dutch negotiated cease-fires, fortified villages, and in some cases, moved entire populations to safer locales (V. King 1985, 62–70). A famous 1894 peace conference in Tumbang Anoi (present-day Central Kalimantan province), whereby warfare, slavery, and headhunting were outlawed, exemplified these efforts (Rousseau 1990, 35). By assembling Dayak representatives from all parts of Borneo, the regime fostered among attendees a growing ethnic consciousness of a common fate and, of course, a familiar recognizability (Usop 1994).

Religious conversion was another important means of forging an indigenous political identity. As noted above, the spread of militant Islam disconcerted the Dutch. Finishing their war in Aceh,[13] yet witnessing the growth of a pan-Islamic movement elsewhere, colonial officials— short on manpower (Schrauwers 2000, 42)—turned to missionary work to staunch its advance. In this context, Bigalke (1984) has observed that the Dutch focused on areas with significant Islamic coastal populations and "still unconverted groups of highlanders. . . . Islam was perceived as an advancing tide that could only be stopped by building a bulwark in the highlands; isolation was the only way to preserve the heathens from Islamic conversion and to save them for later conversion to Christianity" (1984, 85). In central Sulawesi, this process led to a dichotomization between the "coastal" inhabitants (Bugis) and the "heathens" or "highlanders" (Torajan). The former were cast as the oppressors, the latter the oppressed. In West Borneo, in the case of Dayaks and Malays, a parallel development was underway.

Still, reliance on missionaries required a change in attitude, for the colonial authorities had once balked at efforts to convert the heathens.

It was thought that proselytizing might compromise the regime's primary objective: economic exploitation. However, with the introduction of the humanitarian-inspired ethical policy in 1901, which strove to morally and materially elevate indigenous society, the authorities softened their view of missionaries (Kipp 1993). Alternatively, viewed as an outcome of state expansion backed by military force as a way to secure raw materials to fuel the world's capitalist economies, the ethical policy also justified greater interference in outer island, indigenous societies. In the end, both viewpoints facilitated significant "cultural transformations of traditional societies" (Coté 1996, 89).

Missionary Influences

As in central Sulawesi (Aragon 2000), Flores (Prior 1988), and elsewhere, in West Borneo missionaries and the Church formed the bedrock of this civilizing mission. These efforts would focus, though not exclusively, on upper Kapuas non-Muslims. They were, it was believed, the group least corrupted by Islamic influences and most free of oppressive Malay rule. Paradoxically, in the indirectly ruled areas Dutch support enhanced the princes' repressive capacities. Nevertheless, missionaries seized upon what they saw as an opportunity to civilize and Christianize upper Kapuas populations. In 1890 a tiny station opened in Semitau (today's Kapuas Hulu district), which was soon followed by a school-church combination built in nearby Sejiram.

Missionary success progressed slowly. Insufficient institutional support dogged these early efforts. Not until 1905, when the Capuchin Order of the Roman Catholic Church was granted exclusive access to West Borneo, did missionary efforts gain evident momentum.[14] Incongruously, the very same freedom these populations enjoyed that had attracted missionaries frustrated the Church's advances. But as more children began to attend missionary primary schools conversions invariably rose. Although in absolute numbers this growth was glacial, ultimately the Church's influence on its few converts and the broader Dayak community far outstripped the actual number of conversions. Importantly, missionary education was the medium through which Western idealism—democracy, egalitarianism, and empowerment—was inculcated to the educated elite and eventually to the founders of the Daya Unity Party (commonly abbreviated PD). The expanding school network laid the structural basis around which a provincial Dayak elite coalesced.

Missionary education not only laid the foundation for an emerging common identity: it also helped to transform it into a political consciousness. For a handful of elites, a key institution was located not in the upper Kapuas but in a small village immediately north of Singkawang called Nyarumkop. In 1917 missionaries opened a tiny school that quickly grew into a five-year program with some fifty students; a little less than half were full-time boarders. A teachers' course (Cursus Normaal) soon opened, which later expanded into a teachers training program (Cursus Volksschool Onderwijzer, CVO).[15] Its graduates staffed inland primary schools or continued their studies at a junior seminary in Pontianak or a Catholic teachers' college (*normaalschool*) in North Sulawesi.[16] The geographical, educational, and ideological extent of this missionary instructional circuit expanded noticeably during the 1920s and 1930s. Out of this network there arose a select and increasingly distinct group of Dayak leaders who hailed from various ethnic subgroups. Notable were Augustinus Djelani (1919–77) from the Taman subgroup and a graduate of Nyarumkop's CVO and Pontianak's junior seminary; F. C. Palaunsoeka (1923–93), a Nyarumpkop CVO graduate and also a Taman; and J. C. Oevaang Oeray (1922–86) from the Kayaan subgroup and a graduate of these two institutions. Scores of schoolteachers who would staff missionary and PD schools in West Borneo's vast countryside were also products of this expanding missionary-led educational network.

A final important feature of colonial state formation and the construction of a Dayak political identity was the colony's complicated legal system. In the early twentieth century, a small but influential part of the colonial bureaucracy inspired by ethical policy principles and led by Cornelius van Vollenhoven — Professor of *Adat* (Customary) Law at Leiden University — committed great intellectual and ethnographic energies to compiling and codifying local customary law (*hukum adat*). In so doing, they sought to protect these "traditional" and erroneously conceived closed communities from the onslaught of capitalist-driven westernization (Kahn 1993) and from Islam (Lev 1985). This aided the growth of a pluralistic legal system based on race (Hooker 1978) and difference (Harwell 2000) in which Indonesians — particularly those in rural outer island areas — were subject to customary law and Europeans were subject to Dutch law.[17] This drive to promote tradition — no matter how well intended, as Lev observed — was "suffocatingly conservative and at times even reactionary" (1984, 150). And nascent nationalist mobilizations, including the abortive communist revolts of 1926/27 — which had their roots, the Dutch believed, in the dislocations caused by modernization—further convinced colonial officials of the righteousness of their increasingly conservative efforts and the repressive political climate. As the so-called ethical period passed, indigenous hierarchy and tradition came to be seen as practical bastions against anticolonial radicalism (Benda 1958, 60–68). As Li puts it: "The concept of the 'adat community' assumed, as it simultaneously sought to engineer, a rural population separated into named ethnic groups with 'traditions' stable enough from person to person and context to context to serve as definitions of group identity, and centralized political structures with recognized leaders capable of articulating a single 'tradition' on behalf of the whole" (1999, 10).

With concepts of *adat* undifferentiated within constructed ethnic entities (Burns 1989), the juridical foundations of the Dayak identity were laid. Belief and trust in the existence of such a recognizable "*adat* community" took hold and have persisted well beyond the period of its colonial creation. As the following chapters will show, in West Kalimantan the *adat* community has come to define the parameters of the politicization of ethnicity and its attendant collective action and violence.

A Catholic schoolteachers' retreat held in Sanggau in July 1940, organized by the young seminary student Oevaang Oeray, is seen by some as the genesis of an organized Dayak movement in West Borneo (P. Donatus 1946). It was the first time Dayaks regionwide were called to gather in service of Dayaks themselves and not on behalf of the government or the missionaries.[18] Yet by the end of the following year the Japanese Imperial Army had invaded West Borneo, momentarily quashing the development of this incipient movement. As we shall see, the nascent Dayak elite greatly benefited from the war and the political dynamics of the Indonesian revolution.

The Japanese Occupation and Its Aftermath

> West Kalimantan invites many difficulties.
> Djawatan Penerangan Propinsi Kalimantan
> (Kalimantan Bureau of Information),
> *Republik Indonesia*

The Japanese occupation of West Borneo during World War II (1942–45) was a time of great hardship. It devastated the local economy, as the Allies blockaded the shipping lanes. Despite the Japanese policy of regional self-sufficiency, a disrupted flow of goods was perilous, for, as was seen above, the region was heavily dependent on imported rice. Widespread starvation ensued.[19] In 1943, having uncovered an underground resistance movement in South Kalimantan, the Japanese "found" a similar intrigue in Pontianak. From late 1943 to early 1944, Japanese naval officers engaged in a series of roundups and executions, events that are collectively known as the Mandor Affair. The victims included the sultan of Pontianak (Syarif Muhammad Alqadri), some twenty-five members of the high aristocracy, intellectuals, party leaders, and merchants from multiple ethnic groups—including ethnic Chinese who constituted the largest number of victims. The Japanese buried their victims in mass graves in Mandor (Usman 2000, 40–47). Months later some 350 Chinese individuals accused of anti-Japanese activities were executed (Maekawa 2002). The official death toll is cited today at 21,037, although a more realistic figure is probably closer to 2,000. With local elites nearly wiped out, the external state authorities would be afforded ample room to interfere in and dominate local affairs. Paradoxically, this situation also created favorable conditions for a new elite—in this case, Dayak leaders—to play an unanticipated role in regional politics.

In late August 1945, Australian soldiers arrived in the region, seized Japanese munitions, and sought to restore order.[20] Some seven weeks later they surrendered their authority to the Netherlands Indies Civil Administration (NICA). Almost immediately, NICA authorities placed a staunch supporter, Syarif Abdul Hamid Alqadrie, on the throne at Kadriah palace in Pontianak, at which point he became known as Sultan Hamid II. A graduate of the Royal Military Academy in the Netherlands (Breda) and a Royal Netherlands Indies Army (Koninklijk Nederlands Indisch Leger, or KNIL) colonel, Hamid had spent the duration of the war jailed in Java, where he had been stationed (Persadja 1955, 5–7; *Kalimantan Berdjuang*, April 11, 1950).

For Dayak leaders, the revolution was a propitious time. The Mandor Affair left this elite unscathed perhaps because of their scant presence in the lowlands or perhaps because the Japanese considered them inconsequential. Whatever the case, the loss of local elites—including many Malay aristocrats—cleared the way for new ones to emerge and capitalize on an unforeseen opportunity. The first step occurred on October 30, 1945, amid the ruins of the crumbled Japanese administration in Putussibau (Kapuas Hulu district). With the help of a Javanese pastor named A. Adikardjana, leading personalities, principally schoolteachers, formed the Daya in Action (DIA). Headed by F. C. Palaunsoeka, a highly regarded schoolteacher, a year later the DIA was transformed into the Daya Unity Party.[21] Its center of operations was moved some 450 miles downriver to the region's administrative and political center, Pontianak, where PD sought close collaboration with NICA in hopes of becoming a prominent regional player.

NICA too courted members of the increasingly "modern" political Dayak elite. Apart from being politically sound, their cooptation was consonant with the ideals of furthering the Dutch civilizing missions and helping Dayaks overcome their backward status in local society.[22] The number of Dayak schoolteachers rose markedly, and members of the political elite were given respectable civil service posts. Palaunsoeka worked in the resident's office in Pontianak. Djelani served in the Department of Religion, and Oeray headed the newly established Kantor Urusan Daya (Dayak Affairs Office) (Balunus n.d., 38).

With an unstable security situation on Java (and Sumatra) and negotiations stalled with leaders who sought a unitary republican form of government, by November 1945, the Dutch, led by Lieutenant Governor-General H. J. van Mook, decided to concentrate their energies on more orderly and peaceful eastern Indonesia. Van Mook's strategy included a military element—restoring order with limited personnel—as well as a political one. He became a tireless champion for federalism in Indonesia, an idea endorsed at the Dutch-led Malino (South Sulawesi) Conference of July 1946. The delegates consisted of aristocrats, key ethnic leaders, and Christians, that is, beneficiaries of colonial rule who were "predictably anxious to retain a strong Dutch connection" (Reid 1974, 108). The Dutch hoped that the states of Kalimantan and East Indonesia (Negara Indonesia Timur, or NIT) would form a bulwark of conservative support vis-à-vis Republican-held Java. Those who opposed Van Mook's plan saw it as a continuance of the colonial policy of divide and rule.

Consonant with its drive for a federal solution, in October 1946 in West Kalimantan, NICA created a forty-member governing council, comprising representatives of the main ethnic groups and colonial officials. The former included a reconstituted Malay aristocracy whose autonomous administrative regions were known as *swapraja*. The council was headed by Sultan Hamid II (A. Arthur Schiller 1955, 123). Van Mook had sought to use the council as a way to create a single state of Kalimantan within the framework of a federal Indonesia, as he had done for the NIT in December 1946. Yet a Kalimantan-wide state never materialized. Enmity between Hamid II and Sultan Parikesit of Kutai (East Kalimantan), as well as the pro-Republican stance of the Malays from the south and east coasts, flummoxed Van Mook's designs.

The formation of some federal states met with stiff resistance but not in West Kalimantan. With Hamid representing the Malay aristocracy, PD, and Chinese factions' cooperative stance, and with viable challengers from political parties and intellectual circles missing due to the aforementioned Mandor Affair, NICA kept a tight grip on the situation. In fact, to break the impasse over the formation of the state of Kalimantan, and to guard his own independence, Hamid—supported by the council—asked that West Kalimantan be designated an autonomous region. Van Mook granted his request, most likely because the Dutch were interested in stability and placating elites who sat on the council would help realize this goal. Accordingly, on May 12, 1947, the area became known as the Daerah Istimewa Kalimantan Barat (West Kalimantan Special Region, or DIKB). Meanwhile, more than two years later, on December 29, 1949, the Dutch surrendered sovereignty to an entity called the Republic of the United States of Indonesia (RUSI), bringing the nearly five-year-long revolutionary war to a close. In West Kalimantan Hamid continued to head the DIKB until he was arrested in April 1950, charged with complicity in Westerling's abortive coup of January 23 in Bandung.[23] A month later the DIKB was disbanded and authority was transferred to a resident of the federal government. On August 17, 1950, RUSI was dissolved and the unitary republic was born.

Partai Daya and a Conflict of Allegiances

In October 1946 seven PD leaders were appointed by NICA to the forty-member West Kalimantan Council.[24] Half of the DIKB's administrative board also hailed from PD: Oeray, A. F. Korak, and Lim Bak Meng—a Catholic Chinese but a PD member (*Keadilan*, May 15, 1948; A. Arthur Schiller 1955, 123; and Balunus n.d., 38). Clearly, PD enjoyed the ardent support of NICA (Harmsen 1947, 21–22). An emerging Dayak political consciousness would continue to be molded in the institutional context of PD and the DIKB bureaucracy.

PD, and in particular Oeray, the party's principal spokesperson, strove to strike a balance between cooperating with the Dutch authorities and preserving the ability to criticize them. Understandably, this delicate game produced a certain amount of ambivalence in Oeray's rhetoric and the party's platform. Despite PD's place in the federal camp, Oeray chided the Dutch for the wretched state of Dayak affairs, and he condemned colonialism for reifying differences and creating hostility between "Daya" and "Malajoe," although the two "shared the same origins and blood [*seasal dan sedarah*]" and had once enjoyed cordial, peaceful relations.[25] But Oeray was not blind to the political realities of colonial rule in West Borneo, and he saved his deepest scorn for indigenous collaborators and partners in the suppression of Dayak rights and freedoms, that is, the Malay princes. He lashed out at these rulers whom he derisively referred to as feudal lords, declaring: "Colonization by Feudalism is worse than Dutch colonialism."[26] Taken together, a principal theme running through Oeray's writings (and later PD publications[27]) is what he called *pendjadjahan berlapis-lapis* (multi-layered colonialism), which describes how Dutch and Malay elites teamed up like "husband and wife" to oppress the true indigenous sons of Borneo ("Mandau," c. 1947–50). Part of a bombast written by Oeray in late 1947 and addressed to West Kalimantan's Dutch resident echoes these sentiments: "Daya are Kalimantan's indigenous people but in everyday life they are treated like foreigners, newcomers. . . . Daya . . . have become the water buffalo that has had to work and sacrifice for king [*radja*] and government. . . . Obviously, the abomination and backwardness of Daya are not only the result of their own *ignorance* but also the result of the wicked politics of feudalism, which was strongly supported by the Dutch government for its own interests" (1947, emphasis in the original).

But Oeray never confused idealistic indignation with practical politics, and he seized on NICA as the vehicle through which PD's elite could obtain the necessary resources and power to challenge the Malay aristocracy. Oeray made his desire to work in tandem with the Dutch clear: "*Only* with and *by* the Netherlands might the fate of Dajak be enhanced" (ARA 1947, emphasis in the original). How, then, should Dayaks go about challenging their Malay counterparts? For Oeray, democracy was the sword that would slay the feudal dragon. Citing democracy as feudalism's *moesoeh jang terbesar* (biggest enemy), he declared: "Feudalism weeps at seeing a people that is bright, smart, prosperous and happy" ("Mandau," ca. 1947–50). At PD's first party congress convened in Sanggau in July 1950, this type of political philosophizing infused the party's ideology and platform, which contained such statements as "all men as God's creatures are created equal [*bahwa tiap2 manusia dijadikan oleh Tuhan atas dasar: Sama2 harga dan deradjat*]" (*Usaha2* 1950).

Needless to say, this kind of Jeffersonian idealism did not square with a party that in reality was unabashedly ethnic in orientation. Neither did it sit well with the way in which PD's elites so forthrightly attached themselves to NICA, which had few democratic pretenses and sought to retain Dutch influence in the archipelago by propping up conservative, aristocratic, and ethnic elites. The acceptance by PD of cushy positions on NICA's West Kalimantan governing councils, headed by feudalism's most powerful symbol, Sultan Hamid II, highlights these contradictions.

Ambivalence also colored PD's internal dynamics, which are exemplified by the personal rivalry between Oeray and Palaunsoeka. An extroverted, fiery orator, the former proved to be a political opportunist. He appended his political fortunes to whatever regime currently held power, first the Dutch and then Soekarno and later the New Order. In contrast, Palaunsoeka was more introverted, bookish, and less swayed by changing political winds. Their personal animosity also stemmed from traditions of intra-Dayak warfare. Oeray and Palaunsoeka hailed from two upriver communities (Kayaan and Taman, respectively) that shared an antagonistic history of feuding (Rousseau 1990, chap. 11; Sellato 1994, 23–25). Finally, the split revolved around the question of who epitomized PD. A party man, Palaunsoeka helped found the DIA in Putussibau and later served as PD's chair, while Oeray, stationed in Pontianak, disdained the daily grind of party politics. Rather, he saw himself as PD's leading personality and emanating spirit, preferring the role of grand adviser in the pursuit of provincial-level aspirations. For some time, the institutional context and symbolic weight of PD ably contained and partly diffused the antipathy, but once this framework was dismantled in the early 1960s—as we will see—the promising PD bifurcated along Oeray/Palaunsoeka lines.

Due to PD's federal stance and its associations with the DIKB, the party's political aspirations were nearly eclipsed when Republican factions won out. Oeray was "kicked upriver" to act as the Kapuas Hulu district executive (*bupati*) from 1951 to 1955. Fortunately for PD, processes of decolonization—in this case, the 1950s elections—rescued the party. In its campaign, although it was financially constrained,[28] PD relied on a strong grassroots network of teachers, the Oeray-Palaunsoeka-Djelani triumvirate, and the easily recognizable Daya name.

Bolstered by the decisive weight of identity politics—and in a province where at that time the nascent self-identifiable Dayak population roughly stood at 45 percent and its Malay counterpart at 33 percent[29]—PD won 31 percent of the vote in the 1955 general election. As a result, it placed nine representatives in the transitional provincial People's Representative Council (DPRD Peralihan), a number surpassed only by the modernist Islamic Masyumi party, which placed ten.[30] In the follow-up 1958 provincial election, PD eclipsed Masyumi, winning twelve seats to the latter's nine. It also gained *bupati* posts in Sanggau, Sintang, Kapuas Hulu, and Pontianak districts.[31] Then, in alliance with the Indonesian National Party (PNI) in 1959, PD obtained the provincial executive post for Oeray, who a year later assumed the governorship when the two posts were merged.[32] Just as important, these electoral dynamics helped to transform "Dayak" as subordinated subject into a charged political identity, a symbol of pride for the masses of nonelites. Tens of thousands of inland denizens, perhaps for the first time, were informed or realized themselves that they "represented" a new, broad-based, ethnically defined identity known as Dayak.

No Malay Counter

While the selection of Oeray drew the ire of the Malay and Islamic factions, they did little to oppose the PD. Why did Malays not mobilize as Dayaks had done? Why were there no Malay counterparts to the PD? As in the Dayak example, we need to explore the dynamics of the formation and orientations of political identities and colonial state formation. As for the former, there was the strong legacy of coastal Malay elites (and aristocrats) looking outward to orient their views and identities. And although they were enmeshed in a regional "Malay" cultural milieu, as was noted above, Muslim took precedence over Malay as an identity marker. Complicating the matter locally was the fact that the Islamic identity was not wholly identifiable with Malay. In coastal West Borneo (as elsewhere), it constituted other such ethnicities as Javanese, Madurese, Bugis, or Minangkabau. With regard to the Netherlands Indies, Anthony Reid records this dynamic: "The colonial cities . . . represented a sort of melting pot where people from diverse origins came to see a common adherence to Islam as the most important thing that separated them from Europeans, Chinese and stateless unbelievers. . . . This new identity was generally called 'Islam,' though in some of the cities and coastal areas of Sumatra, Borneo and the Peninsula it might also be called 'Malay'" (2004 18, 19).

Here rulers and elites in essence continued to derive authority and legitimacy from Islam and to gain recognition within this regionally exalted network. In similar fashion, the heterogeneous ethnic lineages of its royal families eroded the political efficacy of a Malay identity. Bugis and Dayak blood was prevalent in the Mempawah aristocracy, Dayak and Chinese ancestry in the Sambas court, and Arabic ancestry in Pontianak's palace (Heidhues 1998; Van Goor 1986). A claim to rule or mobilize politically based solely on Malayness would have been an oblique assertion.

Colonial state formation also played its part. Because the Dutch did not view Malays as objects of pity, the latter were never subjected to colonial civilizing efforts as Dayaks were. In fact, as was mentioned above, although colonial officials were suspicious of Islam, they used the Malay aristocracy to govern much of the territory. As these conservative aristocrats became dependent on and complicit with colonial rule, in the early Republican period they were discredited as feudal federalists and Dutch lackeys.

In this way, Malay elites were more closely associated with "national" politics than their Dayak counterparts were. This is reflected in the region's first formal political organizations, many of which were established by disgruntled members of the lesser aristocracy, merchants, and intellectuals. In 1914 a regional branch of the Sarekat Islam (Islamic Union)—Indonesia's first mass-based political movement, which had been organized three years earlier in central Java—was formed; in 1922–23, a Sarekat Raykat (People's Association, or SR)—the mass base of the Indonesian Communist Party and organizationally its junior partner—was founded;[33] and in 1925–26 the modernist Islamic organization Muhammadiyah established a branch in West Borneo.

Congruent with their strategy of divide and rule and the politicization of ethnicity, the Dutch founded the region's sole internally oriented, "Malay" organization, although it was not explicitly identified as such. Called the Persatuan Anak Borneo (Union of Borneo Natives, or PAB), its nativist motto was "Borneo for Borneans."[34] Colonial officials rather unsuccessfully encouraged members of the local aristocracy to join the PAB to cleave this conservative elite from upstart nationalists, many of whom hailed from outside West Borneo. In 1936 the latter had formed a local branch of the new Parindra (Greater Indonesia Party), a union of conservative associations that, against the jailing or exiling of non-cooperative leaders, espoused cooperation with the Dutch (Ricklefs

2001, 239). Despite this, Parindra's nationalism, albeit lukewarm, still disconcerted the Dutch in this colonial outpost.

Furthermore, during the revolution local Malay youths formed nationalist, Republican organizations, although resources were lacking and resistance against the Dutch was fleeting (Davidson, forthcoming). As such, unlike what they had done for Dayaks, the colonial authorities forestalled the creation of mass-based, Malay organizations. Once again they opted to rule through the conservative aristocracy, whom the Dutch convinced to support a federal Indonesia. The appointment of representatives of the royal *swapraja* to the West Kalimantan Council was emblematic of this policy. To be sure, a generation of Malay intellectuals and elites was lost due the Mandor Affair. Yet none of the above indicates that any of these leaders would have championed regional Malayism. Finally, countering PD with a Malay movement would have placed the Malay identity in an awkward position vis-à-vis the Dayak identity. Placing Malay elites in a defensive position, it would have forced them to acknowledge the political threat these "primitives" posed. This would have been an untenable maneuver considering their condescending attitude toward Dayaks.

Thus, with no Malay political parties, the choices for Malay voters in the 1950s elections seemed settled: support either nationalist or Islamic parties. The modernist, Islamic Masyumi—the preeminent outer island party—fared best in Sambas district, the "traditional" homeland of Malays. It gained more than two-fifths of the vote in the 1958 regional election. All told, in contrast to that of Dayak, Malay as a political identity was subsumed by exogenous national and religious forces. As chapters 4 and 5 will show, not until the early post-Soeharto period was a Dayak threat acknowledged and countered with avowedly Malay organizations.

PD's Demise

As often happens, external, national shocks have the capacity to overwhelm regional politics. Although Oeray served as governor until 1966, his provincial power base was dealt a serious blow almost as soon as he was appointed. In the mid-1950s, regional rebellions materialized, the first legitimate threat to the young republic's existence. The reasons for the rebellions are complex, but economic grievances lay at their roots. The central government was maintaining distorted exchange rates and granting import licenses that favored industrialists and politicians in

Jakarta while disadvantaging the outer islands, whose small-scale commodity export economies ran a brisk trade with Singapore and Penang, not Jakarta. The December 1956 resignation of Vice President Mohammad Hatta—a Minangkabau from West Sumatra and defender of outer island interests—and the growing stature of the PKI on Java further exacerbated the situation. Tensions between the colonial mode of indirect rule, combined with regional autonomy and Jakarta's centralizing tendencies, were coming to a head (Dick 2002, 175, 179–83).

In December 1956 local army commanders in West Sumatra assumed power and announced the establishment of a rebel, counter government (the Revolutionary Government of the Indonesian Republic, known by the Indonesian acronym, PRRI). Dissident military leaders in North Sulawesi followed suit. After a year of failed negotiations, the central army put down the main forces of both rebellions (Kahin and Kahin 1995). This success increased the political influence of the army and gave its chief of staff, General A. H. Nasution, an opportunity to rationalize and centralize army control (McVey 1971, 1972). The suppression of the regional rebellions also had serious political ramifications for the country. For one thing, it epitomized the country's growing disillusionment over the Republic's failure to live up to the great hopes and promises of the early independence period. Furthermore, the regional crisis led to the emasculation of Indonesia's party system. President Soekarno and the army's top brass seized this occasion to act on their ingrained aversion to liberal, multiparty democracy. In 1959 under the pretext of martial law, Soekarno—prompted by the army—banned Masyumi due to its involvement in the rebellions (Lev 1966b). Then he outlawed regional parties by presidential decree (No. 7/1959). With respect to West Kalimantan, in rapid succession, its two political powers, the ethnoregional PD and the Islamic modernist Masyumi, were forced to disband.

In the wake of this reversal of fortune, PD's leadership scrambled to stay politically organized. The inner strife that had dogged the party since its inception finally burst forth, however. Once described as a figure for "the Dayaks what Soekarno was once for the Indonesians" (Feith 1968, 134), Oeray established a provincial chapter of Partindo (Partai Indonesia). He chose Partindo in part because it was regionally weak, which would ensure the erstwhile PD leadership control, and in part because its secular (as opposed to sectarian) orientation would retain PD's non-Catholic (Dayak and Chinese) support. Just as important, Partindo was leftist and thereby Oeray took advantage of the nation's leftist swing, led by Soekarno. Having been backed by Soekarno for the provincial executive position, Oeray now sought to take advantage of his relationship with the president. Palaunsoeka did not follow Oeray into Partindo. Unable to reconcile his devout Catholicism with the party's communist sympathies, he joined forces with the small Catholic Party (Partai Katolik). Although he was aware that this might alienate PD's non-Catholic constituency, Palaunsoeka reasoned that PD's very existence was largely owed to the Catholic Church. Meanwhile, the personal rivalry between these two Dayak heavyweights did little to ameliorate the split.

The division pervaded Dayak society. It implicated the Church, whose pastors used provocative sermons to urge parishioners to avoid Partindo (Kadir 1995, 17–18). As governor, Oeray exploited his position to corral erstwhile PD *bupati* and civil servants, including public school teachers. He toured the province denouncing his absentee rival, Palaunsoeka, who as a national parliamentarian resided in Jakarta, which made him less visible locally. All told, the split eroded the Dayaks' political prominence within the region and its bitter legacy has not been reconciled to this day. The rift also figured immensely in the 1967 Chinese pogroms, the subject of the next chapter.

2

Konfrontasi, Rebellion, and Ethnic Cleansing

We have lived for years, with the Dayaks. We've intermarried. Look at these people, many look just like Dayaks. There is no racial hatred between us.

A former Chinese store owner and victim of the 1967 pogroms,
quoted in J. Williams 1967

This chapter recounts a period of tremendous upheaval, one more tumultuous than Dutch colonialism or the Japanese occupation. Here central state intrusion reached unprecedented depths and laid the foundation for the region's postindependence ethnic strife. This period is when the chief forms of violence crystallized. In 1966, following the end of *Konfrontasi* (Confrontation)—a campaign waged by the Indonesian army and bands of volunteers to disrupt Sarawak's incorporation into the newly formed Malaysian state—an armed insurgency broke out in the heavily forested stretch of West Kalimantan between the Malaysian border and the Kapuas River. It was the first rebellion against Soeharto's authoritarian rule. Ten years later, the Angkatan Bersenjata Republik Indonesia (Armed Forces of the Republic of Indonesia, or ABRI) declared an end to military operations. Between these dates lies a brutal but virtually unknown history of military operations, ethnic cleansing, ethnic engineering, environmental degradation, aggressive capital accumulation, and coercive centralization.

Critically, Madurese-Dayak violence first developed during this rebellion, precipitated by the expulsion of rural Chinese from inland

Sambas and Pontianak districts. Here, as local social relations were solid and did not signal the impending violence (Coppel 1983, 145), the importance of state institutional collapse, the politicization of ethnicity, and strategic elite manipulation in igniting ethnic massacres comes to the fore. Two powerful forces, the army and certain Dayak leaders, working in tandem, were required to spark the violence; one party alone would have been ineffectual. Happenstance and interest brought these two forces together to generate horrific bloodshed.

Konfrontasi in National Capitals

The origins of the rebellion in West Kalimantan lie in the creation of the Malaysian state, which comprised the former British territories of Malaya, Singapore, Sarawak, and North Borneo (Sabah). The overriding concern for the British was how to reduce their forces (and hence their costs) while maintaining political and military influence in the region (Subritzky 1999, 53–55). Prior to the formation of Malaysia, in their three northern Borneo protectorates (Sarawak, Brunei, and Sabah), the British developed a decolonization policy known as "closer association." Its principal components included increased interprotectorate trade and a gradual political liberalization. It was hoped that in time this managed decolonization would facilitate the formation of a quasi-independent yet pro-British Borneo Federation. Only then would the question of whether this entity would join the larger Malaysian Federation, which consisted of peninsular Malaya and Singapore, be considered. Unfortunately, developments in northern Borneo forced the British to shelve its benign federation plan and pursue more coercive measures.

A primary concern for the British was maintaining unfettered access to Brunei's vast oil reserves, which were vital to Britain's postwar economy (Poulgrain 1998, 133). Never a sincere supporter of enhanced political autonomy for Brunei, the British Malayan Petroleum Company ran the protectorate's oil industry. In return, the sultan received huge sums of oil-derived money and sufficient British political and military support to keep his anachronistic regime in power. The rapid rise of Sheik A. M. Azahari's populist People's Party of Brunei (PRB), founded in mid-1956, disrupted this cozy relationship, however. Native to Brunei but a veteran of the Indonesian Revolution, Azahari, upon his return from Indonesia in 1951, sparked nascent Brunei nationalism, championed democratic reforms, and publicized royal corruption. His intent was to establish a constitutional monarchy loosely based on the British system that would unite all three Borneo territories in an entity called Kalimantan Utara (North Kalimantan).

From the outset, the British Colonial Office branded Azahari a troublemaker. More pointedly, Azahari's popularity and political ideals threatened Britain's oil interests. Thus, behind the facade of democratic reform, the colonial office sought to circumscribe the PRB's political latitude. Although the party swept all contested seats in Brunei's 1962 legislative council elections, British subterfuge denied it control of the government. Authority would ostensibly remain in colonial hands.

As the PRB's popularity grew and its leadership contemplated seizing power, the British authorities arrested PRB officials in northern Sarawak. Fearing a similar fate, on December 8, 1962, the PRB leadership, despite Azahari's absence, launched a revolt in Brunei. The sultan sided with Britain. Within days and before masses of people could be mobilized, British and Gurkha troops arrived and crushed the uprising, which was led by the Tentara Nasional Kalimantan Utara (North Kalimantan National Army, or TNKU), the PRB's armed wing of some two to three thousand troops. Having reinstalled the sultan on the throne, the British were forced to seriously reconsider their decolonization plans (Easter 2004, 35–36).[1]

Although Sarawak was not as vital to British interests as Brunei, the situation there nonetheless caused considerable consternation for British authorities. Sarawak was home to a resilient Chinese communist movement that had survived the so-called Emergency and the collapse of the Malayan Races Liberation Army (MRLA) in the late 1950s in Malaya (Porritt 2004).[2] The communists—the grassroots backbone of the Chinese-dominated Sarawak United People's Party (SUPP)—steadfastly opposed the Malaysian Federation proposal.[3] In fact, SUPP and its affiliated Sarawak Communist Organization (SCO) joined forces with Azahari's PRB in an effort to form a united North Kalimantan free of British influence.[4] Following the abortive Brunei revolt, the SCO refocused its energies on liberating Sarawak from British control. It also switched its emphasis from a legal to an armed struggle (Sarawak Government 1972, 19).

For the British, the SUPP leadership, which included a handful of broadly pro-British moderates, was of secondary concern. The main threat consisted of the twenty-five hundred core members of the SCO and its networks among students, teachers, peasants, and trade unionists.[5] Like its counterpart on the peninsula—the Communist Party of Malaya—the SCO was heavily (if not wholly) Chinese. The SCO's failure to garner support across ethnic groups—and even among large sectors of the Chinese population—inhibited its spread and efficacy.[6] But in Sarawak the Chinese comprised roughly 31 percent of the population and had a birthrate appreciably higher than those of other ethnic groups. So the SCO still posed a formidable challenge to the British. A communist Sarawak, either as an independent state or one aligned with Azahari in an anti-British North Kalimantan, would threaten British access to Brunei's oil reserves and create a stronghold for communism, which could then be exported throughout the region. Throughout 1961–62 British authorities clamped down on SCO cadres. Detentions became more numerous after the authorities accused the SCO (and the more radical factions of SUPP) of complicity in the PRB's abortive revolt. To evade incarceration, by mid-1963 some seven hundred cadres had fled Sarawak to find refuge in the neighboring Indonesian province of West Kalimantan (*The origin and development* ca. 1974, 2).

National Politics in Indonesia

In addition to SUPP and SCO, the British (and the new Malaysian elite) accused President Soekarno in Jakarta of backing and even instigating the Brunei rebellion (Easter 2004, 28).[7] Following the revolt's outbreak, Soekarno did publicly declare his support for Azahari, and in January 1963 Foreign Minister Subandrio announced the initiation of a vague policy known as *Konfrontasi* that would comprise political, economic, and military struggles against what Soekarno perceived to be Britain's neocolonial Malaysia plan. Seen in this light, the unfolding of *Konfrontasi* is best understood in the context of Indonesian domestic politics at the time.

In the early 1960s there emerged an unstable and increasingly acrimonious political dynamic described by Feith (1964) as "the triangle." One leg was the Indonesian army. On the eve of *Konfrontasi*, the army was enjoying unprecedented unity among its ranks and a burgeoning confidence, the result of a series of successful military operations against the rebellions in West Sumatra and North Sulawesi, the Darul Islam insurrections (notably in West Java), and the "liberation" of West Irian, which was wrestled from Dutch control.[8] The prospect of domestic security, however, threatened the political influence its leadership had fought hard to acquire. Martial law—as a result of the regional rebellions—was revoked in May 1963, but another military campaign would ensure substantial military budgets and enhance army influence in the political (and business) affairs of the state save for one important caveat. The army leadership backed *Konfrontasi* as long as the tactics of this "undeclared war" were characterized by sporadic, low-intensity raids (Crouch 1978, 59; Penders and Sundhaussen 1985, 166, 169). In other words, army leaders did not want a full-fledged war. Indonesia's struggling economy could not underwrite such an enterprise, and the army doubted its abilities to defeat an alliance of Commonwealth forces. An increased commitment of troops north along the border in Borneo would also leave the army vulnerable on Java, where the influence of the PKI, the army's principal adversary, was waxing and rumors of a possible coup was widely circulating.

The second leg of this political triangle, the PKI, found its strength neither in the army elite nor in the upper echelons of Jakarta's political bureaucracy, but among urban workers and peasants in Java's densely populated, agricultural heartland. Throughout 1964–65, conflict over land and land reform on Java heightened, exemplified by the *aksi sepihak* (unilateral actions) led by the communist-affiliated Barisan Tani Indonesia (Indonesian Peasant Front, or BTI) (Feith 1964; Lev 1966a; Lyon 1970).

Somewhat contradictorily, the PKI over time came to support the *Konfrontasi* campaign. Why would it back *Konfrontasi*, whose putative aims was to "crush Malaysia," if, as some believed, the Chinese would come to dominate Malaysia and turn the new nation-state into a communist-oriented "second China" (see Hatta 1965)? In short, the answers are threefold. First, the party (correctly) believed that procapitalist, not communist, forces would hold sway in a newly constituted Malaysia. Second, the party leadership argued that civilians should be trained and armed to participate in the campaign. In the context of the fierce PKI-army rivalry, this was seen as a means of arming a "fifth force" outside of the military, thus enhancing the PKI's strength vis-à-vis the army. This was one element of a broader radicalization of the country's politics that the PKI was trying to achieve (Mortimer 1974, 203–5, 380–87). Finally, the PKI's support for *Konfrontasi* derived from its close relationship with President Soekarno, the third leg of the triangle and the principal spokesperson of the anti-Malaysian crusade.

Soekarno branded "Malaysia" a neocolonial, puppet state of the British that would unnervingly encircle Indonesia. His vehemence stemmed from a complex and muddled set of motivations (Subritzky 1999, 41–42). For one thing, Soekarno was wholly consumed with the ideal of nation-building, a daunting task in a young, extraordinarily

heterogeneous country spanning thousands of islands. External enemies around which to rally divergent populations could help serve this
end. The British policy on Malaysia also fit comfortably within the context of Soekarno's indignant, anti-Western, and anti-imperialist ideology and rhetoric, which pushed the idea of "new emerging forces" outside the traditional spheres of dominance. Furthermore, the prospect of
a further military campaign offered Soekarno more latitude among military officers. As an unelected president, Soekarno had mass support
but no way to mobilize it. He was forced to play the army and the PKI
against each other to stay in power (Hindley 1964). The British suspected that Soekarno had territorial expansion in mind (Easter 2004, 31;
Gordon 1963-64).

In response to and support of the Brunei revolt, Indonesia announced the anti-Malaysia campaign in January 1963. Not until April,
however, did the first Indonesian raiders slip into Sarawak and not until
September did Soekarno's infamous slogan *Ganyang Malaysia* (Crush
Malaysia) become the cornerstone of Indonesian political jargon, although a propaganda campaign had been under way for some time. In
between these dates, a concerted effort was made to settle the Malaysian issue diplomatically.

In May 1963, Soekarno and the premier of Malaysia, Tunku Abdul
Rahman, met in Tokyo for informal talks. Soon a Foreign Ministers'
Conference in Manila was held. In the spirit of Maphilindo, a pact of
solidarity among ethnic Malays, the Manila Accord was signed. One of
its points called for a United Nations (UN) commission sponsored by
Secretary-General U Thant to conduct a survey to ascertain the views
of North Borneans concerning the Malaysia Federation. In the meantime, British and Malaysian leaders had decided that on August 31 Malaysia would be officially proclaimed. Significantly, this agreement was
signed on July 9, prior to the UN commission's arrival in north Borneo.
The maneuver infuriated Soekarno, who interpreted it as an example of
British arrogance and Tunku duplicity (M. Jones 2002, 278-79, 289).

Consequently, in late July 1963 in Jakarta the first of a series of *Ganyang Malaysia* demonstrations was held at the British embassy. In the
face of aggravated tensions, in early August a summit in Manila gathered the Filipino, Malaysian, and Indonesian heads of state. There the
Tunku—as he was known—agreed to delay Malaysia's independence to
allow the UN commission to conduct its work. A negotiated end
seemed possible, but Soekarno—"whose dominance on the issue of
Crush Malaysia was virtually complete" within Indonesia—rejected the

commission's findings, which confirmed the population's support for the Malaysian Federation (H. Jones 1971, 289, 290–92). Similarly, after the new Federation of Malaysia was proclaimed on September 16, Indonesia refused to recognize it. The Tunku responded in kind by severing diplomatic ties with Indonesia. For the next two days anti-British demonstrations rocked Jakarta, culminating in the destruction of the British embassy and the organized looting of dozens of British homes throughout the capital. The *Ganyang Malaysia* campaign had reached the point of no return (Bunnell 1969, 622–32; Mackie 1974, 157–94).

The breaking of diplomatic ties severely affected the Indonesian economy. Its trade embargo on Malaysia, which included Singapore, its largest trading partner, forced Indonesia to abandon its strict monetary policy and stabilization scheme, which had been instituted in May 1963 at the behest of the United States and the International Monetary Fund (IMF). But the embargo, which precipitated a dwindling of foreign reserves and the takeover of British firms in Indonesia, led the United States and the IMF to suspend much needed aid and credits to Indonesia. Add an increased military budget to this dire situation and the country's precipitous economic slide became inescapable (Mackie 1974, 136–37, 179–94, 217–21).

Militarily, the coordination of *Konfrontasi* was placed under Komando Siaga (the Alert Command, or Koga), which was headed by an air force commander, Vice Marshal Omar Dhani, a Soekarno loyalist. Throughout 1963 and the first half of 1964, despite worsening diplomatic relations, from an operational point of view *Konfrontasi* was maintained at a satisfactory level for the army leadership, primarily as a series of periodic, low-intensity raids into neighboring Sabah and Sarawak (Crouch 1978, 69–70; Easter 2004, 133). These raids, conducted largely by Indonesian regular troops and some *sukarelawan* (volunteers), were limited to the Kalimantan–northern Borneo border. The expansion and escalation the army feared, however, soon occurred. In July 1964 ethnic riots hit Singapore and suddenly the peninsula looked vulnerable. Without the army's consent, on August 17, 1964, a small group of Indonesian raiders infiltrated Johor on the southern tip of the Malaysian Peninsula. Although the conflict had little to do with Malaysia (Mortimer 1974, 233), two weeks later Indonesian paratroopers, along with some Malaysian Chinese, parachuted into southern Malaysia. The conflict, some generals worried, was expanding beyond its comfort zone. Their interests and those of Soekarno were beginning to diverge markedly.[9]

These generals took steps to rein in and gain control of *Konfrontasi's* military operations. In late February 1965, they successfully pressured Soekarno to replace Koga with the Komando Siaga Mandala (Mandala Alert Command, or Kolaga). Despite similarities in nomenclature and function, Kolaga's formation benefited the army. An army officer, Major General Soeharto, who had led the campaign in West Irian and who was then commander of the Army Strategic Reserve Command (Pangkostrad), was appointed Kolaga's first deputy commander (Wakil Panglima I). With this restructuring, Soeharto, not Dhani, now held "the real decision-making power" within Kolaga (Penders and Sundhaussen 1985, 171). Under Kolaga, Sumatra and Kalimantan were given their own combat forces and operational names.[10] The left-leaning Brigadier General M. A. Soepardjo, whose appointment was largely perceived as a concession to Dhani, headed the Kalimantan operation.[11] In Sumatra, Brigadier General Kemal Idris, a Soekarno detractor and solid anti-communist, was tapped as commander. Given Sumatra's proximity to the peninsula compared to that of Kalimantan, this arrangement greatly reduced the possibility that *Konfrontasi* would inexplicably engulf the peninsula. Furthermore, Kolaga's authority over troop deployments was at once expanded and circumscribed. Its command was widened to cover all four military services but was restricted to its area of command, namely, Sumatra and Kalimantan. In other words, it had no power to mobilize troops on the crucially strategic island of Java. Finally, troop deployments had to be transferred to the Army Strategic Command Reserve (Kostrad), which was under Soeharto's control. This ensured that the troops either arrived in the field ill-prepared or never arrived at all.[12] In sum, at the expense of the Soekarno-Dhani faction, the Achmad Yani-Soeharto camp was gaining the upper hand.

Insurgency on Borneo

In mid-1963, Indonesian army raids into Sarawak increased in frequency, as did the number of regular troops involved, although Indonesian support for the rebels remained largely furtive. This soon changed, however, as statements by Indonesian officials increasingly alluded to support of rebels in Borneo.[13] Over the course of the next year basic military training and the provision of weapons for several thousand volunteers in West Kalimantan and on Java continued. Recruitment processes culminated in Soekarno's Dwikora declaration of May 1964, which urged volunteers to join the struggle, a campaign behind which the PKI threw its full support (Mortimer 1974, 226, 243). Newspaper headlines exaggerated claims that millions rushed to enlist (see, e.g., the leftist *Bintang Timur,* March 25, 1946), though the number of volunteers that were actually sent to the field from Java remains obscure.

Meanwhile, a year after the failed Brunei revolt, in early December 1963, Subandrio flew to Pontianak and met with Azahari. Shortly thereafter, Azahari arrived in Jakarta to lobby Jakarta's anti-Malaysia factions and garner support for his fledgling force, the TNKU. Upon his return to West Kalimantan, in an upriver town in Sintang district, he and two leading members of Sarawak's SCO, Yap Chung Ho and Yang Chu Chung (a.k.a. Yacob), agreed to form two interdependent rebel forces, the Pasukan Gerilya Rakyat Sarawak (Sarawak People's Guerilla Force, or PGRS), which comprised mainly SCO cadres; and the Pasukan Rakyat Kalimantan Utara (North Kalimantan People's Force, or Paraku), which consisted of members of Azahari's TNKU. Azahari and Yap then returned to Java to meet Subandrio and Njoto, a member of the PKI's Politburo, in Bogor, a cool hill town south of Jakarta to discuss rebel support. Subandrio, in his capacity as head of the Central Intelligence Bureau (BPI), agreed to Azahari and Yap's request to train a core group of rebels in early 1964. After a month's training in Bogor, a group of ten leading SCO figures returned to West Kalimantan to train another group of sixty. These groups would later form the core of the PGRS and Paraku troops.[14] Indonesian support for the rebels did not stop there, however.[15] Fueled by intramilitary rivalries, General Nasution, the army chief of staff and a Subandrio critic concerned about the latter's growing influence over the rebels, also began to equip Borneo-based troops through his own man, the interregional commander of Kalimantan, Colonel Hassan Basri (Crouch 1978, 60).

All told, the "volunteers" who did participate in the raids into Sarawak played a minor role in the fighting between 1963 and 1966. They were of mixed origins: TNKU members who later formed the Paraku; young ethnic Malaysian Chinese from the SCO, the armed wing of which was the PGRS;[16] Indonesian "volunteers" recruited locally and in West Java (many of whom were sympathetic to the PKI); and Indonesian military troops "who had been released from their army units" (Mackie 1974, 211). In fact, many of the latter had simply rebelled.[17] According to military data, in October–November 1965 the number of volunteers totaled 2,313.[18]

These raids aimed to destabilize Sarawak and undermine its incorporation into the Malaysian Federation. But the raiders failed to establish reliable base camps within Sarawak and arouse popular resistance against the formation of the federation.[19] In all, two different investigations—those of the Cobbold Commission (February 1962) and the UN Commission (September 1963)—were conducted to ascertain Sarawakians' wishes vis-à-vis the Malaysian Federation. One observer, however, sensibly warned that "any 'official' expression of public opinion in North Borneo was bound to be a little suspect" (Curtis 1964, 23). We do not know whether these raids created the external threat that convinced the majority of Sarawakians to support the Malaysian Federation, but, as per British designs, Sarawak joined the federation upon its inception.

In the meantime, from late 1964 to mid-1965, in part due to Soeharto's tightening grip over *Konfrontasi*'s military aspects, no meaningful raids on the Malaysian Peninsula were conducted. The status quo—low-intensity, periodic raids into Sarawak (and Sabah)—was maintained. The military seizure of power begun on October 1, 1965, in Jakarta, however, created a political reversal with extraordinary implications throughout Indonesia.[20] Almost immediately the Soeharto-led army instigated massive anticommunist massacres, although Soeharto failed to coerce Soekarno, who officially remained president, into banning the PKI.

The Fallout in West Kalimantan

The virulent anticommunist vibrations emanating from Jakarta were quickly felt in West Kalimantan. On October 10, 1965, three leftist newspapers were banned, and days later the provincial government placed a "freeze" on the PKI and its affiliated organizations (*Kompas,* October 11, 1965).[21] Its party leaders were ordered to report to the authorities. Soon thereafter anti-PKI demonstrators ransacked communist and Chinese property: the PKI's headquarters and its newspaper's office, the secretariat of the Chinese organization Baperki (Badan Permusyawaratan Kewarganegaraan Indonesia), the office of the communist-affiliated labor union Sentral Organisasi Buruh Seluruh Indonesia (SOBSI), and several Chinese-run schools and businesses. Demonstrators also attacked the province's public works department because its head, Bambang Soemitro, was a high-ranking PKI member (*Akcaya,* January 19, 1984). Crowds searched in vain for the head of the West Kalimantan branch of the PKI, Said Achmad Sofyan. Within a day or two, Brigadier General H. M. Ryacudu, the commander of the Tanjungpura

Regional Military Command (Kodam XII), gave Sofyan refuge in his official residence.[22]

Why would Ryacudu, the person most responsible for Sofyan's arrest, protect him? Ryacudu was not complicit with the PKI, despite his staunch Soekarnoism.[23] Student demonstrations held around this time protested Ryacudu's patronage networks and attendant interference in the local economy, which, according to the students, had led to increases in the price of staple goods. But no one accused Ryacudu of being a PKI stooge.[24] The answer is found in the amicable relationship between Ryacudu and Sofyan, a relationship that was well known locally.

Historically, while there were vibrant communist organizations in West Kalimantan, including proletarian miners' associations, the PKI never gained a strong footing there. Given the province's substantial Chinese population and in the context of the 1920s–50s communist-nationalist struggles in China, significant support for Mao and the People's Republic of China (PRC) existed, especially among the Chinese in the greater Singkawang area (Heidhues 2003). But strong communist sympathies did not necessarily translate into PKI backing. The majority felt more attracted to political developments in China than Indonesia, lacked Indonesian citizenship papers, and spoke poor Indonesian.[25] Communism also failed to appeal to many modernist Islamic Malays and animist and Christian Dayaks. For the most part, Indonesian communism remained an import of Javanese migrants whose numbers, prior to the New Order, remained small. In the 1955 general elections, the PKI won 1.7 percent of the provincial vote.

But in the early 1960s the party grew considerably under the able leadership of Sofyan.[26] Hailing from Banjarmasin and of mixed Arab and Madurese descent, Sofyan was a PKI candidate in the 1955 elections in South Kalimantan and by 1959 had become secretary of the party's provincial central board.[27] Sometime later he was assigned to West Kalimantan to galvanize its PKI branch. Pessimistic about the party's potential to attract ethnic Malays, Sofyan argued that recruitment strategies should focus on the large Chinese population. His plans, however, created friction with the Javanese-dominated PKI elite. In particular, the provincial chair, the Moscow-oriented Bambang Soemitro, believed that the PKI should build a *pribumi* (native) base from Dayak and Malay populations. Sofyan eventually won out and in 1960 was named the new PKI leader. According to military sources, the rift endured.

Upon seizing the leadership, Sofyan concentrated his energies on Pontianak's Chinese youth, working closely with Lim Bak Sun, a leader of a youth organization called the People's Youth Organization (Djen Min Tjhin Njin Min Toan in Chinese). Sofyan was well liked among their ranks, where he was known by the Chinese name Tai Ko, meaning "Big Brother" (or "Boss"). Having gained the confidence of the pro-PRC elite, Sofyan was permitted to organize rallies, dances, plays, and sing-a-longs in conjunction with the PKI's cultural organization, Lekra, in the leftist Chinese theater Angin Timur (East Wind).[28] The PKI also coordinated its efforts with those of a Chinese labor union (Lo Kung Hui) and Chung Hwa Kung Hui, the Chinese General Association. Together they established dozens of schools (Lembaga Pendidikan Nasional) and related facilities that offered social, cultural, and educational services to rural Chinese. Thousands of illiterate adults learned to read in these evening schools (Angkatan Darat Kodam XII 1972, 329–30).

Sofyan's popularity extended beyond the local ethnic Chinese population. Interviews unanimously confirm his superior leadership qualities, his engaging personality, and the high esteem he garnered. Sofyan socialized effortlessly with Pontianak's Islamic elite, for his father was a respected *kiyai* (Islamic teacher) in Banjarmasin, and Sofyan was well versed in Islamic teachings. His presence at religious festivals and celebrations was common.[29] Furthermore, due to his competence, Sofyan often chaired cross-party or citywide committees formed at the behest of the government (or the army). Thus, he was well known and liked by Ryacudu.[30] Their relationship was further deepened when in 1963 Soekarno expanded the regional executive committees, called Tjatur Tunggal (Four-in-One), to include a fifth member: the head of the regional National Front, which in this case, was Sofyan. He also chaired Pontianak's 1965 Independence Day Committee.

Back in Jakarta, having engineered a putsch against President Soekarno on March 11, 1966, General Soeharto banned the PKI and moved swiftly to end *Konfrontasi,* although clandestine contacts between pro-Soeharto officers such as intelligence chief Ali Murtopo and Lieutenant Colonel L. B. Moerdani—then the Indonesian military attaché in Kuala Lumpur—and certain Malaysian parties had been underway for nearly two years (Mukmin 1991, 116–58; Pour 1993, 314–43). In January 1966, the Indonesian and Malaysian foreign ministers met in Bangkok to negotiate an end to *Konfrontasi,* and further talks followed in Kuala Lumpur in May.

With his political potency on the wane, Soekarno continued to rail publicly against the Bangkok Proposals, but *Konfrontasi* "was coming to lose the last of its capacity to play an important political function" (Weinstein 1969, 76). With the prospect of the resumption of foreign aid and Soeharto's increasing dominance of the military and the nation's political scene via the ruthless and bloody PKI pogroms, the Jakarta Accords were signed on August 11, 1966, bringing *Konfrontasi* to a close.

A negotiated end to *Konfrontasi* staged in national capitals, however, did not mean that Indonesian-trained rebels in the field would suddenly disappear. Nor did it mean all regular troops and *sukarelawan* would simply surrender or return to their original stations. The Indonesian-Malaysian talks had tentatively directed the "volunteers" in West Kalimantan to return their weapons and disband, but many of them, having been mobilized to participate in armed resistance, disregarded the directive.[31] Instead, these divergent actors coalesced into two more or less distinct groups. On the one hand, PGRS and Paraku relations remained cooperative, demonstrated in the frequently cited PGRS/Paraku appellation. The former was largely concentrated along the western part of the West Kalimantan–Sarawak border (from the coast to the Sikukng mountain complex).[32] The latter was located along the border's eastern reaches (around the Benua Martinus mountain complex). On the other hand, members of the banned PKI and at least some volunteers and regular troops consolidated, first as an urban underground and later in the mountain complexes of West Kalimantan. The PKI was oriented toward West Kalimantan; the PGRS/Paraku, fighting for Sarawak's liberation, was oriented toward Sarawak. Nonetheless, survival necessitated engaging the Indonesian military as well. The PGRS's view toward its potential foe is expressed in a poignant letter putatively sent to Indonesian soldiers sometime in 1967:

> We the people of North Kalimantan are continuing the struggle against neocolonial "Malaysia" for the full national independence of North Kalimantan! The people of North Kalimantan and Indonesia can unite to oppose England, the U.S. and neocolonialism. By fighting our enemies side by side . . . we hope that our mutual assistance and cooperation can continue to be nurtured.
>
> If you don't attack us, we won't attack you. If you attack us, we will be forced to respond and thoroughly annihilate our attackers. If you attack us, the foundations of our cooperation and friendship will have been ruined.

You have troubled yourselves by coming far from Java. Your self-beings [*jiwa*] have to be nurtured as well as possible. If you are hard-hearted and join in the attacks against us, we will be forced to respond. Thus, your sacrifices surely will be great, so how can you go home to Java to meet safely with your families?

By leaving your families and relatives, you came here to fight whom? To fight North Kalimantan guerrillas, no? Those struggling for the full national independence of North Kaliman-tan? If you heedlessly make sacrifices, what about your family's future in Java? . . . Long live the anti-imperialism friendship between the people of North Kalimantan and the people of Indonesia!!!

The PGRS.[33]

Ultimately, the PGRS made good on its promise to retaliate if attacked, and scores of ABRI soldiers never did make the trip home to Java to re-unite with their families.

Military and Rebel Organizing

With Soeharto at the helm, the army branded the PKI sole conspirators behind the "abortive coup" of October 1, 1965, and by mid-month anti-PKI massacres had erupted. Led by the Army Para-Commando Regi-ment (Resimen Para Komando Angkatan Darat, or RPKAD) and in conjunction with youth and religious vigilante groups, killings started in Central Java and were spread to East Java. Massacres eventually ravaged Bali and North Sumatra as well, although substantial anti-PKI violence in Aceh had anticipated the Central Java bloodshed. In West Kaliman-tan, anti-PKI massacres failed to materialize, for the PKI's strength had not reached levels sufficient to threaten vested interests. Despite its growth, its provincial membership was meager; estimates stood at 3,500 members and sympathizers in mid-1965 (Semdam XII 1971, 226). The BTI operated in the region yet made few inroads. The province's vast hinterland and low population density did not (yet) lend itself to intense conflict over land; there are no known reports of unilateral actions undertaken by the BTI. In certain areas, latent or mild conflict over land most likely existed, but well-rooted, organized channels to air re-lated grievances were missing. Arrests of suspected communists were common, but collective violence was exceptional.[34]

This same period also saw some anti-Chinese violence nationwide, although this paled in comparison with the pogroms against the PKI. The presence of left-wing Chinese organizations, coupled with the threatening menace of the PRC looming in the north, made accusations of Chinese complicity in the events of October 1, 1965, all too facile. Aceh and North Sumatra witnessed several large-scale incidents, including forced repatriations (Mabbett and Mabbett 1972, 9). Smaller episodes were reported in South Kalimantan, Bali, Lombok, and Sumbawa. Minor rioting broke out in Jakarta, largely directed at the Chinese embassy and related installations (Mackie 1976).

Again relative calm prevailed in West Kalimantan. The aforementioned incidents make their absence in West Kalimantan—home to Indonesia's largest Chinese population—more surprising than the lack of anti-PKI violence. This development reflected two crucial interrelated aspects, especially in the face of what was soon to come: the most serious anti-Chinese atrocities since the 1740 massacres in Batavia (now Jakarta). First, the lack of anti-Chinese violence during this period demonstrates that social relations were in fact strong and failed to foreshadow the impending massacres. Second, it sheds light on the substantial instigation needed to prompt the soon-to-be violence that finally did erupt in October 1967.

Regardless of the lack of mass violence, new restrictive policies regarding the Chinese population in West Kalimantan were introduced. In March 1966, Singkawang's Chinese General Association was disbanded; a year later some three hundred of its members were ordered to repatriate to China.[35] In April the authorities began an eight-month campaign to compile lists of personnel in all Chinese organizations, schools, and related institutions (Ryacudu 1967b, 8). In May, thousands in Pontianak were forced to attend an *appel setia* (loyalty line-up) overseen by Ryacudu (*Kompas*, May 3 and 4, 1966). Licenses for foreign-run (i.e., Chinese) schools were revoked and in December the authorities banned Baperki (*Kompas*, July 21, 1966).[36]

In early 1967, the authorities forced thousands of Chinese to participate in labor programs. Nearly eight thousand worked on the Singkawang-Seluas road, some three thousand opened rice fields (*sawah*) in Sanggau district, and another 600 built an army barrack in Semitau in Kapuas Hulu district (Ryacudu 1967b, 8–9).[37] Ryacudu also ordered that "Chinese" associated with either the PKI or Chinese social organizations leave the province (*Antara Weekly Review*, December 4 and 11, 1965; Coppel 1983, 112). This action was followed by a half-hearted effort to expatriate five thousand more from the interior. Five thousand individuals was only the tip of the iceberg. The military estimated that there were 450,000 Chinese in West Kalimantan, three-quarters of whom did not have Indonesian citizenship papers.[38]

The relative quiescence at this juncture should not imply provincial stagnation or a radical disconnect from national events. Antileftist student groups in Pontianak (and Jakarta) vociferously called for the removal of Governor Oeray as a representative of the Soekarnoist Partindo party. As Partindo became implicated in the events of October 1, 1965, Oeray's political fortunes waned.[39] The Himpunan Mahasiwa Islam (Islamic Students Association, or HMI) and related organizations held demonstrations at the governor's office and provincial council building.[40] Subsequently, in July 1966 New Order authorities removed Oeray, accusing him of being a Soekarnoist. Oeray's extroverted regionalism did not help his cause either.

Student associations were not the only active local organizations at this time. There was also the PKI. Although favorable social and geographic conditions still prevailed in West Kalimantan, in the face of virulent anticommunism and the massacres being conducted elsewhere, the PKI was not about to await the arrest of its members or simply disappear. Sometime in late 1965 or perhaps early 1966, Sofyan and a group of followers fled from Pontianak to a forested mountain complex in the Bengkayang area, which they called Bukit Bara.[41] The location of Bukit Bara placed Sofyan and his followers in the midst of the large rural Chinese population and within easy reach of their remaining PKI cadres on the coast.[42] The PKI built an extensive underground organization and in April 1967 established a *komite kota* (city committee) in Singkawang. Recruiting and training exercises were carried out throughout Pontianak and Sambas districts, and coordination was strengthened between the urban centers and the nascent resistance in the forests (*Pelita* 1975, 62–63).[43] Sofyan's forces called themselves the Tentara Komunis Kalimantan Barat (West Kalimantan Communist Army, or TKKB).

As the PGRS/Paraku was oriented toward Sarawak, the majority of its forces were located farther north along the Sarawak–West Kalimantan border. While they may have enjoyed some contact during 1966 and early 1967, for a while the PGRS/Paraku and the PKI remained distinct groups. But in April 1967 Sofyan and his PKI colleagues met with members of the PGRS/Paraku in Sanggau Ledo subdistrict (then Sambas district) to form a joint Bara Force to execute a military offensive. Some sources claim that Sofyan sought out the much stronger PGRS/Paraku and joined its struggle (*Laporan-chusus tentang perkembangan gerombolan PGRS* n.d., 5; Porritt 2004, 155), but there is reason to believe that the opposite is true. According to *Pelita 1975,* a book published by Kodam XII/Tanjungpura, PGRS forces in Singkawang sometime after the military seizure of power in Jakarta split over questions of strategy. Some PGRS members argued for a frontal military attack against Sarawak; others wanted to enhance recruitment among the local population. Because of this split, about thirty PGRS members under the leadership of Huang Han and Lim Yen Hwa left Sikukng to join Sofyan's PKI forces in Sanggau Ledo.[44] Over the next several months, a number of young recruits from Singkawang were also sent to join the TKKB, where they were trained in guerrilla warfare strategies (Angkatan Darat Kodam XII 1972, 335; *Pelita 1975,* 61–62; *Penumpasan terhadap geromobolan tjina komunis* n.d., 4–5).

Meanwhile, New Order officials in Jakarta, having signed the Jakarta Accords in August 1966, began to address the problem of "rebels" in West Kalimantan. But without a change in the command structure in Kalimantan the old Kolaga and Kopur commands continued to conduct military operations that, as they were originally established to spearhead *Konfrontasi,* were unlikely to hunt down their former collaborators. Despite the launching of Operasi Tertib (Operation Order) in October 1966, there was little real military activity during the following months. This was in part a result of the Soeharto regime's preoccupation with destroying the PKI on Java and Bali and in part a result of misjudging the nature of the problem in West Kalimantan. In fact, troops deployed under *Konfrontasi* outside of the province were being withdrawn.[45] According to a veteran of these operations, local military officers hoped that the "problem" would simply disappear.[46]

Not until the first half of 1967 did the military begin a series of moves to reorganize the command structure and operations in West Kalimantan. One reason for these rearrangements may have been pressure exerted by Malaysia, which, in the view of the New Order's rabid anticommunism, ironically accused Jakarta officials of allowing communists to operate on Indonesian territory. On February 17, 1967, Malaysia and Indonesia signed a secret security agreement regarding the border. Soon after, the Indonesian military disbanded the Kolaga Command (Ryacudu 1967a, 1). In March military operations in West Kalimantan were placed under the Koanda Kalimantan (All-Kalimantan Regional Command) and Kodam XII/Tanjungpura (West Kalimantan). Furthermore, in conjunction with Malaysia's Third Infantry Brigade, the Kodam XII commander Brigadier General Ryacudu initiated Operasi

Sapu Bersih I (Operation Clean Sweep I), which involved five companies of troops based only in Kalimantan.

Nonetheless, only a limited number of sweeps were conducted, and there is little to suggest that the military took the problem seriously. There were a number of reasons for this: the transfer of combat operations from Kolaga to Koanda and Kodam XII was poorly coordinated; Kodam XII was not provided with information about the location or strength of the alleged communist threat; and the actual operations were conducted by poorly trained troops, many of whom were still *remaja* (teenagers). Kodam XII troops at this point suffered greater casualties than did the rebels.[47] The lack of discipline among Kodam XII troops furthered the difficulties. Individual soldiers were accused of being preoccupied with extorting *sumbangan* (donations) from merchants, setting up roadblocks to collect tolls, and pursuing otherwise *tindakan liar* (illegal means) of procuring money.[48] Overall, Kodam XII admitted that its "military forces and preparedness were extremely minimal" (Semdam XII 1971, 261). With respect to this lapse in military preparedness in the immediate post-*Konfrontasi* period, General Soemadi admitted to a foreign journalist, "This was our biggest mistake" (Schumacher 1971).

Finally, on June 29, 1967, Brigadier General Witono Sarsono replaced Ryacudu as commander of Kodam XII. Having done little to eradicate the rebel presence, it is not surprising that Ryacudu was replaced. But why was Witono—as he was known—selected as the new commander? A Catholic from Yogyakarta, he had served in the campaign against the Darul Islam rebellion in West Java during the 1950s, as chief of staff of Kodam Jaya (Jakarta) in 1965, and as army deputy assistant for logistics during the operations against PKI remnants in Java in 1966–67 (Bachtiar 1988, 468). Witono therefore was appointed as commander of Kodam XII because he had experience with antiguerrilla operations and was well regarded by General Soeharto.

Military Response

On July 16, 1967, Sofyan and his new PGRS allies staged a daring attack on the Singkawang II Air Force Base in hilly Sanggau Ledo, resulting in the deaths of three air force personnel and a civilian guard and the capture of 150 weapons.[49] Describing the attack as "a shocking blow that awoke us [to the seriousness of the problem]," the military moved quickly to respond (Soemadi 1974, 87). From July 26 to 28, General

Soeharto met in Jakarta with all of the Kalimantan commanders to discuss the situation in West Kalimantan and prepare for new military operations (Semdam XII 1971, 260).[50] On August 8, 1967, the military declared West Kalimantan a Daerah Operasi (Operations Area) to which new units from Java and Sumatra were sent.[51] By the end of the month, the military had initiated Operation Clean Sweep II, which brought about a dramatic increase in Indonesian army activity (Semdam XII 1971, 270). Still, military histories maintain that activities between August and December 1967 were not intended as a full-scale campaign against the rebels. Instead, this was merely stage 1 of Operation Clean Sweep II, code named Operasi Persiapan dan Pengintaian (Operation Preparation and Intelligence). The problem was that the army lacked an effective intelligence network in West Kalimantan, as evidenced in this report: "During Konfrontasi, our field intelligence was handled by the Kopur command, but its pullout created a vacuum, completely paralyzing our intelligence network. And many of the people in charge of intelligence during Konfrontasi supported the Peking/Djakarta axis. So it was difficult for this network to be used against the band of Chinese communists [*gerombolan Tjina komunis*]. Furthermore, today our enemy is a distinct ethnic group [*satu ethnis* group *sendiri*] with its own community and language, which we don't understand, making it difficult for our intelligence to penetrate" (*Penumpasan terhadap gerombolan tjina komunis* n.d., 5).

So, instead of penetrating these rural Chinese communities, the army sought to uproot and relocate them by drawing upon a clichéd antiguerrilla tactic: "Drain the water so the fish can't swim." The water, of course, was the huge rural Chinese population.

To do so, the military sought to provoke Dayaks to attack ethnic Chinese and thereby drive them from the interior to the coast where they could be controlled, counted, and prevented from providing supplies to the rebels. Apparently, "the military had been dissatisfied with the earlier response by the Dayaks to the appeal for support against the PGRS" (Coppel 1983, 147–48).

During September and early October, atrocities were committed in the greater Bengkayang region, many of which are now shrouded in myth. On September 3, 1967, a "Gerombolan Tjina Komunis" (Band of Chinese Communists) putatively kidnapped nine villages from Temu village, Sanggau Ledo subdistrict.[52] Two days later a RPKAD unit, working with locals, "found" the bodies. Soon thereafter, the Kodam XII spokesman was quoted in the military daily *Angkatan Bersenjata*

(September 21, 1967) calling on Dayaks to "take revenge for blood with blood." Following the attack in Temu, a *timanggong* (or *tumenggung,* a traditional Dayak leader) was killed in the Bengkayang area in late September by unknown assailants. Stories circulated that his genitals had been cut off and sewn to a pole together with a note in Chinese characters, hence providing "evidence" that this atrocity was committed by "*Tjina,*" the Chinese (Witono 1967, 3). Remarkably, however, there are no reports of Dayaks taking revenge against ethnic Chinese in September and early October. Rather, villagers from the Mempawah Hilir, Mempawah Hulu, and Bengkayang areas conducted a series of *upacara adat pemabang* (traditional ceremonies) in which they vowed: "Each villager, whether Dayak or Chinese or from another ethnic group, takes vows to unite against enemies who come from outside the community. Anyone who does not fulfill this promise will be subject to traditional law or evicted from the village and Dayak society" (Witono 1967, 4).

Meanwhile, additional violence was taking place along the coast. Between August and November 1967 there were a number of "incidents" involving PKI members in coastal towns and villages between Mempawah and Sungai Duri. *Kompas* (August 18 and September 9, 1967, and January 4, 1968) suggested that the distribution of PKI leaflets containing Maoist teachings and anti-ABRI messages was behind these incidents. While this is possible, it seems more likely that these incidents were the result of military sweeps to arrest members of the communist underground (something Ryacudu had failed to do), perhaps with the aid of local informants.[53] These informants may have included former PKI members or sympathizers who in the changed environment of 1967 hoped that by cooperating with the new regime they could avoid arrest.

In October the military increased combat operations against the guerrillas, staging a series of sweeps in the Sikukng complex and from Seluas southward to Sanggau Ledo (Semdam XII 1971, 270–71; see map 2). Continuing southward past Bengkayang, on October 13 at Mount Merebuk[54]—an area in which some rebels (most likely PKI) took refuge after the attack on the air force base in Sanggau Ledo—army troops killed "twenty-five communist PGRS" in a cave using flame-throwers (*Angkatan Bersenjata,* October 23, 1967). They then massacred forty-six "unarmed family members . . . having no connection with the communists at all" (Job 1967). A history commissioned and published by Kodam XII/Tanjungpura admits similarly: "It turned out that some of these were Chinese villagers who had participated in the previous peace ceremonies" (Semdam XII 1971, 276). The first of these killings was reported in the national press as a military success; meanwhile, the military spread word locally that "Chinese PGRS" were responsible for killing the villagers to provoke Dayak revenge against rural Chinese.

Massacres

On October 14, the day after the Mount Merebuk military sweep, in the village of Temu—the same village from which nine villagers had been kidnapped and killed a month before—an estimated sixty Dayaks launched a retaliatory attack on ethnic Chinese, reportedly killing eighty.[55] Soon after, violence was spread westward into Samalatan before turning southward following the Chinese corridor into Pontianak district and hitting the Anjungan-Mandor-Menjalin triangle particularly hard.[56] A Dutch pastor, Herman Josef van Hulten, who worked in the area at the time, described the large-scale attacks as "sudden" yet "well organized" (1992, 280).[57] For several weeks, thousands of Chinese fled toward Pontianak; others found shelter in and around Singkawang.[58]

According to army sources, Dayaks believed that the Chinese had broken the Pemabang Oath and mobilized in revenge by passing the *mangkok merah* (red bowl), which symbolizes a call to war (Witono 1967, 4–5). Oddly, there are also reports that Dayak leaders had placed a prohibition on burning the homes of or killing ethnic Chinese in this area (Van Hulten 1992, 281).[59] While Van Hulten claims that no one was killed in the Anjungan-Mandor-Menjalin triangle during the first month of mobilizations, the army lists 249 deaths throughout the region.[60]

Despite protestations made by the civilian governor Soemadi on November 8 and 9 over state radio to halt the mobilizations (*Kompas,* December 28, 1967), days later massacres erupted on a much larger scale. The first incident occurred in the town of Senakin (central Pontianak district), where a group of Dayaks gathered to threaten the local Chinese. The latter fired "warning" shots to disperse the crowd, allegedly wounding two and killing one. The next day Dayaks took revenge, indiscriminately killing Chinese and burning down Senakin's market (Witono 1967, 6).[61] This incident triggered massive violence along the two major roads in the region, one running east-west along the Mempawah-Ngabang axis and the other extending from Sidas north to Bengkayang. In Menyuke subdistrict, the *Angkatan Bersenjata* (January 17, 1968) reported "a massive killing of hundreds of Chinese." Farther south, the towns of Senakin, Pahauman, and Sidas were "the most dev-astated and had the greatest number of people killed" (*Kompas,* January 1, 1968). And to the west, in the Menjalin region, Pastor Van Hulten re-called "horrifying murders" (1992, 294).[62] Estimates in written accounts of the number of Chinese massacred range from two to five thousand, although these figures exclude deaths that later incurred in detainment camps.[63]

Accounts of the 1967 mobilizations and massacres stress the "sponta-neity" of Dayak actions against the gangs of godless communist rebels. Presenting the mobilizations and their succeeding violence as spontane-ous served several purposes. It distanced the military from involvement in organizing and planning the mobilizations and also suggested that there was a deep-rooted and uniform animosity toward local Chinese. In doing so, it ignored the immense linguistic and cultural variations among Dayaks, glossed over the broad range of relations among com-munities, and portrayed Dayaks as emotional, irrational, primitive war-riors prone to excesses and unable to differentiate between the "good" and the "bad" Chinese.

Despite the repeated claims that the massacres were spontaneous, military histories provide detailed accounts of ABRI involvement be-fore, during, and after the violence. The military actively recruited "traditional Dayak chiefs" to wage war against the PGRS/Paraku/PKI forces, granting them such titles as "War Commanders with the Titular Rank of Lieutenant" (Rozhany March 3, 1973). Weapons were distrib-uted and efforts were made to encourage "traditional" war practices, in-cluding the passing of the red bowl and *mengayau* (headhunting). In the words of General Soemadi, Dayaks were told that "anyone who sides with the PGRS-PARAKU enemies can be beheaded like a pig or a chicken." He further boasts that "the enthusiasm for taking heads [*Ngayau*] flared up everywhere, and the [head-takers] were always es-corted by our soldiers" (Soemadi 1974, 94, 96). Witono maintains that for weeks prior to the mobilizations, he toured the province instructing Dayaks not to trust the Chinese who were complicit with the commu-nists (Alexander 1973, 4). The military also rewarded villagers for the use of violence by holding headhunting feasts: "With each victory of the Dayak people in these villages [*kampung*], we always held tradi-tional victory feasts with dancing and drinking of rice liquor from the skulls of PGRS-PARAKU members killed by the local people" (Soe-madi 1974, 96).

But military encouragement does not fully explain why the violence moved south away from PGRS/Paraku and PKI strongholds. And it fails to explain why the retaliatory attacks began in mid-October. In other words, why did neither of the first two attacks—the early September killings in Temu and the later killing of the *tumenggung*—not trigger an immediate Dayak response? To understand why the violence was largely concentrated in an eighty- to ninety-square-mile triangle between coastal Sungai Pinyuh in the west, Bengkayang to the north, and Ngabang to the east; to understand why the massacres broke out when they did; and to understand the bloodshed's desperate intensity and apparent success, we need to turn briefly to Dayak elite politics at the time.

The key figure was Oeray, who, having been dismissed from the governorship a year earlier, saw the rebellion as an opportunity to make a comeback. Sensing the army's desire to relocate the rural Chinese, Oeray seized the chance to disprove leftist accusations against him and to gain the confidence of the new regime. In an interview years later he claimed that "the initiative" to clear the border region of Chinese "came from me" (Jenkins 1978, 25). The military may have approached him, believing that only he had the capacity to mobilize sufficient numbers of Dayaks to cleanse the Chinese from inland areas. Or perhaps "the process [was] more involuntary . . . with each side discerning its own interests only as the events unfolded" (Feith 1968, 134).

While eager to prove his nationalism and anticommunism, Oeray was also driven by economic motives. Forcing the Chinese out of rural Pontianak district, he calculated, would clear the way for the development of a Dayak-dominated economic zone in the Anjungan-Mandor-Menjalin triangle, which he and his clique would control. This area contained fertile rice fields and a lively trade in the hands of small- to medium-scale Chinese merchants. There is a strong possibility that local authorities promised Oeray financial assistance to invest in the area.[64] Critically, Oeray enjoyed strong support in Mempawah Hulu and Menyuke subdistricts, both of which lie just beyond this prized triangle. It was not difficult for him to mobilize supporters in these areas. Simply put, Chinese peasants and traders would be driven out and replaced with Dayak counterparts.

Following the *tumenggung* killing in late September, a number of Dayak *pemuka* (leaders) from the Bengkayang area came to Pontianak City to meet with Oeray. It is not known what was discussed, but soon thereafter, a "declaration of war" against the Chinese was announced over Radio Indonesia (Witono 1967, 3).[65] Also, a militia called Laskar Pangsuma was established to "lead and channel the spontaneity of the movement . . . according to instructions" (7). Dayak leaders in Pontianak soon announced: "We warmly welcome this Dayak spontaneity in the form of active and physical assistance to ABRI's campaign to eliminate the PGRS gang and its lackeys. This spontaneity has emerged as an awareness of a national duty for each responsible citizen of the Indonesian Republic to help and join in saving one's country and people from danger in any form" (*Kompas,* January 4, 1968).[66]

Laskar Pangsuma

The formation and role of the Laskar Pangsuma is both enigmatic and controversial. Few from younger generations know of the militia, and a number of ex-militia members refused to comment. One elder referred to its existence—and this entire episode—as *sejarah gelap,* the dark side of recent Dayak history, and observed that younger generations prefer to remain oblivious.[67] Written sources pertaining to the specifics of the militia's structure and operations are scant, and oral evidence is patchy. A few participants willingly discussed the militia, however, and through that, combined with scant army and newspaper documentation, we can glimpse its possible mechanics.

Named after the famous war leader Pangsuma who led the daring raids against the Japanese in the Sanggau area during World War II, the militia was an extension of a preexisting Dayak social organization in Pontianak, the Yayasan Mandau Persai (Shield and Sword Foundation).[68] Most of the militia's key actors were members of this organization. Oeray sat atop the militia as its *penasehat umum* (general adviser), and Stephanus Ngo Lahay, the former provincial head of the banned Partindo, ran its day-to-day operations. Two main areas of operation were delineated. One was Sambas district, with its base in Singkawang, and the other, Pontianak district, was centered in Anjungan. A commander was appointed to head each operation, and smaller branches were formed throughout the area.

The militia most likely formed sometime in mid-October 1967, but according to military documents, it was not placed under direct army command until mid-November, that is, not until the Senakin incident, which touched off the horrific massacres (Ryacudu 1967d). Evidently at the start of the mobilizations the army gave the militia room in which to maneuver. The militia recruited members, organized mobilizations, supplied transport to ferry bands around the area, and oversaw the expulsions. For the army, deaths up to this point were reasonable—if 330 can be considered acceptable—and the expulsions were running smoothly until the Senakin shootings. Most likely to contain excesses, the army placed the militias under its command, although little evidence exists with which to evaluate to what extent this move may have stemmed the bloodshed.[69]

This is a probable scenario. But there remains a serious sticking point pertaining to the expectations of violence, especially from the army and militia leaders' point of view. Consider Oeray's original prohibition on killing. Whether the intent behind the prohibition was sincere is not known, but evidence suggests that this command was not fully obeyed. Indeed, the second wave of killings appreciably outstripped the first, but 330 deaths before the killings in Senakin are significant. The participants' justifications for the massacres are likewise troubling. It has been claimed that only those who resisted were killed and that the slaughter began in retaliation for the Dayak blood that had been shed. Evidence suggests that this is not wholly accurate, for there was a massacre of nearly an entire Chinese village in Menyuke subdistrict before Senakin (*Angkatan Bersenjata,* January 17, 1968).[70]

More important, it seems unlikely that the militia (or army) leaders expected utter Chinese submission. Resistance, and even the killings of Dayaks, must have been anticipated. The history of warfare and resistance by the Chinese was well known locally. The success of these mobilizations—the expulsions were accomplished in a matter of weeks—did not stem from prohibitions on killing nor were they due to blind rage in reaction to Dayak deaths. The army could not execute this plan single-handedly. Villagers had not responded en masse to earlier "incidents." Local assistance was necessary, and it came in the form of a specific group of Dayak leaders mainly situated in Pontianak. Simply put, the success—not necessarily the origins—of the mobilizations can be largely attributed to the existence and work of the Laskar Pangsuma. Significant portions of this cleansing were organized, coordinated, and, more important, desired.

In the face of the horrendous violence, one might be tempted to note which ethnic subgroups participated so as not to lay careless culpability across the broad swath of the cultural and linguistic heterogeneity subsumed under the Dayak rubric. In this case, the violence took place in areas dominated by Kanayatn Dayaks, who themselves comprise several dialect or ethnic subgroups. It is more instructive to deconstruct the

Dayak label along political lines, however. In other words, those under Oeray and the Laskar Pangsuma, the ethnic extremists, as opposed to those aligned with Palaunsoeka and the Catholic Party, were more likely to participate in the anti-Chinese mobilizations.[71]

Although the mobilizations cleared the inland areas of Chinese, in two important ways the violence failed markedly. First, from the army's perspective, the strategic objective of cutting supply lines to starve rebels into submission was not achieved. With the guerrillas in retreat, the army had planned to launch the second stage of Operation Clean Sweep II, called Operasi Penghantjuran (Operation Destruction). But the insurgents were well entrenched further north and east along the border where they continued to cultivate their own food and trade with the locals. Moreover, the atrocities drove some Chinese and former PKI members to seek protection by joining Sofyan and the PGRS/Paraku, which further fueled the rebellion.

The second way in which the violence failed, and it was distinctly more abysmal than the army's miscue, was that it did not bring Dayak elites into positions of regional power the way Oeray had hoped. In its efforts to subordinate local politics to "national" concerns, the nascent New Order denied Dayaks key positions. Nor did Oeray and his followers subsequently enjoy any real influence in the new regime. The Laskar Pangsuma was soon disbanded after its purpose was served. Oeray's economic zone never materialized either. In fact, the violence destroyed the distribution and transportation network in Pontianak and Sambas districts, paralyzing the local economy. A British journalist commented that "the Dyaks struggled in vain to take over the running of deserted Chinese stores and businesses. The supply of rice and other staples came to a standstill. Prices soared and the market for the Dyaks' own goods dried up" (Alexander 1973, 5).[72] Laskar Pangsuma and local government teams roamed the hinterlands delivering goods in effort to prevent famine (*Kompas,* December 14, 1967). When asked in 2000 what was achieved from the mobilizations, one Dayak elder exclaimed, "Nothing! Look, go to Anjungan. Who owns all the shops? Not Dayaks!"[73]

With the local economy decimated, the hard-pressed Dayak peasants, the majority whom rejected the violence, suffered greatly. In the end, they endured severe economic hardships, and in many cases, lost friends and family due to the expulsions. In fact, some fled with Chinese relatives while others bravely hid Chinese in their villages. Neither the army nor the Dayak elite in Pontianak bore the bloodshed's heaviest burden.

The army's goal of removing the Chinese and Oeray's of gaining control of rural trade were not compatible in all respects. The army worried that amid the bloodshed the situation might escalate beyond its control. One internal report stressed the need for political parties and social organizations to form a *konsensus* (consensus) vis-à-vis the mobilizations so that extraneous interests—individual, ideological, and ethnic alike—would not exploit the volatile situation. In particular, it stressed that other ethnic groups were *membontjeng* (coming on board) (*Penumpasan terhadap geromobolan tjina komunis* n.d., 13).

Subsequent events proved that the army's fears were justified. In the midst of the anti-Chinese campaign, the first (substantiated) Madurese-Dayak riot broke out. With large numbers already in the area, many working on rubber plantations or road construction projects, the Madurese were best positioned to compete for the new "opportunities" left behind by the fleeing Chinese. As they began to occupy the now empty land, their trading networks threatened Oeray's designs. Madurese would challenge Dayaks for control of the Anjungan-Mandor-Menjalin triangle. This was the source of the first serious riot between Dayaks and Madurese, not the "clash of cultures," widespread logging, or excessive transmigration. It was the direct, though unanticipated, result of the anti-Chinese mobilizations and expulsions.

On December 7, 1967, Madurese homes in a village between Anjungan and Mandor were burned and fliers circulated describing the Madurese as *tjina hitam* (black Chinese) and *pelindung Tjina* (defenders of the Chinese) and demanding they leave the area. A week later a Madurese village outside Pontianak was threatened with violence (*Kompas,* December 28, 1967). Two days after that a Madurese killed a Dayak named Sani, a *penghubung* (coordinating officer) in the subdistrict office of Sungai Pinyuh (Pontianak district), and severely injured his son. In revenge, a group of Dayaks attacked the Madurese. Van Hulten recalls that roughly thirty Madurese were killed (1992, 296). One recent pro-Dayak account not surprisingly blames the riot on Sani's attacker (Petebang and Sutrisno 2000, 201),[74] suggesting that he had occupied Chinese land after the expulsions and when his demand for a deed was refused he stabbed Sani to death. This version conforms to the dominant local discourse that riots are *always* precipitated by the killing of a Dayak by a Madurese. It fails to mention, however, the prior burnings of Madurese homes, the inflammatory fliers, or the possibility that Sani was killed in retaliation. But blame is not the issue here. More critically, the Madurese pursuit of their agenda in this prized area threatened the domination Oeray's gang hoped to achieve. This conflict of interests sparked the riot and unwittingly initiated a vicious cycle of violence—the subject of chapter 3—which ebbs and flow to this day.

Relocation and Internment

The massacres of late 1967 and early 1968 were accompanied by the massive relocation of ethnic Chinese southward to Pontianak, and westward to the coast. Some fled under heavy duress, some of their own accord, while others were "escorted" by the military. Most refugees were housed in Pontianak and Singkawang, with smaller numbers in Mempawah, Sambas, and Pemangkat. Government statistics published in late 1968 show that there were nearly sixty thousand refugees; others place the number as high as seventy-five thousand (Soemadi 1974, 177). The most striking feature of the data is the comparison between Pontianak, where the number of refugees in camps fell dramatically by August 1968, and Singkawang, where it remained virtually unchanged (see column A in table 1). This sheds light on the manner in which the military perceived these two groups—as distinct from one another—despite its propaganda, which painted the entire rural Chinese population as conspirators allied with the PGRS/Paraku/PKI rebels. The military knew that rebel strongholds were in Sambas district and not Pontianak district, which is one reason why the ironic southward spread of the violence was highlighted. So when the time came to resettle the refugees, the military balked at resettling those in Singkawang. This caution suggests that from the outset the military viewed the Sambas Chinese as detainees, not refugees.

Visitors to the camps described horrifying conditions. Extreme overcrowding, pitiful food rations, scant medical supplies, leprosy, malaria, children with bloated stomachs, assaults by guards, and suicide were all common (Feith 1968; *Kompas* December 7, 1967; *Harian Kami*, March 25 and 26, 1968). In January 1968 in Pontianak alone 508 refugees reportedly died, and by April 1968 nearly 1,500 children had starved to death (*Harian Kami*, March 26 and April 15, 1968). One British journalist who visited the camps maintained that by early 1968 nearly four thousand Chinese had perished (Alexander 1973, 3). Another observer reported that refugees in Pontianak's camps were free to come and go, but in Singkawang, Pemangkat, and Sambas they could not. One such detainment camp was in Pemangkat, a small town at the mouth of the Sambas River estuary. It held more than 2,619 individuals charged with "involvement

Table 1. Refugees in West Kalimantan, 1967–68

	November 1967			Reregistration May 1968			Post-resettlement August 1968		
	A	B	C	A	B	C	A	B	C
Singkawang & surroundings	14,161	8,501	22,662	14,161	4,240	18,401	12,788	4,240	17,028
Pontianak	18,186	7,483	25,669	10,775	7,483	18,258	2,759	7,483	10,242
Mempawah & surroundings	—	11,519	11,519	—	7,282	7,282	—	758	758
Total	32,347	27,503	59,850	24,936	19,005	43,941	15,547	12,481	28,028

Source: Progress report, propinsi Kalimantan Barat 1968, appendix VI.
Note: A = refugees in camps; B = refugees with families; C = A + B.

in PGRS/Paraku." Another account described a "barbed-wired camp for North Kalimantan People's Guerrilla Force and Communist detainees" on the outskirts of Singkawang (Rozhany April 4, 1973).

The magnitude of this crisis simply overwhelmed local officials, who were ill prepared and underfinanced. In November 1967 the government formed a Badan Kontak Urusan Tjina (Contact Body for Chinese Affairs) at the provincial and district levels to replace a leadership vacuum caused by the involuntary closures of Baperki and the Chung Hua Tsung Hui (Chinese Central Association).[75] But aid to the refugees was not quickly forthcoming. One foreign correspondent noted that the government was "doing virtually nothing for them" (J. Williams 1967). Not until April 1968 was the Panitia Chusus Masalah Pengungsi (Special Committee on the Refugee Problem) established. Poor communication between officials and refugees, many of whom spoke little or no Indonesian, also hampered relief efforts.[76] Meanwhile, corruption at Pontianak's notorious port and among the distribution committees prevented aid—international and national alike—from reaching the refugees. It was estimated that as much as 80 percent of the supplies were sold for private gain (*Kompas*, February 26, 1970). Army personnel and officious local politicians provided additional headaches for relief workers. The former insisted that relief efforts were not to obstruct their operations, which included "screenings" of refugee camps to search for suspected rebels, while the latter used disturbances in the camps caused by the arrival of supplies as an excuse to expel relief workers.[77]

With Pontianak's mayor promising a city "free of refugees" by May 1968, the government began to move refugees into permanent locations. The army wanted the resettlements to conform to the ideals of *pentjampuran* (mixing) and *pembauran* (assimilation) with local populations, an ironic notion since many Chinese had done just that (*Lampiran C, isi laporan tahun Kodam XII Tandjungpura Tahun 1968*, 2). Plans were made for nine projects accommodating nine thousands families surrounding Pontianak City in a "huge area of unhospitable [*sic*] mangrove swamps" (*Sarawak Tribune*, February 2, 1968). Another would house fifteen hundred families in Ketapang, and five would accommodate four thousand families in Sambas (*Harian Kami*, March 26, 1968). These plans never fully materialized, however, and no more than a few thousand people were resettled on agricultural estates.[78] While several thousand returned inland to towns such as Bengkayang and Ngabang, the vast majority became laborers, peasants, fishermen, and small-scale traders in and around the coastal cities of Singkawang, Mempawah, Sungai Pinyuh, and Pontianak. Still others left for Jakarta and elsewhere.

As the rebellion dragged on during the late 1960s and early 1970s, the military undertook further relocations, principally in areas not affected by the original spate of violence. In October 1970, seventeen thousand were forced from the border regions in Sanggau, Sintang, and Kapuas Hulu districts to areas south along the Kapuas River (*Kompas*, March 11, 1971; Mabbett and Mabbett 1972, 10; Soemadi 1974, 91). In December 1972, at least ten thousand more were moved from the northern interior of Sambas to areas along the Pemangkat-Tebas-Sambas road (Komandan Korem 121/ABW 1993, 10).

In sum, when the Soeharto regime sought to address the rebellion in West Kalimantan, it did so on the basis of sweeping social categories, labeling all Chinese as rebels or potential rebels and all Dayaks as primitive headhunters. In the face of limited state capacity and weak legitimacy, the army responded by organizing, instigating, and rewarding the massacre of ethnic Chinese. Between 1967 and 1972, some one hundred thousand were relocated from the rural interior to coastal cities and towns. The scale of these operations is almost as astonishing as the success of the regime's cover-up.[79]

In this context it is instructive to quote at length a letter written by a PKI member sometime in late 1967 or early 1968.

> Even before the blood on their hands [from the 1965-66 massacres] had dried, and at the command of their imperialist

American masters, [Soe]Harto and Nasution cruelly set about dividing the people's unity and pitting one group against another. This has been done mainly by setting the Chinese against other ethnic groups. These actions are intended to fan a racist anti-Chinese movement. By using racism, Harto-Nasution divert the people's attention and anger from the criminal and treasonous deeds that they themselves have committed. In so doing, the people's anger is not aimed at Harto-Nasution but redirected along ethnic lines, and in particular against the Chinese. . . . Consequently, it is the people who suffer. Harto and Nasution easily tricked and incited a small group of people who, escorted [*dengan kawal*] by their wicked army, are the ones who rob, destroy, burn, torture, and savagely murder Chinese. (*Kompas*, January 4, 1968)

Among the many deleterious consequences of this anti-Chinese crusade, I have already mentioned the massive loss of life and property, a damaged local economy, and the first serious Dayak-Madurese riot. But this poignant letter highlights one more result. By playing the ethnic card, by stigmatizing the rural Chinese as "Chinese," and by helping to mobilize divergent communities as "Dayak"—Dayak in stark contrast to Chinese despite the fluidity of ethnic relations among these communities—murderous New Order policies in West Kalimantan facilitated a hardening of ethnic differentiation. The Chinese huddled along the coast and unwittingly unsettled local coastal fishing communities, which, in the presence of large numbers of new neighbors, became decidedly "Malay." And as migrants clashed with Dayaks over the spoils of the anti-Chinese violence, they became distinctively "Madurese." As will be shown in the coming chapters, these dynamics would have dire consequences for the province in the form of recurrent ethnic riots.

Military Operations Continue

Under the name Sapu Berish II (Operation Clean Sweep II) and with a force of nearly 6,300 troops from outside the region, military operations continued.[80] They succeeded in capturing or killing a number of PGRS/Paraku leaders. Between July 1967 and July 1968, ABRI killed at least 397 rebels and captured 209; another 409 surrendered (*Angkatan Bersenjata*, July 16, 1968). By the time the operation ended in February

1969, hundreds more had joined this list. Dozens more were found dead of starvation in the interior. It is likely that many of these individuals were not armed guerrillas but ethnic Chinese who had refused to leave their homes or who had fled farther into the forests after the 1967 massacres.[81]

But both the PGRS/Paraku and the PKI survived, becoming "an embarrassment for Jakarta" (Conboy 2003, 192). This was in part due to the industriousness of the rebels who tended to dry rice fields. In July 1968, more than six months after the anti-Chinese violence, the army admitted that the enemies' logistics were *masih teratur* (still in order) (*Laporan umum Operasi Saberda, tahun 1968* n.d., 6). The rebels also maintained close relations with villagers, especially the Iban, in the forested and mountainous interior. They often lived near settlements, buying food from and trading medicine with the locals (Soemadi 1974, 94). In contrast, relationships between the army and Dayaks were more troubled. The former often forced the latter to perform coolie labor such as hauling rice and equipment for little or no pay. Villagers were also coerced into helping track the PGRS/Paraku/PKI cadres.[82] In 1971 alone, army data list some 180 villagers having perished in these operations (Angkatan Darat Kodam XII 1972, 306–12).

Despite functional Dayak-rebel interactions along the border, in Pontianak district relations with the Chinese had been shattered. The purges drove many to join the rebellion. One refugee was quoted as saying that the Dayaks "went after the wrong people. They should have gone north to the border where the PGRS . . . is. Why us?" (J. Williams 1967). And the *Kompas* daily reprinted an extraordinary letter sent by a Chinese man to a Dayak village.

> Beloved Dayak Brothers!
>
> Our best wishes to you. We hereby ask you a thousand pardons, and we are sending you this letter. Over the past centuries we Tiong Hwa [Chinese] and you Dayaks have never killed one another.
>
> But today many of us have been killed. Our possessions have been looted, and our homes burned to the ground. Now even planting for food is still a real mess. So we are forced to look after our own safety. We hope that you our Dayak brothers grant us this today. Don't any longer believe the reactionaries (the lies of wicked people).

> But if you persist in listening to these reactionary criminals
> and keep killing us, and destroying our crops, we will have to
> take strong action. That's it!
>   Signed: Sian Sui Kong (*Kompas*, December 11, 1967)

It is believed that the author of this letter fled to join the rebels in
Sarawak.[83]

In March 1969 the army initiated Operation Clean Sweep III and
brought in new army units from Java. Operations were concentrated in
the western sector, particularly around Bengkayang, around Mount
Puah in the northwestern corner of the province, and in the Sikukng
complex, where ABRI forces killed two top PGRS leaders, Yap Chung
Ho and Yacob (Semdam XII 1971, 327-30). Although the military
claimed that these campaigns were a success, this was largely illusory.
PGRS/Paraku and PKI rebels would flee across the border into Sarawak, only to return if they were attacked by Malaysian troops or when
the Indonesian troops had withdrawn. Under intense attack, Sofyan
and his PKI forces chose a different strategy, eventually giving up the
guerrilla struggle in the interior and taking refuge near relocated Chinese in coastal Sungai Duri south of Singkawang (*PKI gaya baru pimpinan SA Sofyan* n.d., 2; Pusat Sejarah dan Tradisi ABRI 1995, 167). If the
1967 massacres and relocations were intended to separate the fish from
the water, Sofyan and the PKI chose to follow the water.

Throughout 1969 and 1970 the army, with the help of student groups
such as KAMI/KAPPI and the Laskar Ampera, began to arrest scores
of coastal Chinese traders and businessmen, this time considerably dis-
rupting rebel supply lines.[84] Meanwhile, military operations along the
Kalimantan-Sarawak border were becoming more effective. The Indonesian and Malaysian militaries, both supported by their Western allies,
cooperated in their pursuit of the insurgents, holding frequent meetings
and staging joint operations (see e.g., *Sarawak Tribune*, October 31,
1969).[85] The British and Australian militaries conducted a photographic
aerial survey while the military operations were taking place, which resulted in the production of superb topographical maps, the military uses
of which were all too apparent (*Kompas*, February 27, April 4 and July 11,
1970).[86]

During this period the Australian government also commissioned a
detailed seven-volume survey, ostensibly for the purpose of road building in the province (Government of Australia 1973). For its part, the

United States was providing Indonesia with military hardware and officer training. Following the deaths of Yap and Yacob in the western sector, the Indonesian military shifted its focus to the Paraku rebels, who were located in the province's mountainous eastern region. In 1970 the air force heavily bombed the Benua Martinus mountain complex north of Putussibau and then dropped platoons of paratroopers to hunt down the guerrillas (Semdam XII 1971, 306).

The rebellion soon dissipated after an amnesty deal, christened Sri Aman, was reached in October 1973 between the Sarawak government—represented by Rahman Yakub, Sarawak's chief minister—and Bong Kee Chok, a top rebel strategist. Having survived warfare and innumerable depredations in the mountainous forests for nearly a decade, nearly five hundred Malaysian insurgents finally gave up the struggle, surrendered their weapons, and returned home.[87] Soeharto's government offered no such amnesty and continued to hunt down the PKI whose leader, Sofyan, remained at large.

Hunting Sofyan and the New-Style PKI, 1970–74

The 1965–66 massacres devastated the PKI. Hundreds of thousands, if not millions, of the group's members and sympathizers and those accused thereof were either slaughtered, jailed, or forced to flee the country. In the wake of the massacres, two main PKI exile groups emerged, a Maoist faction in China and a pro-Moscow group in Delhi, India. The two traded vitriolic charges and countercharges over the ultimate responsibility for the events of October 1, 1965, and the subsequent tragedies. Domestically the party demonstrated impressive resilience and soon began to reorganize. In rural Blitar (southeastern Java) in early 1968, for instance, the party's new armed wing, Tentara Pembebasan Rakyat Indonesia (Indonesian People's Liberation Army), led raids on local officials, religious teachers, and landlords. The army easily crushed the uprising. There were reports of similar movements elsewhere in East and West Java and southern Sumatra (Lampung), but as the 1970s approached, unambiguous evidence of party activities dissipated as urban underground strategies were pursued.[88] During this period, in fact, the party's most active branch may have been located in West Kalimantan, a perennial PKI backwater.

After giving up the guerrilla struggle in the Sanggau Ledo forests, sometime in 1969 Sofyan fled to the coast, where many refugees had been forcibly relocated. Although little is known about PKI activity during this period, it appears that he set up a training center in Sungai Duri and formally reestablished the PKI. During the next several years Sofyan continued to operate in the greater Pontianak area. The PKI's presence was not limited to Sofyan and his activities, however. Army reports contain a detailed chart showing the PKI organizational structure between 1972 and 1974, which lists eighty-five party officials by name and eight regional committees in addition to a central command.[89] In an effort to make itself known, in May 1972 pamphlets were distributed to celebrate the PKI's "birthday" and numerous hammer and sickle flags were mysteriously raised along the coastal road from Pontianak to Sambas.

For the local authorities, the problem was not simply one of armed insurgency. They were also concerned about the large ethnic Chinese population that was now concentrated along the coast between Singkawang and Pontianak, which they feared could become a breeding ground for an insurgency. One form of social control involved language. In September 1969 ethnic Chinese were *diijinkan* (permitted) to use Indonesian, while special language courses were set up in Chinese ghettoes. Instructions posted on homes read "Use Indonesian" (Angkatan Darat Kodam XII 1972, 341). Frustrated at the lack of progress, the authorities later banned the use of Chinese languages over the radio and on the telephone (*Angkatan Bersenjata*, June 22, 1970). Officials also pushed the Chinese to assimilate and integrate into "Indonesian" society by moving them out areas dense with Chinese. For example, seven thousand "refugees" were moved to the province's southernmost district, Ketapang (Ryacudu 1967b, 51). Later, in the early 1970s, the military sent hundreds of *tahanan* (detainees) again to Ketapang where they were housed in "rehabilitation installations." According to Brigadier General Hartono, at that time Kodam XII commander, Ketapang was to function as "a kind of laboratory" (*Tempo*, August 17 and October 26, 1974).[90] Local officials later clamped down on Hartono's lab—perhaps fearing its success—and banned the employment of laborers from outside Ketapang and from outside Indonesia (*Utama*, March 22, 1973). This restriction implicitly meant ethnic Chinese laborers.

Restrictions on labor extended beyond Ketapang. As the insurgency dragged on, ABRI was convinced that Sofyan and the PKI were receiving "support from Chinese timber workers" (Soemadi 1974, 108). It insisted that insurgents along the border were doubling as timber workers and smuggling wood into Sarawak in exchange for supplies (*Perkiraan keadaan intell* 1969, 3). The authorities responded by introducing ad hoc labor regulations. Such coastal subdistricts as Sungai

Pinyuh, Pemangkat, and Tebas were designated *daerah pengawasan* (regions under supervision). Farther south in Pontianak district, Segedong and Teluk Keramat subdistricts became *daerah tertutup* (closed areas). In the Mempawah area Chinese timber workers were required to obtain work permits from the district military command (*Utama*, March 5, 1973).[91] The forested swamplands of Segedong and Teluk Keramat were, of course, one of the last redoubts of Sofyan and the PKI between 1972 and 1974. Telok Air, the busy timber port located ninety-five miles south of Pontianak, was of particular concern. To be sure, the large number of Chinese dockworkers led the port to be listed as a "region under supervision." But in reality the army took pains to "supervise" Telok Air because it was an exit point for timber smuggling. By 1972, nearly two million square meters of plywood were being "exported" through the port (Rozhany April 5, 1973). Phantom timber companies were nicknamed PT. Kayu Hanyut (Drift Wood Ltd.) (*Tempo*, August 17, 1974). Undoubtedly, army officers played an active role and benefited handsomely from this lucrative yet illicit timber trade.

But labor control was not enough, and despite the army's insistence few rebels had remained; in mid-1970 the army announced that there were still 8,825 former communists in West Kalimantan (*Angkatan Bersenjata*, August 6, 1970). As the army needed the help of locals to hunt down the communists, cash rewards were announced, with a sliding fee scale for such jobs as supplying information and the capture of weapons, culminating in a reward of 500,000 rupiahs for Sofyan's capture (*Harian Kami*, March 26, 1968). In July 1973, Hartono went so far as to appeal to the population to report the whereabouts of "S. A. Sofyan and his gang because they are a thorn in our side" (*Utama*, July 5, 1973).[92]

In 1973 the military began to employ a new tactic, the infamous *pagar betis* (fence of legs), whereby villagers were made to march side by side in pursuit of the rebels, facing the grim prospects of being shot from the front by rebels or, should they refuse this duty, from behind by the military. In September the use of this tactic in a village at the mouth of the Sambas River resulted in the discovery and torching of an alleged "communist nest." Continued military operations and foreign assistance eventually paid off. In October 1973 ABRI units captured several PKI leaders, including Sofyan's wife, their seven-month-old baby, and a number of Sofyan's couriers.[93] Finally, on January 12, 1974, Sofyan was captured and promptly executed in the forests of Sungai Kelambu (Terenteng subdistrict), roughly fifteen miles upriver from Pontianak

(Hartono 1974).[94] Sofyan's death marked the end of the roughly nine-year PKI rebellion in West Kalimantan against Soeharto's rule.[95]

Operations against PGRS/Paraku forces in the eastern sector continued throughout the mid-1970s, as did Malaysian operations in Sarawak's Third Division. Finally, in 1976, ABRI formally ended military operations and turned provincial security over to the Kodam XII/Tanjungpura (*Kompas,* July 18, 1977). Nevertheless, there were scattered reports that "communists" were being arrested in West Kalimantan during the 1980s and that PGRS/Paraku forces were still operating in the eastern sector.[96]

Why did the rebellion last as long as it did? Four broad sets of factors contributed to its protraction. First, in contrast to the fate of the PKI in Java and elsewhere, Sofyan and his comrades survived for so long because of West Kalimantan's particular features. With a vast and heavily forested mountainous area, a large ethnic Chinese population, an indigenous populace generally resistant to interference by a central state, a land border adjacent to Malaysia, and a fellow movement sharing the same border, the West Kalimantan PKI had opportunities largely unavailable elsewhere.

Second, it is likely that Sofyan enjoyed some protection from local army officers. Recall that Soepardjo—who was implicated in the events of October 1, 1965, in Jakarta—commanded *Konfrontasi* operations for nearly two years. This afforded him ample opportunities to cultivate a sizable following among his subordinates. A prime example is Colonel Kistam, who was arrested in January 1969 for having dealings with the PKI. He was the highest-ranking officer in West Kalimantan during the rebellion to be so charged; a number of his subordinates were subsequently arrested.[97]

Third, it furthered the army's interests to nurture a drawn-out rebellion. Officers profited handsomely. From coastal ports to border posts, they controlled both legal and illicit trade flows, squeezed Chinese businessmen, collected "taxes," and required the purchase of "permits," all of which created tension among competing army units over the fruits of these counterinsurgency operations. West Kalimantan also provided the army with an expansive training ground on which to experiment with new weapons and expose officers and troops to combat.

The final point concerns the allure of patriotism, which has been obscured by New Order historiography. Sofyan and his colleagues did not fight for so long because they were communists or part of an international communist network. If that was their motivation, they could have either joined the PGRS/Paraku in the struggle for Sarawak or fled to the PRC. Rather, they waged a guerrilla struggle against the Soeharto regime for nearly nine years against overwhelming odds because they were *Indonesian* communists. When Sofyan returned to the coast in 1969, he reestablished the PKI, not a Chinese Party of West Kalimantan or a branch of the Chinese Communist Party. He was a communist *and* an Indonesian. In fact, Sofyan's execution could not have come at a more opportune time for ABRI. A year later it invaded East Timor, initiating more than two decades of brutal operations and a military occupation of that region. Many of the army units, commissioned officers, and even tactics (such as the fence of legs) employed in West Kalimantan were to play formidable roles in East Timor.[98]

3

Regional State-Building and Recurrent Riots

It has become conventional wisdom that large states traditionally and typically have viewed their expansive, resource-rich peripheries through rapacious and greedy eyes. Almost uniformly, they have run roughshod over the physical landscape and populations that inhabit these "empty lands." This is especially so in new or postcolonial states struggling to climb out of positions of dependent development in the world economy. Desperate to earn enough in foreign exchange to develop an industrial base in its core, to fund a repressive security apparatus, or to stow away in private foreign bank accounts, state actors assume full control over these regions' natural resources, such as timber, and auction them off to international capital. To secure control, authorities often settle these outer regions with loyal and pliable migrants (called "pioneers") who are familiar with the state's core values, ideology, and practices.

This internal colonization creates a precarious situation for local populations. Threatened with demographic swamping and putatively unfamiliar with state rule and the attendant fruits of modernity, they are deemed irrevocably "different" from the state's dominant ethnic group or groups. "Primitives," foreigners in their own land, they are accused of having contributed little to the nation's glory, particularly to its founding, when daring revolutionary heroes threw off the colonial yoke. Given the ethnocidal implications of this state-building project, an inherently volatile and increasingly untenable situation is produced, especially when the ethnic group in question has a tradition of warfare.

West Kalimantan under the New Order fits this description well, leaving one to conclude that the infamous Dayak-Madurese riots that have occurred were a logical outcome of it. This chapter, however, seeks to challenge the assumptions underlying this line of argument, which could be called the basic tenets of the critical development school. As I discussed in the introduction, this school places New Order development at the heart of the province's recurrent riots. But the limitation of this thinking is clear once we examine the evidence more closely, as we began to do in chapter 2. Small-scale Dayak-Madurese clashes occurred both before the adverse effects of development took hold and in areas removed from the principal development components of logging and transmigration. This chapter shows that a host of contextual factors born out of the New Order army's counterinsurgency campaign are far more useful in explaining the genesis and protraction of the riots than a perspective that sees these events as primarily the product of the New Order's development strategy.

This chapter also extends the examination of the massive 1997 unrest, the greatest ethnic riot under the New Order in some thirty years. This violence drew national and international attention to West Kalimantan's "special problem," and gave rise to the critical development school. By 1997, New Order development had taken its toll and may have contributed to the unanticipated intensity of the violence. By then, however, years of periodic riots had already determined the targeting of Madurese — a fact that adherents to the critical development school cannot explain.

Rather than blaming it on development, my argument situates the 1997 violence in the increasing politicization of the countryside, especially the growth and effects of a Dayak ethnopolitical movement, whose beginnings can be traced to the early 1980s. This dynamic spawned a more oppositional, activist-oriented NGO movement, which drew on the discourse and practice of the international indigenous peoples' movement. In its attempt to explain the intensity of the 1997 riots, the missing link in the critical development perspective is the local politics of this Dayak movement. With this mind, this chapter takes a thorough look at Dayak-New Order state relations, as well as the 1997 bloodshed itself. The irony and tragedy are clear: even as the Dayak movement transformed an imposed ethnicity into an indigenous protest movement, empowerment became equated with the butchering of equally vulnerable people.

Recurrent Riots

The involuntary relocation of ethnic Chinese from the interior to the coast in 1967 introduced a new regional dynamic by opening considerable agricultural space and creating opportunities in small-scale trade. Local Dayaks responded in various ways. Some showed little interest; others occupied Chinese land, houses, and stores.[1] Some remained in their new locations permanently; others vacated the land and returned to their villages.[2] Madurese migrants also took advantage of these opportunities and soon came to blows with Dayak communities in precisely the same places where the 1967 massacres had been orchestrated to such brutal effect. By late 1967 and early 1968, they were battling over the land and other spoils abandoned by the fleeing Chinese.

This now new form of violence continued intermittently in roughly the same locations. The number of riots is unclear, especially those that took place in the 1970s and 1980s for which little documentation exists. A Human Rights Watch (HRW) report lists eight clashes prior to 1997; yet, it judiciously qualifies its findings. Their sources "make no distinction between a single murder that was settled without erupting into communal violence, and attacks that led to ethnic riots" (HRW 1997, 8). A more recent study of Madurese-Dayak relations chronicles seven incidents in which Dayaks were stabbed by Madurese assailants in Salatiga (then Sambas district) between 1976 and 1989, although tellingly none led to a riot (Giring 2004, 74–75, table 2).

Attempts to verify the number of riots confront a number of problems, three of which are substantial. One is the poor quality of media reporting in this vast province. In the 1970s and 1980s, not only were some areas hard to access but the New Order authorities frowned on the reporting of violent incidents. The local New Order newspaper of record, *Akcaya*, for instance, failed to report a single disturbance during the 1970s. Its first mention of a clash comes in 1983 and uses euphemistic terms such as "incident" (*kejadian* and *peristiwa*) rather than more alarming ones such as "violence" (*kerusuhan*) or even "conflict" (*konflik*). A second problem relates to attempts to chronologically list Dayak-Madurese riots, which became a popular activity during the 1996–97 incident. In general, "conflict chronologies" are of two types: those produced by the media and those constructed by researchers connected to local Dayak organizations.[3] The former contain scant and conflicting data, while the latter are tainted with bias. For these chroniclers, there was the temptation to exaggerate the timeframe and number of Madurese-Dayak incidents to bolster the popularly held view that the unwillingness of the Madurese to assimilate and adapt to local cultural conditions lay at the roots of the recurrent riots.[4] The dominant local discourse blames the Madurese for the habitual strife.[5]

The final problem concerns the social processes of memory formation. To be sure, the relevant literature suggests that participants tend to recall violent incidents well (Wood 2003, 33–35). But there are two important caveats to this as it relates to the inability of informants in West Kalimantan to remember the details of the minor riots of the 1970s and 1980s. First, compared with the events of 1996–97 and 1999, the riots were not very intense, so residents remembered them less well. Nor were they always associated with unpleasantness. In fact, people seem to enjoy reminiscing about the anti-Madurese violence. Not only do informants take pride in the violence Dayaks can generate when necessary—what one researcher calls "self-righteous narratives" (Tajima 2004, 16)—but their stories serve to "prove" that the innate mischievousness of the Maudrese lies behind the violence. Moreover, as is typical of social movements and other forms of contentious collective action, participant stories over time tend to cluster around neatly prescripted themes (Tilly 2003, 31–32). In West Kalimantan, the standard stories revolve around the carrying of knives by Madurese and their propensity to stab adversaries from behind—a cultural practice known as *carok*.

The second caveat stems from the fact that the more serious clashes—the 1996–97 and 1999 affairs—had recently transpired when I began my fieldwork. These conflicts relegated earlier incidents to minor importance. More importantly, they also flooded informants' memories with images of anti-Madurese violence, which drowned out memories of earlier incidents. The blending and blurring of once discrete episodes into almost seamless narratives became commonplace. Ethnographies of violence elsewhere have encountered similar problems. In reference to a horrifically violent incident in a dense neighborhood (Pakka Qila) in Hyderabad, Pakistan—which touched off years of subsequent violent conflict—one chronicler admits that "considering the number of discussions I have had with Pakka Qila residents about the events of May 1990, I know surprisingly little about what actually happened in Pakka Qila during those days" (Verkaaik 2004, 142). In West Kalimantan, as current attitudes regarding anti-Madurese violence are read into past, smaller cases, memories are drained of reliable detail. That locals trust in the heritage of Dayak-Madurese violent conflict is what matters, and stories are related accordingly.

That said, although the data are sketchy, we can establish a pattern of Dayak-Madurese riots from the late 1960s following the Chinese pogroms to the 1980s.

1967: In early December, following the razing of Madurese homes in a village between Anjungan and Mandor (Pontianak district) and the circulation of fliers demanding that Madurese leave the area, a Madurese killed a Dayak civil servant and severely injured his son. Dayak retaliation left some thirty Madurese dead.

1969: An internal army report commented on a series of "local skirmishes" (*bentrokan lokal*) in Pontianak district about which we know little else (*Rentjana Operasi Sapu Bersih III-Tahun 1969* n.d., 15).

1975: In late May or early June, a Dayak-Madurese riot broke out in (or near) the coastal town of Sungai Pinyuh (Pontianak district). Stores and houses were destroyed. While we do not know the precise number of deaths (or the fighting's immediate cause), one account reported "many victims" (*Angkatan Bersenjata*, June 10, 1975).

1977: Possibly in early August in Singkawang, a Madurese man by the name of Maskat killed a Dayak police officer (Robert Lanceng) over an argument related to their children. Despite the paucity of detailed information, there appears to be sufficient corroborating evidence to label this incident an ethnic riot. Perhaps five or so died and a few dozen houses were destroyed (Giring 2004, 168; HRW 1997, 8; Petebang and Sutrisno 2000, 201).[6]

1979: One of the better documented riots began on November 8 in Sendoren village (Samalantan subdistrict, then Sambas district). There Sidik, a Dayak man, had asked a Madurese man named Asmadin bin Ariman, who was cutting grass to feed his cows, to be mindful of Sidik's rice stalks. A war of words ensued and Sidik was fatally stabbed. A subsequent raid on Asmadin's village (Sansapi) by friends of Sidik led to violence in surrounding villages. According to official estimates, over the course of two or three days, these clashes resulted in about twenty deaths (roughly fifteen Madurese and five Dayaks) and the torching of forty to sixty-five houses. Local security forces were called in. Asmadin was later sentenced to twenty years for instigating the violence (*Kompas,* November 19, 1979; Sudagung 2001, 126, 140–44; *Tempo,* December 8, 1979 and April 5, 1980).

1983: On November 20, in Sungai Enau village in Sungai Ambawang subdistrict (Pontianak district), a fight between a Dayak and a Madurese, whose origin lies in obscurity, escalated into a three-day riot. The fighting was spread to Mandor, Toho, Menjalin, and Karangan subdistricts (*Akcaya,* December 1, 1983).

Conditions for Violence

A complex and enduring set of elements and circumstances lies behind the tensions that led to these outbreaks of periodic violence. In all, they relate more to local politics and the aftermath of the New Order's counterinsurgency campaign than they do to New Order development or Dayak frustration at being excluded from the national, institutional model.

The first factor was the destruction of the region's economy and distribution networks caused by the expulsion of the inland Chinese. Immediately following the expulsions, teams of government officials and members of the Laskar Pangsuma were forced to traverse the area distributing foodstuffs to ward off famine. The situation continued to deteriorate, however. In early 1970 news reports commented on the near faminelike conditions in inland Sambas district (*Kompas,* January 22, 1970). As late as 1971 similar reports emerged—this time noting the hundreds of deaths due to epidemics and starvation (*Kompas,* September 10 and 25, 1971; *Tempo,* October 16, 1971).

Second, the Laskar Pangsuma mobilizations and the unofficial yet forced "conscription" of villagers during the counterinsurgency campaigns further destabilized an evidently militarized environment. An internal military report from 1969 describes the northern Pontianak district as an area of "tumultuous conditions that is being exploited by instigators playing one ethnic group off another." The report refers to disconcerting rumors that "Dayas will attack Madurese. . . . Catholics will attack Muslims" (*Rentjana Operasi Sapu Bersih III-Tahun 1969* n.d., 14–15). Clearly, this depiction marks Dayaks as the aggressors. It is likely that in their attempt to consolidate control over the area, elements associated with the Laskar Pangsuma were behind many of these disturbances. Subsequent to the Chinese pogrom, the militia's main coordinating body in Pontianak City was dissolved, but we do not know precisely when. It is possible that in the interior either its dismemberment was delayed, or its members remained loosely organized along networks that had developed prior to, during, or after the mobilizations.

The third factor during this period was the marked increase in Madurese migrants to the region. Most migrated on their own, rather than as participants in any government relocation program — a phenomenon known as "spontaneous migration" (*migrasi swakarsa*). They came in search of jobs created through New Order development projects, especially in road construction. In 1971 the area had 1,830 kilometers of roads, of which 336 were asphalted. Within ten years, these numbers doubled and trebled, respectively (Sudagung 2001, 86-87, table 3.12). Three large road projects — the coastal Mempawah-Singkawang road, the inland Singkawang-Montrado extension, and the road connecting Bengkayang to the border (see map 2)[7] — attracted significant numbers of migrants, who were unfamiliar with local conditions and norms. Contemporary news reports remark on the increases in the number of imported cows and the number of pedicab (*becak*) drivers in Pontianak City — two niches in the local economy that came to be dominated by Madurese (*Kompas*, March 4 and April 12, 1972). Revealingly, another article explained that all this "wild [*liar*] transmigration can create unwanted social problems" (*Utama*, September 19, 1973). Here the term *social problems* undoubtedly meant heightened ethnic tensions.

Fourth, the increasing numbers of Madurese in the area gave organizers for the Islamic Nahdlatul Ulama (NU) party opportunities to flex their electoral muscles, at least at the district level, although the provincial population of Madurese at this time was estimated at 0.6 percent (Riwut 1979, 49). In Jakarta, following Soeharto's 1966 putsch against Soekarno and his being named president by the Provisional People's Consultative Council (MPRS) the following year, lively debates ensued among political parties, government ministries, the armed forces, and Soeharto's closest advisers on when and what form elections would take. One commentator noted that NU officials "did want an election as quickly as possible, since they were confident of their mass support after the destruction of the PKI and wished to be in a stronger position to check the rise of New Order forces" (K. Ward 1974, 7). In this way, at the local level, fractious campaigning and electoral jostling would have been likely in 1968 and 1969. In fact, as late as December 1969 when the electoral legislation was enacted, the "general opinion was that the elections would in no way alter the existing political arrangements, that they would maintain the *status quo* of a parliament in which the majority of seats were held by parties with no single party dominant" (Reeve 1985, 264). In other words, party leaders in West Kalimantan most likely expected the upcoming elections would be competitive, akin to Indonesia's first democratically run election in 1955.

Meanwhile, the military reported that, although the nationalist party IPKI (League of the Supporters of Indonesia's Independence) was dominated by Dayaks in Pontianak district,[8] the Laskar Pangsuma remained the primary mobilization vehicle. Its aim was to "demonstrate to the government its strength." Thus, it is within this context an internal military document commented: "There are frequent local skirmishes [*bentrokan lokaal (sic)*] between the Daya and Madurese. These circumstances are used by the Madurese in their NU shirts to demonstrate their mass support" (*Rentjana Operasi Sapu Bersih III-Tahun 1969* n.d., 15). Although the report glosses over the nature of these "local skirmishes," evidently tensions must have been strained and certain forms of collective violence were frequent.

The fifth factor involves the fact that the local state apparatus did little to ameliorate tensions. Although ABRI officers were replacing civilian *bupati*, lower-ranking Dayak civil servants unofficially aligned with Oeray's Partindo were still well represented in district bureaucracies.[9] These bureaucracies were neither capable nor neutral enough to help assuage ethnic tensions. The military was still focused on the communist insurgency—recall that Sofyan was not killed until January 1974—and accruing handsome profits from such development projects as logging. Not until the widespread riots in Samalantan subdistrict in 1979 did the violence attract the military's attention. When it finally did address the issue, it did so by forcing both sides to sign an ineffectual peace accord and by erecting a gaudy, thirty-foot monument. The statue's tribute to the official state motto, "Unity in Diversity" (*Bhinneka Tunggal Ika*), was a vain attempt at conflict resolution. In fact, the statue's ominous presence exacerbated the situation by monumentalizing the conflict.[10]

Nonetheless, by 1979, several riots had already taken place, which led to the sixth factor, a "routinization of violence" (Tambiah 1986, 118) among combatants materialized (see also Laitin 1995). Within a specific geographic location and among particular belligerents, as one riot succeeded another, an internalization of violent impulses vis-à-vis a certain

Other crystallized. This internalization may not have necessarily caused the violence, but it materialized as one of its unfortunate effects. Violence became the means through which people resolved disputes.

Similar dynamics have been noted in recurrent insurgent wars, in particular, ones that implicate cultural or ethnic identities and that end without a proper resolution. It has been shown that these violent conflicts exacerbate cleavages and complicate future cooperation; the chances of violence recurring is thereby increased (Doyle and Sambanis 2000; Gurr 2000, 66; Rothchild and Groth 1995). Certainly, this was the case in this specific area in West Kalimantan. While our knowledge of these early riots remains rudimentary, it is clear that they did not stem from nebulous "ancient hatreds." Rather, they were generated by the expulsion of the Chinese from inland Sambas and northern Pontianak districts in 1967.

Violent Development?

These factors, which favor political processes and the diachronic unfolding of collective violence, have implications for the critical development school popular with environmental and human rights NGOs and institutes, which blames New Order development for the bloodshed (Down to Earth 1997, 2001; Linder 1997; Samydorai 1997). Heavy-handed, capital-intensive development, so the theory goes, altered the region's physical and social landscape to the detriment of marginal indigenous populations. These transformations fed Dayak grievances, which ignited the massive 1997 riots. This reasoning captures part of the truth with regard to the intensity of the unrest, although there is no evidence that increasingly acute struggles over resources proportionately lead to greater amounts of violence. This resource competition argument also works less well when it is proposed as the cause of the violent conflict itself, because it deflects attention from the riots that occurred before New Order development took place or from the fact that some areas affected by New Order development did not experience clashes. Here it is revealing to unpack the critical development school's argument into its key components to see how it relates to the temporal and spatial dimensions of the riots.

At the outset, the New Order regime saw economic development as a remedy for both the communist insurgency and the "backwardness" of the area and its people. Accordingly, considerable sums of money were poured into the province. From 1969–70 to 1974–75, central government subsidies increased by a hefty 1,200 percent.[11] Through this development program, dubbed the Roads and Rice campaign, the regime sought to eradicate shifting dry-rice cultivation, which was deemed inefficient, backward, and environmentally destructive,[12] and develop wet-rice agricultural systems, thereby limiting villagers' movements, making them more governable and restricting access to such common resources as forests (Peluso 1996). But the poor rainforest soil in newly cleared areas was generally unable to support intensive wet-rice cultivation, resulting in the spread of unproductive grasslands. Consequently, the province remained a rice importer (*Utama,* October 31, 1973; Gayo 1990, 649).[13] The promotion of wet-rice agriculture and new trading networks linking the border regions to Pontianak (i.e., away from Sarawak) required extensive infrastructural improvements, the most important of which was road building.[14] It was not lost on the military, of course, that an improved road network would facilitate counterinsurgency efforts.

Whereas new infrastructure was ostensibly intended to promote economic development, it also opened opportunities for national and military elites. With the passage of foreign and domestic investment laws in 1967 and 1968, the Jakarta elite encouraged the exploitation of Indonesia's vast natural resources. The forests were among the top attractions for domestic and foreign investors. Indonesia's dependent position in the world economy, its structural weakness, and the late stage of its industrialization intensified its need to catch up and "leapfrog" other similarly situated economies. This, combined with the increased demand on the world market for rain-forest timber, pushed New Order policymakers to pursue rapacious policies in extracting timber from resource-rich regions, including West Kalimantan. Before the first oil boom of the early 1970s, forests were a top foreign exchange earner (Ross 2001, 166–78).

Prior to the New Order, granting licenses to private logging companies in West Kalimantan was common. In 1963, for instance, permits for nearly sixty-two logging concessions—ranging from fifty to five hundred hectares—were extended. The authorities granted another twelve permits of five thousand hectares apiece (see *Laporan Kerdja Tahun 1963 Gubernur Kdh. Kal-Barat* n.d., appendix XXVIIIa, XXVIIb). Soeharto's regime altered this practice by granting fewer but incredibly large forest concessions (Hak Pengusahaan Hutan, or HPH). In 1969 the first four HPH's totaled 370,000 hectares. Through early 1974, sixteen concessions, many of which were backed by foreign-capital, were issued, covering roughly 1.3 million hectares.[15] Accordingly, between 1968 and 1973, timber production increased twenty-five fold.[16]

Commonly involving a combination of highly placed bureaucrats and military officers, HPH allocation took place in Jakarta, where much of the money accrued from the logging wound up. Military engagement in business, however, required partners with capital, local knowledge, and managerial skills. Despite repeated charges that the PGRS/Paraku/PKI insurgents were Chinese, and despite the brutal treatment of this population in general, it was logical for officers to turn to local ethnic Chinese as business partners.

Over time, large-scale logging has deprived indigenous communities of now ruined ancestral lands. It has also wreaked great environmental destruction, which these groups have born disproportionately. These claims are unassailable and figure prominently in the critical development school. That these factors may have contributed to the intensity of the 1997 violence is one thing; situating large-scale logging at the riots' roots is another. Simply put, massive logging alone cannot explain the Madurese-Dayak violence. Incipient clashes occurred prior to and contemporaneously with the granting of the first massive logging concessions. This hardly leaves time for the deleterious social consequences of logging to take effect (neither of these groups were fighting over the logging spoils). Finally, most of the original concessions were located in the swamplands of southern Pontianak and northern Ketapang districts, areas not afflicted with riots.[17]

Capital accumulation through large-scale logging was only one means by which the New Order regime altered the province's landscape. There was also the program known as transmigration, an integral part of the military's "territorial management" (*pembinaan wilayah/teritorial*) of troublesome outer islands. In West Kalimantan, as the insurgency dragged on, the authorities came to view the area as ideal for transmigrants from overcrowded Java. Its extremely low population density (thirteen people per square kilometer in 1971) and the relocation of tens of thousands of Chinese left large tracts of open land. During the 1950s and early 1960s, an army transmigration program had settled a few thousand revolutionary fighters and former servicemen near the Sarawak border and farther south in Ketapang (Djawatan Penerangan Propinsi Kalimantan 1953, 166–67; Tobing ca. 1953, 130–50).[18] Interestingly, due to security concerns, West Kalimantan was left off the New Order's official transmigration list.[19] Not until 1973 did Governor Kadarusno, hoping that an influx of Javanese would counterbalance the large Chinese population and "civilize" the rural Dayaks (*Utama,* February 27, 1973), lobby to have the province made a transmigration destination.

The authorities responded by opening a number of transmigration sites in "strategic" areas. One was along the coast. Sites were established south of Pontianak (at Rasau Jaya and Sungai Kakap) and others near Mempawah.[20] In the words of one military officer, these schemes were designed to "balance and neutralize Chinese cultural influences and to create loyalty toward Indonesia" (*Angkatan Bersenjata,* August 1, 1970). The border area was also designated. There, officials hoped that the transmigration initiative, in conjunction with the Roads and Rice campaign, would materialize into a security belt (*wilayah aman*).[21] Plans were announced to send nearly 1,300 military families, termed "transmigrant battalions," each year.[22] In 1971, transmigrants constituted a minute portion of the province's population (0.5 percent); by 1985, this figure had increased fourteenfold (Fasbender and Erbe 1990, 136–37, tables 33–34).

As in the case of large-scale logging, transmigration clearly fueled Dayak grievances, which included the fear of becoming minorities in their homeland and resentment over the preferential treatment transmigrants receive (e.g., the receipt of two hectares of free land per family). Government attempts to extirpate cultural distinctions while "modernizing" so-called isolated tribes (*suku terasing*) through transmigration have been well publicized and documented (Colchester 1986a).

Yet, linking transmigration directly to the riots is a leap of faith, as it glosses over a host of intervening variables and ignores the lack of violence in most transmigrant-native relations. But blaming transmigration for violence did serve the political purposes of pro-indigenous rights campaigns, which highlighted the complicity of Western governments (through aid) in the transmigration program. The mid-1980s testimony of an associate of Survival International, which promotes the rights of indigenous peoples worldwide, is exemplary. It notes that "the local Dayak have reacted to the takeover of their traditional lands with violence. . . . [P]opular resistance to Transmigration continues. In 1984, some twenty transmigrants from Madura were killed in bloody clashes over land" (Colchester 1986b, 109). Tellingly, this statement dismisses several key elements. If resistance to transmigration was popular, why were only Madurese who rarely participated in the government-sponsored transmigration program singled out? Why was the violence geographically concentrated? While misrepresenting the Madurese as transmigrants, this statement also ignores the fact that Madurese and

Dayaks had clashed before the province became an official transmigration site. Finally, when official transmigrants did arrive, the majority were placed in coastal sites (such as Rasau Jaya) west of Pontianak City, again, areas free of widespread bloodshed. While Sambas district did house several transmigration sites that Madurese had inhabited—they bought plots from transmigrants quitting the sites[23]—these sites were opened in the mid- to late 1970s, after the relevant critical juncture in this violent conflict. All told, these incongruities destabilize the links among popular resistance, transmigration, and the killing of Madurese.

Problems of place and time handicap another apart of the critical development package: the expansion of large oil palm estates. Despite the rapid growth of agribusiness under the New Order, these plantations were not established until the mid-1970s and became pervasive only in the early 1980s. In addition, the earliest plantations were located in eastern Pontianak and Sanggau districts, areas beyond the bounds of the early riots.[24]

One final limitation of the theories of the critical development school involves the case of Ketapang. This book stresses that coming to grips with the aftereffects of the New Order's counterinsurgency campaign to account for the timing and geographical concentration of Madurese-Dayak riots is critical to an informed understanding of the ethnic violence in West Kalimantan. It is not happenstance that Ketapang, the province's southernmost district and home to considerable (rural and urban) Dayak and Madurese populations,[25] did not experience ethnic riots in the time period under consideration. What accounts for this? A brief sketch of the social and political relations in this counterfactual case is meant to show that the New Order's counterinsurgency and subsequent anti-Chinese mobilizations were decisive intervening variables.

Madurese began migrating to Ketapang in the mid- to late nineteenth century. Some continued north; others settled along its littoral, particularly in the town of Ketapang and Teluk Melano–Sukadana areas. Rivers in Ketapang lack the sizable gold deposits that attracted an influx of Chinese miners farther north in Pontianak and Sambas districts. Geographically, this district—the province's largest—is somewhat isolated from the rest of the province, whose rivers flow east-west not north-south. Consequently, the Kapuas River, Indonesia's longest, links upland West Kalimantan with Pontianak but bypasses Ketapang. Swampy marshes and sloping mountains form another barrier between Ketapang and Pontianak and Sanggau districts.

Collective violence in Ketapang has been scant. In 1933 some twenty Madurese indentured servants revolted against their master, causing a minor disturbance. A decade later, during World War II, violence was minimal except for limited engagements against Japanese troops along the coast (Semdam XII 1971, 112–18). Ketapang was also largely removed from the PGRS/Paraku rebellion. Aside from coastal naval patrols, few if any intensive counterinsurgency operations were conducted. Consequently, neither land grabs nor other destabilizing events occurred.

On the other hand, like its Sambas and Pontianak counterparts, Ketapang district has been marred by New Order development, though belated due to its geographical isolation and the fact that the rebellions were located farther north. Not until the mid-1980s did widespread logging in northern Ketapang and the opening of massive oil palm plantations in the south commence. In particular, the latter has intensified land conflicts (Walhi Kalbar and Down to Earth 2000). Moreover, from 1990 to 1996, some thirty-five transmigration sites were built to contain nearly 42,000 inhabitants. Only Sanggau district received more transmigrants during this period (Departemen Transmigrasi dan Pemukiman Perambah Hutan 1999, appendix 4, 53–58).

What, then, explains Ketapang's lack of riots?[26] The critical development argument holds little weight, for Dayaks in Ketapang have been as susceptible to New Order development as their more northern ethnic brothers. Neither were they less marginalized by and less frustrated over the New Order institutional makeup. Is the answer found in conflict prevention attempts by local government? During the 2001 riots in Central Kalimantan, officials in Ketapang made a public spectacle of ethnic peace accords to prevent a spillover of violence. Yet in 1997 when the massive riots of Pontianak and Sambas districts *should have* buffeted Ketapang, similar accords were not implemented. Finally, one could construct a cultural argument along the lines that Dayaks and Madurese in Ketapang are naturally or culturally more passive than northern counterparts. These are, I believe, unfounded presumptions. To the contrary, Madurese and Dayak communities in Ketapang have coexisted in relative harmony for more than a century.

The Great Riots of 1997

The 1997 unrest in Pontianak and Sambas districts was the last in a series of exclusive Madurese-Dayak clashes extending from 1967. This time, the once-characteristically-contained fighting reached massive dimensions. At the time, it was Indonesia's largest outbreak of communal violence in nearly thirty years. More critically, they set the stage for the extensive regional clashes that proliferated in the early post-Soeharto state and during Indonesia's transition from authoritarianism.

In the years preceding Soeharto's downfall, explanations of collective violence in Indonesia invariably explored the incendiary role of outside provocateurs who engineered unrest for political gain. Commonalities among local disturbances in this period (mid-1990s) — the timing (nearing elections), locations (oppositional strongholds), targets (churches and/or Chinese-owned property), lax security forces, and precipitating events (rumor mongering and the conspicuous presence of "troublemaking" non-locals) — impelled observers to consider the provocateur hypothesis.

The large-scale 1997 violence in West Kalimantan did follow two riots on Java. One hit in Situbondo (East Java) in October 1996; the other in Tasikmalaya (West Java) in December. And in May, immediately before the 1997 elections, deadly campaign-related clashes rocked Banjarmasin in South Kalimantan (Salim and Achdian 1997). The features listed above fit these incidents. Specifically, heavy speculation that the 1998–2003 term might be the aging Soeharto's last redoubled the jockeying for strategic positions in the run-up to the 1997 general elections.[27] It is within this context that many observers see these riots as attempts by certain cliques in ABRI and hard-line Islamists associated with the Association of Muslim Intellectuals of Indonesia (ICMI), the Indonesian Committee for Solidarity with the Islamic World (KISDI), and the Indonesian Council for Islamic Predication (DDII) to disgrace the head of NU (and the president from October 1999 to July 2001) Gus Dur, and corner the (Muslim) Development Unity Party (PPP) by inciting violence in NU strongholds (Aspinall 2005, 198; Eklöf 1999, 68–74; Hefner 2000, 189–93; Sidel 1998; N. Schulte Nordholt 2002).

The Madurese were PPP supporters, but semirural West Kalimantan lacks national electoral significance, unlike East and West Java. Nor is semirural West Kalimantan a major outer island city like Banjarmasin.[28] "Third party intervention" (HRW 1997), for some, does point to possible military involvement. A regional disturbance at this time would have benefited ABRI by justifying the continuation of its *dwifungsi* (dual function doctrine), which allowed it to play a dominant role in civil and political state functions. Similarly, it would have reconfirmed the perceived necessity of deploying a repressive "security approach" in its territorial management of the country. While other aspects of military policy and ideology were being debated within ABRI, one scholar maintains that its "territorial doctrine was an area of 'non-debate' during the late New Order era" (Honna 2003, 154). One reason for this was that military predominance in the outer islands would safeguard well-entrenched business interests.[29] Yet Soeharto fell unexpectedly. It would be overly conspiratorial to imagine that ABRI could have known some sixteen months after the killing began in West Kalimantan that Soeharto would no longer reign and that the army would be scrambling to protect its interests in a *post*-Soeharto state. Instead, influential riot lineages and a rountinization of violence contributed immeasurably to the recent history of Dayak-Madurese bloodletting. Its principal modalities— ascriptive "ethnic" descriptions and geographical location—materialized well before 1997. Thus, it is more pressing (and illuminating) to explicate the incident's immense scale rather than the violence per se. To do so, we must place the changing political environment of Dayak society-state relations at the center of the analysis.

In describing the 1997 unrest, HRW reported that "Dayaks waged what appeared to be a ritual war against Madurese communities, burning houses, killing inhabitants, and in some cases severing heads and eating the livers of those killed" (1997, 3). The violence subsided by early April 1997, but not before it had left a toll of hundreds (if not thousands) dead and deepened a legacy of bitter hatred. Rather than offering a blow-by-blow account,[30] I sketch a cursory outline of events that help inform the key features of the violence: its unanticipated intensity and scale. An attempt to explain these key features follows.

In the early hours of December 30, 1996, in the village of Tanjung (Ledo subdistrict, Sambas district), following a pop concert, a gang of young Madurese men, in retribution for a scuffle earlier that month, attacked two Dayak youths,[31] one of whom was rushed to a nearby clinic with stab wounds. Crowds began to gather and the police were given until noon to arrest the assailants. As local authorities and Dayak and Madurese leaders tried to resolve the matter, a crowd of some one hundred persons gathered. According to HRW, the police had made five arrests but were reluctant to announce them for fear that the suspects would be lynched (1997, 13). As the police and local leaders tried to moderate rising emotions, drawn by the rumor of the deaths of the two Dayak youths, more people from the south (Ledo) and the north (Seluas) converged on Sanggau Ledo. By the morning of December 31, a crowd of some two thousand strong began burning Madurese houses in Sanggau Ledo as security forces evacuated hundreds of Madurese to a nearby air force base. Roving gangs then rampaged through Madurese enclaves south toward Bengkayang and west toward Montrado. In Singkawang, Madurese burned the houses of a few well-known Dayaks.

By January 5, 1997, the killings had dissipated. As some six thousand Madurese who had fled the violence slowly returned to rebuild their burned houses, local government officials, ethnic elites, and two members of the National Human Rights Commission (Komnas HAM) held a traditional peace ceremony in Tujuhbelas subdistrict. Days later a government-sponsored peace accord was signed. In all, the rioters razed some twelve hundred houses and killed roughly twenty Madurese. Reportedly, Dayaks had suffered no casualties. Yet circumstances dictated that this "typical" West Kalimantan riot would be different.

Past violence rarely had disturbed religious sanctuaries, as if the combatants strove to deny these episodes religious significance. The riots involved Christians and Muslims, but had little to do with Christianity or Islam. In fact, following the first phase of these riots, local military officials and a member of Komnas HAM proclaimed that no mosques had been destroyed (*Republika*, January 14, 1997). An apparent exception, however, would have grim consequences. The motives behind a premeditated attack on a Dayak Catholic school, the St. Francis of Assisi Junior High School, are contested, but the earlier destruction of a small Muslim prayer house (*surau*) in Sinduh (Samalantan subdistrict) may have been a contributing factor. Whether the *surau* was purposely razed or it inadvertently caught fire as adjacent homes burned is unclear. Nevertheless, the keeper of the *surau* traveled to Pontianak to meet with some Madurese leaders, which included a religious leader (*kiyai*) from Madura who was visiting the region to survey the destruction wrought upon his ethnic brethren. At this meeting they chose the school and an adjacent boarding house in Siantan (a Pontianak suburb and Madurese stronghold) as the target of retribution.[32] Both targets were run and operated by the Pancur Kasih (Fount of Love) Social Foundation, the province's most prominent Dayak organization. The attack was calculated to strike at the heart of Pontianak's Dayak community, a minority and patently vulnerable population in the provincial capital.[33]

Before dawn on January 30, a group of at least forty Madurese raided their targets, severely injuring two young female students in the process, although news spread that they had died (Soetrisno et al. 1998, 37–38). This incident and rumors about it sparked broader clashes. In Pahauman (Pontianak district), some 150 Madurese perished. Meanwhile, about twenty-five miles north of Pontianak, in Peniraman, Madurese erected roadblocks and over two days killed five Dayaks pulled from passing vehicles.[34] As we shall see, the deaths of two of these victims—Martinus Nyangkot, a head villager from Tebas subdistrict (Sambas district), and Djalan, who hailed from Batang Tarang subdistrict (Sanggau district)—measurably affected the riots' geographical distribution.

The roadblock killings triggered substantial bloodshed along the two major roads in the region, one running east-west along the Anjungan-Ngabang axis and the other extending from Sidas north to Bengkayang (see map 2). Riots also erupted again in Ledo, Bengkayang, and Samalantan subdistricts. It is no coincidence that the spread of the violence eerily recalls the earlier Chinese expulsions. Indeed, many Madurese inhabited areas from which the Chinese had fled three decades before.

This time the killings spilled beyond their usual parameters. Dayaks rampaged through Madurese areas in the usually peaceful Tebas subdistrict, north of riot-prone Samalantan, where the Madurese were to pay for the earlier slaying of Martinus Nyangkot. Reprisals for the death of Djalan forced the fighting farther east than usual. Mobs razed houses along the main thoroughfare in Sanggau district as thousands sought protection at military posts. The fighting continued to spread. From central Sanggau, bands headed north toward the border and sparked rioting in Balai Karangan and Entikong. Never before had Dayak-Madurese riots spread so extensively.

The unprecedented scale of the bloodshed was matched by its exceptional intensity. Recorded death tolls for prior riots—data that should be viewed with suspicion due to chronic underreporting—had never surpassed thirty. In 1997, the figures ranged from four hundred (official) to seventeen hundred (unofficial) with the Madurese accounting for the lion's share of the fatalities (Soetrisno et al. 1998, 27). There were also fierce clashes between Dayaks and government security forces. Most deaths of the former were the result of these confrontations that took place at army roadblocks (HRW 1997; *Kabar dari Pijar,* March 12, 1997).

In addition to their physical (perhaps repressive) approach to quelling the violence, the authorities also deployed "cultural" tactics such as holding "traditional" peace ceremonies. Typically, such local personalities as subdistrict and district heads, army and police commanders, and ethnic elites would attend ceremonies to sign peace accords. Starting in mid-February, the government arranged a slew of ceremonies in each afflicted subdistrict, later to be conducted at the district and provincial levels. With all the pomp and circumstance surrounding the one held in Pontianak City on March 15, 1997, HRW reported that this government-managed stage show "could have been an election rally for GOLKAR" for the upcoming May elections (1997, 32).

Two aspects of these ceremonies require elaboration. First, they were solely "traditional" in terms of contemporary Dayak views on what traditional should mean and how it should be portrayed. They were devoid of Madurese cultural trappings. By incorporating only indigenous cultural symbols, the ceremonies reinforced the native versus migrant distinction and implied that Madurese culture lacked characteristics that could contribute to conflict resolution. How can it be represented, the argument goes, if it is the culprit? The perception in West Kalimantan continues to be that Madurese culture would have to change if future outbreaks of violence are to be avoided.

This leads us to my second point. On the one hand, government-sponsored ceremonies are deservedly ripe for criticism. As the HRW report notes, they had little in common with traditional Dayak end-of-war ceremonies and involved local elites of questionable legitimacy. This exacerbated already sensitive situations in which pacts were "quickly broken, amid mutual recriminations and charges of bad faith" (1997, 33). On the other hand, if viewed broadly, the peace ceremonies could be surprisingly constructive, although the conventional wisdom suggests that the New Order undermined local social institutions and leadership to the point where traditional mechanisms for mediation became pointless. Despite the fact that violence flared for nearly a month following the first of the peace pacts of mid-February, many on both sides widely acknowledge the ceremonies' and pacts' legitimacy. For Dayaks, *hukum adat* (customary law) demands that peace ceremonies conclude violence, while the Madurese have become accustomed to, and in fact, demand such ceremonies.[35]

Over the years, peace ceremonies have kept minor incidents minor. They do not address more substantive issues, but they do provide a sense of finality to a specific incident. Following violence, members of these communities had typically returned to their previous stations and resumed their lives, often coexisting, a situation that is characteristic of riots elsewhere (Tilly 2003, 11). In West Kalimantan, this had been reflected in the norm of the Madurese returning home following the conclusion of fighting. While this norm began to dissolve following the 1997 violence, it did not fully dissolve until the 1999 unrest.

Dayak-State Relations

Why did these riots' intensity and scale far outstrip those of prior Madurese-Dayak clashes? The answer to this important question stems from changing Dayak-state relations and in particular the rise of a politicized, indigenous consciousness sparked and nurtured by a long-standing ethnopolitical movement. To substantiate this argument, we need to revisit incipient New Order–Dayak relations in the context of the counterinsurgency and early New Order state building efforts.[36]

In the late 1960s, during the early stages of the insurgency, the New Order authorities were aware of their tenuous legitimacy and minimal control in this vast hinterland. The army admitted that "only the trust-worthy obedience of the Dayaks toward government has prevented a violent, negative reaction toward us. If not for this, it is possible that we could experience what the Japanese army did during World War II" (Witono 1969, 2). Confronted with this situation, the authorities resolved to supplement military operations with "political" efforts. At a meeting held in July 1967, led by General Soeharto, a program known as Consolidation and Development (Konsolidasi dan Pembangunan) was initiated. It involved converting the Chinese and Dayaks of West Kalimantan into obedient and loyal citizens of the Indonesian Republic via state building and development. Exterminating the insurgents was never simply a matter of military operations.

The military was fully aware of the long history of close relations between Dayaks and Chinese, including intermarriage, which meant that it was crucially important for ABRI to prevent Dayaks from siding with the "Chinese" communists.[37] The military noted their amicable relations: "If viewed from an ethnological viewpoint, Dayak-Chinese relations actually are better and closer with each other than with other ethnic groups . . . because of mutual economic and societal interests. Moreover, their religions and the fact that both are of 'Mongoloid stock' facilitate integration. In fact, for a long time the two have physically assimilated. It is customary for Dayaks in the hinterland to call the Chinese "good friends [*sahabat*]" (Witono 1969, 1). Moreover, the military was convinced that as long as lives and trade were oriented toward Sarawak, borderland inhabitants would remain susceptible to communist influences. It sought to combat this situation by "planting a national feeling" and "spreading the influence of the government of the Republic of Indonesia" among the "backward" (*terbelakang*) inland inhabitants

(Semdam XII 1971, 267, 299). So the state set out to count, organize, and control almost every aspect of these villagers' lives. By April 1971 a large survey team consisting of dozens of "experts" from Jakarta had arrived in the border area to produce detailed reports on its populations and to help plan development projects.[38]

Ideologically, the military proceeded along two tracks. First, it was concerned about the lack of formal, state-controlled education among border populations. "The very low level of education," according to the governor's report on border development, was incapable of "cultivating the consciousness of a community steeped in Nation, in Government and in Pancasila [the state ideology]" (Kadarusno 1974, 10). Accordingly, ABRI built dozens of schools and posted some three hundred soldiers as teachers. A standard curriculum was not always taught.[39] Recalcitrant locals who were unwilling to help ABRI search for rebels were schooled in "social education" programs. Those classified as "serious" underwent "mental education programs to induce an *opinion change* [*in English*] so as to side with [what is] right and to oppose the PGRS-PARAKU enemy" (Soemadi 1974, 124). Reportedly, as many as 250,000 border-area residents underwent military education programs (*Kompas*, October 30, 1969).

Second, ABRI also believed that the lack of established religious belief among indigenous communities made them susceptible to communist influence. For state elites, local, traditional beliefs (*kepercayaan*) did not comprise a religion. "I don't care which religion [they belong to]," one regional commander was quoted as saying, "as long as they have one" (*Tempo*, October 26, 1974). Accordingly, the authorities brought community leaders to military headquarters in Pontianak where they were instructed: "The PGRS and PARAKU are communists and communists don't have religion. Dayaks are part of the Indonesian nation, which is a religious nation, and Dayaks cannot live together with communists. So the PGRS-PARAKU must be crushed" (Witono 1967, 3).

To ensure compliance with state religious policies, the military undertook missionary work to convert the predominantly animist indigenes. A Catholic Church report admits to their slow progress in the 1960s but explains that in the early 1970s "a development began under the leadership of ABRI and later under civil authorities which channeled this religious movement toward the border area." In Bengkayang Parish, for instance, in a mere six years (1969–75) the church converted fourteen hundred indigenes, equaling the total number of converts during the parish's first thirty-five years. In the nearby Sambas Parish, there were twice as many converts during these same six years than had been brought into the church from 1913 to 1968.[40]

In essence, the military instigated a race between religious leaders to convert border populations. Catholic priests and army chaplains scoured the area distributing thousands of yellow cards (*kartu kuning*) to be posted on dwellings to mark their inhabitants as Catholic. In most instances these "Catholics" had never met a priest. As the archbishop of West Kalimantan, Monsignor Hieronimus Bumbun explained, the goal was to distribute as many cards as possible and later worry about conversion.[41] Although the authorities had hoped Islam would compete, they eventually conceded defeat, blaming the Islamic leadership's engagement in politics (*mementingkan bidang politik*) rather than attending to its religious duties. This accusation is misplaced. Decades-old missionary networks gave Catholicism a strong institutional advantage, leading the military to snipe, "Dayaks know white people better than their own people (*bangsanja*)" (Witono 1969, 4).[42] Today the term *Dayak*, particularly in the province's western-half, has become synonymous with *Christian*.

The New Order authorities' efforts to contain and control Dayak leaders rivaled their attempts to corral the masses. The extensive 1967 mobilizations evidenced the potency of this elite's influence over its flock. While a strong Dayak leadership served New Order interests in 1967–68, this was no longer the case. Oeray's removal from the governorship was only the first step. By 1968 the regime had replaced all four (former) PD district heads;[43] the heads of Sintang and Kapuas Hulu district assemblies were similarly removed. This "renewal" (*peremajaan*) of provincial government would ensure unflagging loyalty to Jakarta. According to the military, this was an "absolute requisite" (*sjarat mutlak*) for state building (Ryacudu 1967c, 6).

The authorities also clamped down on leaders in Pontianak. Palaunsoeka and his Catholic Party's anticommunist credentials were unassailable. Not so for Oeray's Partindo group. Although they were hardly ideologues, at the national level Partindo was unquestionably leftist. Furthermore, no matter what their motives—business opportunities or ideological affinities—some had joined the now banned Chinese organization Baperki.

The political expediency of Partindo (and Baperki) fizzled with the rise of General Soeharto and his reactionary New Order regime. In

West Kalimantan, by mid-1966, provincial military authorities had coerced this Partindo elite to join another political party, IPKI.[44] As the 1971 elections neared, they were again forced to hitch their political fortunes to another electoral vehicle, this time the government-backed Golkar party. Pressure was applied frequently in the form of arrests, including those of Stepanus Ngo Lahay and Rachman Sahudin, both of whom were instrumental in the Laskar Pangsuma.[45] In the end, without protection from its most powerful patron—Oeray had been transferred to Jakarta in March 1971 (Tanasaldy 2007)—Oeray's gang acquiesced to the New Order's demands.[46] In time, a local Dayak Golkar elite coalesced. While it never had genuine policy or decision-making influence in government, it enjoyed local notoriety and benefited from Golkar-associated largesse.[47]

State policy toward rural Dayak leaders differed markedly. Whereas urban elites were largely under the pressure from "the stick," rural leadership frequently was lured by "the carrot." The authorities rewarded rural leaders for services rendered in hunting insurgents. Village headmen were paid handsomely for mobilizing villagers to help track the insurgents;[48] others received honorary military titles (Pelda Kehormatan).[49] Another twenty-one were brought to Jakarta to meet with President Soeharto. There they were told that "the government of the Republic of Indonesia has now corrected the mistakes toward West Kalimantan made by past leaders."[50]

In the end, the New Order authorities treated the urban, party elite with suspicion, emblematic of their inbred aversion toward party politics. Worse, they viewed rural leadership as simpletons easily wowed by excursions to the big city or empty honorific titles. Local "elites," to the military, were mere derivatives of a politically "blind" (*buta*) populace that, being ideologically "empty and clean" (*kosong dan berish*), could be manipulated into pliable Indonesian citizens (Ryacudu 1967a, 7; Ryacudu 1967c, 2).

Golkar Dayaks and Budding Opposition

Against this backdrop, by the mid-1970s, a small of coterie of leaders—willingly or unwillingly—were working on behalf of Golkar to represent the Dayak masses.[51] Derisively known as "Golkar Dayaks," they were awarded with seats in the largely ceremonial national, provincial, and district assemblies.[52] While some held semiprominent civil service positions, none was allowed higher than subdistrict head.[53]

This elite functioned to secure the Golkar vote in its stage-managed elections. Whereas Golkar's victory was predetermined, its margin of victory was somewhat contestable. A former governor of West Kalimantan, Soejiman explained that the size of the Dayak population rendered its vote pivotal. "Don't forget," he remarked, "victory in West Kalimantan was not unconditional [*tak mutlak*] like in Sulawesi."[54] For the 1977 election, Oeray shouldered the burden of culling this Golkar vote. The government-controlled local newspaper, *Akcaya* (March 24, 1977) describes tens of thousands of supporters meeting the former governor with ecstatic cries of "Long live Oeray! Long Live Golkar!" Another article mentions a crowd of one hundred thousand supporters (March 30, 1977). Having campaigned assiduously, Oeray was rewarded with a seat in the national People's Representative Council (DPR).[55]

The regime's strategy of overly relying on Oeray was exposed when he passed away in 1986. In response, the authorities sought to institutionalize the delivery of Dayak votes. Its domination of local politics had foreclosed the rise of genuine *adat* (customary) leaders, making necessary a change in strategy that would co-opt a slightly larger swath of this elite. The formation of a Dewan Adat (Customary Council) at the district level and later subdistrict levels was exemplary. In 1985 the first council was formed in the densely populated and electorally strategic Pontianak district. Its name, the Kanayatn Customary Council, reflected the domination of the Dayak subgroup of Kanayatns in the district. A year later, with government backing, the council organized the first of several large harvest festivals (Gawai Naik Dango).[56]

In Pontianak City, another development was underway that would have more influence on indigenous society than politicking for Golkar or organizing festivals. In 1981 a group of urban educators, led by A. R. Mecer, formed a social works foundation popularly called Pancur Kasih (Yayasan Karya Sosial Pancur Kasih). It sought to open a junior high school (the future St. Francis of Assisi) run by Dayaks for Dayaks. Inspired by the ideal of self-sufficiency, Pancur Kasih's leadership maintained that for decades foreign missionaries or the government—though rather poorly—had been responsible for Dayak education.[57] It was time, they felt, to wean themselves from this dependence and show that they were not the backward and lazy natives that the New Order authorities (and others) deemed. Pancur Kasih's mission statement underscores the importance of self-sufficiency: "'Dayak' society has the capacity to determine and to manage its political, economic, cultural, and social existence in a self-sufficient manner of loving togetherness within the framework of acknowledgement, respect, and protection afforded by Pancasila and the 1945 Constitution."[58] Over time Pancur Kasih's motto, school, and activities would galvanize a self-empowerment movement that would far exceed New Order expectations to which "backward" Dayaks could aspire.

Aspiring to educational independence is laudable, but tangible self-sufficiency would require economic security. Investments by Dayaks in institutions owned and operated by Dayaks, it was hoped, would foster informed decision making and enhance economic opportunities. Savings and access to small-scale capital also might buttress the shock of those on the frontline of New Order development, those whose land was being expropriated by logging concessions, oil palm estates, and transmigration sites. To achieve this end, in 1987 Pancur Kasih opened a credit union that over time has evolved into the cornerstone of this self-determination movement. By late 2004, it had some twenty thousand members with assets totaling Rp. 30 billion—making it Indonesia's largest—and has spawned at least fifteen similar credit unions in the province (*Kalimantan Review*, November 2004). What differentiated Pancur Kasih from previous self-help efforts and accounted for its early success, was its commitment to long-term social change. It did not seek rapid, grand change, nor did it rush to fund-raise among external—either Jakarta- or international-based—donors, organizations to which it then would have been beholden.

Pancur Kasih was spearheading what became a rather remarkable story—an inspirational, textbook civil society and social capital case. But at this point, the organization did not have autonomous, oppositional status. Particularly at its peak in the early to mid-1980s when the "totalitarian aspirations of the regime came to the fore" (Vickers 2001, 73), the New Order brooked little criticism or "destabilizing" activity. To criticize was to risk the dissolution of the organization and personal harm to its members. Its leaders were cautious, and in some ways continued the arrangement under which Dayak elites served Golkar's interests.[59] Some preferred to effect social change from within the system and saw little contradiction in supporting both organizations. Others kept a foot on either side to hedge their bets against an uncertain future. Or perhaps identification with Pancur Kasih lessened the stigma of being branded a "Golkar Dayak" and New Order lackey. This conservative-progressive tension would continue to dog Pancur Kasih as younger, more critical activists joined and expanded the organization's reach into the countryside.

Indigeneity and Pancur Kasih's NGOs

To situate Pancur Kasih in its proper political context, we need to demonstrate how this movement overcame substantial obstacles to become a regional political force. In doing so, we must explore the mediating, middle ground (often missing in accounts of rural politics) between the microscopic, daily grind of resistance and the macroscopic yet infrequent revolutionary experiences (Fox 1990). This narrative also confirms the supposition that the creation (or, at least in this case, the revitalization) of ethnicity is regularly a phenomenon of an urban elite under the conditions of interethnic competition (Bates 1983).

The oppositional, counterhegemonic practices and discourse that Pancur Kasih would foster commenced in the early 1990s with the establishment of Dayak-oriented NGOs in Pontianak. Staffed and run by a young breed of activists, these NGOs were autonomous units underneath the Pancur Kasih umbrella. The first to be formed, in 1991, was the Institute of Dayakology Research and Development (IDRD). Although the background of and inspiration to establish IDRD are varied and diverse, the presence of Pancur Kasih was key. At first, some older, conservative members balked at the idea, believing that such an NGO would be exclusionist and would be perilously stamped an ethnic or racial (SARA) organization.[60] Ironically, these were the very same objections that Pancur Kasih's founders had confronted ten years earlier. But once Mecer agreed, the organizational and institutional support Pancur Kasih afforded IDRD was invaluable.

The lively 1987 anti-logging campaigns in Sarawak (Bevis 1995; Brosius 1997) and a visit to Pontianak by Sarawak activists inspired some young Dayaks in Pontianak to begin advocating on behalf of West Kalimantan's indigenous community (*masyarakat adat*). Soon, exchange visits were initiated, which enlarged these urban-based Dayaks' contacts and gave them access to the literature critical of capitalist development paradigms that was available in Sarawak.

Significantly, through this literature and these contacts, activists were introduced to the discourse of the burgeoning international indigenous peoples' movement. By the 1980s, after decades of organizing and lobbying among North and South American networks—and aided by the unparalleled ease of global communications—the term *indigenous peoples* was in vogue, just as *ethnicity, ethnic group,* and *peasant* had been beforehand (Niezen 2003, 3). By the time this movement and its associated political identity, known as *indigeneity*, penetrated activist circles in Indonesia in the early 1990s, a political sea change had taken place in the world at large, whereby indigenous peoples had "reentered the arena of power" (Wiessner 1999, 58). Seen in this light, as will be shown below, there is nothing natural or inevitable about the fact that today many Dayaks see themselves as the indigenous peoples of West Kalimantan. The politics and notion of indigeneity and the attendant rights that come with them were pushed, pursued, and promoted by activists embedded in national and transnational indigenous rights networks.

Two developments in particular spurred Dayak students at the state-run Tanjungpura University (UNTAN) in Pontianak to establish a Dayak-oriented NGO. One was the participation of Stephanus Djuweng, an UNTAN student, at a workshop on customary law held in Chiang Mai, Thailand, in 1993. Another was a report written by a Belgian researcher who chronicled the adverse impacts of New Order development on Dayaks in Sintang (Rokaerts 1985). The type of research reflected in the report, grounded in factual knowledge yet ardently advocating traditional land rights and ways of life, impressed these students. Reading the report fired their enthusiasm (*membakar semangat*) and in May 1991, with the help of an English-language professor, Albert Rufinus, they formed IDRD.[61]

As Djuweng later explained, outsiders—government officials, foreign missionaries, and researchers—have always spoken for and on behalf of Dayaks. It was time, he was convinced, for Dayaks to speak for themselves. Solidarity would be forged by defending a particular traditional way of life predicated on customary law (*hukum adat*) and land rights.[62] A year after its founding, IDRD made a name for itself by holding a three-day conference on Dayak culture in Pontianak; it was the largest gathering of Kalimantan wide Dayaks since the 1894 Tumbang Anoi meeting (*Kalimantan Review*, November 2004). One of the conference's important outcomes was an agreement to standardize the spelling of Dayak. The fixity of and the popular support for the spelling of Dayak—rather than, for example, Daya—kicked off a process in which a word that once signified contempt and subjugation would be transformed into a charged, politicized term. Marc Edelman's discussion of the changing connotations of the term *agricultor* in the 1980s Costa Rican peasant movement is germane to what was happening in West Kalimantan in the 1990s: "[T]he label *agricultor* increasingly took on a new meaning in local discourse. . . . [T]he term was suddenly being asserted in a new adversarial context assuming connotations of persecution and dignity, and becoming almost synonymous with a punishable offense" (1999, 146).

On the heels of the successful conference, the organization's visibility and networking capacity grew, especially among those in the blossoming NGO movement on Java (Eldridge 1995). Soon IDRD received generous grants from such international donor agencies as the Ford Foundation and the Dutch Catholic Cebemo organization.

IDRD and its spin-off NGOs have been active members of the Indonesian indigenous peoples' movement. They were represented at a 1993 meeting in Tana Toraja (Central Sulawesi) that is seen as the organizational origins of this national movement.[63] And in 1996 one of the first regional indigenous peoples organizations in the country—the Alliance of Indigenous Peoples (AMA)—was formed in West Kalimantan. In sum, IDRD rapidly became *the* organization representing *the* Dayak voice in the many national and international forums its activists attended, albeit problematically, for other Dayak organizations (and points of view) lacked access to such forums and these agencies' resources.

IDRD's original research focused on preserving, documenting, and revitalizing Dayak cultures. They were unambiguously essentialist cultural projects. One recorded and published oral stories and histories in local languages. Buoyed by the 1992 conference's success, and following the Tana Toraja meeting, it was decided that more grounded activism was needed; it was time for the activists to get their hands dirty in community organizing. To serve this end, two new NGOs were established, LBBT (the Institute for the Defense of the Talino Homeland) and SHK (the People's Forestry System). LBBT stressed the legal rights of Dayaks to make customary land claims;[64] SHK concentrated on the design and promotion of alternative economic strategies to counter large (and small) government-backed oil palm estates.[65]

Gradually, a campaign of rural activism, advocacy, and agitation unfolded. Information was disseminated and local dissent facilitated and—as necessary—fomented. Traditional ceremonies were also funded. Yet, in a vast, sparsely populated region with an anemic road network, more efficient communication was needed. Activists could not adequately organize a region that was larger than Java. Hence, informed news reporting was introduced. Coverage of Dayaks in the government-controlled local newspaper, *Akcaya,* was essentially absent.[66] One glaring example was the paper's silence on the formation of the Kanayatn

Customary Council. This situation soon changed thanks to IDRD, which worked to make "Dayak" mainstream.

The 1992 conference drew the attention of the national press. The publishing wing of the national daily *Kompas* published the conference's articles (Florus et al. 1994), and another national paper, *Suara Pembaruan*, hired Djuweng and another IDRD associate, Vincent Julipin, to report on the plight of indigenous communities (see *Suara Pembaruan*, June 9, 1992). While these newspapers were not reaching audiences in rural West Kalimantan, the articles, in conjunction with IDRD's growing local stature (and that of Pancur Kasih), affected *Akcaya*. Local newspapers—in Indonesia and elsewhere—take cues from influential national papers on what is considered newsworthy. Fortuitously, the Surabaya-based Jawa Pos New Group had recently purchased *Akcaya* and brought commercial imperatives to bear on the government-controlled newspaper. This tied it more closely to national reportage trends. In the early 1990s, the regularity of articles featuring Dayaks, though hardly garnering daily headlines, visibly increased.[67] Fueled by infusion of new capital and an improving road network, *Akcaya*'s distribution network also expanded, which bolstered its visibility in rural areas.

The final part of this transformation was the publication and rural distribution of IDRD's own magazine, *Kalimantan Review* (KR).[68] *Akcaya* was devoting more space to Dayak concerns in its papers, but important (or politically sensitive) issues and cases still went unreported. KR filled this gap. Again, Pancur Kasih was instrumental. The purchase of its own printing press facilitated the formation and dissemination of a discourse that challenged the New Order's developmental ideology.[69]

Originally found to publish current indigenous-oriented research, KR evolved into an alternative news source that generally supported the budding Dayak resistance.[70] Its coverage of violent acts will be discussed shortly, but its reporting of small, peaceful protests—such as submitting a letter of complaint to a subdistrict head over a local development project—alerted distant communities to activities that previously went undetected.[71] It also ran regular features on Pancur Kasih's credit union, the benefits of small-scale rubber cultivation, and the perils of oil palm. All told, KR helped to foster, borrowing from Anderson's work on nationalism, a notion of "simultaneity" among previously disparate groups (1991). With the latest information in hand, Dayaks increasingly empathized with each others' concerns and responses, which in turn engendered a thickening of reciprocal identification and an increase in coordinated action. Less ideational than Anderson, the neoresource mobilization school would call this development "scale shift," whereby "a change in the number and level of coordinated contentious actions lead to broader contention involving a wider range of actors and bridging their claims and identities" (McAdam, Tarrow, and Tilly 2001, 331). In other words, the movement was making inroads in the West Kalimantan countryside.

It would be disingenuous to suggest that resistance only began once the Pontianak NGOs were established. Despite the paucity of documented materials, cases in Ngabang (Pontianak district, 1979), Sayak (Sintang district, 1981), and Nobal (Sintang, 1984) predate their founding.[72] Evidently, frustrations were not new. But if not what was the purpose of establishing Pancur Kasih and its NGOs? New developments were under way, namely, an evident web of politicization of the region's indigenous communities. Not surprisingly, the government authorities remained highly suspicious of these groups and watched them closely. There were other adversaries as well. As the NGOs continued to condemn "Golkar Dayaks"—Customary Council members were common targets (Bamba 2000)—opponents retaliated, countering that the NGOs exploited Dayak poverty by selling its images abroad for material gain. Evidence of well-funded operations such as computers and jeeps fueled these accusations. Furthermore, they were accused of condoning, and even fomenting, violent protest. Some of Pancur Kasih's conservative elders shared likewise views.

Beyond reporting resistance, KR's staff and related Pancur Kasih activists were engaged in the process of protest itself. Roles ranged from fomenters and facilitators to informal consultants. Critically, the external support that these committed urban-based activists gave local communities galvanized sustained, organized resistance (Fox 1996). As the frequency of violence against state property increased, news about it was disseminated widely. The protests and violence exhibited a budding political reawakening among these rural communities.

One early example of protracted (and successful) protest occurred prior to IDRD's existence, but involved future IDRD activists. In late 1987, university students from Simpang (Ketapang district) returned home from Pontianak to prevent the opening an integrative oil palm–transmigration site on sixty thousand hectares of land. Once the students convinced locals to participate, a petition was sent to the subdistrict head protesting the project. No violence erupted, but threats to the subdistrict head stalled the project's inception.[73] Similar examples followed the NGOs' founding. In September 1992 in Mukok subdistrict (Sanggau district), locals razed the living quarters and warehouse of a state-owned industrial tree estate company (PT. Inhutani). The arson was triggered by the rejection of inquiries made by the head villager from Empurang about assurances the company had made (*Kalimantan Review* January–March 1994).[74] The drawn-out case of Petai and Nangka (Sengah Temila subdistrict, Pontianak district) demonstrates the leverage local communities enjoyed due to external support. In 1992 protests prevented the Kota Niaga logging company from cutting trees on sacred land. A year later when the company's loggers returned to the contested spot, Pancur Kasih NGOs got involved. Locals seized chainsaws and axes and on January 6, 1994, they held a sizable protest in Saham village. Notably, Pancur Kasih's NGOs helped formed a local *adat* organization to defend land claims (*Kalimantan Review*, January–March 1994).

Two more incidents ended in violence. Dayak students in Pontianak sought LBBT's help in pressing legal claims against the Tri Eka Sari Company—a subsidiary of the large Bumi Raya Utama Group—in Sandai (Ketapang district). For two years, locals had been embittered by the company's logging practices. Eventually, in the early morning of August 11, 1994, the company's base camp and equipment were set alight.[75] A case in Belimbing (Ledo subdistrict, Sambas district) also ended in violence. For a year, villagers who had been forced from their fields attempted to solve their dispute with the Nitaya Idola Company legally. This included a trip to the district DPRD in Singkawang. Having exhausted legal channels, on November 1, 1995, villagers burned down the company's base camp (*Kalimantan Review*, January–February 1996).

While a further incident ended in violence, its significance lies in the drawing together of this activist-led, empowerment movement and the Golkar Dayaks. As long as Soeharto remained in power, the two formed a loose but strategic alliance that sought to gain Dayaks better political (and bureaucratic) representation. The incident that sparked unrest was a botched *bupati* selection process in 1994. In brief, roughly a quarter century had elapsed since a Dayak had last held a *bupati* post in a province where they accounted for some 40 percent of the population. Accordingly, having faithfully delivered the Golkar vote for more than two decades, Dayak leaders began to press for representation. Governor Aspar Aswin heeded their demands, and tapped L. H. Kadir—the provincial head of village development (Kadit Bangdes) and the highest-ranking Dayak civil servant—for the Sintang *bupati* post. Although

New Order district councils conventionally rubber-stamped government directives, in this case, Sintang's DPRD members voted twenty-one to sixteen in favor of Abdillah Kamarullah, a Sintang Malay and head of the district's planning agency (Bappeda) (*Kompas*, February 12, 1994).[76] Angered at the results, hundreds blocked the main road between Ngabang and Sanggau, smashing the windows of passing cars. Lobbying efforts by members of the Dayak elite in Jakarta fell on deaf ears. To allow the situation to cool, authorities delayed Kamarullah's inauguration for nearly a month. While leaders pointed to this fiasco as another example of Dayak persecution under the New Order,[77] it equally attested to a political awakening and incipient revitalization under an increasingly distinct Dayak banner.[78]

Empowerment and Violence

All things considered, the situation was in flux, and a politicization of the countryside was underway. The Pancur Kasih NGOs tapped into Dayak frustration and grievances against the pervasive cultural, economic, and political marginalization of West Kalimantan's indigenous communities, mainly the result of the New Order's ruthless and destabilizing transformations of Indonesia's upland societies (Li 1999). With organized and sustained advocacy, it began to reawaken the political awareness of people who identified themselves as Dayak, as IDRD and associates strove to redress colonial and postcolonial wrongs. Significantly, it is in this context that the 1997 violence broke out and subsequently gained immense proportions. Pancur Kasih activists neither engineered nor instigated this bloodletting, but in large part its intensity was a result of this ethnopolitical, indigenous rights movement. Of course, the jumping-on-the-empowerment-bandwagon by Golkar Dayaks in Pontianak City and other district capitals also fed the riots' intensity.

The link between large-scale violence and empowerment—which becomes very evident subsequent to the 1997 "victory" in the "Dayak and Madurese war"—is laid bare in an English language article published in KR under the name IDRD. Putting forth a cultural perspective championing the cultural, collective rights of peoples, IDRD's polemic underscores the sacred need for Dayaks to uphold *hukum adat* (customary law) traditions, particularly in the face of imminent threats to their community's well-being. When these laws are violated—in this case by the killing of a Dayak, exacerbated by the perpetrator's refusal to submit to *hukum adat* sanctions—the entire community, in order to protect itself, is required by *adat* to retaliate collectively and punitively against the perpetrator's community. The organization's views on the riots are equally explicit. "[T]here is probably not one Dayak person who will tell you that the number of causalities inflicted upon the Madurese was just, but that is not to say that it was unjust either. . . . And despite the number of Madurese causalities, there is not one Dayak who will say that there was another way" (IDRD 1999, 40). More tellingly, in its conclusion, it draws together of the notion of *adat*-based empowerment, collective violence, and resistance to development. "Already there have been several successful, but violent responses, based on adat ritual, to plantations. . . . The role of adat, in the lives of the Dayak who live in the villages and the bigger cities in West Kalimantan, can only be seen to be getting stronger. . . . Although there is not yet the case of a collective adat response to development as was seen against the Madurese, given the plans of the Government to take a further three million hectares of mostly Dayak land for plantations in West Kalimantan alone, there may be the kind of Dayak movement that cannot wait for future generations" (44).[79]

In all, it is this backdrop that informs this movement, which while fueling the violence against the Madurese, gained formidable momentum and voice in the postconflict period. Beside victory in war, it was appreciably aided by the unexpected resignation of the longtime authoritarian ruler Soeharto in May 1998 and the political freedoms that followed. Unwittingly, it also sparked Malay (and later) Dayak violence against the Madurese in Sambas district once again. These developments are explored in greater detail in the following chapter.

4

Reform, Decentralization, and the Politicization of Ethnicity and Indigeneity

Thus we begin to see how the "demonization" of the enemy is produced. . . . An increasing alienation and polarization between the self as a "son of the soil" and the other alien develops, and much that was previously shared now gives way to a suspicion-ridden separation and dehumanization of the other, so that to treat him as nonhuman and deserving of degradation and destruction becomes imperative and justifiable. So the aggressor community in attacking its enemy finally comes to perceive its actions as defensive and protective.

Stanley J. Tambiah, *Leveling Crowds*

In mid-June 1998, a month after Soeharto fell, in the pouring rain a band of armed Dayaks held up the bus I was riding in near the mountainous West Kalimantan–Sarawak border. To cries of "Long live the reform movement!" (*Hidup Reformasi!*), they boarded the bus and the pungent smell of *arak* (rice whiskey) quickly filled the confined space. The young men put a homemade rifle to the driver's head and urged each passenger to contribute Rp. 5,000 (about 35 U.S. cents at the time) to their cause.

This single event forced upon me a sudden realization: the popular movements that had coalesced under the reform banner and swept Soeharto from office contained multiple meanings, contingent not just on one's political and economic position but on a geographic vantage point as well. In Jakarta, student organizations had presented a core of reform-oriented demands; the dissolution of the government party Golkar and the eradication of collusion, corruption, and nepotism (known as KKN) topped their lists. They made no demands for greater autonomy for the country's regions. Instead, it was left to a team of technocrats in government offices in Jakarta to initiate a deliberate program of decentralization, which would soon become the touchstone of reform in post-Soeharto Indonesia. Their chief goals were to put an end to the coercive and excessive centralization of the New Order and to dampen separatist aspirations in resource-rich regions. This program amounted to no less than the "biggest administrative reorganization in the history of the Indonesian state" (H. Schulte Nordholt 2003, 564).

For local and regional politics in Indonesia, the political implications of decentralization have been enormous. Regional autonomy has precipitated a rash of an intensely public — though not necessarily transparent — form of politics. Some of these political actions have been violent, some not, but nearly all of them have stirred conflict of some kind.

Acute and financially costly competition for the country's four-hundred-plus *bupati* positions has arisen. In the outer islands especially, decentralization has unleashed a potent form of identity politics: the politics of indigeneity and a related revival of *adat*, at least as a basis for mobilization and staking claims. Aside from the impact on parties and local elections, indigeneity has heightened demands for respect of "the local," which had been trampled by the centralized New Order. At the same time, more darkly, this localism has fed growing ethnocentrism and palpably xenophobic nativism.

Nowhere have these dynamics played out more strikingly than in West Kalimantan, where an unmistakable ethnopolitics came to the fore. As we saw earlier, urban NGO activists sparked an indigenous movement *before* regional autonomy (*otonomi daerah*) became prominent in Indonesian political discourse. The Dayak "victory" in the widespread ethnic battles of 1997 and the euphoria of reform in 1998 created new space in which Dayaks could mobilize politically. These Dayak movements grew so strong that provincial power holders could not ignore them. Through protest and selective acts of violence, these movements succeeded in gaining the appointment of several Dayaks to the office of *bupati*. This was extraordinary. Only once during the thirty-two years of the New Order had a Dayak held such a prestigious political post in West Kalimantan. By mid-1999, they held four of the province's seven *bupati* posts.

Dayak political success was also reflected in the countermovement it spawned. Malay elites feared that they would be bypassed as groups jockeyed for positions that would give them access to the new riches promised by regional autonomy. These elites understood the importance of generating an ethnopolitical resurgence to counter the Dayak movements. And, as the Dayak example had shown, mass violence against a scapegoat can galvanize a movement, fortify ethnic identities, and deliver institutional power. Comprehensive explanations for the anti-Madurese riots of 1999 in Sambas must thus encompass the convergence of two larger, complementary political forces: the Dayak resurgence and the anticipation of decentralization.

Centuries of conversion to Islam and the outward orientation of a coastal Malay ethnic consciousness had long eroded Malay claims to being autochthonous. Thus, anti-Madurese violence became a way to stake a claim to indigeneity, the sine qua non of decentralized, local politics. In this way, "Malay" could rightfully challenge "Dayak" for the attendant patronage and largess associated with the decentralized state.

Before more fully examining these political movements, one final word about the 1999 riots is in order. These riots confound the literature on violence in West Kalimantan. Unlike the 1997 unrest, foreign observers have either ignored these events or mentioned them only tangentially. The problem is that Malays—unlike Dayaks—were not seen as victims of New Order development nor have they been placed by international and domestic urban activists in Indonesia's conventional "tribal slot" (Li 2000). Standard explanations of violence, and especially those focusing on Dayak frustration due to either New Order development or institutional political arrangements, work obliquely in this case. To understand mass violence in West Kalimantan, we must more concretely trace past violent lineages and expose explicit regional political processes.

Dayak Political Mobilization and *Reformasi*

Nearly a year prior to the national emergence of the reform movement in April and May of 1998, a once repressed voice in West Kalimantan's hinterland began to be heard. Under the New Order, customary lands (*tanah adat*) had been consistently stripped from Dayaks in the name of development. Yet, it was following the 1997 riots, in which thousands of Dayaks were mobilized, particularly in the province's western half, that these hinterland rumblings grew increasingly audible. "Victory" in war sparked a self-assertiveness that materialized in increasing public demands based on customary legal claims that fell outside the narrow limits imposed by the New Order. The grievances were old, but with organized NGO backing they were now spoken with greater confidence and audacity. The province's notoriously corrupt and inept formal legal system was bypassed as the application of customary law (*hukum adat*) sanctions against natural resource extraction companies became prevalent.

In June 1997, in Kendawangan subdistrict (Ketapang district), *adat* sanctions were applied against three plantation companies, all owned and operated by the mammoth Benua Indah Group. Two months later, in Ambalau subdistrict (Sintang district) the logging company Batasan Ltd. was fined following the destruction of a local cemetery. Eventually it paid Rp. 18.6 million in restitution, some 15 percent of the original demand.[1] In September villagers in Simpang Hulu subdistrict (Ketapang district) brought *hukum adat* charges against the Wahana Stagen Lestari logging company. Their demands included: 1) an *adat* ceremony to evidence the company's good faith 2) a Rp. 160 million fine 3) the right to hunt on the disputed land and 4) a halt to the logging. After a month of intense negotiations that included government officials, the company acceded to the demands, although the fine paid was one-third of the original demand. In the same month, villagers from Engkaning (Air Besar subdistrict, Pontianak district) fined the Kusuma Perkasa Indah Timber Group an exorbitant Rp. 6 billion (nearly U.S. $2 million at the time) over the felling of nearly three thousand illipe nut (*tengkawang*) trees. In January 1998 locals from Keranji Birah (Pontianak district) brought *hukum adat* charges against the Agro Mas and Batasan Ltd. companies (*Kalimantan Review*, October 1997, November 1997, December 1997, and March 1998).

Hukum adat charges were also brought against officials whose demeanor or actions were deemed provocative. In mid-1997—again, immediately following the 1997 riots—the first case against a provincial-level official took place. Karsan Sukardi, the head of the plantation department, had publicly blamed small-scale inland cultivators (Dayak peasants who burn their holdings for dry-land planting) for the province's frequent forest fires. Incensed at his accusations, demonstrators regularly gathered at his office. Customary legal fines were then levied against Sukardi (*Akcaya*, September 18, 1997; *Kalimantan Review*, October 1997). Largely ignored in the New Order press but celebrated in the *Kalimantan Review*, these incidents indicated that tensions were mounting between indigenous communities and local power holders.

But not until the impact of Soeharto's fall hit West Kalimantan did this ethnopolitical revitalization become something provincial stakeholders could no longer dismiss.

Fueled by a financial crisis that began in mid-1997, the reform movement that helped to topple Soeharto in May 1998 had unmistakable implications for the country's outer islands. Divergent parties translated the various understandings of reform to suit local needs. Events in the capital opened the door to reform, but had little say about who would or would not step through. In West Kalimantan, the impetus for reform among a coalition of Dayak movements took advantage of opportunities the national political slogan *Reformasi* afforded them.[2] Backed by urban elites, these mostly rural movements stepped forcefully and decisively into the space that had been opened by the political turbulence surrounding *Reformasi,* thus transforming this incipient dynamic into a bold political movement. To reverse their long-standing economic, political, and cultural marginalization, two principal short-to-medium-range goals have been discernible; both of which represent the ambition to claim a kind of redistributive justice: 1) getting more Dayaks into the province's highly prized bureaucracy—critical in typical outer island economies, which are acutely dependent on government largess and patronage—and 2) pressing the government to recognize Dayak land rights. It should be emphasized, however, that the omnipresence of *Reformasi* created diffusion within these movements. While the Pancur Kasih NGOs had hitherto facilitated protest and resistance, in the early reform era with the New Order putatively a thing of the past, the activist faction and "Golkar Dayaks" began to part ways, although both exploited the reform movement's dynamics to promote politically motivated, Dayak-based claims.

Much as in 1997, *tanah adat* claims fueled this revitalization, but the reform era also saw new forms of opposition. Following the 1997 violence, petitions and negotiations had predominated, but reform triggered a barrage of more public and forceful displays of protest, including lively demonstrations, threats of violence (which were occasionally carried out), and political attacks on select members of the elite, Dayak and nonindigenous alike.

Starting in May 1998, nearly every week some form of visible protest against rural symbols of state-backed, large-scale capital enterprises was staged. On July 30 and August 6, 1998, for example, more than a thousand locals demonstrated against the Wira Rivaco Mandum rubber plantation in Ngabang (Pontianak district). In the same district in

August 1998, two logging bulldozers were confiscated in Air Besar, and in the following month villagers in Tebas subdistrict (Sambas district) seized eight trucks of the Rana Wastu Kencana company. On October 7, some two hundred villagers protested at and then sabotaged the facilities of the Timah Investasi Mineral Company in Toho subdistrict (Pontianak district). On November 25, more than five hundred protested at the Inhutani III plantation, shouting "Burn!" And in early February 1999, the Halisa and Alas Kusuma plantation companies in Ketapang suffered damage caused by arson.[3]

These developments soon heightened intra-Dayak tensions as well. One fault line split the so-called pro-reformers from those deemed New Order lackeys. This division occasionally converged around the planning of ceremonies to ward off evil (*tolak bala*). Once devoid of overt politicking, these ceremonies became sites of political contestation. Most notable was the one staged in August 1998 to renounce Ketapang's Customary Council. Largely initiated (and funded) by Pancur Kasih, the organizers accused the council of complicity in government expansion of oil palm plantations. Roughly three hundred shamans (*dukun*), spiritual guardians of indigenous cultural belief systems, attended the *tolak bala*. It was the largest gathering of *dukun* in over forty years. In front of more than three thousand onlookers, the three-day ceremony culminated in the placement of an intricately carved wooden statue, six meters high and festooned with traditionally martial and Christian iconography, planted in the town's center. The statue signaled the resurgence and watchful presence of reform-oriented Dayaks in Ketapang (see figure 1).[4]

Once rare, demonstrations at regional councils (DPRDs) now became common. On June 30, 1998, Dayaks held their first large-scale protest in recent memory at the provincial assembly in Pontianak.[5] From October to December 1998, demonstrators met regularly at the Sanggau DPRD building to demand recognition of their land rights.[6] Protests at these sites and the overall aggressiveness of these mobilizations centered over the question of representation in *bupati* posts, although Dayaks were equally underrepresented in other high-profile bureaucratic positions as well.[7] As in the Kadir fiasco in Sintang, these positions were considered coveted prizes and bellwethers of change *before* the shift to regional autonomy enhanced political power at the district level, which precipitated conflict over these posts nationwide. In Sanggau, for example, when infantry Col. Mickael Andjioe's name disappeared from the *bupati* candidate list in favor of the governor's

Figure 1. The "Reform" Dayak Statue, Ketapang.

handpicked candidate, infantry Col. Soemitro, locals jumped at the chance to support Andjioe. If appointed, he would be the first Dayak *bupati* in Sanggau since 1967. From April to June 1998, demonstrations were held regularly—accompanied by occasional threats of violence— at the Sanggau DPRD. This persistent pressure "from below" eventually led to Andjioe's appointment.[8]

Protest also helped put Cornelius Kimha in the Pontianak district *bupati* post. In early February 1999, more than one hundred protestors gathered outside the DPRD building in Mempawah. Angered that Cornelis, the Dayak subdistrict head of Menyuke, was not included among the final three candidates, demonstrators burned several cars and razed the building. Following the DPRD's deadlocked decision a few days later between Agus Salim, a Malay, and another Dayak, Cornelius Kimha, security forces stationed at Anjungan prevented hundreds from storming Mempawah.[9] Meanwhile, in Pontianak, frequent demonstrations were held at the governor's office in support of Kimha's candidacy. The Ministry of Home Affairs eventually broke the tie, choosing Kimha. The mobilizations had convinced the government to take steps that would diminish the likelihood of more violence erupting "from below," possibly against the government itself. In the language of contentious politics, these *bupati* selections "certified" the Dayak movement, that is, the external authorities had validated its actors, actions, and claims (McAdam, Tarrow and Tilly 2001, 145).

Two final points warrant attention before we turn to the 1999 violence and the subsequent Malay revitalization. First, mentioned above, these mobilizations have not been monolithic. They have been an amalgam of multifarious, sometimes contentious, collective perceptions and actions. Consider rifts along party lines. In the 1999 general elections— administered under the Habibie presidency and Indonesia's first free and fair elections since 1955—Dayaks headed numerous parties. Notable examples were the Indonesian Democratic Party for Struggle (PDI-Perjuangan, or PDI-P, led locally by the late Rudy Alamsyahrum),[10] the Indonesian Unity in Diversity Party (PBI, headed locally by the late Herbertus Tekwaan, Oeray's adopted son), the PDI (led by Sebastiantos Khapat), and the Love Thy Nation Democratic Party (PDKB, headed by Cosmas Damianus Yan Kay). Golkar also listed Arsen Rickson (then a member of the national People's Consultative Council, or MPR), as its legislative candidate for Sanggau. These fractures contributed to a scattered Dayak vote in the 1999 elections, leaving many to joke warily that only in fighting the Madurese are they united. Second, the directions that this political revitalization was taking drew criticism from within Dayak circles, particularly from the same NGOs that helped to spark its resurgence. Some activists feared growing ethnocentrism and an entrenched "culture of violence." They preferred to use legal, less violent methods and wanted to empower both Dayak and agrarian-based non-Dayak people (*rakyat*) alike. The destruction of forests and the rapid proliferation of oil palm plantations hurt other similarly situated ethnic communities. Likewise, activists also doubted the ability of the new *bupati* in countering this New Order–inspired, capital-intensive transformation of West Kalimantan's economy. What is the good of Dayak *bupati*, they have asked, if the forests continue to disappear, "development" strategies bring in more oil palm estates, and capital continues to strip land from the people? These are well reasoned, but largely unheeded, concerns expressed to date.

The "New" Sambas

Dayak demands for their rightful place in the post-Soeharto state inspired other ethnic groups to follow suit. Unfortunately, but not altogether surprising, this precipitated more violence: the 1999 riots in which Malays (and later Dayaks) targeted the Madurese in Sambas. Before examining this unrest, which Malay elites used to galvanize a political countermovement, it would be beneficial to relate aspects of Sambas's recent past and social structure to the 1999 violence. Unlike its inland counterpart, coastal Sambas was unaccustomed to widespread violence. Local accounts maintain that this tranquility stemmed from a culture of kind, self-effacing, soft-spoken Malays (Effendi April 11, 1999; Purwana 2003, 31, 109). I find the dynamics of the communist rebellions more telling. Although anti-Chinese expulsions in the late 1960s took place in inland Sambas (and the northern part of Pontianak district), they skirted the coast, sparing it from significant economic disturbances, social dislocations, and the involuntary mobilizations of the populace. The few coastal Dayak communities were not receptive to intrusive Laskar Pangsuma influence. And, with insurgents ensconced along the mountainous border, locals there were coerced into hunting and fighting the rebels in markedly greater numbers than were the coastal inhabitants.

    Coastal Sambas was not completely devoid of insurgent activity, however. The PKI moved among coastal Chinese, and supplies were frequently smuggled from Sarawak. But in all, the area remained free of the hazardous consequences of forced mobilizations.[11] In the early 1970s, though a few thousand coastal Chinese were forced to relocate, they did so peacefully and were not stripped of their land. In Jawai subdistrict, for example, they were moved closer to the area's main north-south thoroughfare but continued to return by day to tend their fields.[12] In all, there were no explosive land grabs in coastal Samba nor were its local trading networks destroyed.

Long-term pressures on Sambas's social structure did have an effect. Following the expulsions, tens of thousands of Chinese refugees arrived from the hinterland. While a few thousand were detained in Pemangkat, many others resettled locally, although acute land pressure did not materialize because refugees were too poor to buy large holdings. Others moved to Pontianak or elsewhere. Those who remained settled in or near towns and were absorbed into the local retail trade, service, and informal sectors.

Increased Madurese migration also intensified local demographic pressures. The migrants' relative economic prosperity opened opportunities to buy land, and areas of Madurese concentration soon materialized. "Colonies" were soon found in Pemangkat, Tebas, and Jawai subdistricts. Based on the 1999 evacuations from Sambas to Pontianak, we can estimate that the Madurese population in coastal Sambas was about 55,000 (or 10 percent of the whole).[13] The presence of Madurese contributed to the area's population pressure.[14] Estimates of the three aforementioned subdistricts' population densities in 1999 were 305, 167, and 212 people per square kilometer, respectively.[15] These numbers far surpassed the provincial figure of 26. Moreover, during the 1997 clashes, hundreds of Madurese had arrived from inland Sambas and opted to stay.

Although Sambas's economy grew at an impressive clip,[16] population growth outstripped job creation, which created a tight labor market. Coastal Sambas has few rubber mills and plywood factories; tourism lagged. While the area is known as West Kalimantan's rice bowl, with increased population pressure the agriculture sector could no longer sufficiently absorb the working population, and social strains soon materialized. An upward trend in crime and hooliganism (*premanisme*) was evident. Madurese toughs dominated criminal networks and, backed by local police, ran gambling and protection rackets targeting Chinese traders and merchants. Gang-related violence was vicious and common; one infamous area (Rambayan, Tebas subdistrict) was dubbed "the Texas of Sambas."[17]

Out-migration to Java, Pontianak, and Sarawak was also common. In the latter, migrants mainly worked in the booming plywood industry. This trend became acute after the once flourishing local orange (*jeruk*) industry was destroyed, the result of failed attempts of the Bima Citra Mandiri Group—owned by one of Soeharto's sons, Bambang Triatmojo—to monopolize the local trade. The collapse, which began in 1992, was disastrous for the 28,000 or so farming households whose livelihoods depended on the crop. Hordes of farmers, who once could afford to send children to universities and perform the pilgrimage to Mecca, sought work in Sarawak; some went as far as Hong Kong and Taiwan. At first, although unemployment rose, out-migration proved to be an adequate outlet. Officially, in 1995-96 nearly 5,500 people left Sambas for Sarawak; unofficial estimates ranged from 10,000 to 15,000.[18] Later they were deported when the regional economic slowdown, which began in mid-1997, hit Sarawak (Suara Independen 1997). With thousands suddenly returned to Sambas with little prospect for work, gloom enveloped the region.

At first, for export-oriented, outlying regions, the crisis was a boon. Farmers sold primary commodities on the world market at competitive prices. The weak rupiah also drew waves of Malaysian tourists to Pontianak and the "surprise market" (*pasar kaget*) that sprung up at the Entikong border crossing (*Gatra*, July 25, 1998). But in general these short-lived advantages benefited inland farmers and bypassed Sambas's rice bowl. It drew no waves of tourists, and its export boon was limited to copra, the cultivation of which was concentrated in Jawai subdistrict.

But these difficulties were not unique to West Kalimantan; other regions suffered similarly. As the economic crisis that beset Sambas was not exceptional, it cannot fully explain the 1999 violence, for riots rarely combust spontaneously in areas unaccustomed to mass violence. Such macrofactors as strains on the local social structure account for neither the timing of the violence nor its principal forms. Two other critical developments must be considered: reactions of the Malay elite to resurgent Dayak mobilizations and the anticipated arrival of regional autonomy. Before investigating these political dynamics, let us turn to the riots themselves.

The Raid on Parit Setia

At about 1:30 in the morning of January 18, 1999, locals in Parit Setia—a small, nondescript village in Jawai subdistrict—tied up Hasan bin

Niyam, a Madurese who hailed from nearby Rambayan (administratively Sari Makmur village, Tebas subdistrict). The police were informed, but before they could respond a few of Hasan's acquaintances, including Jabak bin Punel, a notorious local thug (*preman*), arrived on the scene. They released Hasan and took him to a local clinic. Beyond these bare facts, the events of this night are contested. Rumors and conflicting versions are bountiful, and participants have engaged in accusations and counteraccusations. Accounts related by Parit Setia informants display two chief variants. Whereas one denies that the beating took place, the other admits to the assault. The latter's proponents insist that, in the light of Hasan's actions—possible attempted burglary—his thumping was justified. Madurese narratives are more diffuse, elaborate, and entertaining. Notwithstanding their diversity, most agree that Hasan was extremely drunk and was beaten by Malays.

Subsequent events are equally murky. At his trial, Jabak claims to have personally seen to the matter, for Hasan was one of his underlings (*anak buah*). Jabak testified that he tried to settle the matter peacefully but was rebuffed by the Jawai police and the head (*kepala desa*) of Parit Setia. The latter testified that he was never approached (*Berita acara lanjutan* 1999, 42–44). Jabak and Hasan's parents, incensed at police indifference and "Malay" arrogance, took matters into their own hands. At about three in the afternoon on January 19 during Idul Fitri, the holiday marking the end of Ramadhan, the Islamic fasting month, Jabak gathered about two hundred of his companions in Rambayan. They climbed into three trucks and onto a handful of motorbikes. Armed with an assortment of knives and sickles, they stormed Parit Setia. Their twenty-minute raid resulted in three Malay deaths. According to court records, Hasan's mother and father committed two of the three murders.

In the attack's immediate aftermath, the (in)actions of Jawai's police came under scrutiny. Apparently, it was known that an attack was imminent. In fact, that morning, Jabak had told a police officer in a bus terminal that a raid was coming. According to the officer's testimony, he escorted Jabak to the police station to relate the information to his superiors, who did not take the threat seriously. They did not detain Jabak and assigned only two (possibly four) officers to guard the northern entrance to Parit Setia. The attackers easily overwhelmed the guards. An officer's single warning-shot affected nothing, save for having his pistol seized by the raiders. On their retreat to Rambayan, the pistol was returned to the officer (*Berita acara lanjutan* 1999, 42–44).

As news of the raid spread, there was a public outcry for the assailants to be apprehended. To many, this attack more than vindicated the ubiquitous perception of Madurese as arrogant, hot-tempered belligerents keen to take the law into their own hands (*main hakim sendiri*). Incessant bouts with Dayaks had given this view local currency, but this incident was perceived as different. In fact, Sambas Malays saw it as much worse. They argued that pious Muslims could not commit such acts on Idul Fitri; the Madurese had therefore proven themselves to be irreligious, savage. The actions of the Madurese served to further demonize and dehumanize the Madurese community in the eyes of local Malays, signaling an important change in consciousness that would later justify Madurese expulsion. Confirming the importance of justification, Horowitz notes that "justification motivates violence; it frees up otherwise inhibited participants for violence" (2001, 528). Meanwhile, rubbing salt into Malay wounds, the Jawai police dragged their feet on arrests. Nearly a month after the attack, the provincial police chief admitted that only one arrest had been made (*Akcaya*, February 28, 1999). If the police will not protect us, Malays began to feel, then "we" will be forced to protect ourselves.[19] Following the attack at Parit Setia, government officials and ethnic elites met to ease tensions (*Akcaya*, January 29 and February 4, 1999). An informal meeting in late January among elder and "concerned" Malays in Singkawang would have greater impact, however.

At this meeting of the "Team of 11" (*Tim Sebelas*),[20] under the direction of Zulkarnain Bujang—a retired civil servant who had worked in such departments as sanitation and public works—it was decided to form an organization capable of confronting the Madurese in Sambas. They chose the name Forum Komunikasi Pemuda Melayu (Communication Forum of Malay Youth, or FKPM), capitalizing on the revolutionary élan and mobilizing potential of *pemuda* (youth). Zulkarnain explained that, while Malays were fearful of Madurese, they needed to be masters of their own house (*jadi tuan rumah di rumah sendiri*). Moreover, like other ethnic groups, it was time, he added, that Malays had their own umbrella organization (*wadah*).[21]

So Zulkarnain and younger associates like Ikhdar Salim and Jamras—the latter known for his fiery oratorical skills—toured Sambas to mobilize youths. Speeches were made, meetings held, and strategies discussed on how to best solve the Madurese problem, and in late February, FKPM branches were formed at the subdistrict level throughout Sambas. Their leaders included Supido, a converted Dayak, in

Figure 2. This statue, locally known as the Ketupat Berdarah (Bloody Rice Cake), was built to commemorate those killed at Parit Setia, Jawai subdistrict.

Pemangkat; Uray Kamaluddin, a retired ABRI serviceman, in Jawai; and Haji Nazumi, a school principal, in Tebas. Meanwhile, Erwin Saputera, a thirty-something son of one of Pemangkat's more prominent businessmen, and a young street thug we will call "Bob" were instrumental in mobilizing youths. Many young people were already loosely organized in New Order–related youth groups like Pancasila Youth (Pemuda Pancasila), the Communication Forum of Sons and Daughters of Indonesian Veterans (FKPPI), and Panca Marga Youth (Pemuda Panca Marga). When asked who would be responsible for the actions they would undertake, Zulkarnain claims to have responded: "Don't worry. We'll take responsibility."

So young men procured weapons, sharpened bamboo spears, and produced homemade shotguns in local smelters. They patrolled neighborhoods at night to guard against Madurese reprisals and got themselves into shape (*mengisi badan*). Preparations were begun, but FKPM waited for an opportune moment to strike.[22] The slow buildup to the 1999 bloodshed recalls Horowitz's observations that riots are "commonly preceded by . . . a time of apprehensive quiet during which rumors and warnings may circulate . . . while preparations for the attack go forward in inconspicuous ways" (2001, 16).

The Riots Erupt

> By force of example, bystander groups are enabled to overcome their own initial inhibitions on the use of violence.
>
> Donald Horowitz, *The Deadly Ethnic Riot*

The recklessness of a Madurese youth presented FKPM with a moment to strike. On February 21, 1999, a young bus passenger, Rudi bin Muharap, refused to pay his fare as he alighted in Pusaka (Tebas subdistrict). Annoyed, the fare collector, a Malay youth named Bujang Lebik bin Idris, stared the youth down. Rudi took offense and vowed to exact revenge. As Bujang stepped off his bus at the end of the day, Rudi stabbed him in the stomach and slashed his right hand. Friends brought a bleeding Bujang to the Pemangkat hospital. Inquisitive crowds gathered by the hour.

By two o'clock the next morning, rioters had struck. One mob of a few dozen—wearing yellow headbands to signify "Malay" and armed with knives, machetes and spears—burned down seventeen houses in Semparoh (Pemangkat subdistrict).[23] Later, they killed two Madurese in Sungai Kelambu (Tebas subdistrict). As the sun rose on the morning of February 22, a third corpse was found in Pemangkat. That day stores in Pemangkat remained closed. As hundreds stood armed on street corners guarding entrances to neighborhoods, the security forces quickly came under attack. A Molotov cocktail was thrown in the direction of the local military commander and police chief as they toured the damaged area (*Akcaya*, February 23, 1999). On the night of the February 23, FKPM-led rioters unsuccessfully stormed the Tebas police station where some two hundred Madurese were being sheltered. This incident convinced the authorities to order their forces to shoot rioters on sight (*Kompas*, February 24, 1999).

At this point, it was reported that rioters had slain seven people and destroyed fifty-eight houses. The acute violence in Jawai subdistrict went unreported, however. Separated by the Sambas River estuary, Jawai is not as accessible as Pemangkat or Tebas. But on February 26 reports circulated that the headman of Sentebang, the subdistrict's capital, had been detained for his role in mobilizing (*menggerakkan*) rioters (*Media*, February 27, 1999). As local troops and police seized weapons in Tebas, local ethnic elites, at the behest of the authorities, signed a statement of concern.[24] This resulted in a temporary pause, but strangely, the security apparatus continued to escort Madurese out of Sambas and into Singkawang and even Pontianak. Over the next two weeks, increasingly sporadic and constrained violence occurred, but overall a fragile calm prevailed.

Following this ominous lull, on the night of March 14, fresh violence erupted in and around Pemangkat. Over a two-day period, possibly eight people were killed and dozens of houses were razed (*Akcaya*, March 17, 1999). Then, on March 16, a mysterious murder ignited massive violence. Outside of Pemangkat on his way home to Samalantan subdistrict, Martinus Amat, a Dayak, was killed. Unknown assailants stopped the pickup truck in which he was riding. Thirty or so passengers escaped, everyone except Amat (*Kalimantan Review*, May 1999). The killing triggered widespread Dayak participation and transformed the sputtering coastal clashes into a six-week paroxysm of violence that engulfed most of Sambas district. Within twenty-four hours of Amat's death, over three hundred Madurese houses along the Kulor-Samalantan road were razed. Dayaks mobilized in the inland subdistricts of Samalantan, Ledo, Sanggau Ledo, Bengkayang, and Tujuh Belas, that is, in areas intimately familiar with anti-Madurese clashes.

Galvanized by Dayak inclusion, FKPM mobilizations grew apace. With the former mobilized on the eastern front, FKPM commanders pushed for more rioting. On March 21, skirmishes erupted in Sukaramai, a Madurese enclave north of Sambas town. As FKPM-led raiders moved north into Paloh subdistrict, nearly four hundred Madurese fled on boats to Kuching, Sarawak.[25] Not wanting an international refugee crisis on its hands, the Sarawak government quickly transported the refugees to Pontianak (*Tempo,* April 5, 1999). Meanwhile, some seven thousand had reached Surabaya (East Java) (*Suara Pembaruan,* March 14, 1999; *Republika,* April 29, 1999).

Attacks on trucks ferrying women and children out of Sambas convinced authorities to call in crack anti-riot police units (PHH) from Java.[26] By late March, nearly twenty-five thousand refugees had reached Pontianak,[27] and another three thousand were being sheltered outside Singkawang near Pasir Panjang beach. Countless others were hiding in the area's forests. In early April, having completed missions farther north, FKPM commanders retraced their steps and sparked violence in the district's southern reaches, around Singkawang and in Sungai Raya subdistrict. Like its northern counterparts, these areas had been peaceful until FKPM commanders decided to stir up trouble.

Shortly thereafter, a serious run-in with the PHH took place. On April 7, the FKPM led a convoy to Singkawang to demand the release of their arrested ethnic brethren. About five kilometers north of Singkawang at Sungai Garam, PHH troops met the convoy. Leaders from each side were engaged in heated negotiations when shots rang out. Both sides denied shooting prematurely, but after the mayhem had settled down a dozen passengers lay dead. Scores more were injured (*Akcaya,* April 8, 1999) (see figure 7). Coming under heavy criticism, officials pulled the PHH from escort duty. Instead, Malay and Dayak civilians were assigned to escort refugees out of the district (*Akcaya,* April 13, 1999).

Increasingly, sporadic violence continued in areas where Madurese were left: in the vicinity of Singkawang and in Sungai Raya. By early May, with the Madurese expelled from Sambas district, the combatants ran out of intended targets and the mobilizations ceased. One account places the government figures at four hundred deaths; unofficial estimates are twice this figure. The same source lists more than four thousand houses razed (Purwana 2003 68, 70, tables 3.2, 3.3). Estimates of the number of Madurese displaced due to riots ranges from 34,000 to 62,000.

Malay Political Revitalization and Regional Autonomy

Characteristics commonly found in "deadly ethnic riots" were prevalent during this bloodshed: gratuitous violence, decapitations and the parading of impaled heads, blood smearing, mobs in trance-induced frenzies believing that they were invincible, shrill war cries, predominance of young males, ritual incantations, torched homes, discriminate killing of belligerents, indignant justifications of the brutality, and the symbolic use of signifiers (Horowitz 2001). In this case, color was prominent, red for Dayak, yellow for Malay. And, as usual, the blame was laid solely on the Madurese, who again suffered the most casualties.

To place the riots in their proper political context, two points should be made. Foremost was *Malay* participation; several accounts erroneously claim that Dayaks were the instigators, but only after the violence was underway did Dayaks participate on a massive scale. Second, like the expulsion of the Chinese some thirty years earlier, the cleansing of the Madurese from Sambas was not inevitable or historically determined but forged out of contingent events.

Adequate explanations of the 1999 violence must situate the riots at the confluence of two broader, complementary political forces: the Dayak resurgence and the anticipation of regional autonomy. Designed as a desirable antidote to the New Order's overly centralized rule, decentralization devolves substantial administrative and fiscal authority to the district level.[28] Promising the groups that controlled district bureaucracies remarkable political and monetary windfalls, it has sparked violent competition nationwide at the district level, especially over *bupati* posts.[29] Despite efforts to invest DPRDs with increasing authority, strong institutional legacies have not been undone by mere "reformist" rhetoric. Locally, *bupati* still reign supreme. Concurrent with this competition, decentralization has precipitated a virulent form of identity politics: the politics of nativism. Staking a claim to indigeneity became paramount, as it is seen as a means to secure benefits and rights that would come with decentralization. These converging dynamics in large part explain the forms the rioting took in Sambas.

Malay leaders feared being left behind as other groups jockeyed for positions. To understand their anxiety, one need only recall the 1998 appointments of Dayak *bupati* in Sanggau and Pontianak districts. And the disdain in which they held these "primitives" made their gains particularly galling. A "Malay" resurgence was perceived as an effective means to resist Dayak advances. Malay elites needed to demonstrate their status as original inhabitants (*penduduk asli*), which was becoming critical in high-stakes local politics. Although his words are historically dubious, this anxiety concerning the disputed indigenous status of "Malay" is wonderfully conveyed in the statement of a Madurese elder: "Malays don't have the right to expel the Madurese. Malays are newcomers; they come from Brunei. If Dayaks expel us, we can accept that because they are the indigenous people" (cited in Petebang and Sutrisno 2000, 31).

Yet without the capacity to mobilize, the Malays would be hard pressed to physically confront the Madurese or politically compete with Dayaks. To be sure, the 1999 violence involved subduing and expelling the Madurese, which entailed a necessary aggressiveness. The actual intended audience of this outburst, however, was the Malays' Dayak counterparts. Prior mobilizations had placed Malay elites in a noticeably defensive and reactive posture. Thus, the riots in Sambas reflected Dayak-Malay political tussles, not deeply held anti-Madurese sentiments.

One of the unintended consequences of the decentralization program in Indonesia has been a race to redistrict administrative units, a process known as *pemekaran*. At the outset of decentralization, the number of districts in the country stood at 292; by 2003, it had rocketed to over 430.[30] Behind the redistricting craze are essentially "the political ambitions of regional elites and the flow of funds they want to control" (H. Schulte Nordholt 2003, 565; see also Fitrani, Hofman, and Kasier 2005 on bureaucratic rent-seeking). That much of the *pemekaran* has been along communal lines is reflected in the West Kalimantan case, where by 2005 six districts and one urban municipality had been transformed into ten districts and two municipalities.[31] While some experts rightly worry about the impact excessive redistricting may have on service provisions, in this volatile province the incipient phase of redistricting had particularly deadly consequences. Under the auspices of regional autonomy, Sambas was divided into inland Bengkayang and coastal Sambas districts. This was a crucial development. Ideally the split—a foregone conclusion by late 1998, yet officially implemented after the June 1999 elections—was envisioned as a way to create a Dayak-dominated Bengkayang and a Malay Sambas (see map 3). As a result of the recurrent anti-Madurese violence, most notably in 1997, Dayak control of Bengkayang was irrefutable; at issue was the latter. Haunted by the ambiguity of their position, despite a Malay majority of roughly 70 percent, Malay leaders needed to stamp Sambas emphatically

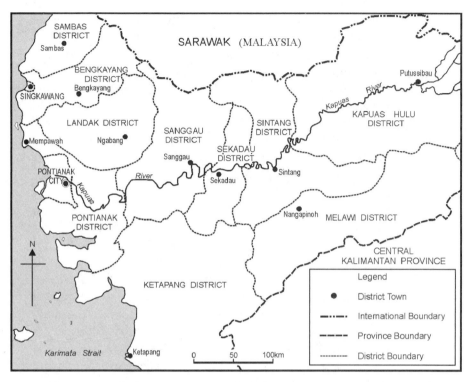

Map 3. The Districts of West Kalimantan, as of 2005 (with district towns noted)

as their own.[32] The Madurese were already demonized as hotheaded criminals and perennial instigators of ethnic unrest. A district population of 11 percent prior to the 1999 violence and the redistricting, they posed little threat in any formal political sense. At issue was not the regional DPRD or the *bupati* post. For the Malay elites, the problem concerned "the street." If Madurese thugs (*preman*) continued to control local gambling, extortion and protection rackets, other criminal activities, and informal service sectors such as transport, how could Sambas be considered "Malay"? In other words, as long as Madurese thugs roamed and operated in Sambas, Malay elite domination would be tenuous at best.

Here, though seemingly immaterial, the stereotyped caricatures of Malays by Madurese as *pengecut* (chicken), *krupuk* (rice crackers), and *penakut* (coward) took effect. In an atmosphere where politics is determined not only by the control of high-end business "concessions" and low-end informal revenue sources but also by the ability to mobilize masses, these disparaging tags weighed heavily. A decentralized Sambas, the "homeland of the Malay," needed to be controlled by Malays, not Madurese. More accurately, as the stewards of Sambas, the identity Malay needed to demonstrate that it would formidably compete with "Dayak" for bragging rights. So violence directed against a vulnerable enemy to harness mobilization energies and fortify identities would ignite this "Malay" resurgence. In other words, through anti-Madurese violence, the Malay identity *proved* its indigeneity to be one par with the Dayak identity in this politicized field of ethnicity. In the words of many Malay, they may be *krupuk,* but the longer it is fried the harder *krupuk* becomes.

This is not meant to imply that the local politics of decentralization and redistricting necessarily sparked the violence. An informed report from South Sulawesi states that redistricting there has been peaceful because local ethnic identities are "too fragmented to be a significant basis for political mobilisation by unscrupulous politicians" (ICG 2003a, i). In West Kalimantan, the prominence of a small number of identifiable ethnic groups and a history of collective violence has ensured the hardening of these identities and the opportunistic use of mass killing.

FKPM exploited its instrumental role in the riots to become the dominant local force in post-riot Sambas. Its roots, not incidentally, are deepest in the riots' epicenter: Pemangkat, Tebas, and Jawai. In Tebas and Pemangkat markets, FKPM set up "communication" or security posts (*pos komunikasi,* or *posko*). As the defender of "Malay" ideals, FKPM declared itself the champion of Sambas's downtrodden, its peasantry, and petty traders (*Pontianak Post,* March 15, 2000). Its motto read: "Malays Shall Not Disappear in the Sands of Time" (*Takkan Hilang Puak Melayu Ditelan Zaman*).[33] Members of FKPM sought material gain from the violence. Some took over the former Madurese gambling and extortion rackets, while the top leadership extended its reach into the district's prized bureaucracy.[34] It essentially handpicked the next Sambas *bupati,* Burhanuddin Rasyid, who was elected by the DPRD in May 2000.[35] Haji Nazumi, the head of FKPM-Tebas, ran Rasyid's successful electoral campaign (*tim sukses*) for southern Sambas. Rasyid's victory was impressive for two reasons. First, FKPM is not a political party; the two strongest parties, Golkar and PDI-P, backed separate candidates. Second, Rasyid had headed Sambas's agriculture department, which is not a highly lucrative position or typically used for grooming future *bupati.*

Figure 3. This black and yellow sign, and many like it, cluttered Jawai's landscape. It reads: "Welcome, You've Entered Matang Terap Village." Following the riots, FKPM changed its name to PFKPM (see chapter 5).

Despite its visibility, FKPM's local prominence should not be over-stated. In the end few benefited greatly from the Madurese violence. Although it is the most visible organization in Sambas, FKPM pales in comparison to ethnic-crime militias made up of youths elsewhere, as in urban Jakarta (Wilson 2006), Medan (Hadiz 2003; Ryter 2000), or the semirural "protection service" organizations of Lombok (ICG 2003b; Kristiansen 2003).

Immediately following the violence, youths in Sambas saw them-selves as war heroes and acted accordingly. Small gangs sought to extort money from Chinese shop-owners, though their disorganized efforts produced meager results. Several of the riot leaders I met were consis-tently strapped for cash. To be sure, FKPM's uniformed guards (*satgas*) make appearances at prominent local weddings or other public ceremo-nies, and its *posko* still stood in Pemangkat in 2004. Yet, it was usually left unattended while the one in Tebas had already been dismantled. Like memories of the riots themselves, FKPM is starting to fade. Many of the group's leaders admitted that its related activities have waned. With-out convenient adversaries, and as formal politics gains saliency—the second post-Soeharto parliamentary elections were held in April 2004—the relevance and need for FKPM has been questioned. This view is shared not just among the populace, but among its own leaders.

Ethnic Cleansing Revisited

The 1999 riot's most controversial and shocking aspect was the expulsion of Madurese from Sambas.[36] As was seen earlier, Madurese generally had returned home following clashes. Not since 1967 had ethnic cleansing occurred in the province despite the prevalence of riots. This recent expulsion reintroduced a worrisome form of collective violence that requires elaboration.

The physical scars left by the violence evidence a more permanent ethnic cleansing. Unlike past riots, which pitted Christian Dayaks against Muslim Madurese, Malays this time razed Madurese mosques. What is the purpose of a mosque, FKPM leadership claimed, without a religious community (*ummat*)? Another scar was the total destruction of Madurese dwellings. Typically, the concrete foundations of homes that have been burned remain intact in these kinds of clashes. In inland Sambas (now Bengkayang), Dayak squatters built makeshift shacks on top of the foundations (see figure 4). In coastal Sambas, the concrete foundations were removed with extreme effort to erase any reminders of Madurese presence. This was neither inadvertent nor accidental; reducing foundations to rubble requires strenuous labor (see figure 5). Developments in Sambas resonate with what one historian of Europe's recurrent ethnic battles has written: "The intention of ethnic cleansing is to remove a people and often *all traces* of them from a concrete territory" (Naimark 2001, 3, emphasis added).

There is little evidence that ethnic cleansing was an a priori aim of the violence. Zulkarnain and other FKPM leaders have claimed that the expulsions were not conceived from the outset; they only wanted to get "the bad ones" (*yang jahat*).[37] Most likely, the idea of expelling the Madurese came in the course of the fighting itself, confirming one of Michael Mann's hypotheses in explaining ethnic cleansing: "Murderous cleansing is rarely the initial intent of perpetrators" (2005, 7).

In this context, the killing of Amat, which precipitated broad-based Dayak participation, merits attention. Given the sputtering violence prior to his murder, his death raises three critical questions: who were the assailants? did they act on their own or on someone else's behalf? and was Amat targeted as a Dayak or inadvertently mistaken for a

Figure 4. An example of a Dayak squatter house, Bengkayang district.

Figure 5. Crumbled foundations of a former Madurese house, Sambas district.

Malay? Dubious eyewitness accounts finger Madurese as attackers, claims Madurese leaders refute. For either the FKPM leaders, local authorities, or both, if Madurese expulsion had been a priority, achieving it would have likely required Dayak aid.[38]

The security forces evacuated the Madurese with exacting efficiency, even in areas that had experienced little violence. Although their actions might be considered appropriate within the context of the situation, there were evident, and revealing, distinctions between the actions of local Kodam XII troops (and their colleagues, the police) and those of external troops. The PHH troops from Jakarta more physically confronted the rioters than did the members of local security forces, who often stood idly by, assiduously "safeguarding" Madurese property, including thousands of cows, in order to resell them.[39]

Local commanders also were enthusiastic evacuators. Days before violence afflicted Sungai Raya subdistrict, local troops urged Madurese to evacuate to nearby Pasir Panjang beach. These communities balked at relocation. When violence broke out, external troops prevented these communities from being uprooted. Because of external—not local—troops, many Madurese remain in coastal Sungai Raya.[40] Whereas provincial and district commanders were likely influenced by local discourses of Madurese criminality and culpability, commanders and troops from elsewhere were less affected. This partly explains their different approach to the violence.

In two important ways the ethnic cleansing puzzle also stemmed from the political dynamics of the early post-Soeharto state. One was electoral pressure. With the June 1999 general elections rapidly approaching and the security forces' general reluctance to confront the rioters, it was likely calculated that quelling the violence would require the removal of its targets. To save the elections, the Madurese were thoroughly and efficiently evacuated from Sambas (and inland Bengkayang). This indicates the importance local elites placed on the elections, mindful that regional autonomy would magnify the spoils of electoral success. Moreover, the local authorities must have figured that removing the "cause" of Sambas's recurrent ethnic strife would resolve the issue once and for all.

The second piece of the puzzle was the nationwide politicization of issues related to ethnicity and religion. Local elites emphasized that Malays could no longer live peacefully with Madurese, whose actions and behavior warranted their exodus. Expulsion from a few subdistricts, they maintained, would be inadequate; all of the new Sambas district needed to be free of Madurese. Local authorities and politicians whole-heartedly supported the evacuations (*The Economist,* March 27, 1999). Even the governor publicly condemned the Madurese (*Akcaya,* April 10, 1999; detik.com, April 9, 1999). In my interviews, the sentiment came across strongly that this sequence of events was but a correction to the decades of injustices.

Nationally, the flourishing of discussion, demonstrations, and de-mands related to ethnicity and religion in the incipient post-Soeharto state contributed to the purges. As was touched on in chapter 3, the New Order snuffed public representations of SARA. But the weakened state could no longer patrol the public realm as coercively as it formerly had done. As one commentator remarked, the politicization of SARA gave "birth to a monster of Frankenstein" (H. Schulte Nordholt 2000, 50). With the old facade of "unity in diversity" having rapidly disintegrated, manifestations of politicized SARA have come in multiple forms. Fore-most has been the blossoming of claims to territorially based indigen-eity. These claims have been exploited to mask such pressing political problems as control over regional bureaucracies, gubernatorial or *bupati* posts, and "the street"—or customary lands in rural areas. In some cases, as happened in Gorontalo (northern Sulawesi) and Banten (west-ern Java), new provinces were formed peacefully. In others, these dy-namics had more perilous consequences. Ethnoreligious cleansing, once unimaginable, had become thinkable. In early 2002, some 1.3 million refugees, who had fled areas as far-flung as Aceh, Central and West Ka-limantan, the former province of East Timor, North and South Moluc-cas, and Central Sulawesi, were "temporarily" housed in as many as nineteen separate provinces, including West Timor, Southeast and North Sulawesi, and East and Central Java (A. Williams and Rosen-blatt 2002). Almost the entire country was affected by the imaginations and realizations of SARA-based expulsions.

Two final developments in postviolence Sambas bolsters the argu-ment that the 1999 violence against the Madurese was about the iden-tity Malay making a claim on indigeneity to justify its rightful place in a decentralizing Sambas. One has been the efforts to revitalize the Al-wadzi Koebillah palace (*kraton*) as the mainstay of Malay culture. Dur-ing the eighteenth and nineteenth centuries, the *kraton* was a vibrant re-gional force. But its sultan pledged his allegiance to the Dutch to ensure its survival. In the 1950s, the newly constituted government of Indone-sia stripped the dozen or so provincial sultanates—which were seen as feudal holdovers and pro-Dutch—of their authority. In Sambas, the

Figure 6. Wimpi had two paintings commissioned on themes related to the anti-Madurese violence in time for his coronation ceremony in July 2000. For several years they hung in the Alwadzi Koebillah *kraton*. This painting, entitled *Musibah Sosial di Sambas* (Social Catastrophe in Sambas), celebrates the killing of Madurese and the burning of their houses. In this portion of the painting, the foreground spotlights a Malay hero—wearing a yellow headband with long hair that evokes the revolutionary valor of Indonesian youth *(pemuda)*—single-handedly subduing three middle-aged (hence staid) Madurese, who are comically festooned in traditional Madurese customs. One adversary holds a sickle *(clurut),* the Madurese weapon of choice, but it is facing downward, as if to symbolize the rendering limp of Madurese aggressiveness. In the background, amid the burning of Madurese houses, notice the fleeing cows. Madurese are renowned cattle herders.

district capital was moved from Sambas to Singkawang, and the *kraton* fell into disrepair. The heir to the throne, then known as Raden "Wimpi" Winata Kusumah—the grandson of the last reigning sultan—worked in relative obscurity as a low-level civil servant in Sambas's tourism bureau.[41]

As the 1999 riots waned, Wimpi became a recognized local figure *(tokoh masyarakat)* almost overnight by publicly denouncing actions of the PHH in the aforementioned Sungai Garam incident (see figure 7). Some suggest that he may have mobilized rioters (Petebang and Sutrisno 2000, 26), a charge Wimpi denies. In fact, so too do many FKPM leaders of southern Sambas district (Tebas, Pemangkat, and Jawai) whose contempt for Wimpi is palpable. Invariably, they decry his unwillingness to act during the height of the riots.

Figure 7. Wimpi also had this painting, called *Tragedi di Sungai Garam* (Tragedy at Sungai Garam), commissioned. This portion depicts the shootings of Malay raiders by the security forces. While many in the trucks were armed and their leaders were engaged in heated negotiations with the security officials in front of the convoy when shots rang out, these "facts" are occluded in this rendition.

Nonetheless, capitalizing on Wimpi's new (and wholly surprising) status, a first-ever purification ceremony (*upacara tepung tawar*) was held at the *kraton* in July 1999, which drew hundreds of onlookers (*Akcaya*, July 7, 1999). Heralded in the local press in the context of a resurgent Malay identity, Wimpi a year later was installed as the crown prince (*pangeran ratu*) (*Equator*, July 19, 2000). Fortuitously, Wimpi's ascent rode the winds of the revival of sultanship in the country's regional autonomy era.

The reasons for this rise are complex, but they range from economic interests (such as the reclaiming of lost lands) to a growing emphasis on local identity, place, tradition, and culture, and a societal nostalgia for order, clarity, and comfort that hierarchy evokes in times of political instability and social uncertainty (Van Klinken 2007). With over twenty recent revivals, this development is a real, if unintended, consequence of decentralization.[42] Unfortunately, in West Kalimantan, like so much else in this province, it is also a result of riots against a vulnerable minority.

Secondly, discussions of mass violence in Indonesia and in West Kalimantan especially require mention of government efforts at conflict resolution, or as we saw in chapter 3, state-forged peace pacts. In this case, that no elaborate peace ceremonies were held was striking, and the reasons for not doing such equally revealing. For one thing, holding a "traditional" peace ceremony as in the Dayak-Madurese example was beguiling given the novelty of violence between these two groups. More significantly, such a ceremony sensibly would have been infused with Islamic ritual and symbols, save for the fact that religion complicates the matter by emphasizing Madurese-Malay affinities rather than underscoring their *ethnic* differences. Regrettably, without a peace pact in place, further recriminations were fueled. Locally there was a strong sense that the 1999 riots, though the killings had ceased, had not yet come to an end. Ultimately, such sentiments proved prescient and fed the violent anti-Madurese incidents of 2000 and 2001 in Pontianak City, the subject of the next chapter.

5

Refugees, a Governor, and an Urban Racket

Under the Dutch, the Japanese, we were never driven out. Why now that we are free? This is really a step back.

Local Madurese historian

Me, I'm genuinely Sambas. I will go home because that's where I'm from.

Madurese refugee, *Kalimantan Review*, August 2002

While trying to decipher the logic underlying contemporary violence in West Kalimantan, this book has also devoted considerable attention to discontinuities in the forms of collective strife. Chapter 2 stressed the expulsion of the Chinese from inland Sambas and Pontianak districts, which gave rise to intermittent Dayak-Madurese riots. Chapter 3 investigated why these periodic yet restrained clashes gained immense proportions in early 1997. Chapter 4 documented the central role of Sambas Malays in the 1999 riots.

In the early post-Soeharto state, this persistent violence took on new spatial and demographic dimensions. Two short spells of violence convulsed Pontianak, which had hitherto been free of such disturbances. Suddenly, the city was plunged into a deadly cycle of politicking, perpetrator-victim formation, and recrimination. Erupting in late October 2000 amid pervasive ethnic politicization, Pontianak's inaugural ethnic riot was touched off by a traffic accident—a typical instigator of riots—between a Malay and two Madurese in areas of extreme ethnic politicization and recurrent violence (Tambiah 1996; Wilkinson 2004). In this case, ethnic chauvinism was exploited to mask the riot's truer purpose: to quash efforts to remove Governor Aspar Aswin. A prototypical New Order general-cum-governor-cum-millionaire unaccountable to the province's populace, Aswin came under attack by legislative members and ethnic leaders who sought his ouster in the name of reform, regional autonomy, and nativism. Calling upon figures of the city's underworld to orchestrate the riot, Aswin vanquished his challengers and rescued his lucrative patronage network.

This riot and the lack of closure characteristic of Malay and Madurese violence fed the city's next riot. The June 2001 clashes featured coordinated attacks on the fifty thousand or so Madurese refugees from Sambas who by this time had been housed in makeshift camps for more than two years. Whereas most of the refugees sought a return to Sambas, the government, determined to capture the bonanza of massive construction and development monies, preferred the policy of permanent relocation in marshy sites built thirty or so miles south of Pontianak. Also favoring permanent relocation were Malay leaders who feared the erosion of Malay economic footholds—for example, in the city's markets. Add Madurese elite connivance in the construction of the relocation sites to the mix and one begins to sense the insuperability of the refugee crisis. This chapter closes with extrapolations on potential trajectories of strife along three lines: Chinese victimization, Malay-Dayak animosities, and intra-Dayak tensions.

The Urban Malay Countermovement

In mid-October 2000, Pontianak experienced its gravest violence since minor, anti-Chinese riots broke out in late 1945 following Japanese capitulation (Heidhues 2003, 211–12). In the years that followed, while deadly collective violence scarred semirural Pontianak and Sambas districts, the city was free of "deadly ethnic riots." But this recurrent dynamic gained a new urban dimension when the traffic accident noted earlier was swiftly transformed into a three-day spate of clashes between Malays and Madurese. At first glance, this episode appeared to be a mere appendage to the 1999 Sambas riots. Yet this assertion overlooks mutually reinforcing political developments introduced in the last chapter: an ethnic politicization of and competition between Malay and Dayak elites exacerbated by the forces of decentralization. These ethnic tensions, in fact, surfaced in Pontianak prior to the 1999 Sambas riots.

In Pontianak, Malay leaders responded to the Dayak revitalization that occurred in the wake of the 1997 clashes by forming the Majelis Adat Budaya Melayu (Malay Cultural and Customary Council, or MABM). Although it had provincial aspirations—thus making it West Kalimantan's first provincial "Malay" organization in postindependence Indonesia—it was in essence a Pontianak-based association. In particular, MABM sought to counter the growing abundance of Dayak customary legal claims. It voiced concern against what it saw as increasingly deliberate sanctioning of non-Dayaks. This, they averred, was contributing to a politicization and commercialization of *hukum adat,* which ironically echoed the concerns of urban Dayak activists (*Kalimantan Review,* January–February 2001).

MABM's striking resemblance to the Dayak example was not coincidental, for it was modeled on the provincial-level Majelis Adat Dayak (Dayak Customary Council).[1] To spur its own ethnopolitical movement, MABM engaged the Dayak movement through a multifaceted approach, which included a complicated interplay of difference and recognition. Foremost was a campaign to elevate the identity Malay to legitimate *penduduk asli* (original inhabitant) status.[2] As was seen earlier, this claim was exceptionally expedient for garnering *bupati* posts in a decentralized West Kalimantan (and elsewhere).

These leaders precipitated a tussle to gain a share of the monopoly Dayaks had on indigeneity, the hallmark of decentralizing, local politics. As was covered in chapter 1, the origins of the Malays are contentious, and settling this debate is not pertinent for the present argument's purposes. Instead, it was significant that, after their perennial denial of commonalities and a conscious distancing from the "uncivilized" Dayaks, Malay leaders began *publicly* to acknowledge a shared ancestry and express a desire for recognition as Dayaks. Put simply, as one proponent wrote in a local newspaper, "The Malays of West Kalimantan are either indigenous peoples or Dayaks who converted to Islam" (Effendi December 11, 1999). Thus, it was argued that ancestral conversion to Islam should not preclude claims to indigeneity (*Pontianak Post,* December 23, 1999).[3] The impetus behind this discursive change, of course, was the Dayak movement. It not only transformed the Dayak identity into a politically charged badge of honor, but it also threatened elite Malay interests by exploiting the indigenous people's tag to place its representatives in choice government positions.

The contest over cultural reproductions of indigeneity soon became politically commodified. One example was the *adat* (customary) house, which in Indonesia constitutes an unmistakable stamp of local indigenousness (K. Robinson 1997). Because the Dayak version—the longhouse—has been integral to a traditional Dayak cultural repertoire, it was argued that Malay customary houses should also be built to establish a claim to regional indigeneity (*Pontianak Post*, June 5, 2001). Amid pomp and pageantry and attended by Vice President Jusuf Kalla, Pontianak's first Malay *adat* house was opened in late 2005.[4] Dismayed and disturbed, Dayak urban elites asked for government funds to renovate Pontianak's existing longhouse (*Pontianak Post*, May 28, 2005).

MABM held uniform views on Malay discursive and cultural rights to indigeneity. Of concern, however, were its political implications: how would MABM maneuver vis-à-vis its Dayak counterparts? Here the organization demonstrated some internal divisiveness and weakness. Chairil Effendi, one of MABM's founders and a professor of Malay literature at UNTAN, thought it should emulate and be the Malay answer to Pancur Kasih.[5] Effendi observed that Pancur Kasih's experience and professionalism accounted for the recent Dayak gains. The organization's commitment to long-term social change, which, of course, was politically significant, impressed Effendi. Akin to Dayak experiences, large swathes of the Malay farming and fishing populations were being squeezed by the liberalization of West Kalimantan's economy. Establishing and nurturing dedicated Malay-oriented NGOs not only would rival Pancur Kasih, Effendi believed, but would also empower economically hard-pressed Malays.

Effendi's long-term, social strategy did not win out, however. Members of MABM either did not understand his vision or ignored it. As political and business elites who sought immediate political gratification, these people instead wanted to safeguard their interests in the upper echelons of local bureaucracies. Not surprisingly, *bupati* posts were targeted, and a power-sharing deal mediated by the governor's office was struck between the Dayak Customary Board and MABM. Now that under decentralization *bupati* were elected by the DPRD rather than appointed by the central government,[6] each *bupati* and vice *bupati* candidacy would contain a Malay and a Dayak in either position. In this way, representation would be reasonably balanced. Subsequent *bupati* elections in 2000 and 2001 in Sintang, Ketapang, Kapuas Hulu, and Landak districts reflected this compromise.[7]

Mobilizing the Grass Roots

At one level, MABM neutralized early Dayak gains by ensuring that Malay elites would hold *bupati* or vice *bupati* posts. But in Indonesia, elite jockeying over chief executive positions does not exhaust the range of political activity; the ability to mobilize masses is also essential. This was MABM's failing. An elite consortium, it lacked a loyal and reliable grassroots following capable of intimidating or physically engaging Dayaks. Two incidents brought this limitation to the fore: in September 1998 when Dayaks descended upon Pontianak City to protect Chinese-owned warehouses during a few days of looting;[8] and in February 1999 when the mobilizations led by Cornelis ultimately won Kimha the Pontianak district *bupati* office (see chapter 4). For young, eager, urban Malays, the escalation of ethnic tensions required new and different forms of organization. It deserves reiteration that, in the aftermath of anti-Madurese violence, the sights of this Malay movement were focused on Dayak, not Madurese, antagonism and momentum.

 Malay organizations with the ability to mobilize would come in different forms. In November 1999 capitalizing on the momentum generated by the Sambas violence, meetings were held in Pontianak to establish a provincial Malay organization (*Pontianak Post*, November 26, 1999). FKPM members from Sambas and those in similar networks percolating in Pontianak formed the Persatuan Forum Komunikasi Pemuda Melayu (Union of Malay Youth Communication Forums, or PFKPM). Nonetheless, the Sambas faction stymied efforts to form a hierarchical, province-wide organization centered in Pontianak. Guarding its independence, it did not want to be dictated to by Pontianak elites. In essence, this was a turf war. Naming the new forum was also contentious. Recognizing that their long-term adversaries were in fact Dayaks, the Pontianak faction wanted to replace FKPM because of its association with the anti-Madurese violence. So, another compromise was reached: PFKPM.[9] MABM's youth wing—the Pemuda Melayu Kalimantan Barat (Malay Youth of West Kalimantan, or PMKB)[10] joined the new organization, which then opened branches throughout the province.

 Whereas PFKPM sought a provincial domain, another organization—Lembaga Adat dan Kekerabatan Melayu (Malay Brotherhood and Customary Institute, popularly called Lembayu)—was formed with Pontianak as its operational base. Besides providing another barrier to Dayak advances, Lembayu's mid-1999 formation was note-worthy for two reasons. First, akin to the Sambas example, its founders were royal descendants of the Kadriah *kraton* in Pontianak, which by that time was practically defunct.[11] Here Lembayu sought to profit from heightening ethnic tensions and the phenomenon of reviving "traditional"—or in this case royal—authority in Indonesia. Although Malay and Dayak ethnic elites were staking claims to indigeneity and contesting bureaucratic posts, their respective movements lacked effec-tive provincial leadership, a consequence of the New Order's eviscera-tion of local leaders. To fill this gap, Lembayu turned to the legacy of Sultan Hamid II, the last sultan of the Kadriah *kraton* (see chapter 1). Serious efforts followed, which included extravagant conferences, a bar-rage of media reports, and lobbying efforts in Jakarta, to rehabilitate the sultan's name. Lembayu refashioned, albeit problematically, Hamid's image as a local "Malay" champion, one who understood "regional au-tonomy" and the dangers of an overbearing political center long ago.[12]

Second, besides dabbling in the symbolic realm of politics, Lembayu pursued more tangible ends, namely, constructing a network suitable for mass mobilization. Controversially, Lembayu appointed nine Malay *panglima* (war commanders) responsible for recruitment and security in their respective sections of Pontianak. The controversy behind these ap-pointments was threefold. First, the appointment of war commanders, many feared and argued, would facilitate more violence. Second, there was debate over whether *panglima* was a traditional Malay term (and position) or simply another Malay attempt to appropriate a Dayak sym-bol in the campaign to claim indigenous status.

Finally, the appointments generated resentment among those not selected. Foremost among them was Abas Fadhilah, a midsized con-tractor, prominent gangster, and one of many in Aswin's stable of bene-ficiaries enjoying the munificence of the province's public works depart-ment. Disenchanted with Lembayu for not having appointed him a *panglima*, Abas withdrew from the organization and in October 1999 established a *pencak silat* (self-defense) center called Ya-Qohar. Backed by Aswin, Ya-Qohar quickly grew into the city's largest, and Abas began declaring himself "Malay War Leader of the Undertow" (Panglima Melayu Arus Bawah).[13]

The roles Ya-Qohar and other martial arts centers play in Pontianak's criminal rackets have been notable. Primarily, they extort money from Chinese-owned natural resource extraction companies headquartered in Pontianak (and Sungai Raya, an adjacent suburb) in return for security and protection. Abas claimed to have some seventy *anak buah* (under-lings) posted at such companies as Bumi Raya Utama, Benua Indah, Kayu Mukti, and Batasan Ltd.[14] Al-Faqar, another martial arts school, was alleged to have provided security at similar companies: the Lyman Group, Rimba Ramin, Liberty, and New Kalbar Processor.[15]

In October 1999 rancor over the selection of provincial represen-tatives (*utusan daerah*) to the national People's Consultative Council (MPR) sparked a limited clash that both highlighted Malay-Dayak tensions and portended the October 2000 riots. There was an under-standing that the DPRD members would elect two Malays, two Dayaks, and one Chinese to reflect the province's ethnic composition (and polit-ical balance). The selection of Zainuddin Isman, a PPP activist and for-mer *Kompas* correspondent, complicated matters, however.[16] Dayaks rejected Isman, for, although he claims Dayak ancestry, he is a Mus-lim and thus considered "Malay."[17] Therefore, for some, the tally was three Malays and one Dayak. Angered by such duplicity, dozens of Dayaks tried to storm the DPRD building but were met by Abas's goons. The symbolic potency of the fracas far surpassed the actual fighting. Whereas it demonstrated that future Malay-Dayak distur-bances remained a possibility, it also indicated that Pontianak's looming "ethnic" clashes would, in fact, mask elite politicking. But this form of ethnic animosity was momentarily sidelined as Malay and Madurese thugs (featuring Abas), politicians, and Governor Aswin took center stage.

The Politics of the October 2000 Riot: Party and Ethnic Interests

The most conspicuous feature of the riot that began on October 25 and lasted until October 27 was its local, elite-led mobilizations. The poli-tics underpinning this incident reflected the complexity of shifting al-liances within Malay and Dayak ethnopolitical movements. Whereas tensions primarily resonated between these two groups broadly defined, the riot shortly diffused these animosities and redirected them toward convenient victims, the Madurese. Dayaks and Malays were found on both sides of the political divide that precipitated the violence. In the end, Governor Aswin, fighting the battle of his political career, deftly manipulated all challengers and emerged victorious.

Galvanized by the reform movement and the vibrancy of demon-strations in Jakarta, students in Pontianak gathered forces starting in mid-April 1998. They congregated regularly at the UNTAN traffic circle strategically located between the governor's official residence and the DPRD building on Achmad Yani Boulevard (see map 4). At their peak, following the shooting of six students at Trisakti University in Jakarta on May 12, these demonstrations marshaled an estimated crowd of two thousand. Occasional clashes did break out between student demonstrators, on one hand, and security forces and *preman* (thugs) mobilized to intimidate students on the other. The latter were culled from three New Order youth organizations: Pemuda Pancasila, Pemuda Panca Marga, and FKPPI. No casualties were reported.

From the outset, the students demanded Governor Aswin's ouster. To them, he epitomized New Order rule and was seen as the provincial ringleader of "corruption, collusion, and nepotism" (KKN), the reform movement's most popular antiregime slogan.[18] Without his removal, students believed, attempts at meaningful, local reform would reach a dead end. A prototypical New Order governor, Aswin was a retired three-star major general who served the center's interests while enriching himself, his family, and his friends.[19] Unaccountable to electoral constituencies, Aswin cultivated an impressive patronage network nurtured via the granting of licenses for such development projects as road construction, logging concessions, and oil palm plantations. Smuggling and illegal gold mining and logging were similarly pertinent. Most politicians, contractors, wealthy businesspeople, and government-sanctioned organizations were in some manner parties to this network. When it began to fray as certain figures betrayed their patron and sought his demise, Aswin responded by calling upon local underground figures to rescue his lucrative gubernatorial racket.

When *Reformasi* burst onto the national stage, only a few student groups demonstrated and called for Aswin's ouster. Soeharto's resignation had failed to spark a chain reaction in the provinces; governors (and even *bupati*) largely remained entrenched in their positions. Without the benefit of precedent, politicians in West Kalimantan were not yet ready to renounce Aswin, their patron. Moreover, during the first half of 1999, the riots in Sambas and the June electoral campaigns temporarily derailed the students' anti-Aswin designs.

The active students remained undaunted, however, and soon thereafter renewed their efforts.[20] This time their demands gained greater currency when some local figures changed course to pursue Aswin's removal. Publicly, they reproached Aswin for failing to solve the province's chronic ethnic strife and the concurrent refugee crisis (see below).

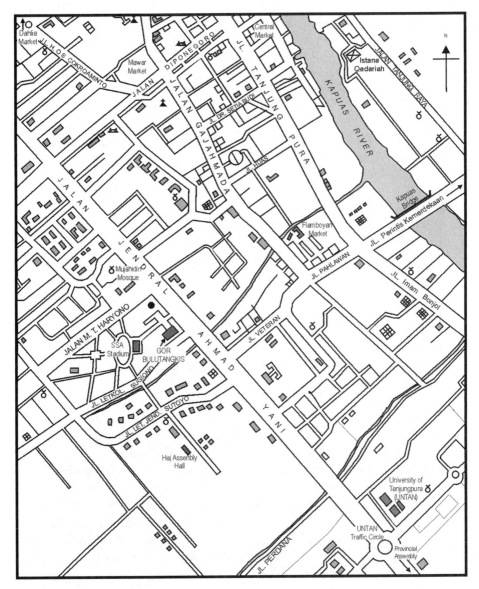

Map 4. Central Pontianak City

Privately, the motives behind this change were more complicated. The role played by Gusti Syamsumin was telling. The provincial leader of Golkar, head of the provincial DPRD, and a native-son Malay, Syamsumin was well positioned to succeed Aswin. Although as governor Aswin headed Golkar's Board of Advisers, the Golkar faction in the DPRD backed Syamsumin.[21] Politicians from lesser parties who were visible in ethnic organizations also jumped ship. Ismet Noor—head of PAN (National Mandate Party) and MABM—and the late Herbertus Tekwaan—PBI's chair and a member of the Dayak Customary Council—headlined this group. All told, five DPRD factions (Golkar, PPP, PDI/PDKB, PBI, and Pembaharuan) conspired to impeach Aswin while the PDI-P and military/police factions stood by him.[22]

Exclusion from patronage networks can also foster animus. Despite the breadth of Aswin's network, the fiery and unscrupulous Oesman Sapta Odang, a wealthy businessman and at the time one of the province's three "Malay" MPR representatives, felt slighted. In fact, he harbored a florid contempt for Aswin and Pontianak's richest Chinese businessmen. Odang believed that an Aswin-ABRI-Golkar-Chinese business oligarchy marginalized native Indonesian (*pribumi*) entrepreneurs. While big Chinese businessmen, Odang submitted, controlled large-scale projects, *pribumi* contractors were thrown the crumbs. To embarrass his rival, Odang, who contemplated succeeding the governor, furtively funded parts of the anti-Aswin campaign; in particular, the student group Solmadapar was a beneficiary of his largesse (*Pontianak Post*, May 19, 2000).[23]

To achieve their goal, anti-Aswin factions sought recourse in a new law on regional government that laid the foundations for Indonesia's decentralization program, No. 22/1999. A technocratic attempt to instill horizontal accountability between the executive and legislative branches, a section of the law stipulated that the relevant DPRD could legally impeach a chief executive (governor, mayor, or *bupati*) by rejecting the official's annual accountability speech/progress report. Here the distinction in terms reflected the confusion that permeated the incipient phase of decentralization.[24] Predicated on New Order precedent when the report was perfunctory, pro-Aswin factions maintained that the speech was merely a *laporan progres/kemajuan* (progress report) and therefore provided inadequate grounds to impeach Aswin (*Equator*, June 8, 2000).[25] Opponents countered that, as was made explicit in the new law, it was a *laporan pertanggungjawaban* (accountability speech), and thus could constitute grounds for dismissal.

With their new elite backing, student demonstrations proliferated, but so did antistudent aggression. Loyal Aswin clients, Abas and Ali Anafia, mobilized *preman* to intimidate demonstrators and stage pro-Aswin rallies. Tellingly, Anafia, a Golkar functionary, headed Pontianak City's DPRD. Thus, if we recall Syamsumin's defection, we witness how Aswin ably split Golkar and isolated his adversaries at the provincial level while anchoring support in Pontianak City (and in districts across the province).[26]

On June 14, 2000, the day Aswin delivered his annual address to the DPRD, a student named Syafruddin, one among a restive horde of some eight hundred protestors gathered outside, was killed, most likely by sniper fire.[27] As cascades of condemnations of Syafruddin's death flooded the local press, Aswin's days in office appeared numbered. Perhaps thinking that public opinion was on their side, rather than rejecting the governor's accountability speech—the legal route set out by Law No. 22/1999—the five dissenting factions signed a *mosi tak percaya* (vote of no confidence) calling for Aswin's removal.[28] A vote of no confidence, however, was beyond the new law's bounds.[29] Predictably, PDI-P and the military/police factions rejected the measure, and a stalemate promptly ensued. Intense lobbying efforts by both sides in Jakarta followed, paralleled by escalating tensions in Pontianak.[30] On October 10, the central government gave Aswin three options, all of which tended toward his ouster: 1) resign, 2) be recalled to Jakarta, or 3) be impeached via the appropiate mechanism (*diberhentikan sesuai dengan mekanisme yang berlaku*) (*Pontianak Post,* October 11, 2000). Two weeks later, a riot broke out.

The Riot

The triggering event was a traffic accident between a bus and a Malay moped driver at around nine o'clock in the morning on October 25, on Perintis Kemerdekaan Avenue, the main thoroughfare connecting Pontianak proper and all the arteries heading north and east (see map 4).[31] Brandishing tire jacks, the bus driver and conductor, who happened to be Madurese, chased the moped driver into his neighborhood. A war of words erupted, though nothing else. The bus driver and conductor reboarded their bus and headed to Siantan, the location of the region's primary transport hub (Batu Layang) and a Madurese stronghold. Almost immediately, mysterious yet strategically placed phone calls were made to a few Malay and Madurese figures, each of whom were informed that the other side was about to attack. Whether either side was actually mobilizing forces apparently was immaterial. Word spread that Malay and Madurese tensions were spiraling: this was what mattered. The perfidy of rumor in the production of ethnic clashes reared its ugly head once again (Brass 2003).

By ten o'clock, a thousand or so people had converged at the site of the traffic accident. "Madurese" from Siantan were mobilized and congregated on the site's northern side. Opposite (closer to the Kapuas Bridge — see map 4) was the "Malay" crowd in which yellow headbands bearing the name Ya-Qohar were prominent. Sandwiched in between stood the police separating the two. Here quotation marks are deliberately used to draw attention to the crowds' mixed characteristics, although "Malay" and "Madurese" is how they came to be perceived, thus providing fodder for the escalation of violence. Clearly delimiting the two opposing sides following a "trigger event" is critical to the unfolding of riots. On this topic, Keith observes that "the reading of the significance of the trigger event must be sufficiently clear to induce collective action. Within the 'social language' of a particular area at a particular time the trigger is read similarly by a large number of people. . . . Trigger events are not epiphenomenal or incidental to the development of violence. They provide a key element in the signification of action, the meaning of *the riot* set against its spatial and social context" (1993, 168–69, emphasis in the original). In this case, the context of Madurese domination of the city's transport sector signified what a "traffic accident" in Pontianak could mean.

The next eight hours or so can be best described as a stalemate. The accumulated tension climaxed at sundown when Abas's forces crossed the Kapuas Bridge into Pontianak proper to unleash the violence. They attacked Madurese *becak* (pedicab) drivers and burned dozens of the Madurese-owned kiosks that cram the Flamboyan market area adjacent to the Kapuas Bridge. That night, during which perhaps as many as six people were hacked to death, Ato' Ismail, the head of PFKPM-Pontianak, and his associates distributed alcohol to embolden the rioters. Aswin was also seen touring the town, surveying the damage, and conversing with some of the riot's leaders. As the sun rose the next morning, marketgoers saw hundreds of empty plastic bags of alcohol and boxes of *nasi bungkus* (takeout) littered about the area.[32]

During this first day, the actions of the security forces were strategically ambiguous.[33] The moment crowds gathered on Perintis Kemerdekaan Avenue, access to Pontianak north of Siantan was blocked. The security forces stood by once night fell as crowds wreaked havoc unimpeded in the Flamboyan market area. Later that night, however, Abas-led forces, moving east from the market area, were prevented from storming nearby refugee camps. As this was taking place, locals set up innumerable makeshift blockades throughout the city, and thousands stood outside their neighborhoods to prevent the inadvertent spread of violence.

On the morning of October 26, two Madurese in southern Pontianak were slain and Madurese houses in Jeruju (eastern Pontianak) were razed. In the early afternoon, each side, with diminished numbers, reassumed its position on Perintis Kemerdekaan Avenue, again separated by security forces. Fighting also flared in Sungai Raya Luar (southern Pontianak) and areas surrounding the Flamboyan (central Pontianak) and Dahlia (western Pontianak) markets. As Kijang jeeps circled Malay strongholds, alcohol, weapons—mostly machetes—and money were distributed. Meanwhile, armed Madurese spilled out of a refugee camp (GOR Pangsuma) to blockade Achmad Yani Boulevard in order to protect themselves. Later that night, they once again faced attacks.[34] October 27, the riot's third day, was mercifully its last. While sporadic clashes revisited areas already afflicted, three companies (Satuan Setingkat Kompi, or SSK) of the Police Mobile Brigade (Brimob) arrived from Jakarta to curb the violence. Shortly thereafter, Abas disappeared, perhaps fearing arrest.[35] Altogether, the riot claimed about forty lives, with Madurese victims accounting for some thirty-five.

The riot's most conspicuous feature was its mobilizations. *Preman* networks led by Abas and Anafia—"the riot captains" (Tambiah 1996, 99)—that had coalesced to confront student demonstrators now assumed an unmistakable Malay identity. They exploited anti-Madurese sentiments to serve Aswin's political interests. Nonetheless, just as salient was the fact that, although thousands mobilized to guard neighborhoods, only a handful of people committed acts of violence. Well cognizant of the executive-legislative tussle and the conspicuousness of the mobilizations, most residents rejected violence.[36] In addition to the arrival of Brimob troops and Pontianak's small size and geography, which make it easy to cordon off, this refusal dampened the riot's fury.

All told, the riot was semiorganized and purposive. Contrary to the fears of many, it did not turn Pontianak into a second Ambon, that is, a site of massive Christian-Muslim killings (Van Dijk 2001, 395), but it successfully silenced Aswin's legislative opponents. Following the unrest, provincial DPRD intransigence rapidly fizzled. Legislative efforts to depose Aswin ceased,[37] while the anti-Aswin students had reached the end of their tether.[38]

Several points concerning the riot and the Aswin debacle warrant mention, some of which facilitated Aswin's survival. For one thing, whereas most residents rejected the October violence, they also maintained an indifference to the political mudslinging. Pontianak's insipid civil society may have accounted for some of this apathy, but most people saw it for what it was: elite maneuvering over a lucrative office that in the end had little resonance in people's lives. Moreover, the tussle was not perceived in stark status quo versus reform terms. To be sure, Aswin unequivocally represented the New Order's legacy; yet no one anointed his challengers as progressive reformers. It was painfully obvious that few trusted them to solve the region's social problems, which were blamed on Aswin. The way in which Aswin's legislative opponents handled this crisis failed to inspire confidence in their ability to create "good governance," the mantra of democracy and civil society advocates everywhere.[39]

Aswin not only staved off assaults on his governorship; he also prevailed in safeguarding his succession. To be sure, provincial elites had adopted the ethnic power-sharing model on the district level, which in this case meant a Malay governor and a Dayak running mate.[40] And it was significant that the succeeding governor, Usman Djafar, was backed by the then-vice president, national head of PPP and West Kalimantan native son Hamzah Haz, who visited Pontianak to lobby for Djafar. Remarkably, PPP, which officially nominated Djafar, controlled only six out of the forty-five seats in the provincial DPRD.[41] But two other features reflected Aswin's success. One was that Djafar did not come from the DPRD, the home of Aswin's "reformist" challengers. Djafar is a businessman who had been residing in Jakarta.[42] Second, the new Dayak vice governor, L. H. Kadir, had been a top Aswin assistant. Syamsumin, Golkar's nominee and Aswin's nemesis, finished a distant second in the December 2002 balloting by the DPRD.

Finally, from a national viewpoint, one lesson learned from the October 2000 riot was that regional elites never did intend to follow the decentralization laws to the letter. Although regional autonomy has precipitated a rash of troubled elections across the country over *bupati* posts, few naively believed that governors would be reduced to mere patronageless referees as power devolved to the district level. In fact, the Megawati administration's (2001–4) disdain for decentralization was well known.[43] One action undertaken to staunch the program's tide was to reach out to the governors, whose positions the decentralization laws largely bypassed. Megawati actively intervened in the election of governors in key provinces, while central government regulations were enacted to keep authority (and thus resources) in central and provincial government hands. Tellingly, the revised law on regional government (No. 32/2004) passed under Megawati enhanced the power of gubernatorial authority, especially with respect to the determination of regional budgets (article 25d).

Refugees, Relocation, Riot

The city's economically and politically underprivileged—Madurese petty traders, *becak* drivers, and kiosk owners—bore the disproportionate brunt of the October riots. Another group of vulnerable Madurese—victims of the Sambas clashes—were likewise targeted, although this orgy of violence did not involve the refugees per se. Instead, the refugee issue lay at the core of Pontianak's cascading riots of June 2001. At the time, this violence was the climax of a three-year saga of near catastrophic proportions, redolent of government corruption, ineptitude, intensifying urban economic competition, and the further dehumanization of a victimized population.

Following previous clashes with Dayaks, including the massive 1997 episode, most Madurese returned to rebuild their razed homes. But the Sambas riots unleashed a new and troublesome dynamic. Starting in mid-March 1999, escorted by military trucks and boats, an estimated fifty thousand traumatized Madurese arrived in Pontianak,[44] thus furthering their dehumanization. Most were placed randomly in holding camps, sports stadiums, athletic fields, warehouses, and a religious facility. Others—perhaps as many as ten thousand—were shipped and then housed (in camps) in East Java and Madura; an equal number found lodging in Pontianak. Of the latter, those better-off rented accommodations while others found shelter with family or friends. Also, not all refugees were Madurese. Dayak, Javanese, Bugis, and Malay spouses were involved as well.[45]

The provincial government was content to feed and shelter the refugees until the June 1999 elections, evidently to avoid "unnecessary" controversies that might, in turn, disrupt the implementation of the electoral results. Thus, for the moment the authorities failed to relocate the refugees to "permanent" houses built about thirty miles south of Pontianak in Tebang Kacang and further south in Padang Tikar (see map 2), the only option the government entertained. Officials blamed *oknum* (troublemakers) for spreading fear among the refugees over issues ranging from poor soil to unsafe conditions in the relocation sites (*Equator,* June 10, 1999). In reality, they would have preferred to return to Sambas. Although in time more and more of them would have liked to remain in Pontianak (though not in the camps), the majority still wanted to go home to Sambas.[46] Going to Madura was never considered an option, as some 97 percent had been born in West Kalimantan.[47] For the residents of Pontianak, the lingering refugee crisis served as a reminder of violence past and a foreshadowing of violence to come.

The deplorable conditions in the camps prompted little in the way of public outcry or sympathy. Madurese are not considered native sons, and a belief persists that Madurese belligerence is the root cause of the chronic unrest.[48] Although women, children, and the elderly composed the majority of the refugees, they were uniformly stigmatized as "Madurese" and thus considered responsible for their wretched fate. Accordingly, few to no local support groups were formed to aid the refugees.[49] On hand from the outset, the international aid organization Médecins sans Frontières (Doctors without Borders, or MSF) became the main pillar of nongovernmental assistance, despite stern government intransigence. MSF projects concentrated on upgrading infrastructure, such as sanitation facilities, rather than food distribution, which caused consternation among government officials. The latter felt that these improvements would buoy spirits and provide incentives to prolong their stay. In this way, the camps' squalor was politically constructed.

These decrepit conditions soon produced social ramifications. With disheveled facades and poor lighting, the areas surrounding the camps were soon deemed troubled and crime infested. In essence, camps in central Pontianak, with permeable yet recognizable boundaries, became Madurese ghettoes. Local newspapers did their part to reinforce these perceptions by featuring crimes that occurred nearby the camps; whether the perpetrators were refugees was usually obscure in the reports (see *Equator,* July 17, 2000; and *Pontianak Post,* November 15, 2000).

The random placement of refugees upon arrival tore asunder social networks and leadership structures.[50] Attempts to establish representative committees met with internal fissures and derision among a divergent refugee population spread across some nine separate locations. Their overall failure, however, can be traced to the duplicity of Sulaiman, then West Kalimantan's wealthiest and most visible Madurese figure. The head of the leading Madurese organization, Ikatan

Keluarga Madura (Madurese Family Association, or IKAMRA), Sulaiman was an infamous champion of Aswin who once held a monopoly on the salt trade.[51] With Aswin's approval, Sulaiman won contracts to help construct the relocation sites. His enthusiasm for relocation can be gleaned from statements he made in the press; for example, he described relocation as "a policy we respect and we put our full trust in the provincial government to carry it out" (cited in *Kompas,* April 22, 1999).

Most notable, however, was the magnitude and pervasiveness of government corruption. The presence of refugees in Pontianak created problems; the convenient combination of government incompetence, corruption, and vested interests made these problems into a crisis. Subsidies for refugees consisted of Rp. 1500 worth of rice and vegetables per person per day, although what percentage of this sum the refugees received was open to debate. Local officials inflated the refugee rolls to increase the amount of central government subsidies circulating among their offices (*Kalimantan Review,* September–October 2001). But corruption figured most prominently in the construction of the relocation sites. These projects would require thousands of new houses and miles of new roads, bridges, and irrigation ditches. It was a treasure trove for the bureaucrats.

Such government departments as public works, village development, transmigration, and Bappeda fought among themselves for control of planning and construction, foiling attempts at interdepartmental coordination. Atop the bureaucracy sat Aswin. His thirst for development monies was unquenchable.[52] Construction monies also vanished at a remarkable rate. On-site investigations suggested that no more than one-quarter of the budgeted construction costs for houses were actually used as they were intended.[53] The number of houses built was grossly overreported, and officials recurrently falsified soil suitability reports (*Pontianak Post,* March 16, 2001). Again the local press participated in this farce. It published pictures of proud Madurese settlers displaying their prodigious amounts of produce and ran such disingenuous headlines as "Refugees in Tebang Kacang Are a Success" and "4,000 Refugee Families Want to Be Relocated."[54]

The Refugee "Time-Bomb"

The refugee "time bomb" to which the local press and aid workers had alluded finally exploded. On June 23, 2001, a robbery gone awry outside

Figure 8. Razed refugee shacks, GOR Bulutangkis, Pontianak.

the GOR complex of refugee camps resulted in the death of a young boy. The perpetrators were four Madurese youths, although whether they were refugees was unclear. It hardly mattered. Their ethnicity and the crime's location signified *pengungsi* (refugee). Once word spread at dawn that the boy had died of a head wound, accumulated frustration over the government's inability to resolve the crisis was vented on the refugees. Locals mobilized at the GOR camps (see map 4). A contingent of police officers kept the two well-armed sides apart but could not prevent the firebombing of the refugees' wooden shacks, hundreds of which were reduced to ashes (see figure 8).[55] Women and children fled to the relative safety of the nearby GOR Pangsuma and Sultan Syarif Abdurrahman Stadium camps. PFKPM gangs adorned with yellow headbands then spread the violence, so that it consumed sites affected by the October 2000 riots. In particular, they torched scores of kiosks and *becaks* and lynched two *becak* drivers near the Flamboyan market.[56]

As police forces cordoned off the GOR complex of camps, and patrols were doubled, a war of wills materialized between the refugees, on the one hand, and the government and Malay and Dayak groups, on the other. Aswin warned: "There are no more negotiations concerning the refugee issue. They have to be relocated soon or kicked out of GOR. We will not heed offers or demands from refugees" (*Pontianak*

Post, June 25, 2001). Accordingly, on the morning of June 26, ten trucks arrived at the Sultan Syarif Abdurrahman Stadium to evacuate the refugees to the relocation sites. But they refused to cooperate and the trucks left empty. One refugee was reported to have said, "Enough, Sir. Don't continue to cajole us. We don't want to be evacuated. Not until the last drop of our blood has been spilt" (*Pontianak Post,* June 27, 2001). Faced with refugee intransigence, PFKPM announced an ultimatum: exit the camps within five days or risk *perang terbuka* (open war) (*Pontianak Post,* June 27, 2001). Shortly thereafter, the Dayak Customary Council, in response to two attacks on Dayaks in Siantan, issued a similar ultimatum.[57]

Firm in his resolve, Aswin called on the security apparatus to evacuate the refugees by force. The army balked. In a rare public spat, infantry Col. Simanjuntak, then the new Danrem (Subregional Military Commander), refused to brook Aswin's bravado. He reminded Aswin of the sensitivity of the situation, which included well-armed refugees who had displayed a desperate obstinacy. Undermining Aswin's authority, Simanjuntak calmly declared: "I am an instrument of the state, not of the governor. What happens in the field is not as simple as the governor has decided" (*Pontianak Post,* June 26, 2001). So, the ultimatum deadlines passed without incident. A hundred or so refugees chose relocation, though the majority remained ensconced in the camps.

The prospect of tens of thousands of additional Madurese settling in and around Pontianak and the increasingly acute economic competition it would create unnerved the city's Malay elite. While Madurese predominance among Pontianak's transport sector is well documented, their growing visibility in the city's markets has eroded Malay strongholds. An energetic team of assistants and I mapped the ethnic composition of the city's four largest markets: Central, Mawar, Dahlia, and Flamboyan (table 2). The data highlight the economic competition underlying the rancor vented on the Madurese refugees.

Table 2. Ethnicity of Traders (4 markets combined)

| | Size of Operation | | | |
	Large	Medium	Small	Total
Malay	54	287	107	448
Madurese	39	251	102	392
Total	93	538	209	840

The slight advantage Malay traders enjoyed is rendered less significant when the fact that Malays in Pontianak outnumber Madurese by almost three to one is taken into consideration (BPS 2000a, 73, table 10.7). It requires emphasis, however, that, based on scores of interviews, traders for the most part discount the relevance of ethnicity in the markets. This is one reason why, despite the fact that markets became violent flashpoints in the riots, they were not razed.[58] Both times traders banded together to keep the marauders out of the marketplace. Nonetheless, Malay leaders perceived the markets as the crux of heightened economic competition, one in which Malays were losing ground. The riots' trajectories—both times striking market areas but sparked by interests external to the markets—reflect this alarm. For Malay leaders, thousands of newly permanent Madurese in Pontianak would further erode Malay economic footholds. All told, the June 2001 riot was limited in scope and largely spontaneous, but it exploded in a context of wider political and economic meaning. Rampant government corruption, intensifying economic competition, and raw ethnic sentiments were all operative.

Nearly a year later, a few months before Aswin's second (and final) term was to expire and following a visit to Pontianak by Hamzah Haz, a deal was struck by which refugee families in resettlement sites would be granted Rp. 2.5 million each; others would be given Rp. 5 million (ostensibly to leave the camps).[59] Importantly, there were no restrictions placed on resettlement. Starting in mid-May 2002, refugees of their own accord began exiting the camps to build new homes and lives on the outskirts of town—a minor victory indeed. A final cathartic explosion had been averted. While these Madurese are no longer in camps, they retain their refugee status until a safe return to Sambas is permitted.[60]

Shifting Alliances, Shifting Identities

The urban dimension of these riots induced urgency among the province's elite to seek reconciliation, or at least minimize the likelihood of future outbreaks. Despite the massive size of the 1997 and 1999 clashes, the provincial (i.e., Pontianak) elite still tended to feel disconnected from the bloodshed and suffering that had occurred in the semirural districts. Moreover, no matter how extensive and horrendous, these affairs had disturbed but did not destroy the provincial economy. It risked devastation, however, now that Pontianak loomed as the new locus of violence; the economy would not survive a ransacking of the city. The

then-recent Dayak-Madurese bloodshed in neighboring Central Kalimantan (see chapter 6) provided a haunting lesson of what could
happen when a region's primary distribution center was destroyed. For
months following the riots, denizens of upland Central Kalimantan
suffered under faminelike conditions.[61]

So, in Pontianak on April 24–25, 2001, an attempt at rapprochement
was launched among representatives of nine ethnic groups. Expecting
tangible outcomes from this elite conference held in the air-conditioned
auditorium of the governor's office would have been sanguine. Con-
versations about essentialist ethnic cultures and characters dominated
the proceedings. Nonetheless, the meeting can be used heuristically to
understand the fears of the various groups and explore the trajectories of
potential strife. Predicated on the 1999 riots, ill-informed assumptions
were drawn about local politics, suggesting that the structure of violence, Malay-Dayak versus Madurese, mirrored local political constellations. Indonesia's leading news weekly, *Tempo*, misread the political situation, editorializing that "feelings of animosity are very thick, with
Dayak and Malays on one side, and Madurese on the other" (October
22, 2000). My account seeks to dispel such uncritical simplifications.

Tensions within the meeting reflected the contingency of provincial animosity, a kind of shifting triangulation among combatants. One
formulation pitted Malays and Dayaks (the sons of the soil) against
the Madurese (the newcomers), the scenario of the Sambas bloodshed.
If religious sentiments were manipulated, however, then Malays and
Madurese would join forces to confront the Dayaks.[62] The spillover
effects of then-ongoing religious fighting in Poso and the Moluccas
weighed heavily on the minds of the participants. Finally, given the continuing Malay-Madurese tension, some envisioned a scenario in which
Dayaks and Madurese would confront Malays.[63] These shifting alliances evoke an axiom drawn from realist international relations theory:
"The enemy of my enemy is my friend."

In fact, even this fluid triangle of contestation glosses over the complexity of local politics. One shortcoming of the meeting was the rele-
gation of Chinese representation to observer status on a par with that of
ethnic groups such as the Bugis, Bataks, and Javanese. To be sure, out-
right reconciliation with Chinese would have been superfluous, as since
1967 Indonesians of Chinese descent have not been targeted in bouts of
collective violence. There are at least two reasons for this. The first
comes from "above." Despite internal fissures, Chinese leaders, with
1967 pogroms seared in their memories, have understood the necessity

of maintaining working relations with multiple provincial power holders and others in a position to threaten their interests. Put simply, anyone and everyone who matters is paid.[64] A second reason comes from "below." Socioeconomically, most Chinese in West Kalimantan are worse off than those in Java and Sumatra. To subsist, semirural Chinese in Sambas district, for instance, wallowing in poverty, frequently marry their daughters off to affluent Taiwanese men. Their hardships not only distort stereotypical images of the monolithic Indonesian Chinese pariah economic class. Locally, it also ameliorates social jealousies and animosities, complicating the construction of the Chinese as scapegoats. Moreover, because local scapegoats—the Madurese—already exist, the imperative to create another is lessened.

Nonetheless, the influence of the Chinese is substantial, and engaging them as full partners would appreciably bolster the reconciliation process. Lately, a more worrisome development has been brewing. With the impact of decentralization and a more competitive political system, local balances could shift and jeopardize Chinese security. Like their Malay and Dayak counterparts, West Kalimantan's Chinese are in the midst of a political revitalization. Whereas former movements are the products of violence, these new developments can be traced to Chinese *nonvictimization* in recent riots. A small sense of comfort among local Chinese has materialized. Coupled with the easing of legal restrictions in the post-Soeharto state,[65] they have stepped gingerly into the province's public sphere.

This was first noticeable during the 1999 electoral campaigns, which galvanized these communities by providing them an opportunity to protest and demand reforms at officially sanctioned party rallies. More competitive elections forced parties to vie for the substantial Chinese vote. The 1999 campaigns (and subsequent ones as well) were awash with such suppressed Chinese-oriented symbols as the colorful and fiery *barongsai* (lion dance).[66]

This was followed by the blossoming of Chinese organizations. Compared to the Malay and Dayak examples, however, this movement was understandably more guarded. Its conservative elite feared a rapid pace that might draw the ire of its ethnic counterparts, the government, and the security apparatus. To downplay their "political" significance, most were "cultural" in orientation, including a plethora of new *barongsai* committees. Ceremonies of all kinds now open with lion and dragon (*naga*) dances, while *barongsai* festivals have become common. In 2001, Chinese New Year and other religious festivals such as Cap Go Meh were celebrated along the province's seaboard with festivities not seen in decades. In August 2002 the first ever Chinese Cultural Week was held in Pontianak.

Increasing Chinese political participation worries non-Chinese elites, however. The Malay-Dayak elite tussles over bureaucratic positions, often viewed through a zero-sum prism, will most likely deny Chinese demands for greater inclusion. To keep the Chinese communities isolated politically, non-Chinese could resort to inciting anti-Chinese sentiment. One path might be to evoke memories of the last time the Chinese were engaged politically: the tumultuous 1960s and the communist insurgencies.[67]

Internal fissures also threatened to undermine the relative security the Chinese have attained. New political dynamics—decentralization, a freer competitive political system, and ethnomobilizations—have exacerbated rifts within the Chinese elite. New Order discrimination and exploitation forced a certain cohesiveness among factions. For instance, the majority of the province's Chinese population became Indonesian citizens in the mid- to late 1970s (Heidhues 2003). Government corruption and inertia produced a tortuous and expensive citizenship process (Mabbett and Mabbett 1972, 8; *Tempo,* August 17, 1974). Nonetheless, over time speedier processing of citizenship papers was exchanged for Golkar electoral support.[68] Consonant with the New Order policy of corporatism, the government mainly dealt with its new "citizenry" through Pontianak's most visible Chinese organization, Bhakti Suci,[69] which was headed by the late Tan Liem Hian, known by his ethnic Javanese name Adijanto, then the community's foremost business leader.[70] This stable arrangement padded the buffer zone wherein the Chinese were protected when violence struck.

But deferred antagonisms resurfaced and have been magnified by democratic processes. The 1999 elections were telling, when members of the Chinese elite backed different parties, principally PDI-P, Golkar, and the small PBI. The primary fissure and most public dispute, however, did not concern political parties. It involved Adijanto and his longtime business adversary Budiono Tan, the chair of the large Benua Indah Group.[71] This crystallized publicly over the "Chinese seat" for provincial representation (*utusan daerah*) in the MPR.[72] Budiono relished the position, while Adijanto—due to his poor Indonesian language skills and lack of formal education—campaigned for his "young wife" (*isteri muda*), Rosye Anggela. In late 1998, to pursue his aims, Adijanto quit Bhakti Suci and established his own social organization,

Figure 9. Close-up of a new archway in Sambas district with Chinese symbols, marking the Chinese identity as native son. Underneath the dragon, it reads "Welcome."

Figure 10. A statue outside one of Pontianak's newest shopping centers, depicting the province's three "native sons"—Chinese, Malay, and Dayak men—each festooned with stereotypical cultural trappings.

Marga Bhakti, dragging much of Bhakti Suci's board along with him. In the end, the provincial DPRD opted for Budiono, infuriating Adjianto. All told, internal and external forces alike threaten the protection the Chinese once enjoyed. Whether key interests can continue to be satisfied may determine their future security.

On the other hand, although it is controversial, the association of the Chinese identity with *putera daerah* (native son) status provides them with some shelter, which may prevent future attacks. Examples abound. The Chinese in Sambas are increasingly seen as native sons, particularly vis-à-vis the dehumanized Madurese. New archways displaying Chinese cultural markings that have been built along the district's main thoroughfare capture this sentiment (see figure 9). So, too, does the frequent cultural festivals in which Chinese trappings are featured alongside Dayak and Malay symbols.[73] In Pontianak a Chinese-Malay-Dayak Brotherhood Forum was organized in 2000, while a statue outside a new shopping mall depicts a Chinese man sitting comfortably among his "native son" Dayak and Malay companions (see figure 10).[74] In mid-2005 Chinese, Dayak, and Malay spokespeople were equally represented at a seminar on *hukum adat* coorganized by UNTAN's law faculty and Komnas HAM. And Yansen Akun Effendi, a local businessman of Chinese descent, was selected *bupati* by Sanggau's DPRD to succeed Andjioe whose term expired in 2003.[75]

Brewing Tensions

By emphasizing ethnicity, the 2001 reconciliation meeting in Pontianak also overlooked deteriorating religious relations. Dayak leaders interviewed never disparaged the "Maduraization" of West Kalimantan, but they poured scorn on its "Islamization." They singled out abundant state subsidies for the construction of mosques, the favoring of Islamic over Christian teachings in schools, increasing numbers of Muslim transmigrants, and intense pressure to convert to Islam if a Dayak (i.e., a Christian) civil servant fancies promotion.[76] In December 2004 the *Kalimantan Review* expressed alarm at the 2000 census results, which tallied the province's percentage of Muslims at 57.6 percent. Instructively, no mention was made of the 5.4 percent who called themselves Madurese.[77] Local Islamic leaders hold Christianity in equal contempt. Their derision focuses on supposed missionary efforts to make West Kalimantan a bastion of Christianity.[78] Calls for the expulsion of Madurese from West Kalimantan (and their purge from Central Kalimantan in 2001) fueled, and, for this elite, substantiated their views. The belief that Christians engineered the 1999 Sambas clashes to embarrass Muslims and sow discord (*memecahbelahkan*) among them was prevalent.

This friction was reflected in the formation of two post-Soeharto organizations in particular. First was a provincial branch of the Majelis Ulama Indonesia (Council of Indonesian Islamic Scholars), the first attempt to draw all Muslims into a single organization. Second was the Ikatan Keluarga Dayak Islam (Muslim Dayak Family Association). Formed in December 1999, the organization's controversy stemmed from the attempts of some Muslim leaders to appropriate Dayak identities and symbolism. The case of the late Rudy Alamsyahrum, at the time the provincial head of PDI-P, is exemplary (see chapter 4). Here, use of the terms *Dayak* and *Islam* is intended to attract separate audiences. *Islam* resonates nationally and is associated with the blossoming of Muslim movements. *Dayak* signifies the local, and attempts to capture and rechannel the growing symbolic potency of the Dayak identity (which is ironic given its longtime primitive and backward connotations). This Muslim-Dayak movement is truly a post-Soeharto phenomenon.

This development leads one to ask: could future violence—for instance, Malay-Dayak clashes—be spun in explicitly religious webs of meaning? It would behoove Dayaks to prevent this. To date, violent mobilization along religious lines has not occurred. Such warfare traditions as passing the red bowl and issuing shrill war cries (*tariu*) are associated with Dayak ethnic identities, not Christian ones. A prominent split between Catholic and Protestant Dayaks in West Kalimantan could also interfere with religious mobilizations. Finally, and most important because violent ethnic mobilizations have a strong and successful history, mobilizing along alternative lines would be risky.[79]

Finally, ethnic representation at the reconciliation meeting in the governor's office falsely conveyed an impression of unanimity within each group. Conflicts among Golkar members, other party elites, and NGO activist Dayaks; between members of FKPM Sambas and Pontianak Lembayu Malays; and between Marga Bhakti and Bhakti Suci Chinese are just some examples that query such clean categorizations. To conclude this chapter, I explore briefly one of these intraethnic rivalries: fractured Dayak relations.

As was noted earlier, the term *Dayak* is but an exonym used to describe and simplify a diverse indigenous population. At times, external pressures and circumstances have provided opportunities for unification. Most instructive was the PD (see chapter 1). Yet, once the broader political landscape changed, the movement split into Oeray and Pa-launsoeka camps, a demarcation whose ramifications continue to reverberate today. This trend in part appears to be repeating itself. Throughout the 1990s, Dayaks largely overcame fissures to entertain uniform aims; securing traditional land claims and obtaining *bupati* posts were foremost. Whereas the former is a complex process that is still going on, the latter was indisputably successful. Success bred new concerns, however. One was palpable disappointment with the first group of Dayak *bupati*. Critics saw them as dressed in New Order clothing, despite their putative reform credentials. Little changed in the way in which these *bupati*, who once enjoyed groundswells of support, governed their districts. When locals were asked to explain or describe their discontent, their answers were often couched in subgroup terms in statements such as: "Of course, the *bupati* has done little for us; he is not of our subethnicity [*sub-suku*]."[80] Complaints concentrated on corruption and the poor condition of local roads (see *Kalimantan Review*, March 2005).

The invocation of subgroup ethnicity is telling, because it relates to two significant differences between PD's decline and the current ethno-movement. One is the issue of leadership. While PD split into only two competing camps, without a discernable provincial leadership, today's movements threaten to splinter into a myriad of minor factions, some aligned along subgroup lines. Decentralization has facilitated this trend by concentrating greater authority at the district level. Dominant ethnic subgroups such as the Kanayatn in Pontianak district may come to dictate district politics. In districts without a dominant sub-Dayak majority, such as Sintang, increased subethnic friction is likely.

The other issue is violence. Whereas PD gained sustenance through electoral competition, in large part the present movements owe their momentum to mass killings. As internal tensions increase, so does the possibility of low-intensity but sustained intra-Dayak violence. Two serious clashes over illegal timber—one in March 2000 on the Sarawak border and the other in mid-2003 in Ketapang (Tumbang Titi subdistrict)—portend this disturbing trend (*Pontianak Post*, March 22, 2000; *Kalimantan Review*, October 2003).

6

Collective Violence in West Kalimantan in Comparative Perspective

It is hard to discern how characteristic the pattern of mass killing in West Kalimantan has been of collective violence in Indonesia. Peluso and Harwell (2001) make a compelling case for its uniqueness, a viewpoint to which I am sympathetic to a point. The upsurge in regional violence in the early post-Soeharto state, however, compels us to situate the riots in this vast, peripheral province within this broader phenomenon. Violence in West Kalimantan provides only one example of nonseparatist, civilian riots, and only one example of how complicated center-periphery relations and struggles for status and power become implicated in bloodshed.

To view mass violence in West Kalimantan in comparative perspective, I underscore two themes this book has developed. First, I emphasize the descriptive and explanatory power of the forms of violence. This is done to draw together the regional cases of massive, post-Soeharto riots in light of the absence of a single framework that adequately explains their varied spatial and multiform modalities. The ways in which Muslims or other ethnoreligious groups sought to make claims on the state in a period of rapid democratization may account for some of the mass violence that occurred from 1999 to 2000 (Bertrand 2004; Sidel 2001). However, as I mentioned in the introduction to this book, existing arguments shed little light on *why* the Moluccas and Poso turned extraordinarily violent while locales endowed with such similar causal factors as religious tensions, acute competition over local government posts, endemic corruption, influxes of official and voluntary migrants, criminal gangs, eviscerated traditional government systems, and land conflict did not. Neither did the country's nonseparatist regional violence begin with the Moluccas in 1999; rather, it began in West Kalimantan in 1997, that is, prior to Soeharto's resignation and the kickoff of the "post-Soeharto scramble."

The second theme I use in this comparative look is the usefulness of the study of ethnic riots over time. Such diachronic vantage points amply capture the complexity behind the genesis, protraction, and marked fluctuations that characterize incidents of mass violence in a given locale. In other words, this exercise seeks to explain not why violence emerged in these cases but why in a historical or contemporary context the identities underpinning violent mobilizations became politicized, and how those identities critically affected the principal modalities of the fighting.

In proposing two correctives to the ethnic violence literature, I organize this chapter as follows. First, a comparative perspective of regional riots in post-Soeharto Indonesia demonstrates the efficacy of ascriptive framings of violence. This is contrary to the common convention in the broader literature. In Indonesia's regions, the contrast pits lethal yet brief ethnic riots (in West and Central Kalimantan) against protracted religious clashes (in the Moluccas and Poso). The latter gained their lengthy dimensions due to the way religious framings aggregated opposing sides to demographic parity. This in turn attracted religious militants from elsewhere. To bolster the argument, I then explain why ethnic identifications predominate in Kalimantan and religious framings in the Moluccas and Poso. Second, I compare West Kalimantan with recurrent riots beyond Indonesia to help bridge a prominent divide in the literature: the oft-cited elite versus mass-led dualism in the sparking of riots. It is shown that in areas of recurrent riots over significant periods of time the instigation of collective violence has the capacity to obtain shifting qualities that oscillate between the two dyads. While one may predominate in provoking any given riot, the igniting of mass bloodshed over time need not be unidirectional. Although the case of West Kalimantan cannot definitively resolve these controversies in the scholarship, it does provide new and revealing evidence.

Ethnic versus Religious Riots

Comparing West Kalimantan with other Indonesian cases is best done with reference to the collective violence literature. These studies axiomatically use ethnicity as a broad categorical imperative to embrace racial, religious, regional, linguistic, tribal, and other signifiers of difference (Horowitz 1985; Kaufman 2001; Weingast 1998). Accordingly, diverse violent conflicts are construed as "ethnic" — for instance, Hindu-Muslim riots in India, Protestant-Catholic bloodshed in Northern Ireland, or Tamil-Sinhalese killings in Sri Lanka (Varshney 2002, 4–5). It is presumed, perhaps rightly in some cases, that more fine-grained descriptive ascriptions have no bearing on the principal forms or outcomes of violence. In other words, variance does not arise from the riots' ascriptive framings. Ethnic violence is thereby no more or less violent, deadly, or intense than its religious, linguistic, regional, racial, or tribal variants.

Riots in Indonesia's regions question the assumptions underlying this convention. The framing of violence tellingly mattered and the pivotal distinction rested with the ethnic or religious ascriptions of the fighting. This difference influences the duration of bloodshed. To illustrate this distinction, I draw on the four primary cases of nonseparatist, extensive riots in the outer islands following Soeharto's ouster: West Kalimantan, Central Kalimantan, the Moluccas,[1] and Poso. Assessments have persuasively shown that economic or political competition, not religion or ethnicity per se, were integral to the violence. Some have even suggested that the indigene versus settler dynamic is the most revealing (Acciaioli 2001). While I am in accord with these views, I aim to demonstrate the ways in which the framing of the violence dramatically and meaningfully altered the riots' trajectories regardless of their root cause. Here religion or ethnicity was dominant.

This contrast involves a prominent puzzle regarding Indonesia's post-Soeharto, regional unrest: ethnic clashes rocked West Kalimantan (1999, 2000, 2001) and Central Kalimantan (2001), and thousands died, but they were short-lived affairs. None lasted more than a few weeks. In contrast, similarly intense, "religious" violence in the Moluccas and Poso lasted some three and five years, respectively.[2] What accounts for this vital difference?

The answer is twofold. One is endogenous to these cases, the other exogenous. Internally, ethnic mobilizations in West and Central Kalimantan resulted in substantial demographic imbalances between combatants: majority Dayaks versus minority ethnic Madurese. The situation thus created was typical of civilian-on-civilian riots, in which one side almost always suffers disproportionately (Horowitz 2001). In both provinces, religious violence would have involved a wider range of participants and yielded a more even demographic distribution of them.

A quick glance at population statistics confirms this point. Ethnic Madurese men make up 5.4 percent of the male population in West Kalimantan.[3] In contrast, the province's Muslim male population is some 57 percent and about 64 percent if we restrict our purview to the province's conflict zone (BPS 2000a, 60, 24, 33, tables 9.3, 5.3, 6.3, respectively).[4] In Central Kalimantan, the same categories read 7.1, 74.2, and 78.4 percent (BPS 2000b, 58, 24, 33, tables 9.1, 5.3, 6.3, respectively).[5] While approximations, these percentages clearly demonstrate that had the violent mobilizations in West and Central Kalimantan had been along Muslim rather than ethnic Madurese lines, they would have yielded significantly different violent dynamics and outcomes.

Meanwhile, in the Moluccas[6] and Poso, religious violence aggregated various ethnic groups on opposing sides to relative parity to degrees greater than in the case of Kalimantan. Consider Ambon City, the epicenter of the Moluccan tragedy. Its male population was recorded at 32.8 percent for Muslims, and 63.4 percent for Protestants (BPS 2000c, 31, table 6.1). Moreover, similar parity was reflected in the male population in Poso, which was 55.8 percent Muslim and 39.6 percent Protestant (BPS 2000d, 33, table 6.3).

It is equally important to demonstrate how the different characteristics of the mobilizations in these riot cases affected the ensuing violence. We start with the case of the Moluccas. In Ambon City in January 1999 during Idul Fitri, the festive end of the Islamic fasting month, frenzied electioneering—highlighted by the movement of Protestant elites from Golkar to Megawati's PDI-P—provided the immediate context, in which a nondescript fight between a bus driver and local youths inexplicably escalated into citywide riots. At first, the selective targeting of native Christian Ambonese was along ethnic lines. They attacked such migrants as Butonese, Makassarese, and Bugis from Sulawesi, all of whom are Muslims (ICG 2000, 5). Soon thereafter, as the police stood by and the fighting engulfed the city, Ambon Island, and its nearby islands, the targets widened to include local Muslim Ambonese. By the time of the city's succeeding riot in July, which featured the burning of Catholic and Protestant churches, the clashes' Christian/Muslim ascriptions were fixed. Importantly, religious—not ethnic—demographic parity led to "an equilibrium of strength" on both sides (Aditjondro 2001, 113). In the meantime, a stalemated quality of violence prevented either side from gaining meaningful ground (Van Klinken 2001, 4).

Events in Poso unfolded in a fashion similar to those of Ambon City. A fight among youths in December 1998 curiously escalated into a riot that afflicted Poso Town. Competitive electioneering was also implicated. At stake was the vacant—and now under decentralization highly prized—*bupati* post. With a Muslim and a Protestant vying for the job, mainly Bugis Muslims were mobilized from surrounding areas and attacked Pamona Protestants. The latter were aided by members of a Pamona Protestant church from nearby Tentena. Fueled by apparent police indifference (HRW 2002, 15), these weeklong clashes led to a significant exodus of Pamona residents to Tentena—the capital of now North Pamona subdistrict—and as far north as Manado (Aditjondro 2004, 2). A sixteen-month lull ensued but was shattered by events reminiscent of the first riot when acute competition over a top government position precipitated attacks on Poso's Protestant inhabitants. Clashes dissipated once some six hundred soldiers from Makassar arrived. Again Christians suffered disproportionately.

Weeks later local Christian militias retaliated. In late May 2000, they slaughtered scores of Muslims and in the process marked Poso in the international arena (alongside the Moluccas) as a hot spot of "extremist" religious violence. By this time—commonly called the third phase of the violence—the battle lines in identity formation had been drawn: indigenous Christians from upland ethnic groups such as the Pamona, Lore, and Mori coalesced; likewise, on the Muslim side of things: the Makasarese, Tojo, Luwu, Bugis, and Gorontalo came together (Aditjondro 2004, 3; Aragon 2001). As in the Moluccas, thick religious framing and attendant mobilizations had contributed to a balanced demographic dynamic that underpinned the riots' seesaw characteristics. This was in marked contrast to the one-sided affairs in Kalimantan.

Exogenous Factors

The second factor that contributed to the contrasting duration of violent conflict was external to these four cases. In Kalimantan, *ethnic* riots kept the killers local. Despite its affective command, ethnicity's symbolic resonance—and the discourse surrounding the riots' interpretations (Brass 2003)—proved more parochial. Simply put, it was easier to contain than that of religion's symbolic resonance. This was particularly so in a country where religious politicization had been spiraling precariously, and in particular, where political Islam was making greater inroads and claims on state power (Hefner 2000). Incidents in Kalimantan, therefore, were devoid of mass mobilizations of ethnic brethren from external areas to prolong the violence. Spectacularly, such was not the case in the Moluccas and Poso.

In the former, the equilibrium noted above was "totally destroyed" (Aditjondro 2001, 113) when these religious clashes drew Muslim militants to the region (see also Huxley 2002, 58). The arrival in mid-2000 of some three thousand members of the Java-based Laskar Jihad militia marked a distinctly new phase. The perception that the Wahid administration was indifferent to Christian killings of Muslims prompted militias to depart for the Moluccas. In particular, a massacre of some five hundred Muslims in late December 1999 in Tobelo, Halmahera (North Moluccas) instigated massive demonstrations in Jakarta. Subsequent organizing and the formation of militias received tacit support from well-known political personalities in Jakarta. More provocative was the aid the military provided the militias. Militia members were allowed to set sail from Surabaya—despite threats of arrest by President Wahid—and upon reaching the islands were equipped with weapons (ICG 2001b; ISAI 2000).[7] Whether security forces consciously ignored or backed the Laskar Jihad (and other similar militias), both facilitated a systematic campaign of terror to create local enclaves of Muslims and Christians across the southern islands of Moluccas (ICG 2000, 12). There are still many unanswered questions and controversies surrounding this tragedy, which left more than eight thousand dead and perhaps as many as half a million displaced.[8] One thing is certain, however. The religious symbolism of and the concomitant discourse generated by the fighting contributed greatly to its protracted nature. This was also in part a result of the parity of opposing sides, which was then altered by the drawing of militant non-Moluccans into the morass.

In Poso, religious riots also drew a number of radical militias to defend besieged Muslim communities and wage war on Christians.[9] As in the Moluccan case, uninvolved in the fightings' incipient stages, they arrived in response to well-publicized killings of Muslims. A massacre at an Islamic boarding school south of Poso Town in late May 2000 brought members of the Jemmah Islamiyah and the high number of Muslim deaths in Buyung Katedo village a year later prompted Laskar Jihad associates to arrive. Again, as in the Moluccas, their presence tipped the balance in favor of Muslims and subsequently resulted in an upsurge in anti-Christian attacks (HRW 2002, 11-12, 21, 23). In fact, due in part to the presence of militias and in part to pressure applied to the Indonesian government by the United States, which in an immediate post-9/11 environment sought to close down a potential "factory" of Islamic terrorists (Van Klinken 2005, 85), a peace pact was signed in December 2001. While the accord halted the mass mobilizations, it did not snuff the killings completely. Targeted shootings and periodic bombings continued well into 2005 and 2006.

Religious identifications influenced the fighting in these two cases in two ways that complicate this picture. They still, however, buttress the argument that religious framings prolonged and worsened the killings. First, such ascriptions not only tied the violence closely to national politicking and sectarian polarization but also implicated international actors. In the Moluccas, Muslims received material and (likely) personnel support from the Middle East and the southern Philippines, while Christian groups based in Europe (where exiles of the former separatist movement in the Moluccas [Republik Maluku Selatan, or RMS] and their descents are numerous) and Australia gave Ambonese Christians material aid. In Poso, religious networks not only extended to Java and Jakarta (Van Klinken 2005, 83), but they also reached beyond the country. Gunrunning from the southern Philippines was routine (Sangaji 2004, 6), and the establishment of terrorist training camps with links to al Qaida became a matter of public debate (HRW 2002, 12–14).

The second complication was the fact that police and army personnel became involved in the fighting to degrees far greater than they did in Kalimantan. Beyond efforts to gain materially, security force involvement was a result of emotional attachments formed along sectarian lines. This became evident in the early stages of the riots. In the Moluccas, the police, comprising mainly locals, sided with Christians, while army reinforcements from Sulawesi sided with their religious (and ethnic) brethren (HRW 1999). More detrimentally, as the violence dragged on and attendant enmities deepened, so too did security force participation. Military personnel were frequently seen providing cover for Muslim rioters, particularly once the Laskar Jihad arrived. A military spokesperson admitted that a considerable number of security personnel were "emotionally involved" (quoted in ICG 2000, 10). Moreover, implications of sectarian cleavages among the security apparatus led to a complicated matrix of military-on-military, police-on-police, and police versus military confrontations and killings.[10] Although less evident (and publicized) than in the Moluccan case, the militias in Poso received tacit and implicit backing from the security forces. On occasion the latter fought alongside Muslims and benefited from the selling of arms

(Aditjondro 2004; Huxley 2002, 62; Sangaji 2004). At other times, Christian groups were favored (HRW 2002, 23, 28).

Thus, the evidence suggests that the ethnic or religious ascriptions applied to collective violence in Indonesia's regions matter. Here the religious violence lasted far longer than its ethnic counterpart. Two dynamics contributed to this difference. First, the ethnically aligned combatants were not demographically balanced. In terms of religious identifications, in contrast, the groups were relatively balanced, which contributed to the protracted nature of the fighting. Second, the symbolism of ethnicity tended to keep the violence local, precisely what religious symbolism did not do. In a country of polarizing religious tensions, religious sentiments resonated in national (and international) spheres, which resulted in the participation of militants from elsewhere.[11]

Historical Lineages

The pattern described above begs the question of why. What explains *ethnic* violence in Kalimantan and *religious* clashes in the Moluccas and Poso? Answers to this question relate to themes developed in this book in two important ways. First, that Indonesia's worsening religious strains precipitated the bloodshed in the Moluccas and Poso has been well established; these were two hitherto peaceful, though not tension free, places. Observers point to the violent manifestations of the late New Order to substantiate this politicization at the national level: church burnings in Surabaya in 1996, anti-Christian riots in Situbondo (East Java) in October 1996 and in Tasikmalaya (West Java) (December 1996), gang-related yet religiously ascribed clashes in Ketapang (Jakarta) in November 1998, and retaliatory attacks against Muslims in Kupang (West Timor) days later. Their writings, however, fail to consider why *ethnic* violence erupted in Kalimantan amid this maelstrom of religious politicization.

Second, answers to the question posed above can be found in the approach this book has adopted: underscoring the contextual historical factors that regulate social relations while prefiguring the choices actors and collectivities make in violent collective action. The presence or absence of recurrent riots (or related mass mobilizations) is particularly telling. In West and Central Kalimantan such violent lineages established the ethnic characteristics of the post-Soeharto violence. In the Moluccas and Poso the absence of recent mass strife made these areas more susceptible to the national politicization of religion, thus bringing the sectarian identifications of the bloodletting to the fore.

As this book has shown, ethnicity in West Kalimantan as a mobilizing marker is a product of Dutch colonial practices and domination, which forged an increasingly monolithic Dayak ethnic identity out of a diverse autochthonous population whose greatest commonality at this time was its non-Muslim beliefs. Ethnicity as a political cleavage was embodied in the vibrancy of the Daya Unity Party (PD) in the 1950s (see chapter 1). More important was the decisive role of collective violence. The Dutch deployed "Dayaks"—not "Christians"—to quash local unrest, as did the early New Order authorities when they wished to raid Chinese villages. Given the minor Dayak-Madurese riots of the 1970s and 1980s, by the time the extensive anti-Madurese clashes occurred in the late New Order and early post-Soeharto periods, their ethnic underpinnings—not the violence itself—was determined.

In what is now the province of Central Kalimantan, ethnicity has also been the politically dominant cleavage. Decades prior to the emergence of the PD in West Kalimantan, an elite group of educated Dayaks had formed in Central Kalimantan. With the help of Protestant missions (Ukur 1971) and concerned over growing links between Banjar Malays and Java-based Muslim organizations such as NU and Muhammadiyah, the urbanites established associations that were ethnic in orientation. Formed in 1919, the Dajakbond (Dayak Union) was later transformed into the Serikat Dajak and the Pakat Dajak. In 1938 the latter became the Comite Kesadaran Bangsa Dajak (Committee for Dayak Tribal Awareness) (Riwut 1958; Van Klinken 2004). Ethnicity, not religion, defined the boundaries of membership in these organizations, despite their Protestant leadership and support from the Christian missions.

Here, as in West Kalimantan, collective violence was also crucial, although it came in different forms. The 1950s witnessed a violent struggle to create a province separate from the existing one of South Kalimantan. Framed ethnically, the battle was fought in the name of the Ngaju Dayak, the area's dominant ethnic subgroup. This was so in light of the movement's Protestant leadership and the fact that this movement, which won its province in mid-1957, was in part a reaction against the religiously inspired Darul Islam revolt in South Kalimantan, whose aim was to establish an Islamic state (Miles 1976; Van Klinken 2006).

Finally, recurrent riots in West Kalimantan helped to determine ethnicity as the mobilizing marker in its neighboring province. To be sure, Madurese-Dayak tensions were taut, as both sides fiercely competed in Central Kalimantan's thriving black market economy of cutting and smuggling timber (and illegal gold mining) (McCarthy 2004). It was in this context that occasional gang fights and individual murders took place, none of which, it should be stressed, escalated into deadly riots. But, the latest incidents in West Kalimantan impressed such Dayak ethnic leaders in Central Kalimantan as K. M. A. Usop,[12] a member of the province's most visible Dayak organization and the one that was most responsible for the anti-Madurese bloodshed—the Central Kalimantan Dayak and Regional Consultative Institute (LMMDD-KT).[13] For instance, LMMDD-KT's version of the 2001 riots—a two-volume compilation known as the *Buku Merah* (Red Books)[14]—opens with reference to the lesson the LMMDD-KT learned from the expulsion of Madurese from Sambas in 1999, namely, that negotiated peace with the Madurese was doomed to fail (*perdamaian-perdamaian yang gagal*). We can thus only imagine that the LMMDD-KT leadership was enticed by the "solution" that events in Sambas presented, that is, the expulsion of the Madurese. This is not to say that the Dayak-Madurese violence simply spread from West to Central Kalimantan—a far too common misperception that ignores the fact that two years separated these incidents. As a source of inspiration, however, the link was unmistakable. In fact, if the events in Sanggau Ledo (1996–97), and especially Sambas in 1999, had not taken place, it is doubtful that the riots in Central Kalimantan would have assumed the scale that they did, with some 150,000 Madurese expelled from the province, leaving anywhere from 1,500 to 3,000 dead in the process (C. Smith 2005, 1).

To be sure, the expulsions that began in mid-February 2001 were not predetermined.[15] One viable argument holds that LMMDD-KT escalated the conflict to dispatch a prominent competitor from the region's vibrant black market economy and as a means of capturing the newly empowered and lucrative regional administration under the auspices of decentralization (Van Klinken 2002). While these are likely, two other dimensions of the violence were more certain; in fact, they were utterly predictable. One was the targeting of the Madurese. West Kalimantan's recent history made this so. While the Madurese represented entrenched competition for Dayak associations involved in the illegal (and legal) timber trade, these illicit economies consisted of *multi*-ethnic actors and networks. Viewed from the perspective of economic competition, presumably other ethnic groups *could have* been targeted.

The second certainty is that Usop and his gang would mobilize followers along ethnic lines. If they wished to actualize their designs, they had no other option. For one thing, Usop himself is Muslim. In Central (and East) Kalimantan, being Dayak *and* Muslim creates less dissidence (psychologically, discursively, and politically) than it does in West Kalimantan. More important, however, was the legacy of Central Kalimantan's history of collective action and the recent riots in West Kalimantan. Having seen in the Moluccas and Poso what *religious* violence can do—like draw militants from elsewhere—LMMDD-KT was at pains to stress the ethnic framing of its anti-*Madurese* mobilizations. Revealingly, a statement from late February 2001 signed by Usop (and one Bahing Djimat) in the aforementioned Red Books concluded with the message: "This is an *inter-ethnic conflict,* not an *inter-religious one*" ("adalah *konflik antara etnik* dan *bukan antara agama*") (emphasis in the original).[16] All told, a contingent history of politics, collective violence, and mobilizations in West and Central Kalimantan produced a teleology: the determined nature of ethnicity as a mobilizing tool in collective violence.

The Moluccas and Poso

In contrast, the sociohistorical forces and political factors that molded the religious ascriptions of violence in the Moluccas and Poso were more complex and variable than those in Kalimantan. Here the malleability of ascriptive identifications exposed these regions to the winds of religious politicization that have been sweeping the country. Divides along religious lines in these cases were not fixed a priori but solidified once the riots gained unprecedented proportions.

In the Moluccas, religious cleavages were a result of the region's long history of interaction with European colonialism. Due to early Christian influences—from both Portuguese and Dutch sources—colonial authorities relied heavily on these converts who legally became "Dutch" citizens. Many served in the colonial army (KNIL) and others as domestic help (at one point as slaves) in Batavia (today's Jakarta). Locally, the civil service was the domain of members of the local Christian elite, who were beneficiaries of Western, missionary education. Ambonese Muslims, though prominent in trade, were marginalized.

One theme of this book is that collective violence is rarely, if ever, historically determined. In the case of the Moluccas, neither were its religious identifications. The intensity and scale of these riots were unprecedented. Nothing is comparable in the region's recent past. By the same token, the Moluccas does entertain a history of separatism. This ill-fated movement—known by the initials RMS (Republik Maluku Selatan, or Republic of the South Moluccas)—was launched following Indonesia's independence, when Christian Moluccans feared the loss of privilege and of being a minority in a majority Muslim state. Reprisals against Moluccans in Java, especially against KNIL soldiers, in the chaotic and brutal period following the Japanese surrender and the proclamation of Indonesian independence—known as the *bersiap* period—were severe and traumatic. This said, secessionism was not divinely inspired alone, for local Ambonese Muslims also participated in the failed movement (Chauvel 1990).

To be sure, politics in the Moluccas under the New Order tended to develop along religious lines, particularly in the late 1980s and early 1990s, when Soeharto turned to Islamic groups to cultivate new bases of political support (Bertrand 2004, 118–21), which consequently exacerbated tensions between Muslims and Christians (HRW 1999). What the "greening" of Jakarta's politics meant locally was the opening of significant—and for the Christian elite threatening—inroads for Muslims into the Moluccan bureaucracy (Van Klinken 2001).

Yet relations between indigenous Ambonese Christian and Muslim migrants (mainly from Sulawesi) constituted another axis of conflict (HRW 1999, 10). Despite a long history, migration of Muslims from Sulawesi to the Moluccas grew appreciably under the New Order. This influx gave Muslims in Ambon a slight numerical advantage in what was traditionally seen as a Christian stronghold (HRW 1999, 2). Thus, as was mentioned above, Protestant Ambonese first viewed the incipient clashes through an antimigrant prism (Sukma 2005, 2, 5; Van Klinken 2001, 4). Small-scale fights of this kind were commonplace (HRW 1999). This time, however, the violence escalated suddenly and shockingly, engulfing first the city, then the island, and finally the region. Amid escalation and expansion, which tied the violence closely to national political developments (Bertrand 2004), the religious framings of the riots consolidated. Patricia Spyer notes that "much has been written about this conflict which *over time* consolidated two polarized religiosities—one Christian and one Muslim—as the war's main obvious opponents," and that with the arrival of Java-based militias the violence was "further characterized by a deepening of the religious definition of the opposing parties and the crystallization of relevant extremist discourses" (2002, 22, 26, emphasis in the original). Another commentator similarly observes that dozens "if not hundreds, of small, localized battles, not exclusively fought out between Christians and Muslims [became] part of a single major struggle between Islam and Christianity on the presentation level" (Bräuchler 2003, 126–27). Regarding this struggle, it is widely believed that figures in networks based on Java (ISAI 2000)—supported by inflammatory tabloid and sectarian reporting on the disturbances, the wide distribution of video and digital imagery of the bloodshed (Spyer 2002), and battles fought in cyberspace (Bräuchler 2003)—worked to encourage this violence and frame it as religiously inspired. Many elites in Jakarta, and some in the Moluccas, sought to gain from such sectarian framings (Aditjondro 2001).

Poso is the most difficult case. The social and colonial history of present-day Central Sulawesi has parallels with that of West Kalimantan (see chapter 1). Interactions between stateless upland communities and Muslim coastal powers figured prominently. Later, facilitated by the introduction of the Dutch-led ethical policy, missionaries introduced Christianity into the highlands to form a bulwark against encroaching Muslim proselytizing. In the process, supravillage social and ethnic groupings coalesced, yielding such ethnicities as the Pamona (Aragon 2001; Coté 1996). In addition, this region has long attracted Muslim migrants. Consistent with the three other violent conflict cases, this migration increased noticeably under the New Order. In Central Sulawesi in particular, the opening of the highlands following the construction of the trans-Sulawesi road was instrumental.

So, as in the Moluccas, Central Sulawesi constituted a complicated matrix of ethnic and religious divides. The region's social distance from Jakarta, however, distinguished it from the Moluccan case. Due to their long-standing relationship with the Dutch authorities, Moluccan descendants and migrants are prominent and numerous in the nation's capital, which ties the islands more closely to social and political developments there. It does so far more than in Central Sulawesi (or West and Central Kalimantan). The high visibility of Ambonese gang members in Jakarta, hundreds of whom were deported to Ambon after the fights in Ketapang (Jakarta) in November 1998 that preceded the outbreak of clashes in Ambon, is a case in point. There are no Pamona gangs (or Dayak gangs for that matter) in Jakarta. Thus, as in the case of Kalimantan, the social distance between Central Sulawesi and Jakarta would plausibly favor ethnic mobilizations. Indeed, reports on the riots noted the saliency of ethnic alliances (Aragon 2001; HRW 2002; Sukma 2005, 5).

By the same token, Central Sulawesi had not experienced bloodletting on this scale. Its last major disturbance dated from the 1950s, when its peoples were caught between two separatist yet religiously inspired movements—the Permesta movement in North Sulawesi and Kahar Muzakkar's Darul Islam insurgency in South Sulawesi. Forced to defend themselves, villagers in the Poso Lake region formed an ethnically oriented security militia called the Youth Movement of Central Sulawesi (Aragon 2001, 52–53). But the organization (and its attendant movement) was short-lived and did not embark on massive, long-lasting mobilizations.

As in the Moluccas, while religious tensions in Poso worsened under the New Order, so did indigenous-settler relations as migrants poured into the area to buy land and take advantage of the high price cacao was fetching on the world market due to the severe depreciation of the Indonesian rupiah (Acciaioli 2001; Aragon 2001, 56). In all, as in the Moluccan case, lacking recent histories of mass violence, Poso was riddled with multiple, crosscutting tensions, a situation that left it susceptible to the influence of national-level, religious politicization. In the interest of certain actors, and with the help of a partisan media, a complicated affair of religious, ethnic, economic, and indigenous-settler dynamics was turned into a straightforward religious clash, as reflected the headbands worn by the raiders—white for Muslims, red for Christian (HRW 2002, 16–17). On this point, Van Klinken puts it clearly: "The identification of 'Muslim' and 'Christian' as the key categories of familiarity was not foreordained. Place-of-origin ethnicity was . . . another possibility. . . . But the choice of religion to shape categories in the public mind . . . clearly created greater scope for coalition building. . . . It was a choice made by the urban brokers with a vision not tied to the land. The rural farming folk were mainly interested in resisting the expansion of Bugis settlement, and would have been better served by an indigenous peoples' or a land rights discourse" (2005, 84). Tragically, this redirection and simplification—Muslim versus Christian—perpetuated the bloodshed, tragically taking hundreds, if not thousands, of lives in the process.

Beyond Indonesia

What can attention to these cases illustrate about the phenomenon of collective violence more generally? Thus far, this chapter stands as a small corrective to the ethnic violence literature. In short, ascriptive markings of violence can be determinative, and in this case, the duration of the bloodshed was decisive. Rather than using them broadly, ethnic signifiers require careful and contextual circumscription when applied to collective violence.

This corrective to the literature is consistent with a theme this book has stressed: understanding the salient forms of violence in a diachronic framework. Using the same approach, I put forth a second corrective by placing the case of West Kalimantan in comparative perspective with recurrent riot cases elsewhere. This is done to surmount a prevalent dichotomy in the literature: the elite-mass dichotomy. Some studies underscore the role of the former in collective violence (Gagnon 1994–95; Hardin 1995; HRW 1995; J. Snyder 2000). Meanwhile, others emphasize mass-led dynamics (Daniels 1996; Hinton 1998; Kapferer 1988; Petersen 2003; Posen 1993).[17]

The elite-instigated camp is the outgrowth of a longer tradition of theorizing on ethnic politics. These scholars shifted the mainstream notion of ethnicity as a timeless and immutable essence to a malleable and context-specific tool. Importantly, they saw ethnicity as susceptible to manipulation by traders and political entrepreneurs for their own ends (Bates 1983; Brass 1991; Cohen 1969). Building on this instrumentalist tradition to explain violent conflict, Hardin, for instance, employs a strict rational-choice perspective. He maintains that violence emerges when a self-interested person of power successfully convinces a group that its interests coincide with his or her individual motivations. When this happens, he warns that "the result is often appalling" (1995, 5). Another scholar, Jack Snyder, widens Hardin's narrow methodological individualist approach to place the emphasis on influential groups, but he still highlights the role of pugilistic demagogues in newly democratizing states who revive nationalist sentiments to deadly effect (2000, 19, 32).

Scholars that champion group-led processes in the fomenting of ethnic violence display a wider range of approaches than the (strict or loose) rational-choice perspective that underlines the elite-instigated view. Take the work of the international relations scholar Barry Posen and that of the anthropologist E. Valentine Daniels. Posen's influential security-dilemma hypothesis sees the inadvertent arming of opposing sides and distrust as the root of ethnic conflict. In an environment of state collapse and a concomitant breakdown in communication, one group arms for defensive purposes. An opposing side misreads the group's intentions, however, and arms in turn. This dynamic escalates to the point where violence is inescapable. For Daniels, the struggle over recognition lies at the bottom of ethnic strife. In his discursive-heavy formulation, he notes that ethnic strife "results when the discordance that obtains between epistemic and ontological discursive practices leads to a quest . . . and a plea for recognition of new identities constituted by these practices" (1996, 67). Here, it is not important to dwell on the specifics of dissonance between Posen's and Daniels's approaches. Instead I call attention to a broader similarity, that is, the downplaying of malevolent elites in the initiation of ethnic violence.

By the same token, ethnic riots need not consist exclusively of either manipulative elites or mass-dominant elements. This observation is not novel; it is something a range of scholars from different disciplines has begun to acknowledge. The sociologist James Rule concludes that civilian violence is ordinarily a mix of both "expressive" and "instrumental" elements (1988, 189, 244). The political scientist Paul Brass (2003, 358) seeks an "intermediate space" between spontaneity and planning, while the anthropologist Veena Das (1990, 28) argues for congruency between "highly organized" crowds and those that "draw upon repositories of unconscious images." Informed observers as diverse as Brubaker and Laitin (1998, 446), Stuart Kaufman (2001 12, 205), Arjun Appadurai (1998, 912, note 7), Michael Keith (1993, 168–69), Michael Brown (2001, 15), and Michael Mann (2005, 22–23) have remarked similarly.

In large part, I am sympathetic to these observations; there is much evidence in West Kalimantan to confirm these views. Innovative research conducted by Roger Petersen (2003) that attempts to construct an emotion-based theory of collective violence, however, points in an instructive direction. Petersen nears the mark when he maintains that one direction—strategic elites or masses—will normally prevail. He posits that "the influences go both ways, but it is an important matter to determine which direction is dominant" (35). Petersen's own inclination is clear when he writes that "if this structural and mass-oriented approach is able to identify patterns of ethnic conflict, then the critical explanatory role of elite strategy must be questioned" (35). There is much truth in Petersen's contention, but it is his assertion that, once determined, a singular direction will take hold indefinitely to which I take exception. Evidence presented from West Kalimantan in this book has demonstrated that elite manipulation does not necessarily prevent mass-led factors from containing substantial efficacy at other times. To reiterate, my emphasis here does not pertain to the processes of mass violence as it gains momentum. At this escalation stage, the mix of mass and elite-led elements is undeniable. Instead, I pay particular attention to the outbreak or incipient phase of riots. At these early stages, it can be demonstrated that in areas of recurrent collective violence over a significant period of time, a shifting logic between elite-fomented and mass-led dynamics typically takes hold.

This has been the case in West Kalimantan, where the sparking of mass violence has contained both elements but has done so in shifting balance. Elite-fomented violence was conspicuous in the 1967 Chinese pogrom, in which New Order army and Dayak elites played conspicuous roles. Elites were also prominent in the 1999 FKPM-led riots in Sambas and in the 2000 antirefugee riot in Pontianak influenced by Governor Aswin. Conversely, the province has also hosted incidents without apparent elite instigation. The minor riots of the 1970s and 1980s, the first phase of the 1997 bloodshed in Sanggau Ledo, and the antirefugee fighting in Pontianak in 2001 were illustrative of this phenomenon.

Calcutta

The back-and-forth dynamics in the sparking of riots can be found in recurrent clashes that have occurred over extensive periods of time outside Indonesia.[18] Exemplary is the nearly a half century of riots in the Indian city of Calcutta, whose repetitive riots began in the late nineteenth century as a steady stream of Urdu-speaking, Muslim migrant laborers poured into the European-owned jute factories located along the city's northern fringes. Intensified communal consciousness and tension among mill hands led to minor fisticuffs, especially over the question of cow sacrifices. Shortly thereafter, in 1891, sparked by the demolition of an alleged mosque, Calcutta's "first recorded riot" (S. Sarkar 1983, 60) occurred. Meanwhile similar clashes during religious festivals continued, with sizable incidents noted in 1894 and 1895 (Chakrabarty 1990, 151).

Historians have not detected elite machinations behind these incidents. They have, however, for what is considered Calcutta's "first ever large-scale riot" (Chakrabarty 1990, 164). Like the 1891 episode before it, this riot of 1897 arose from a land dispute over a purported mosque. This time inflammatory roles in the three-day clash played by influential religious leaders—led by a pan-Islamist, Hajji Zakaria, and merchants with connections to labor organizers—were prominent. Using mass violence as a means, the hajjis sought to promote a pan-Islam ideology, while resentful merchants struck back at Hindu Marwari traders—originally from Rajasthan—who had made great inroads in Calcutta and Bengal's countryside (Chakrabarty 1990, 164–77).

Following this elite-initiated riot, Calcutta witnessed a sizable lull in mass violence that is typical in areas that experience recurrent riots. The effects of World War I, however, took its toll on Bengal's denizens. Against the backdrop of the socioeconomic deprivations caused by World War I and the publication by an Anglo-French paper of a provocative anti-Muslim article, large-scale violence broke out. Regarding this riot of 1918, there is a conflict of interpretation. Historians Broomfield (1968) and Suranjan Das (1991) both concur that mounting frustration among Muslim League leaders over anti-Muslim developments on the larger political scene—rumors of a British-backed Hindu Raj were rife, while anti-Muslim clashes earlier in the year had buffeted the state of Bihar—contributed to the bloodshed. They also agree that the reasons for bloodshed can be traced to a widening split in the league between its old guard, which had allied itself with local Hindu gentry (*bhadralok*) in opposition to the British, and younger, English-educated radicals who accused the established elite of craven self-interest. The two historians diverge, however, on what happened in the lead-up to the riot.

For the first time in Bengal's history, Broomfield maintains, "an attempt was made to use mob violence as a political weapon" (1968, 167). He cites evidence implicating local Muslim leaders, who began comprehending organized violence as a means of political action and who selected early September for the riot due to a convergence of several religious festivals. In contrast, Das purports that this bloodshed, which left forty-three dead and caused extensive damage to Marwari property, "began from below and was carried to a point far beyond that which established leaders would have approved" (1991, 74). "Communal excitement, once fanned, developed a logic of its own, quite independent of elite concerns and interests" (66). For the purpose of the argument I am proposing, whether one sides with the Broomfield's elite-led or Das's mass-led viewpoint, when Calcutta's riots are considered diachronically, from the pre-1918 minor incidents to this 1918 event and those to be described below, a shifting dynamic between elite- and mass-instigated violence is undeniable.

In April 1919, a day of protest in which all shops would close—known as a *hartal*—sparked mass-led clashes that left six dead (McPherson 1974, 50). Incidentally, the prospect of further bloodshed led Hindu and Muslim leaders to seek rapprochement, a development embodied in the growth of the Swaraj Party. Joint anticolonial efforts soon fizzled, however, as mass-led incidents grew increasingly frequent, especially over the question of music played before mosques and cow sacrifices (McPherson 1974, 82–83, 87). By the time mass riots ravaged Calcutta in 1926 the bloodshed had "wiped out memories of a common fight" (T. Sarkar 1987, 11–12).

The widespread violence of 1926 would swing the pendulum toward elite instigation. In addition to the aforementioned clashes, local unease grew over the Marwari stranglehold on the distribution of goods, labor unrest, and acute electioneering for Bengal's Legislative Council. While the formation of a distinctly Muslim identity during this period has attracted considerable scholarly attention, Chatterji (1994) reminds us that a parallel process among *bhadralok* kept pace, as evidenced by the mushrooming of Hindu purist and revivalist groups. Not to be outdone, Marwari merchants organized a number of local defense groups to preempt attacks.

Characteristic of ethnic riots (Horowitz 2001), the 1926 bloodletting comprised distinct phases. Sparked by a procession of five hundred persons in front of a mosque, the first wave (April 2–14) left forty-four dead and another six hundred wounded. Later that month a street brawl ignited a deadlier round; the third and concluding phase left thirty dead. Historians point to the conspicuous hand local Muslim elites, led by the Muslim deputy mayor who sought to unite the Muslim vote through the deliberate use of violence, had in fomenting the bloodletting (S. Das 1991, 95–99).

Twenty years later, elite-instigated violence repeated itself on the streets of Calcutta, this time on a grander scale. In the two decades in between, Muslim separatist and Hindu fundamentalist identities and related organizations had crystallized (Chatterji 1994, 103, 192–203), while feverish labor organizing added "considerably to the general militancy of these years" (T. Sarkar 1987, 49). So, too, did the economic hardships that the Great Depression wrought. The situation reached catastrophic proportions when Bengal's "man-made" famine of 1943 drove streams of hungry rural folk into Calcutta's slums.

Amid the sharpening Hindu-Muslim polarization, the Muslim League organized a series of pro-Pakistan rallies in Calcutta, the largest of which took place on Direct Action Day (August 16, 1946) with crowds estimated between one and five hundred thousand. As the protestors dispersed late in the day, an organized few began attacking Hindu shopkeepers. The violence quickly escalated and continued unabated for three days, constituting what was pre-independence Bengal's bloodiest affair. Historians concur that the leaders of such organizations as the Muslim League and the Bharat Sevashram Sangha, the volunteer wing of the purist Hindu Mahasabha association backed by Marwari merchants, orchestrated the slaughters that left some four thousand dead and another ten thousand injured. Suranjan Das, for instance, observes that the riot was "highly organized . . . and [had] direct links with institutional politics" (1991, 176). In addition to the great loss of life in Calcutta, this riot has the dubious distinction of sparking the chain-reaction of killings known as the Partition Riots, that rocked Bihar, Punjab, and elsewhere for months and claimed tens of thousands of lives.

Kano

A brief exploration of the history of riots in the northern Nigerian city of Kano also illuminates the shifting logic of mass-led/elite-led violence over time. The origins of its recurrent riots (and those of northern Nigeria more generally) date from the early 1950s, a time of significant economic, social, and demographic change (Plotnicov 1971, 297). For instance, a historic center of urban trade and Islamic learning, Kano saw its population rise by some 650 percent between 1911 and 1962. In part, an industrial boom turned this town once dominated by the Muslim Hausa-Fulani ethnic group,[19] into a magnet for such southerners as the Catholic Ibo and Protestant Yoruba (Paden 1973, 16, 19, 26–27). Their presence fueled stiff economic competition. Likewise antagonism grew over employment opportunities, especially in government offices where Ibo proficiency in English gave them an advantage. All told, as Paden recounts (1973, 313–17, 335), these dynamics fed the formation of new communal identities — one "southern," the other "northern" where bouts of mass violence would imbue these nascent identities with new meaning.

In April 1953, northern representatives of the federal government were harangued in parliament in Lagos and harassed by street toughs outside the building (Bello 1962, 133–34). In protest, in May the Northern Peoples Congress (NPC) marched against a tour by Yoruba and Ibo parties in Kano. Soon thereafter, dozens of Hausa, having been mobilized from outside Kano by NPC leaders, went on a rampage, killing several dozen Ibo and injuring scores more. Interestingly, the Yoruba were unscathed (Bello 1962, 136–37). "The memory" of these elite-instigated riots, writes Paden (1973, 322), "remained strong in Kano throughout 1950s and 1960s. In many ways this violence crystallized the sense of northern and southern communities in Kano."

During this period northern nationalism grew in Kano in response to strong southern support for a federal framework. The policy known as northernization exemplified the north's desire to retain a degree of autonomy. Northernization featured the barring of nonnatives (read southerners) from owning land, preferential economic policies, and the promotion of the Hausa language. But following the coup of January 1966 in Lagos, concern was rife among party leaders in Kano over southern domination of the federal government (First 1970, 311–12).

On May 28, 1966, with a permit in hand, students in Kano rallied to express their concern over Ibo domination of the national government. The next day organized gangs of Hausa "hooligans" and "uprooted young men" began attacking Ibo (Paden 1973, 333–34). This elite-instigated rioting lasted three to four days and claimed possibly as many as six hundred lives. For Horowitz, that the Ibo, not Yoruba, were politicizing local social relations explains why they were selectively targeted by Hausa elites and rioters. In short, Ibo represented a serious political threat to northerners (2001, 133, 166–67).

Later that September, another elite-led but far deadlier Ibo pogrom occurred in Kano. First reports that proposals at the national constitutional conference to increase the number of northern states threatened the patronage at the state government level upon which party elites and contractors in Kano thrived. In response, they undertook the "deliberate and systematic organization" of mass violence. Planning included the transfer of officials who had helped stymie the May killings (First 1970, 328–29) and a redeployment of the army that brought Hausa troops back to Kano, replacing their Ibo counterparts (Paden 1971, 135). In late September, these troops transformed what was sporadic violence into a torrent of bloodshed by firing on retreating Ibo with automatic weapons (O'Connell 1967, 99, n.2). These shootings fomented horrific killings across the north. A plausible estimate of deaths ranged from eight to ten thousand (Paden 1971, 135); more than one million Ibo who were displaced by the violence fled to the country's Eastern Region.

Subsequently, ethnic riots waned in Kano. Then in the early 1980s, distinctively religious rioting took shape, as did characteristically shifting elite- and mass-instigated rioting. An incident in October 1982, for instance, was sparked by a protest by Muslim students over the proximity of a church to a mosque. The consequent mass-led clash left some forty-four dead, among whom were now included both Ibo and Yoruba

(Boer 2003, 39–41). In October 1991 another anti-Christian riot hit Kano. The bloodshed—this time elite inspired—stemmed from the objection of local Muslims to an evangelistic campaign organized by the Christian Association of Nigeria (CAN), which was the country's most organized and active voice for Christians. That CAN pressed ahead with its program over vociferous protests angered Muslim clerics, who mobilized attacks on Christians (Falola 1998, 211–13). The two to three days of violence took hundreds of lives. Meanwhile, in early 1995 the arrest of two Hausa for burgling a car owned by an Ibo initiated a riot that lacked overt elite instigation. Possibly as many as two hundred perished in the daylong clash (Boer 2003, 46–50).

Kano's volatility persisted into the country's postmilitary period. Like that of Indonesia, Nigeria's transition from military rule, which began in May 1999, was marred by a rash of ethnic riots whose death toll may have been as high as twenty thousand. Reasons cited for the violence are numerous. Popular culprits include the absence of good governance and effective citizenship (Lewis 2003) and the rise of ethnonationalism reflected in the mushrooming of youth-oriented paramilitary organizations (Harnischfeger 2003; Ikelegbe 2001; Ukiwo 2003). One commentator's observation, however, echoes the argument I have put forth here: "[M]uch of this violence has come about spontaneously, [while] some has clearly been planned" (Lewis 2003, 136).

In Kano, a Hausa-Yoruba riot in late July 1999 ushered in the post-military period. This mass-led affair, which left some seventy dead, was precipitated by the arrival of Hausa injured from clashes with Yorubas farther south in Sagamu (BBC, July 23, 1999). Another mass-led incident followed some two years later, when in mid-October 2001 anti-American protests were transformed into two days of attacks against Christian-owned stores and residents in which scores were killed (CNN, October 15, 2001).

In mid-May 2004, another reprisal riot hit Kano; this time, however, it was elite inspired. Hordes of Muslim youths attacked Christians in response to Christian killings of Muslims in Yelwa in the central Plateau State (BBC, May, 11 2004). On the day the clashes in Kano broke out, Muslim leaders held a massive protest for which the governor had granted a permit against the security forces' wishes (HRW 2005, 52). During the rally, Muslim leaders issued the federal government a seven-day ultimatum to hold Christian gangs behind the Yelwa slaughter accountable "or bear responsibility for whatever happens" (BBC, May 11, 2004; see also HRW 2005, 52). In a fashion that has come to typify the actions of Nigeria's security forces, the police used excessive force, including extrajudicial killings of unarmed civilians, in their attempt to quash the mayhem. In all, these elite-instigated clashes left some thirty thousand inhabitants displaced and possibly more than two hundred dead (HRW 2005, 65–73). The shifting elite-led/mass-led dynamics of Kano's riots over time has had truly deadly consequences.

Karachi

"For the sheer repetition of violence," Horowitz comments, "hardly any location approaches Karachi" (2001, 414). Two pertinent characteristics underpin the unrest that has scarred Pakistan's largest city. One is the alternating elite-mass dynamics in the instigation of its frequent riots. And as in the cases of Calcutta and Kano, the other has been a great inflow of migrants into Karachi. Hundreds of thousands have arrived, fleeing violence elsewhere—for instance, from northern India to escape the 1947 Partition-related slaughters, and from Bangladesh to avoid the killings that accompanied its war of liberation from Pakistan in 1971. The social, political, and economic changes the displaced wrought in Karachi contributed significantly to the ethnic fighting that gained alarming regularity in the mid-1980s.

Two elite-instigated clashes anticipate this period, however. In 1965, fall-out from national elections led politicians from the Muhajir (literally, "refugee") community—a mix of Urdu-speaking ethnic groups that fled the urban centers of central India in 1947—to incite attacks against local Pathans, more recent migrants from northern Pakistan (Shaheed 1990, 198). Another elite-led riot followed some seven years later. In Karachi and elsewhere in the province of Sind, relations between the autochthonous Sindhi and the more economically successful Muhajirs were taut. Due to the latter's numerical dominance, Urdu had become the area's lingua franca, leaving Sindhi leaders resentful (Shaheed 1990, 198–99). Acrimony peaked when in 1972, backed by ardent Sindh nationalists, the provincial chief minister pushed a bill through the provincial legislature making Sindhi the provincial language. Muhajir elites objected and instigated large-scale attacks against Sindhis in Karachi and Hyderabad (Rahman 1998, 123–26).

In the mid-1980s, when the frequency of Karachi's ethnic riots—and their shifting elite-mass dynamics—took hold, the radicalization of politics and politicization of ethnic relations were significant factors. These processes ushered in a period of democratization after the military regime relinquished power in 1988 (Verkaaik 2004, 66, 78). Illustrative was the rapid growth of the Muhajir Ethnic Movement (MQM), which had been furtively formed in 1984 by university students who sought to declare Muhajirs a singular nationality and unite them on a single voting platform. Equally relevant was the state's Inter-Service Intelligence (ISI) support for—or, has some would have it, the creation of—the MQM as it sought to undercut Prime Minister Benazir Bhutto's support in her home province of Sindh. For its young supporters, as Verkaaik recounts (2004, 56), the movement was politically and culturally liberating, for it confronted landlords and other elites in the name of the underprivileged. Others accused it of exploiting tense relations between Pathans and Biharis, migrants who traveled from northern India to East Pakistan (Bangladesh) after 1947 and from there to Pakistan after 1971. Accordingly, detractors blamed the MQM for the rise of Karachi's "Kalashnikov culture" of theft, robbery, random "fun" violence, and political assassination (Verkaaik 2004).

The rioting that touched off Karachi's spiral of violence began in April 1985 when police mishandling of a road accident sparked "unplanned" riots between Biharis and Pathans in outlying Orangi district (Tambiah 1996, 186). Problems related to the political economy of public transport had severely strained relations among denizens of this densely populated urban settlement.

The next eighteen months witnessed frequent clashes between residents and security forces, yet it was in October 1986 that the city's subsequent ethnic riot occurred. The MQM turned an accident at an unmanned railway crossing during an antigovernment rally into an opportunity to punish Pathans. Shortly thereafter, in early November, another elite-led Pathan-Muhajir clash broke out following the arrest of MQM leaders (Shaheed 1990, 200–207). At the time it constituted the worst bout of rioting in post-independence Pakistan. A significant difference between the 1985 affair and later incidents, according to commentators, was their increasingly organized and elite-led characteristics. In this development, leaders of the nascent MQM and those of a counterorganization, the United Pathan Front, were influential (Horowitz 2001, 415; Shaheed 1990, 203).

In part due to this increasing organization, the December carnage was unprecedented "in scale and sheer brutality." The two-day affair was sparked by a botched government operation that sought to evict squatters and confiscate weapons from Pathans in the Karachi slum of Sohrab Goth and in Orangi district. In response, local drug barons and slum landlords mobilized Pathans (and Afghans) to retaliate against Muhajirs (and Biharis), who were blamed for the raids (Hussain 1990, 185–87). Meanwhile, these killings in Karachi for the first time directly instigated reprisals in Hyderabad, some ninety-five miles to the northeast. It established what one researcher called a "now familiar pattern" (Shaheed 1990, 207).

From January to September 1987 sporadic violence continued, pulling Karachi's Punjabi community onto the side of Pathans. Two large-scale Pathan-Bihari clashes took place in February and again in July (Tambiah 1996, 163). A year later, and lasting to May 1990, a series of riots ravaged Karachi and Hyderabad. In one incident of note, known as the Hyderabad Carnage, in late September 1988 Sindhi militants gunned down about 250 Muhajirs. It is widely believed the ISI instigated the killings in the hope that the violence would force the government to postpone upcoming elections (Verkaaik 2004, 79, 135). Days later, in reprisal, Muhajirs shot dead sixty Sindhi in Karachi (Tambiah 1996, 173). Then in July 1989, following the shooting death of Muhajir students at the University of Karachi, the MQM broke an electoral accord with a Sindhi party. In response, Sindhi elites unleashed violence on Muhajirs throughout Karachi (Tambiah 1996, 174).

In May 1990 mass violence again featured the Hyderabad-Karachi retaliatory pattern. In a dense Muhajir neighborhood (Pakka Qila) in Hyderabad the police fired upon and killed dozens of Muhajir women who were protesting the suspension of water service (*Karachi Herald*, June 1990). Making matters worse, Sindhi nationalists praised police actions. In Karachi enraged Muhajirs stormed Sindhi neighborhoods, taking revenge (Tambiah 1996, 176–77). Not only were vulnerable Sindhis in Karachi attacked, but Muhajirs shot commuters heading north from the city (Verkaaik 2004, 153). Finally, in June 1992 the Pakistani army launched a massive operation in Karachi—and in particular, in Liaqatabad, a MQM stronghold and "no-go" area for police and non-inhabitants—that brought MQM's "Kalashnikov culture" to heel. Over the next few years, army personnel (and later paramilitary Rangers trained by the police) led a ruthless anti-MQM campaign. Hundreds of supporters were slain, forcing MQM into submission (Verkaaik 2004, 1, 58, 84–86). For a time, thankfully the alternating elite-led/ mass-led dynamics of Karachi's deadly riots were brought to a close.

All things considered, from West Kalimantan and Calcutta to Kano and Karachi, this brief survey of examples of recurrent riots over time in a single site suggests that one must look at elite *and* mass-led scenarios to understand the initiation of collective violence. Elite and mass-led violence can coexist within a given site, but they often do so in shifting balance when viewed diachronically. That said, these cases do not reflect the ultimate nature of riots. This kind of simplification—elite manipulation versus mass-led processes—denies the complexity of the constitutive factors and processes that precipitate to ethnic riots (Brass 2003). No adequate explanation of these episodes can be monocausal. Yet, as the ethnic violence literature proliferates so do attendant questions of appropriate specification, disaggregation, and identity loom (Brubaker and Laitin 1998). It is in this unfolding and messy context that this hypothesis should be situated. It is a suggestive insight that can help us gain comparative traction in our attempt to understand the phenomenon of recurrent ethnic riots. Tracing and accounting for the changing forms of violence over time brings this hypothesis to the fore.

Conclusion

It was the best of times, it was the worst of times.
Charles Dickens, *A Tale of Two Cities*

This book has shed light on the temporal and political processes under-pinning a series of violent conflicts on the periphery of a multiethnic, weak state. Spanning the divide between the cold war and post-cold war periods, the violence in this resource-rich region has taken two related yet distinct forms: counterinsurgency warfare and ethnic riots. The pre-ceding chapters illustrate how the former spawned the latter. Aiming to lay bare the modern origins of the infamous Dayak-Madurese riots in West Kalimantan, Indonesia, this study has also sought to defuse the tenacity of the popular ancient hatreds mantra when it is haphazardly applied to "seething ethnic cauldrons" here and elsewhere. The contex-tual, historical perspective informing this work demonstrates how these riots were forged, how and why they became endemic, and the ways in which signal forms of the violence did (or did not) change over time. In my attempt to capture the region's central tension—namely, the politi-cization of ethnicity and recurrent riots—the complex interplay be-tween central and regional authorities and contests over the distribution of power, whereby such struggles invariably inform violence (or its ab-sence) on the ground, figured prominently.

In this conclusion, three tasks remain. First, I recast my argument against competing explanations of violence in West Kalimantan. A brief discussion of the practical implications of the analysis with an eye to-ward conflict resolution follows. Finally, I conclude with a discussion of the dilemma of democratic deepening and—especially acute in the country's outer islands—the thorny issue of reconciling competing conceptions of rights that Indonesia's newly emboldened and empowered citizenry, indigenous and migrant alike, is striving to possess.

Collective Violence in West Kalimantan

This study found no natural link between violence and ethnic heterogeneity. Neither did it support the notion that violence is historically determined, even in areas of recurrent riots. Rather, tangible political and temporal processes in large part yield violent conflict. To illuminate such dynamics, and the fluctuation and variation characteristic of civilian riots in a given site, diachronic analysis was shown to be a valuable tool (Brass 2003).

In West Borneo/Kalimantan, the historical forces conditioning violence have been exceedingly intricate. Through missionary education, race-based systems of law, the practice of divide and rule, and the use of auxiliaries, the Dutch forged an increasingly monolithic Dayak ethnicity out of a diverse autochthonous population whose greatest commonality at this time was its non-Muslim beliefs. The Dayak identity thus stood (in the colonial gaze) in opposition to the identity of Muslim Malays whose rulers' own authority rested on colonial force and contractual authority. By ossifying these increasingly political identities into exclusive and distinct categories, colonial rule lent its hand in inducing horizontal and vertical violence as social fabrics were sundered and power relations altered. From Dutch-Chinese *kongsi* warfare and clashes between gold miners and indigenes to abortive rebellions, periodic violence in the region reflected these transformations.

That said, it is my view that contemporary Madurese-Dayak riots are not a direct legacy of this nineteenth- and early-twentieth century violence. Rather, they stem from a specific confluence of contingent factors that emerged in the postindependence era. One was the formation of a provincial-level Dayak elite, which, with the help of the returning Dutch, first formed after World War II. This elite was an important new political phenomenon, and its members would play critical roles in the province's coming bloodshed, although they were not automatically connected to the worst of it.

Explaining the endemic riots in West Kalimantan requires a careful and detailed exploration of the early interactions between the region and the New Order army elite. The origins of the Dayak-Madurese clashes were embedded in the broader international context of cold war geopolitics. More concretely, the PGRS/Paraku/PKI rebellions of the mid-1960s and the subsequent anti-Chinese pogroms were the catalyst. Not the spontaneous result of traditional indigenous warfare, these massacres were actively spearheaded by certain actors. Ruthlessly imposing their authority in the region, Soeharto's henchmen—aided by select Dayak leaders—precipitated a destabilizing politicization of ethnicity, followed by horrific violence. And like the 1965–66 anticommunist massacres in Java and Bali beforehand, the timing of the killings in West Kalimantan in 1967 "indicates that the arrival of the army's Special Forces (RPKAD) functioned as the trigger" (Roosa 2006, 29; see also Cribb 1990 and G. Robinson 1995).[1] As solid social relations and civilian state institutions deteriorated, novel modes of action materialized and new boundaries were defended. The deaths of thousands of Chinese— and the tens of thousands displaced—embodied these changes.

Signaling the growing centralization of power in Jakarta and the militarization of local social and political relations, these horrific events constituted a serious rupture in the region's political development and would determine future patterns of ethnic conflict and cooperation. The issues that fed off the expulsion of Chinese from northern Pontianak and inland Sambas districts were new to West Kalimantan. Never before had ethnic Chinese been so thoroughly and permanently expelled from their land, and never before had Madurese become repetitive targets in antimigrant riots. Dayaks and Madurese first came to blows over the land evacuated by the fleeing Chinese. The perpetuation of these riots was informed by an internalization of "us-versus-them" antagonism and a routinization of violence among belligerents (Tambiah 1996).

New Order military terror played an instrumental role in shaping ethnic violence in West Kalimantan through its counterinsurgency campaign. Following the anti-Chinese pogroms, however, the agency and actions of the province's inhabitants in the use of collective violence as a means of settling local disputes gained an autonomy that surpassed the importance of outside provocation. External actors were inconsequential in the region's ensuing violence.

Seeking to demonstrate the value of historically oriented case study research in uncovering new explanations, this book has problematized accepted theories by highlighting the multiform features of causal explanation (Collier and Mahoney 1996). In this light, if we conceive contemporary riots as outcomes of the 1967 Chinese expulsions, then we must reassess our views on the causes of the Madurese-Dayak clashes and ask why these clashes were concentrated in some areas while others, with reasonably similar ethnic demographics, went relatively untouched.

In so doing, I turn away from static notions of culture to concrete political and temporal processes as an explanatory variable. The evidence this book presents undermines the essentialist belief that the region's riots are simply a result of cultural incompatibilities. Other assessments have focused on the environmental impact that New Order development has had on Dayak cultures and ways of life. The resource crunch thus produced, according to this view, inflamed social relations and sparked riots. While the deprivation caused by New Order development practices was undeniable, this perspective sheds little light on the origins of Dayak-Madurese strife. By underscoring the importance of temporal sequencing, this narrative has shown that riots occurred before the deleterious impacts of development took effect. Collective violence also took place in areas unaffected by such development projects as logging and transmigration.

The perspective that concentrates on Dayaks' institutional frustration is also a relevant subject but one that does not exhaust the possible causes of the genesis, persistence, and changes behind these riots. This approach's inability to meaningfully disaggregate the Dayak political identity and grasp the temporal and spatial variation of the riots (or the lack of violence) highlights its limitations.

More contextual analysis was required to explain relevant transformations of forms of violence in the late Soeharto period. Given the contemporary lineage of the riots in West Kalimantan, explaining why Dayak-Madurese animosity exists in the context of the extensive 1997 unrest became secondary. More pressing was illuminating the riots' unanticipated intensity and scale, unmatched since the 1967 anti-Chinese mobilizations. Here, a key change was the politicization of the countryside by urban-based NGO activists, who fostered a greater awareness of marginality among rural Dayaks. As participants in the national and international indigenous peoples' movement, these activists offered rural communities the external support that was critical in sustaining protest. It is against this backdrop that the large-scale 1997 riots, which broke out *before* the Asian and later Indonesian economic crisis began, must be read.

On the heels of this violence, the 1999 bloodletting, though tragic, was not altogether surprising. More unexpected were the participation of Sambas Malays and the expulsion of Madurese from a newly demarcated

Sambas district. In this case, the larger political dynamics of the early post-Soeharto state, namely, the program of decentralization that has devolved significant administrative and fiscal authority to the district level, were crucial. Combined with the growing ethnopolitical Dayak movement, this encouraged Sambas Malays—mobilized in a youth-oriented militia—to use anti-Madurese violence to validate Malay claims to local indigenous status. This maneuver was deemed necessary to compete with the Dayak identity in the heightened local politics that developed in anticipation of regional autonomy.

The messy transition period of decentralization fed another short but deadly riot in 2000 in Pontianak, a city once free of ethnic riots. Opponents to the retired "general governor," himself a New Order appointee, cloaked their challenges in the guise of reform and native son discourse. A power struggle over the governorship ensued, instigating another anti-Madurese riot. While Pontianak was not turned into another Ambon, victims of the 1999 Sambas strife—Madurese refugees housed in makeshift camps—bore the brunt of the city's succeeding violence amid an atmosphere of intensified ethnic chauvinism, recriminations, and economic competition. In all, collective violence in this vast region should not be understood as natural, unique, or static. Furthermore, revisiting the reasons for the bloodshed and the specific forms it took in certain times and places necessitates a reconsideration of the indiscriminate features that have been historically and arbitrarily ascribed to West Kalimantan.

Conflict Resolution

Has the historical context of the violence in West Kalimantan taught us anything that may aid conflict resolution? First let us consider how the analysis developed in this book raises concerns about a number of popular recommendations. One multifaceted proposal would attempt to empower Dayaks by lifting them out of their perpetual marginalization. This prescription involves strengthening claims to ancestral land rights, integrating local language and history content into educational curricula, revitalizing small-scale agricultural cooperatives, increasing political and bureaucratic representation, and reviving nonstate, *adat* institutions as an effective means of dispute resolution.

Some steps have been taken to improve the welfare and dignity of Dayak communities, and they are commendable. Read carefully, however, these remedies essentially place the blame for the persistent violence on Dayaks. Taken together, they imply that Dayaks are the aggressors and ameliorating their frustration would end the rioting. Madurese and Malays are thus absolved of responsibility. So, too, are local and central government authorities, including the security forces. Resolving the dilemma thus becomes a matter of assuaging Dayak dissatisfaction. Ironically, this is a position some of these same groups that champion the above measures would resolutely reject.

Here I would like to briefly expound on a particular avenue of conflict resolution, that of reviving *adat* institutions, whose legitimacy is presumed to flow from their sensitivity to local cultural contexts. This has become a popular approach among international organizations (World Bank 2004) and national indigenous rights activists (AMAN 2003) in the face of what is perceived as the failure of post-Soeharto governments to maintain peace and order. In the context of reasonably closed communities, for instance, reports have noted how such neotraditional *adat* institutions have been able to settle disputes in ways acceptable to both sides (Acciaioli 2002).

In the context of broader intercommunity relations, and regarding such volatile issues as large-scale violence that resonates provincially (and nationally), locally respected modes of dispute resolution have done less well in maintaining social order and integration. "Traditional" peace ceremonies have barely stemmed the tide in such violence-afflicted places as the Moluccas and in Poso (Aragon 2001). The lack of common cultural underpinnings between warring parties highlights part of the problem. Effectiveness demands that one party, typically migrants or outsiders, acknowledge the legitimacy of the traditional customs of the insider or indigene, which in turn will act as a framework for reconciliation that should have been in the interests of *both* parties. In West Kalimantan, what makes this implausible is that, as this book has shown, Madurese culture has been denigrated to the point where it is commonly perceived as the primary cause of the region's persistent riots, and non-Madurese locals question what this violent culture can contribute to *adat*-based arbitration. Another obstacle is the fact that the majority of Madurese either reject solving disputes with Dayaks through *adat* means, or are befuddled by what *adat* actually signifies and how it might be fairly deployed.[2] This distrust has been exacerbated by the increasing commercialization of *adat* dispute resolution in the area (see chapter 5).[3]

Another increasingly popular conflict-resolution approach is the promotion of civil society associations. This recommendation, which has received significant attention in media outlets and among international donor and development agencies, focuses on the advantages that vibrant and active interethnic organizations bring to riot prevention and conflict resolution (Varshney 2002). It is argued that such dense, interethnic associational life facilitates intercommunal communication and trust, which in turn well position these organizations to prevent or cauterize ethnic violence. In times of heightened tension, for example, their leaders can work to quash pernicious rumors, which often provide deadly fodder in riots, or establish something akin to peace brigades. This enticing approach was born in India, where urban-based riots predominate. In this case, in Indonesia it may be plausible to apply it to Pontianak (and Ambon City). Yet it is uncertain how forging such linkages where few exist—as in Pontianak—can be accomplished and whether new linkages are as efficacious as established ones. Such interconnections cannot be assumed. Moreover, for some fifty years Pontianak (and Ambon City) remained riot free *without* effective interethnic peace brigades.

Despite Pontianak's recent disturbances, the province's hot spots continue to be semirural Sambas, Pontianak, Landak, and Bengkayang districts, where daily, face-to-face interactions are more prevalent than in urban environments. It is not certain that an urban-based tactic can be adapted to semirural conditions (World Bank 2004). It remains to be seen how local elites can be persuaded to cooperate, how effective intercommunal associations in these semirural environments of mutual distrust can be built, and what specific mechanisms would be needed to keep the peace—something the interethnic civic life thesis has yet to demonstrate.

I also find a third proposed solution—ethnic partition—to the problem of the violence troubling. By expelling Madurese from Sambas district and restricting them to towns in Bengkayang district, has the real cause of the violence been removed? Does the fact that six years (and counting) have passed since this area's last large-scale riot justify their expulsion? An affirmative answer would force Indonesians and democracy promoters alike to reconsider the meanings of such terms as *citizenship, republic,* and *Indonesian,* and to rethink the interethnic and interreligious foundations (and promises) on which the modernity that is the idea of Indonesia has been built.

Abundant historical and comparative evidence shows that the long-term effectiveness of ethnic partitions is questionable (Kumar 1997; Walter 2004). In the case of West Kalimantan, most telling is the fact that there have been sustained periods of relative peace within riot-prone areas. In fact, there were fewer riots in these districts for longer periods before the Madurese were expelled. Still, future strife remains a possibility (see chapter 5). Conflict trajectories include intra-Dayak tensions over the spoils of office and black market activities, continued aggression directed against Madurese where they remain, and heightened animosity toward ethnic Chinese, whose growing prominence in the province's public and political sphere is undeniable. Malay-Dayak hostilities are also worrisome.

A practical initial step toward conflict resolution would be to revitalize state institutions. This could begin with the police and the formal legal system, which are an integral part of broader efforts to enforce the rule of law in Indonesia. It is no secret that Indonesia suffers from an inadequate police force and an overburdened and corrupt legal system. I acknowledge that this approach may be seen as a long-term solution to a problem that requires immediate attention (Tajima 2004), as most Indonesians are pessimistic about the prospects of establishing the rule of law in their country. But arresting culprits promptly in the early stages of riots could be surprisingly effective in relieving tensions and ending the fighting. Moreover, these preventive measures would not require the generation of new norms and values or the reconstitution of existing institutions. Studies in other countries have shown that a professional police force and a determined police chief can be an effective means of riot prevention (Wilkinson 2004, 5, 19–20).[4] Even a civil society advocate such as Varshney concedes the value of this approach (2002, 293–95) and cites the successful case of a town outside Bombay as an example. In Sri Lanka, Tambiah attributes the lack of anti-Tamil riots in the southern part of the country since 1983—the time of the last major outburst—to a police force that committed itself to putting an end to the violence (1996, 332). "Force," Horowitz concludes, "seems generally to deter" (2001, 363).

In West Kalimantan, local elites entertain similar views. Interviews with leaders of FKPM confirm that if the local police had promptly arrested the attackers of Parit Setia, the likelihood of the 1999 riots would have diminished greatly (see also Purwana 2003, 92–93). In fact, one of its founders, Zulkarnain Bujang, readily acknowledged that the expulsion of the Madurese from Sambas would not have been possible but for the laxity of the security forces.[5] Dayak leaders argue similarly but cast their views in a longer timeframe. In the 1999 *Kalimantan Review* article defending Dayak violence against Madurese settlers, IDRD complains that for decades Dayaks have had little recourse to state law. They have no alternative but to resort to *adat*-sanctioned violence "given the lack of recourse to substantive law or international conventions to support their rights" (44). The implication is clear: if substantive law had been available as a means of obtaining justice, violence in the name of *adat* might not have been necessary.

In this frontierlike province, upgrading the professionalism of the police force is not the pipe dream some might imagine. One prominent local activist cites a December 2002 case in which the spillover from a stabbing incident over a gambling dispute was quickly contained by police action (Bamba 2004, 414, n.16). Here, the seemingly unrelated but high-profile arrests of illegal loggers made by the then new provincial police commander in 2004 gains relevance (*Kalimantan Review*, October 2004). If such arrests can be made in this province's vast and somewhat inaccessible hinterland, detaining the appropriate people during the early phases of a public disturbance in West Kalimantan's lowlands should not be overly burdensome. Ultimately, funds would be needed to bolster police efforts. Unfortunately, this prospect looks less promising. In fact, according to the same activist, as of 2004 no money had been earmarked or spent on reconciliation efforts (Bamba 2004, 405). Like democracy, conflict resolution costs money. Without it, neither is likely to last.[6]

The advent of competitive electoral politics in Indonesia is especially important in this context. In 2005, the country introduced direct elections for regional chief executives (such as the mayor, *bupati*, and governor). And, while the temporary respite from riots in West Kalimantan may stem from power-sharing arrangements between Malay and Dayak elites (Tanasaldy 2007),[7] the introduction of local direct elections (known as *pilkada, pilihan kepala daerah*) has at least prevented local ethnic elites from determining the winners in advance.[8] Accordingly, the influence of ethnic power-sharing pacts has eroded. One way to safeguard the Madurese (and other minorities), as Wilkinson has convincingly shown in his work on electoral competition and ethnic riots in India (2004) — drawing from the seminal work on electoral engineering by Horowitz (1991) — would be to include Madurese constituencies (or their influential elites) in electoral coalitions in localities where Madurese populations constitute an important swing vote, such as in Pontianak district and Pontianak City (and if allowed to return, Sambas). Stiff party competition for Madurese votes between Islamic-oriented stalwarts such as the PPP and the Justice and Prosperity Party (PKS), and even among such secular heavyweights as Golkar, the PDI-P, and the Democrat Party could conceivably favor multiparty and multiethnic interests.

Final Thoughts: Competing Conceptions of Rights

Formally, Indonesia has made great strides toward establishing a rights-based democracy. This is best reflected in an impressive series of constitutional amendments that have introduced a robust charter on universal human rights; established independent judicial and constitutional commissions (with the latter having been granted powers of judicial review); restricted presidential powers (including a two-term limit); bolstered parliament's authorities (among other powers, Parliament can now initiate legislation); dismantled the army's dual function (*dwifungsi*) doctrine, which had justified its intervention in civil and political affairs; and instituted decentralization, which is considered part and parcel of Indonesia's democratization process. Just as significant, the country has successfully held two national legislative elections (1999 and 2004), a two-phase, direct presidential election (2004), and dozens of local elections for regional heads (since 2005). Media licenses have been liberalized, making the country's press one of the freest in Asia. Finally, although periodic terrorist-related bombings continue, the outbreaks of mass collective violence—communal, separatist, and anti-Chinese—that rocked the country's early transition phase have waned.

Nonetheless, all is not right with Indonesia, and few pretend otherwise. While this is not the place to catalog the country's ills, it should be noted that there is a disconnect between institutional reform and the consensual characteristics of high politics in Jakarta (Ellis and Yudhini 2002; Slater 2004) and its violently contested, zero-sum counterpart in the country's regions. Whereas the former may give the impression that Indonesia has eased into a democratic consolidation phase—despite warnings about the country's steady descent into the abyss of perpetually dysfunctional or low-quality democracy—the latter has struggled with an arduous and bloody transition, belying the facade of democratic strides made at the national level.

To appreciate this disjuncture, we should recall the features of West Kalimantan that, while they may be extreme, are not unique in the outer islands: horizontal violence and concomitant refugee crises, expressly political violent conflict, the lack of a tolerant civil society, the disquieting politicization of ethnicity and religion, acute land conflicts, environmental degradation, systemic corruption, rampant smuggling, and a decrepit formal legal system.[9]

What, then, does this incongruity tell us about Indonesia's democratization? For one thing, it requires us to consider these processes in a more geographically sensitive framework, highlighting those "brown areas" (O'Donnell 2004) where efforts to promote democratic rights are thwarted by local elites. In this way, efforts to strengthen a regime that upholds the ideals of citizenship and human rights will determine the quality of local democratic life in Indonesia. Such commitments to reform underpin conceptions of what being Indonesian means at this critical yet anxious moment in the country's political development. In the outer islands, this also means confronting a fundamental and perhaps irreconcilable clash between the collective and cultural rights of groups claiming indigenous identities and the individual rights of those excluded from such communities, especially migrants. Both sets of rights aim to provide security, justice, and a better quality of life for their adherents, but can they be justly realized for each community contemporaneously?

The upsurge of indigenous peoples' movements constitutes a challenge that goes to the crux of democratizing states struggling to enforce human rights. Bolstered by a plethora of international legal instruments (Anaya 1996) and the resources of a transnational civil society and its attendant discourse of community, tradition, and environmentalism, these movements desire to establish the right to control place (Castree 2004, 151), that is, the natural resources and the norms and rules of social and political behavior contained therein.

Decentralization and democratization have created spaces in which marginalized—and in this case indigenous—communities can demand the return of customary lands and the opportunity to revitalize "traditional" law. The rights these movements privilege, particularly those peddled by their urban-based activists who sit at the interface among (inter)national rights organizations, donor agencies, and rural folk, are predicated on group notions of indigenous identity and territory. They seek recourse in the so-called third generation of human rights: collective rights to sustain or maintain specific cultural lives and the right to a clean environment, to name just two.

Indisputably, New Order developmentalism led to the methodical violation of indigenous peoples' rights—notably the systematic dispossession of land and environmental devastation. Backed by reams of data on the country's economic prosperity, New Order advocates suggested otherwise; in fact, they never did recognize indigenous peoples as separate and distinct communities (Persoon 1998). Yet, in West Kalimantan, throughout Indonesia, and elsewhere, optimism is growing. Despite daunting obstacles, indigenous peoples are "getting what they want" (Wilmer 1993). Government policies throughout Southeast Asia are seen to have shifted from "ethnocide to ethnodevelopment" (Clarke 2001) and in Indonesia "from development to empowerment" (Duncan 2004). Meanwhile, the charges of essentialism (Gledhill 1997) leveled against these movements are being turned on their heads. By embracing the positive and strategic aspects of essentialism—its ability to forge allegiances across formerly distinct communities (Levi and Dean 2003)—indigenous voices are being heard in the corridors of power, national, intergovernmental, and corporate alike.

In Indonesia, such gains are reflected in the Alliance of Indigenous Peoples of the Archipelago (Aliansi Masyarakat Adat Nusantara, or AMAN), whose first national congress was held amid much publicity in Jakarta in 1999; a second congress followed in Lombok in 2003. Ultimately, the demands these putatively traditionalist movements place on democratizing states are what Deborah Yashar (1999) labels the "post-liberal challenge," that is, grounding individual rights in a governmental framework that at the same time accommodates group rights, diverse identities, units of representation, and state structures.

The literature on the indigenous peoples' movement, however, has drawn heavily from the South American experience. There the notion of indigenousness predicated on conquest by outsiders is more distinct than in Africa and Asia, where the greater complexity of displacement and movements of peoples and the lineages of liberationist, nationalist movements have complicated the notion of indigenousness (Bowen 2000; Kingsbury 1995).

It is unnecessary here to elaborate in detail the implications of this difference and the other dilemmas these movements pose. These may include unashamedly delimiting the boundaries of inclusion and exclusion, reifying internal power differentials (Benhabib 2002; V. Das 1997), and sealing off nonindigenous groups that share similar class positions and problems (Gledhill 1997). Instead, I wish to focus on another issue, one that the literature on indigenous peoples' movements in Latin America has had less of a need to confront. This concerns the collective violence committed by self-identified indigenous peoples in the name of indigeneity against migrants of the same nationality, one of this book's animating themes. How does this bloodshed affect the issues presented above? As Mamdani (2001) has insightfully asked, "and victims become killers," how do we adjudicate claims of justice and accommodate contrasting notions of rights within highly pluralistic societies? In what ways does mass violence affect these delicate decisions?

Progressive conceptions of indigenous peoples as marginalized "little people" warding off ethnocide and global ecocide are also undermined by such violence. Tania Li perceptibly notes that "ethnic cleansing disrupts the prominent image of indigenous peoples as victims of violence perpetrated by vicious regimes, corporations, or settlers intent on grabbing their land" (2002, 361). The plight of refugees — as victims of indigenous mass aggression — raises concerns that are as pressing and complicated as the issues that give rise to indigenous peoples' movements themselves.

To what extent do voluntary migrants — many of whom have inhabited the areas in question for generations — have the right to seek economic betterment elsewhere within Indonesia? The country's second constitutional amendment, adopted in 1999, provides a partial answer to this question. It states that each Indonesian citizen possesses "the right to choose a residence anywhere in Indonesia [and] the right to leave it and to return to it." Regrettably, as one legal scholar has pointed out, "[T]here is no tradition of respect for or enforcement of constitutional rights in Indonesia" (Bell 2001, 33). Efforts to stymie the return of Madurese refugees certainly contravene these ideals.[10]

Without the solid political and legal ground on which to claim collective rights in the name of indigeneity, these movements would soon flutter and fade. But this observation does not lessen the fact that such rights conflict with and potentially violate the civil, political, and economic individual rights of migrants, who are pursuing livelihoods within a legally recognized framework. While antimigrant riots bring these incompatibilities to the fore, so, too, is the failure of the state to provide security for both vulnerable communities equally exposed. If the corrupt state, embodied in its decayed legal system, continues to be derelict in the execution of its duties, either set of rights will be rendered meaningless; we can but shudder at the thought of the future implications of this delinquency on the ground.

Notes

Introduction

1. For a review of past scholarship, see Rule 1988.

2. Papua refers to the Indonesian-half of the island of New Guinea that under the New Order was known as Irian Jaya. In 2000 the Abdurraham Wahid administration, in the spirit of reform, changed it to its more indigenous sensitive name, Papua. In 2003 the Megawati Soekarnoputri administration divided Papua into three provinces: Papua, West Irian Jaya, and Central Irian Jaya (which at the time of this writing was not yet formalized).

3. Traditional estimates of the province's ethnic composition have been Dayak 41 percent, Malay 39 percent, and Chinese 11 percent. On the 2000 census results, the first since independence to include ethnicity as a category, see chapter 5, note 77.

4. This includes the great Dutch-Chinese gold-mining wars of the 1850s, the colonial creation of a pan-Dayak ethnic identifier, and the buttressing of Malay principalities under the auspices of indirect rule.

5. A 1998 survey of violent conflicts across the country conducted by a team of social scientists from a leading Indonesian university concluded that of all the cases studied West Kalimantan was the most complex. See Soetrisno et al. 1998, 47.

6. This rebellion, the first against Soeharto's rule, is a missing case in accounts of the Indonesian military's operational and ideological history. See Tanter 2000; Cribb 2002; Honna 2003, 9; D. Kingsbury 2003.

7. See *Ummat*, March 4, 1997; Suparlan 2001; *Equator*, July 11, 2001; and the many domestic media reports reproduced in ISAI/IDRD 1999, especially pp. 132–38, 150–55, 155–58, 159–64, and 198–200. For international media reports, among many, see *The Economist*, March 27–April 1999; *Far Eastern Economic Review*, February 20, 1997; *The Independent*, March 22, 1999; and *The Observer*, March 28, 1999. Also relevant is Parry 2005.

8. The characterization of the Madurese as rough and fiercely loyal is immortalized in the figure of Darsman in Pramoedya Ananta Toer's novels of the Indonesian nationalist awakening. In particular, see his *This Earth of Mankind* (1992). On Madurese stereotypes, see also de Jonge 1995, 7–24. On Madurese *carok*, see G. Smith 1997 and Wiyata 2002.

9. See Colchester 1986b; Djuweng 1999; Down to Earth 1997, 2001; Dove

1997; *Forum Keadilan,* March 10, 1997; Linder 1997; Samydorai 1997; and Soetrisno et al. 1998. Its best articulation is Peluso and Harwell (2001); see also Peluso 2006. More than other studies using this approach, Peluso and Harwell aptly consider the historical and geographical patterns of the violence. They also assign exceptional importance to the notion of "violent identities" as explanatory factors in these ethnic clashes. In this case, "Dayak" and "Madurese" are seen as discursively constructed outcomes of New Order territorial politics (2001, 96). That Dayak and Madurese identities are popularly construed as "violent" is hardly controversial; by what mechanisms they spark violence, however, remains vague. As constants, these violent identities cannot account for the riots' variations. And they seem to be at odds with the many Madurese and Dayak communities that have not participated in riots (such as those in Ketapang for one), and less helpful regarding the Sambas Malays, whose identities had not been constructed as violent under New Order discursive practice and territorial politics.

10. Furthermore, it seems incongruous from an institutional frustration viewpoint that Dayaks in West Kalimantan would engage in riotous activities throughout the New Order period while those in Central Kalimantan refrained from doing so in large-scale fashion until after Soeharto fell.

11. Posen (1993), Tambiah (1996, 214), and Horowitz (2001, 395–422) note that past violence increases the likelihood of similar violence recurring.

Chapter 1. Identity Formations and Colonial Contests

1. In reference to the precolonial period, I refer to the area as western Borneo. It became known as West Borneo under the Dutch, and West Kalimantan following independence. Within a broad historical context, I will on occasion use West Borneo/Kalimantan.

2. The evolution of this exonym's spelling is long and complicated, partly due to its Dutch derivatives. Spellings have included Daya, Dayak, Dajakh, Dajak, Dyak, InDayaks, Dayah, Dayers, Diak, NDayak, and Dayakkers. At one time, Daya was considered less condescending and insulting than Dayak.

3. Bugis hail from southern Sulawesi and are renowned seafarers.

4. Two American missionaries who visited the region's coastal areas observed that "Dayaks" were "held in a state of servile subjection by the Malays" (Doty and Pohlman 1839, 285).

5. In 1841 the Sultan of Brunei seceded Sarawak to Brooke as a reward for his help in crushing a local rebellion. Brooke rule, which passed from James to his nephew Charles and finally to Charles's son, Vyner, survived until World War II. Although originally denied official British Crown recognition, Sarawak did become a protectorate in the 1890s. See Walker 2002.

6. Van der Cappellen (rendered "Vander" in this piece) served as governor-general from 1816–26.

7. One traveler estimated Pontianak's population in the early nineteenth century to comprise 3,000 Malays, 1,000 Bugis, 100 Arabs, and 10,000 Chinese (Leyden 1837).

8. Madurese soldiers had helped to quash the Diponegoro rebellion (1825–30) on Java (see "The Insurrection on Java" 1837, 150). Later they were frequently deployed in the colonial regime's pacification campaigns, especially in the outer islands (de Jonge 1995).

9. In 1930, only Medan (35 percent) had a higher percentage of Chinese than Pontianak (34 percent). See Touwen 2001, 339, table 17.

10. On the complementarity of swidden rice and rubber cultivation, see Dove 1996.

11. On a string of minor abortive (and millenarian) rebellions against Dutch-backed Malay rule from the 1850s to the 1910s in what is now Sintang district, see Wadley and Smith 2001.

12. During this time, the Dutch relied on Iban auxiliaries, a practice that eventually was stopped because it was believed to encourage headhunting. As a substitute, they called on other Dayaks and Kapuas Malay principalities for help (Wadley 2004, 613).

13. It took some thirty years (1873–1903) for the Dutch to put down the anticolonial rebellion. Aceh was the last area in the archipelago for the Dutch to conquer.

14. Jesuit missionaries with experience in China settled in Singkawang in the late nineteenth century to proselytize in its large Chinese community. Protestant missionaries arrived thereafter but did not reach the upper Kapuas until the 1960s. See Houliston 1963.

15. Apparently, few Dayak attended (or were accepted by) government CVOs. In 1946 Pontianak's CVO had perhaps two Dayak students; another three studied in Sintang's CVO. See an unpublished memorandum from the Dayak Affairs Office, November 12, 1946.

16. Prior to the war, some eleven students were sent to North Sulawesi, while several non-Dayak graduates from here were sent to West Borneo to teach. See *Buku Kenangan,* ca. 1991.

17. Chinese and other "foreign Orientals" were subject to Dutch commercial law but native criminal law. Indonesian wives of Europeans, mixed offspring, and Christian Indonesians were subject to one code or the other, contingent on circumstances. See Hoebel and Schiller 1948.

18. In what are now the provinces of South and Central Kalimantan, Dayak organizations predate the PD (Miles 1976; Usop 1994; Van Klinken 2004). Links between these associations and the PD in West Kalimantan have not yet been demonstrated.

19. A full social history of the occupation remains to be written. For different aspects, see Davidson forthcoming, M. Effendy 1982, Heidhues 2003, Maekawa 2002, and the historical fiction accounts of Yanis (1983, 1998).

20. On Dayak attacks against retreating Japanese positions in Sanggau district in mid-1945, see Davidson forthcoming and M. Effendy 1982, 72–95.

21. Here, a problem of chronology, nomenclature, and politics of memory exists. There is confusion over when the DIA became the PD and when it officially became a political party. For further details, see Davidson forthcoming.

22. This sentiment is clearly expressed in a NICA report written by H. J. Harmsen (1947).

23. Raymond "Turk" Westerling, a former KNIL captain who led a slaughter of revolutionary fighters in South Sulawesi in 1946–47, commanded hundreds of troops to launch his coup against the young republican government. The failed plans included the assassination of the sultan of Yogyakarta, Hamengku Bowono IX. For more on Hamid's trial, see Persadja 1955.

24. Eight months later the party gained one more seat when the area was granted special regional status.

25. He wrote: "The Dutch are responsible for the wretched fate of the Dayaks [*Bangsa Belanda adalah bertanggoeng djawab akan keboeroekan nasib Daya*]." See "Mandau," c. 1947–50. *Mandau* is a traditional sword and Oeray's probable pseudonym. See also Oeray 1947.

26. The original reads: "Pendjadjahan oleh Feodalisme itoe adalah lebih boeroek dp pendjadjahan Belanda." See "Mandau," c. 1947–50.

27. See, for example, *Anggaran Dasar* 1955, 5.

28. On attempts at raising campaign contributions, see Davidson forthcoming.

29. These are rough estimates; they are the median of figures taken from the 1930 and 1971 censuses. See Tanasaldy 2007.

30. These results seem to confirm Liddle's conclusions (1970) on 1950s party politics in North Sumatra. Ethnic or religious-oriented parties fared well in areas less economically advanced and where fighting in the revolution was light, the latter suggesting lower degrees of nationalist consciousness.

31. The *bupati* were M. Th. Djaman (Sanggau), G. P. Djaoeng (Sintang), J. R. Gielling (Kapuas Hulu), and Djelani (Pontianak district). In Sanggau, PD won 64 percent of the vote and 12 out of 19 district DPRD seats; in Sintang 57 percent and 9 out of 16 seats; in Kapuas Hulu, 49 percent and 7 out of 15 seats; and in Pontianak district 45 percent and 13 out of 30 seats. Taufiq Tanasaldy graciously provided me with this district level data.

32. Soekarno's desire to have native sons govern the regions also helped Oeray's cause. Tjilik Riwut, the Dayak then-governor of Central Kalimantan province and close associate of Soekarno, backed Oeray's candidacy.

33. It is likely that a formal branch of the PKI was established in West Borneo (Lembaga Sedjarah PKI 1961, 49). In 1923, the PKI declared all SR a member, thereby subjecting them to party discipline (McVey 1965, 190–96).

34. The head of the PAB, Raden Muslimun Nalaperana, also held West

Borneo's lone seat on the colonial Volksraad (People's Council) in Batavia (present-day Jakarta).

Chapter 2. *Konfrontasi*, Rebellion, and Ethnic Cleansing

1. On the rebellion, see Mackie 1974, 112–22; and Tham 2000. The full extent of Azahari's role in the revolt is unclear, given he was in Manila when the uprising was launched. In the end, Brunei, not wanting to share its oil revenues with the poorer states, opted out of the Malaysian Federation.

2. The returning British authorities announced a State of Emergency throughout Malaya in June 1948 in response to an insurgency led by the Chinese-dominant Malayan Communist Party, one of whose fighting wings was the MRLA.

3. On May 27, 1961, the Malayan Premier Tunku Abdul Rahman first announced this federation, although the idea had bounced around British policy circles since the mid-1950s (Easter 2004, 5–21). For reactions in Sarawak vis-à-vis the proposal, see Leigh 1974, 7–39.

4. Once known as the Communist (or sometimes Sarawak) Clandestine Organization, the SCO was not a single organization but a government label that covered all "illegal" organizations (Hardy 1963, 4).

5. The movement had emerged from Sarawak's Chinese language schools in the early 1940s (Fujio 2000, 198). Among the SCO's affiliated organizations were the Sarawak Advance Youths' Association, the Sarawak Farmers' Association, the North Kalimantan National Freedom League, and a number of trade unions. The estimate of twenty-five hundred comes from Justus M. van der Kroef (1964, 40). By mid-1965, government figures estimated that the SCO possessed a combat-ready force of thirty-five hundred backed by twenty-five thousand civilians ("Malaysia" 1969, 390).

6. A captured SCO document written in 1959 notes: "Failure to win these loyal supporters [Malays and Dayaks] to our camp will block any hope of success for the revolution" (quoted in Hardy 1963, 29–30).

7. The full extent of Indonesian aid to the rebels prior to the revolt remains controversial. For one skeptical view, see Poulgrain 1998, 256–59.

8. The rebellions in West Sumatra and North Sulawesi were mentioned in chapter 1. The Darul Islam fighters sought to establish an Islamic state in Indonesia. While Aceh, South Kalimantan, and South Sulawesi hosted rebellions, West Java experienced the most intense fighting; there, some leaders were not captured until the early 1960s. Finally, the Indonesian military led a series of operations against Dutch positions in West Irian, which the Dutch had not ceded to Indonesia in 1949. In 1969 the Indonesian civilian and military leadership succeeded in manipulating a plebiscite through which the United Nations recognized their right to integrate the vast territory into Indonesia.

9. It is widely believed that Subandrio, in his capacity as head of the Indonesian Central Intelligence Bureau (BPI), planned these landings (Crouch 1978, 60–61, 70–75; Mackie 1974, 258–64; and H. Jones 1971, 354–55).

10. The operation in Kalimantan was called Mandau, and its combat force was the Alert Battle Command (Kopur III). In Sumatra, the combat force was called Kopur II and its operation was named Rentjong.

11. On Soepardjo's role in the September 30th Movement (see below), see Roosa 2006.

12. Soepardjo later complained of sabotage and of being denied combat-ready troops (Crouch 1978, 70–74).

13. In July 1963, for instance, Nasution, while inspecting troops in West Kalimantan, stated that if *pemuda pejuang* (revolutionary youths) from "North Kalimantan" (i.e., Sarawak) asked for help in their struggle Indonesia would obligingly provide it (Mackie 1974, 156). Nasution, who was already supplying the rebels, also wrote at the time: "We will train every youth from North Borneo who want [*sic*] to fight, and we will not forbid any Indonesian youth wanting to fight there" (1964, 120).

14. *Proses timbulnju PGRS/Paraku* (n.d., 3). See also Semdam XII (1971, 182–83, 233–34). The above is ABRI's version. Sarawak government documents indicate that the decision to form PGRS and Paraku forces was taken on September 17–19, 1965, in Pontianak. It was supposed that the North Kalimantan Communist Party was formed to replace its Sarawak variant. Two weeks later, SCO leaders scattered because of the military takeover of October 1 in Jakarta (*The origin and development* ca. 1974, 3). Porritt (2004, 107) dates the formation of PGRS in between these two versions (March 24, 1964) and states that at the September 1965 meeting a decision was made to form Paraku (134).

15. In a later interview, Bong Kee Chok, a prominent member of PGRS, said that he had received three months of training by the Indonesian army (*Far Eastern Economic Review*, April 4, 1975). Porritt (2004, 107) maintains that a group of ten SCO leaders, including Bong and Yap Choon Ho, were trained outside Jakarta and then left for West Kalimantan in March 1964. Once there, the SCO held military training exercises at three mountainous sites near the border (*The origin and development* ca. 1974, 2).

16. Although estimates of the size of PGRS/Paraku at this time vary widely, the figure most frequently cited in military sources is 850 troops.

17. An army report states that sixty-five weapons were confiscated from troops in the Infantry Battalion 514/Brawiajaya who had rebelled (Ryacudu 1967b, 11). One high-ranking army inspection trip to the border found that one brigade from Central Java was "rife with PKI sympathizers and itching to rebel" (Conboy 2003, 168).

18. The army reported 10,265 personnel in the field at the time (Manaf ca. 1965).

19. The Malaysian government lists 214 raids and 33 "air violations" into

Sarawak and Sabah from April 1963 to June 1964 (*Indonesian Involvement in Eastern Malaysia* ca. 1965).

20. To this day, mystery shrouds these events. In the early morning of October 1, 1965, Lieutenant Colonel Untung headed a group of left-leaning military officers and civilians—known as the September 30th Movement—who either sought to topple the Soekarno government or "save" it from a putative rightwing, U.S.-backed Council of Generals. Then Major General Soeharto led a countercoup to foil the movement's plans. Six army generals were murdered during the course of these events. Subsequently, Soeharto took command of the army and, methodically, of the country. See Roosa 2006.

21. The banned papers were the *Suara Chatulistiwa, Kalimantan Membangun,* and *Ibu Kota* (Pontianak edition). The freeze on the PKI was replaced in December with a ban on the formation of a new PKI (*Kompas,* December 1, 1965). Nationally the PKI was not banned until March 12, 1966, the day after Soeharto's putsch against Soekarno.

22. According to a number of well-placed sources, one of which includes a former governor, two weeks later Sofyan was escorted out of Pontianak and released.

23. Dhani discusses Ryacudu's zealous devotion to Soekarno in Surodjo and Soeparno 2001, 52–56.

24. Interview, former head of Pontianak's Laskar Ampera, Pontianak (July 10, 2001). Ryacudu was well known for distributing trading monopolies to friends and family and fostering "working" relationships with many Chinese merchants.

25. Of this vexing dilemma facing the PKI, McVey notes: "In attempting to engage Chinese sympathies the PKI thus faced the highest cultural and linguistic barrier to cooperation precisely at the point where its ideological attraction might have been the greatest" (1965, 225).

26. Prior to 1965 and before the PKI in West Kalimantan became a threat in the eyes of government, little is known about it, as few sources have survived. Much of this information is based on either military or personal interviews.

27. In 1959, Sofyan attended the PKI's Sixth Party Congress as a member of its presidium. This meant that party thought highly of him (Ruth McVey, personal communication, February 10, 2002). Some sources in Pontianak maintain that Sofyan taught school in Banjarmasin but then moved to Yogyakarta, where he became active in student associations.

28. It is said that Sofyan spoke some Mandarin. Angin Timur, a Chinese communist youth organization, owned the theater that Lekra borrowed on occasion.

29. Various interviews, Pontianak.

30. For example, Sofyan ran West Kalimantan's National Front, a body that Ryacudu, as the top regional military commander, ceremoniously headed. Soekarno set up these provincial bodies to undermine the authority of regional

assemblies. National Fronts gathered representatives from all parties, thereby providing those poorly represented in local assemblies with disproportionate influence.

31. In fact, the day the accords were signed Paraku guerillas received training from the Indonesian military (Pang Handa Kalbar 1967). Sarawak police also noted a marked increase in guerrilla activity (Chan 1966).

32. When the army arrived in the 1960s, it renamed the area (and its people) "Sungkung." While the latter predominates in New Order sources, I employ the local usage. See *Kalimantan Review,* December 2001, English ed., 4–6.

33. This typescript letter was found in the PGRS/Paraku files in the archives of the army's Satria Mandala Museum, Jakarta.

34. As of mid-1967, 1,120 arrests had been made, but more than one-third of the prisoners were soon released on the condition that they *wadjib lapor* (report) to the authorities periodically (Ryacudu 1967b, 5).

35. According to a military source, the ship containing the deportees encountered difficulties, and they all returned to home (Angkatan Darat Kodam XII 1972, 333–34). The policy had a precedent. Following the controversial presidential regulation (No. 10/1959) that prohibited retail trade by Chinese in rural areas, more than nine hundred from the greater Singkawang area were deported to China (Poerwanto 2005, 249, 357).

36. This followed a national ban on foreign-run schools (except those diplomatically related) announced in early May 1966.

37. Resistance to these programs came in the form of flight. On July 29, 1967, 110 ethnic Chinese working on a road outside Bengkayang fled into a village described by the army as hiding place for Chinese communists (*Chronologis kegiatan PGRS* n.d., 3).

38. See Witono n.d., 5; and Semdam XII 1971, 13. This estimate may be high. Based on extrapolations of earlier estimates, the actual number might be closer to 250,000, roughly 12 percent of the provincial population.

39. Calls for Oeray's dismissal by West Kalimantan student organizations were made in Jakarta as early as January 1966 (*Kompas,* January 10, 1966).

40. Other student groups included the Pontianak Student Association (IMAPON), Association of Indonesian Catholic Students (PMKRI), Union of Indonesian Islamic Students (SEMMI), Indonesian Islamic Student Movement (PMII), and Association of Muhammadiyah Students (IMM). Various interviews, Pontianak and Jakarta.

41. *Bukit* in Indonesian means hill. It is possible that *Bara,* which means ember, is derived from the Chinese *Hu Yan Shan,* or Mountain of Flames. Special thanks to Hui Yew-Foong for pointing this out.

42. According to a military document, Sofyan was accompanied by Tan Bu Hiap, a member of Baperki and the PKI's provincial Legislative Council; Pheng Chen Nen, the sole ethnic Chinese on the PKI's Board of Daily Operations; Soekotjo, an ethnic Javanese born in Solo, and the provincial head of the

BTI (and who was captured in November 1967 in Karangan, outside Mempawah and described as Sofyan's "right-hand man" [*Kompas,* November 21 and December 6, 1967]); Tugiman; and Sumadi BsC—an ethnic Javanese—and Djuang. The latter three were members of the PKI's Legislative Council. See *Penumpasan terhadap geromobolan tjina komunis* n.d., 2. Soemitro, Sofyan's rival, did not accompany him to the forest. On October 16, 1967, Soemitro and Saadi Abdullah, the PKI's second assistant secretary, were sentenced to death in Pontianak (*Kompas,* November 1, 1967).

43. According to Soemadi, there were twenty such training centers (1974, 82–86).

44. Sarawak government reports also mention a possibly related split among PGRS leaders, which resulted in some twenty rebels leaving the Sikukng mountain complex to join forces with Sofyan in February 1967. They joined the Bara Force, which had formed in April. See *The origin and development* ca. 1974, 3–4; and Sarawak Government 1972, 2–3. Fujio (2000, 201) notes that the splits began to occur as early as 1966.

45. The last to leave were three companies from Infantry Battalion 514/Brawijaya (the East Java command) in March 1967 (Ryacudu 1967b, 9).

46. Interview, Pontianak, May 16, 2000.

47. Army data indicate that enemy losses were twenty-five dead, two injured, and two captured/surrendered, and Indonesian losses were twenty-nine dead and thirty-nine injured. See *Penumpasan terhadap geromobolan tjina komunis* n.d., 18.

48. The same report blames the lack of reliable transport on the original Kolaga command, which sold much of its transport to traders rather than give them to the Kodam XII (Ryacudu 1967b, 9–10, 12).

49. It is unlikely that Sofyan participated in the raid, a maneuver that might have been related to the appointment of Witono as Kodam/XII commander. Sofyan may have understood that Witono had been appointed to "eliminate" the communist presence in West Kalimantan, and so decided to strike first, both because he needed weapons and to embarrass the new Kodam commander. An intelligence report states that the attack was carried out by the PGRS under Lim A Lim's leadership and mentions neither Sofyan nor the PKI. See Moeljono (n.d.).

50. In fact, RPKAD forces landed in Pontianak on July 22, 1967, two weeks prior to the Jakarta meeting and only following the Sanggau Ledo air force raid. This is important because it gave them time to begin the clandestine operations that would culminate in the October anti-Chinese violence. See Pusat Sejarah dan Tradisi ABRI 1995, 166. Conboy maintains that they spent the first weeks in anticipation of reinforcements, because they were heavily outnumbered by insurgents (2003, 173).

51. Besides RPKAD forces, the new units included Infantry Battalion 328 (West Java), and Paratroop Battalion Raiders 100 (Sumatra). One internal

army report states that Special Forces began operations in the Bawang and Se-balau mountain complexes by August 6. See Ass-2 Kaskodam 12 Tdpr. 1967.

52. Some sources list this village as Tamu. I thank Taufiq Tanasaldy for this. For the dozen or so different appellations the press used to describe the rebels, see Davidson and Kammen 2002, 82.

53. Some of the individuals arrested were military officers with the ranks of major and lieutenant colonel (*Kompas,* August 9, 1967).

54. Merebuk (sometimes spelled Merabuk or Merebukan) does not appear on any New Order maps or in its military publications.

55. Months later, *Angkatan Bersenjata* (January 17, 1968) reported that the PKI and the BTI orchestrated the attack.

56. An army report notes the path of violence as follows:

Oct. 14	villages outside Bengkayang
Oct. 17	village of Tepo in subdistrict Serimbu
Oct. 19–22	villages of Sibakuan Piong and Buduk in subdistrict Selakau
Oct. 26	village of Sebali, Samalantan, Montrado in subdistrict Samalantan
Oct. 27	Sunang village and its surroundings in subdistrict Mempawah Hulu (Pontianak district)
Oct. 28–29	Karangan and its surroundings in subdistrict Mempawah Hulu
Oct. 29–30	Kuala Behe and the surrounding villages in subdistrict Serimbu (Pontianak district)
Oct. 30	villages of Mandor, Tjap Kala (subdistrict Sungai Raya), and Sebadau, and its surroundings in Mandor subdistrict
Oct. 31–Nov. 4	Senakin, Mandor, Pahauman, Ngaruk, Adjungan, Darit, and Sidas
Nov. 3	Sosok and villages surrounding Ngabang and Kembajan in Sanggau district
Nov. 8	Darit
Nov. 11	Sebadau (Witono 1967, 5–6).

57. Whereas Van Hulten maintains the violence reached the Anjungan-Mandor-Menjalin area on October 17, military sources cite October 29.

58. At first, the Chinese fled their homes and gathered in inland towns. By November 1, the army reported 5,150 refugees, 4,000 of whom were in Beng-kayang. See Pangdam 12 TDPR/Panglak OPS Kalbar 1967.

59. In an interview years later Oeray also mentioned the prohibition on killing (Jenkins 1978).

60. Van Hulten (1992, 281–82); and Witono (1967, 6). Military data is as follows. Sambas district: Sei Betung as many as 20 people; Sepatung as many as 9 people. Mempawah (Pontianak) district: Senakin as many as 70 people; Darit as many as 50 people; Sebadu as many as 90 people. This total, which according to the data should total 239, excludes the aforementioned eighty deaths suffered in Temu.

61. Interviews conducted in Pahauman suggest that those shot did not die, but rumors spread that they had. The daily *Kompas* places the Senakin death toll at seventy-seven (December 13, 1967).

62. For a sensationalistic missionary account, see Peterson 1968, 25–26.

63. Given the intelligence nature of the operation, it is not surprising that local officials, unaware of "Jakarta's" plans, arrested scores of Dayaks during the mobilizations. *Penumpasan terhadap geromobolan tjina komunis* n.d., 12.

64. Interview, Jakarta, June 8, 2001.

65. Whether they came on their own initiative or were summoned to Pontianak is not known. A former bodyguard of Oeray's recalls their reception in Pontianak, although he denied that "war preparations" were discussed. Interview, Pontianak, October 2, 2000.

66. See Widodo's series of *Kompas* articles from December 1967 to early 1968, under the strange pseudonym "*Wartawan 'Kompas'*" ('Kompas' Journalist). In an interview, he referred to the Laskar Pangsuma as an *organisasi bayangan* (shadow organization) and recalled that teams of bodyguards prevented him from approaching Oeray. Interview, Jakarta, June 1, 2001.

67. Interview, Singkawang, May 6, 2001.

68. Some knew of the organization as Yayasan Pangsuma (Pangsuma Foundation). It was housed in Pangsuma Hall. There were at least two other Dayak social organizations in Pontianak at the time: Badan Kesedjahteraan Daya (the Dayak Welfare Board) and Kesatuan Aksi Daya Besar (the Union of Greater Dayak Actions) (see also *Kompas,* December 27, 1967). When asked to differentiate among these groups, elder informants invariably remarked: "Ah, they were all the same thing."

69. Once the militia was placed under army command, officers corralled Dayaks to form local militias. The Subregional Military Command (Korem) 121, which covered the province's eastern half, established a few, and these were kept under the watch of District Military Commands (Kodim). See *Laporan tahunan Korem 121/Tdpr* 1967, 13.

70. This report spotlights the role of J. R. Djamin Indjah, who at the time served as a subdistrict liasion officer in Meranti, as the leader of these attacks begun on October 26, 1967. A few days later, Indjah led another attack in Meranti. In an interview, the now-deceased Indjah spoke very vaguely of his role in the killings. Interview, Pontianak, November 12, 2000.

71. Palaunsoeka used his connections at *Kompas* to discredit Oeray. A string of articles made veiled references to Oeray's complicity (November 11, 15, 20, 23, 1967). Palaunsoeka arrived in Pontianak on November 19, 1967, to survey the situation. He is reported to have said that "it is not true that all Chinese are pro-communist and that many have already become citizens and are anti-communist. . . . I urge all Dayaks to stop these actions . . . for they are ruining the good name of the Dayak . . . as a civilized people in the international community." See *Warta Berita,* November 22, 1967.

72. On the economic hardship, see also Van Hulten 1992, 283, 296–97; and *Kompas,* December 14, 1967, and January 4, 1968.

73. Interview, Pontianak, July 31, 2000. One participant recalls a meeting at the militia's Pontianak headquarters where the division of spoils (land and homes) was discussed and even allotted. Interview, Pontianak, July 19, 2001.

74. This account erroneously dates the attack to 1967 and identifies Sani's position as *camat* (head of the subdistrict).

75. The Chinese Central Association was set up as coordinating body of the many Chinese General Associations, which after World War II were established in towns with a substantial Chinese population. I thank Hui Yew-Foong for clarifying this matter.

76. Hamzah Haz, then a student activist with the Joint-Action Front of Indonesian University Students (KAMI) in Pontianak and later vice president of Indonesia (2001–4), was quoted as saying, "The one and only word they [the Chinese] know is 'money'; that's all" (*Harian Kami,* March 26, 1968).

77. Private relief agencies such as the Indonesian Red Cross, the West Borneo Christian Organization for Aid to Refugees, and Bhakti Suci played a role in addressing the refugee crisis. The military argued that the Geneva Convention on prisoners of war did not apply because no declaration of war had been made (*Kompas,* October 7, 1971). On the expulsion of relief workers, see *Harian Kami,* April 15, 1968.

78. Semdam XII notes only four such projects with 6,304 refugees resettled (1971, 284).

79. While some of this was accomplished via a press blackout, the country's Western allies bought into the New Order's anticommunist propaganda. The following is exemplary: "In late October and early November, hundreds of Chinese in Pontianak, West Borneo were killed, reportedly at the instigation of former members of the PKI" ("Indonesia" 1968, 313).

80. The troops included Special Forces (Pasusad/RPKAD, 356 troops), Batalion 328/Siliwangi (1,090 troops), and Batalion 305/Siliwangi (1,000 troops). See *Rentjana kegiatan bidang personil dan moril* 1968.

81. In 1977 the army announced that during the rebellion, there had been 616 insurgent casualties, 716 arrests, and 1,002 surrenders (*Merdeka,* July 19, 1977).

82. Interviews, Sanggau Ledo, Bengkayang district, July 22–26, 2000. See also *Kalimantan Review,* January–February 2002.

83. Interview, Widodo, Jakarta, June 1, 2001.

84. On the arrests in Pontianak, see *Akcaya,* January 19, 1984. Arrests were also made farther north in the Mempawah and Singkawang areas (Witono 1969, 1).

85. Around this time, the Sarawak rebel forces refocused energies to establish bases in Sarawak, where they worked among its rural Chinese and Iban populations. Sarawak Special Forces countered with Operation Jala Raya (Great Net) launched in February 1970, followed by a civil-military action

called Operation Ngayau (Headhunt) in August 1971. See Sarawak Government 1972, 5–28; and *The origin and development* ca. 1974, 5–9.

86. The most relevant map is TPC-L11DG, published by the Director of Military Survey, Ministry of Defence, United Kingdom, in 1973.

87. By the time the secret agreement was finally announced in March 1974, 482 rebels had surrendered, 171 of whom were women. According to government figures, some two hundred were left in the mountains. See Sarawak Government n.d. On Bong's decision to quit the jungle, see *Far Eastern Economic Review,* April 4, 1975.

88. On PKI activities at this time, see the series of reports on Indonesia in the *Yearbook on International Communist Affairs;* Mortimer 1968; Utrecht 1975; Van der Kroef 1970.

89. *PKI gaya baru pimpinan SA Sofyan* n.d., 3–5. This undated document appears to have been written sometime between October 1973 and January 1974. Another military publication lists three PKI camps with sixty-two rebels in 1970 (*Pelita* 1975, 68).

90. See also *Kompas* March 18, 1975. This article mentions that two hundred detainees were sent sometime in 1970 or 1971 and that plans called for another eight hundred prisoners to be sent.

91. This report also mentions that forestry companies were urged to make sure that non-Chinese Indonesians composed at least 50 percent of their work force. See also *Kompas,* December 18, 1972.

92. In an interview years later, Hartono was quoted as saying, "I was given one hundred days to crush the PKI . . . and get Sofyan dead or alive" (Conboy 2003, 193).

93. Sofyan had married an ethnic Chinese woman while in hiding. His first wife had remained in Pontianak with their four children. Interview, Pontianak, June 28, 2001.

94. See *Kompas,* June 13, 1975; and *Akcaya,* July 20, 1979. Stories circulate that his head was taken to Jakarta for military leaders to see.

95. Arrests of suspected communists followed Sofyan's death. According to the military, twenty-six leaders of the *organisasi "malam"* (underground PKI) were arrested and another 380 of its followers were either arrested or shot dead (*Kompas,* February 2, 1974).

96. See *Laporan tahunan kejaksaan tinggi Kalimantan Barat* 1981, 71; *Laporan tahunan kejaksaan tinggi Kalimantan Barat* 1987, 99; and Badan Koordinasi Intelijen Daerah Kalimantan Barat, July 10, 1986, 5.

97. Interview, Kadarusno, Jakarta, June 15, 2001. An intelligence report mentions that fifteen PKI members had infiltrated the Kodam XII. Witono 1969, 2. *Kompas,* while it did not mention Kistam, reported thirteen arrests (January 17, 1969).

98. For officers who served in West Kalimantan and then in East Timor, see Davidson and Kammen 2002, 86, note 149.

Chapter 3. Regional State-Building and Recurrent Riots

1. Impressionistic evidence suggests that Dayaks retained a greater percentage of market shops in smaller towns (such as Karangan) than in larger towns (such as Anjungan).

2. Sources in Sanggau Ledo maintain that many, although they were described as farmers (*petani*), lacked agricultural know-how (*ilmu*). Important decisions concerning cultivation had been made by the Chinese who had owned the land. Various interviews, July 22–26, 2000, Sanggau Ledo (Bengkayang district). Peluso's observations (1996, 534) corroborate this finding.

3. I know of none published by Madurese researchers or organizations. The two types of chronologies are not mutually exclusive. It is likely that some reporters relied on the lists produced by Dayak organizations.

4. Illustrative of this is an incident in 1952 that these organizations typically cite, though the descriptions are curt and never accompanied by a source.

5. See, for example a statement by the governor, Aspar Aswin, which fingers the Madurese for the violence (*Akcaya*, April 10, 1999).

6. These estimates are drawn from HRW 1997, which does not cite a source.

7. On these road projects, see Government of Australia 1973, vol. 6.

8. Another military document lists IPKI and NU followers (as of 1969) at 36,358 and 18,804, respectively (Ba'dullah 1970, 8).

9. This report mentions strong Dayak representation in the Pontianak district bureaucracy (*Rentjana Operasi Sapu Bersih III-Tahun 1969* n.d., 16). Another notes a similar situation in Sanggau and Sintang districts (*Rencana kerja tahun 1969 Kodam XII/Tanjungpura* n.d., 26, 28). On Oeray's involvement with Partindo, see chapter 1.

10. On the monument, see *Kalimantan Review*, November 2003.

11. They increased from Rp. 550 million in 1969–70 to Rp. 6.64 billion by 1974–75. *Pelaksana evaluasi pelita nasional di daerah Kalimantan Barat* n.d., 1.

12. Dove (1985) has shown these attributes to be myths.

13. In 1979 the provincial government imported 83,800 tons of rice (*Kompas*, October 14, 1980), up 30 percent from 1971 (Ward and Ward 1974, 34).

14. An Australian company was commissioned to survey the province and build a road network. See Government of Australia 1973.

15. Dinas Kehutanan Propinsi Kalimantan Barat n.d., Appendix 4a. By 1975, nearly one-third of West Kalimantan's HPHs were backed by foreign capital. See *Laporan gubernur kepala daerah tingkat I Kalimantan Barat kepada wakil presiden* n.d., 63.

16. The total production of logs and sawn timber increased from 127,894 cubic meters in 1968 to 3.2 million cubic meters by 1973. Accordingly, earnings from timber exports rocketed from $2.4 million in 1969/70 to $61.2 million in

1973/74. See Siahaan 1974, 48, table 5; and *Laporan gubernur kepala daerah tingkat I Kalimantan Barat kepada wakil presiden* n.d., 63–64.

17. According to provincial data, the seven HPH's awarded from 1969–71 were located in southern Pontianak and northern Ketapang districts. See Dinas Kehutanan Propinsi Kalimantan Barat n.d., appendix 6a.

18. Data on the number of transmigrants during this period range from some 5,000 to 8,500 persons.

19. The province was excluded from the list as the Second Five-Year Plan (1973–74 to 1978–79) was being prepared. As security concerns lessened, later it was included via Presidential Decree, No. 12/1973 (Hardjono 1977, 77).

20. As of 1974, 1,584 transmigrants had been moved to Sungai Kakap and another 4,227 to Rasau Jaya (BPS Propinsi Kalimantan Barat 1975, 16, table II.12). Moreover, some seven hundred Chinese refugees housed in Singkawang were moved to Sungai Kakap (*Sinar Harapan,* September 26, 1974).

21. On the saliency of national defense underlying transmigration policies, see Budiardjo 1986.

22. See the editorial in *Angkatan Bersenjata* (August 22, 1974) and Government of Australia 1973, vol. 2, 51.

23. Interviews, Sanggau Ledo, July 26–29, 2000. See also *Merdeka,* December 17, 1974; *Kompas,* October 9, 1978 and April 19, 1979; Soeharso 1992.

24. The physical and political restructuring of villages (based on the Javanese prototype) is also sometimes considered a part of this New Order development package. But the law on village government (No. 5/1979) was not passed until 1979, followed by a period of lethargic implementation (Jatiman 1995).

25. According to the problematic 2000 census, the Dayak population in Ketapang is 123,965, or 29.1 percent of the district total; and the Madurese figure stands at 19,582, or (4.6 percent). Some 96 percent of the Dayak population is rural; 63 percent for the Madurese (BPS 2000a).

26. In 1994 in Tumbang Titi (Ketapang), a brief fight between Madurese road workers and Dayaks led to the razing of a police office, but no fatalities were reported. It was a riot narrowly averted.

27. Violence in Java continued as the campaign heated up (*Gatra,* April 19, 1997).

28. It appears that locally and nationally the high army brass tried to pin the violence on the PPP. In Jakarta, General Hartono alluded to such in the press, while Zainuddin Isman, a local reporter for *Kompas* and a PPP functionary, was detained for provocative reporting on the bloodshed (and for having a sharp weapon in his car). In the end, the frame-up came to naught, and Isman was cleared of all charges (HRW 1997, 36–37). As this episode demonstrates, even army generals—let alone scholars—have failed to "fit" West Kalimantan's recurrent riots within a coherent, national framework.

29. To this day, despite the historic changes in the army's relationship to

state and society in the post-Soeharto era, its territorial doctrine has remained firmly entrenched.

30. See HRW 1997; *Kabar dari Pijar,* March 12, 1997 (posted on the "Apakabar" News Service, March 17, 1997); and the large set of media reports in ISAI/IDRD 1999.

31. Interestingly, the prime assailant, Bakrie, was of mixed parentage. His mother is a Dayak, but he assumed his father's Madurese ethnic identity.

32. Various interviews, Pontianak, May 1, 2001 and Singkawang, May 3–7, 2001. This version differs from HRW's account (1997, 19), which points to a possible Dayak attack earlier that evening and a rumor that a Madurese religious leader had been killed. The presence of members of an association of Madurese Islamic scholars (Bassra) sparked the controversy regardless of whether they had come to avenge Madurese deaths (*D&R,* March 1, 1997).

33. According to the 2000 census, they made up some 3 percent of Pontianak's 464,000 population (BPS 2000a, 73, table 10.7).

34. Muhammad Sidik bin H. Baiduri, who led these roadblock attacks, said in his (likely forced) confession that he planned the killings "to avenge the suffering of Madurese in the fighting that occurred in Sanggau Ledo" (*Berita acara pemeriksaan,* ca. June 1997). Sidik was sentenced to three years in prison (HRW 1997, 34).

35. Many Madurese refugees responded to the question of how to solve Malay-Madurese strife by invoking peace ceremonies. One commented: "Put on peace ceremonies, like those in Sambas during the 1997 violence." In fact, the main provincial organization of Madurese elite, IKAMRA, was formed in response to financial obligations incurred due to Dayak customary legal claims resulting from the peace ceremonies.

36. This discussion privileges the Dayak sides of things because the scale of the 1997 violence — though not necessarily its outbreak — was a result of the aggressiveness of Dayak war parties.

37. On intermarriage between Dayak women and Chinese men, see Tangdiling 1993; for a more historical perspective, see Heidhues 2003, 26, 33–39, 130–33, 149.

38. See *Laporan survey kehidupan rakyat perbatasan* 1976. Journalists also accompanied military officers to the border areas to report on "backward" Dayaks. See the series of articles by August Parengkuan (*Kompas,* July–December 1971) and by Masdan Rozhany (*Utama,* March-May 1973).

39. As late as 1974, troops from Infantry Battalion 123 (North Sumatra) were still teaching at border area schools (*Sinar Pagi,* October, 15, 1974).

40. See Boelaars and Sabon 1979a, 29, Table 9; 1979b, 29, Table 9. The quote is from 1979b, 26. These developments also bolstered the influence of Protestantism (Humble 1982).

41. Interview, Pontianak, August 14, 2001.

42. The military authorities continued to prod the Islamic elite to dissemi-
nate Islam to the border areas (*Kompas,* June 18, 1974).

43. Military officers replaced M. Th. Djaman (Sanggau), G. P. Djaoeng
(Sintang), and A. Djelani (Pontianak district). J. R. Gielling (Kapuas Hulu)
was replaced with a non-Dayak civilian.

44. In 1967, IPKI held six of the twenty seats reserved for political parties
in the provincial assembly (DPRD-GR TK I). The remaining seats were divided among five parties. Functional groups (Golongan Karya) were allotted
eighteen seats.

45. Ngo Lahay was detained because of his associations with Baperki and
Sahudin because he rejected Golkar in favor of IPKI. In the 1971 elections,
IPKI won two of the thirty-two contested seats for the provincial DPRD,
while Golkar took twenty-one. The Catholic Party won two seats.

46. Golkar soon drained IPKI's support. In the 1971 elections in Pontianak
district, the former took seventeen of the thirty-two contested seats, while the
latter won only two. The Catholic Party captured three seats.

47. Those who benefited included Oeray, Imam Khalis, G. P. Djaoeng,
Moses Nyawath, and Rahman Sahudin (whose prison experience convinced
him to join Golkar). Those who refused to join Golkar suffered accordingly.
Consider H. M. Baroamas J. Balunus, who had served on the 1957 West Kalimantan provincial preparations committee, on the 1964 provincial governing
body (Badan Pemerintah Harian), and as a raider during *Konfrontasi.* In the
early 1970s he refused to join Golkar, and his trading company was bankrupted.
He went on to lead a life of relative obscurity and poverty.

48. Kadarusno, interview, Jakarta, June 15, 2001. Before becoming
governor, Kadarusno had served as the commander of the Sintang Regional
Military Command (Kodam) (ca. 1969–71), which covered the eastern half of
West Kalimantan.

49. One military publication lists the names of twenty-three *panglima* who
received such honors (*Pelita* 1975, 92–93). Pelda stands for Pangkat Pembantu
Letnan Dua (Second Lieutenant Assistant).

50. The front-page article quips that Soeharto never "explained" which
"mistakes" he had in mind (*Kompas,* March 20, 1972).

51. Dayak leaders excluded from this group were those (such as I. Kaping
and Balunus) who were partisan to the Catholic Party under Palaunsoeka. Following the New Order's forced amalgamation of political parties in 1973, Palaunsoeka and friends joined the quasi-Christian-oriented Indonesian Democratic Party (PDI).

52. Following the 1977 elections, Oeray and Aloyisus Aloi were appointed
to the People's Representative Council (DPR); J. P. Djaoeng and Moses Nyawath sat in the provincial DPRD, and Rahman Sahudin and Willem Amat in
the Pontianak and Sanggau district assemblies, respectively.

53. One prominent example was Jakobus Luna, who served as the head of Samalantan subdistrict and in 1978 as head of Bengkayang subdistrict. In 2000, he became Bengkayang's first *bupati*.

54. Interview, Soejiman, Jakarta June 7, 2001. In our conversation his contempt for "traditional" Dayak ways of life was explicit.

55. In the 1977 election, Golkar won 69 percent of the provincial vote, up 2 percent from its results in 1971.

56. In West Kalimantan such festivals were not new but holding them at the district level was. The early ones were gaudy displays of the council's notional authority, but over the years they have become popular annual events lasting two or three days that draw tens of thousands of onlookers.

57. Some of Pancur Kasih's leaders insisted that this was not an intrinsic criticism of the Church. In fact, they pointed out that a priest, Helio Herman, was one of Pancur Kasih's seven founders. Members of the elder Dayak elite cautioned against founding Pancur Kasih, which they deemed exclusionist and parochial.

58. Since the highest state institution, a kind of super-parliament known as the MPR (Majelis Permusyawaratan Rakyat), repealed the law requiring all social organizations to claim Pancasila as their sole ideological foundation (*azas tunggal*) in November 1998, Pancur Kasih has deleted references to Pancasila and the 1945 Constitution from its mission statement. See their Web site, dayakology.com. My translation slightly differs from theirs.

59. The experience of some its leaders was exemplar. At the provincial DPRD, Arsen Rickson sat for Golkar four times (1982–99) and then in Parliament. In the DPRD, Sahudin was at least a three-time member (1982–97); and Mecer served once (1987–92).

60. SARA stands for *suku, agama, ras dan antar-golongan* (ethnic, religious, race, and intergroup relations). The New Order discouraged public manifestations of SARA in any form, including organizations and discourse.

61. Their initial startup grant came from the Jakarta-based Indonesian Bishops' Council (LPPS-KWI), which for the first few years administered IDRD.

62. Interview, Pontianak, July 17, 2001.

63. Walhi, a well-known environmental NGO based in Jakarta, helped to facilitate the meeting. See Moniaga 2007.

64. The need for mapping ancestral lands is well reflected in Governor Aswin's statement on *tanah adat:* "On a map, you cannot see customary lands. But in reality there are those, such as the Dayaks, who have their own customary lands. The Agrarian Law (UU Pokok Agaria) concerns land issues of ten to twelve hectares. Now lands owned by Dayaks . . . are found in ten to twelve locations. If one family owns ten to twelve hectares and there are one hundred families, how much ancestral land has to be accommodated? How do I, as the provincial executive [*kepala daerah*], accommodate central government

regulations with the aspirations of a community with customs like that?" (*Tiras*, March 20, 1997)

65. By 2003, there were twenty-one autonomous units under Pancur Kasih. For an exhaustive list, see Wardoyo 2003, 290.

66. My survey of *Akcaya* from 1980 to 1990 found a mere six articles on Dayaks. In contrast, there were many staged photos without text of "exotic" Dayaks that featured "traditional" costume and dance.

67. A good example is a July 27, 1992, article on Pancur Kasih, its first mention in the newspaper, although the organization was a decade old.

68. Despite the English-language title, its articles are written in Indonesian. It publishes a biannual English-language edition to enhance its international exposure, especially among the donor community.

69. Pancur Kasih's press also published provocative pamphlets and tracts with titles such as *Manusia Dayak: Orang Kecil Yang Terperangkap Modernisasi* [Dayaks: Ordinary People Trapped by Modernization] (Djuweng 1996); *The Dominant Paradigm and the Cost of Development* (Djuweng 1997); and *Panen Bencana: Kelapa Sawit* [Harvesting Disaster: Oil Palm] (Florus and Petebang 1999).

70. Early topics were the preservation of *adat* ceremonies, customary law, long houses, and oral histories—in other words, "essences" of Dayakness.

71. Some early cases of small-scale protests covered in *Kalimantan Review* occurred in Sekadau Hulu (Sanggau district) (April–June 1994), Sanggau Ledo (July–September 1995), and Jelai Hulu (Ketapang district) (October–December 1995).

72. Information on these protests was culled from various interviews conducted in Pontianak; *Akcaya*, April 8, 1981 (a small paragraph buried in the paper's back pages); and Rokaerts 1985, 26.

73. Interview, Stephanus Djuweng, Pontianak, July 17, 2001.

74. Fourteen locals were sentenced to three months in jail and six months probation.

75. Various interviews, Pontianak; *Akcaya*, August 18, 1994; and *Kalimantan Review* October–December 1994.

76. The provincial Golkar board of directors accused Golkar members of the Sintang DPRD of "deserting" (*membelot*) the party and threatened to have them recalled (*Merdeka*, February 16, 1994).

77. More cynical people blamed Islam for Kadir's defeat. Leaflets were widely distributed stating that Kamarullah's victory was an insult to all Dayaks because during the vote count, people had shouted "Dayaks are infidels!" (*Orang Dayak Kafir!*). Later Kadir would serve as vice governor (2004–8).

78. Dayak leaders also threatened to withdraw support for Golkar in the upcoming 1997 general elections. When the *bupati* position in Kapuas Hulu opened a few months later, it was given to a Dayak civil servant, Jacobus Layang, whose rank was well below that of Kadir's. Some interpreted the appointment as

an example of "any Dayak will do" and suspected that Golkar viewed Layang as one who could do little damage in the province's most remote district. To bolster his legitimacy among the Dayak political community, Layang initiated a provincial-level customary council (Majelis Adat). In 1995, he was named its first head. On Layang's selection as *bupati,* see Tanasaldy 2007.

79. For more on this provocative article, see Davidson 2007.

Chapter 4. Reform, Decentralization, and the Politicization of Ethnicity and Indigeneity

1. This case was one of the few reported in *Akcaya* (August 6, 1997).

2. It should be stressed that the intensity of this political revitalization has varied among communities, loosely corresponding to the extent to which different groups were involved in the violence. A general distinction can be drawn between those in the western, lowland districts of Sambas/Bengkayang, Pontianak, and Sanggau—areas where the violence was heaviest—and those found in the upriver Sintang and Kapuas Hulu districts where the violence was more ephemeral. Ketapang is an exception. This district was spared the violence; yet, because several of the Pontianak-based NGOs has close ties to communities there (several key activists hail from Ketapang) indigenous activism has been apparent.

3. These examples were taken from *Kalimantan Review* September 1998, November 1998, January 1999, and March 1999.

4. For another politicized *tolak bala,* see *Akcaya,* October 31, 1998.

5. Dayak demands included elimination the military's dual function (*dwi-fungsi*) doctrine, the nullification of an array of laws, including Law 5/1974 on provincial government and Law 5/1979 on village government, which have since been repealed, and the resignation of Governor Aspar Aswin.

6. See *Akcaya,* July 1 and October 30, 1998; and *Kalimantan Review,* July 1998, November 1998, and January 1999.

7. For example, as of 1997, there were no Dayaks in the two vice governor and two assistant to the governor positions, and they held only twenty-seven out of eighty-one subdistrict head positions. In 1999, the most powerful regional departments were devoid of Dayak representation. See Soetrisno 1998, 66, and *Kalimantan Review,* August 1999.

8. *Akcaya,* June 3, 1998, and *Kalimantan Review,* July 1998, January 1999. Andjioe had served as a commander of the District Military Command (Komando Distrik Militer, or Kodim) in Central Kalimantan and as the head of staff of the Kodim in Ketapang.

9. After the incident, Cornelis was called to answer to the governor, the regional military commander (Pangdam), and police chief. His apology was printed in *Akcaya,* February 9, 1999. In 2001, he was elected *bupati* of the new Landak district (once part of Pontianak district), while in 2004 Salim was elected *bupati* of Pontianak district.

10. Since he was a Muslim, the fact that he considered himself "Dayak" aroused the ire of many Dayak, who preferred to see him as "Malay." I return to this "Dayak Islam" controversy in chapter 5.

11. The army had complained that in the Paloh area (on the north coast of Sambas) the "*WNA Tjina*" (foreign chinks) were too free and needed closer supervision (Witono 1968, 2).

12. Interviews, Singkawang, December 7, 2000, and Sentebang (Jawai subdistrict), December 9, 2000. See also Poerwanto 2005, 150.

13. Ethnicity was not recorded in New Order censuses. Its inclusion in the 2000 census does not settle this issue since the Madurese were expelled from the region before that year.

14. It was then West Kalimantan's most densely populated rural district. See *Analisa perkembangan kependudukan menurut sensus penduduk 1990* 1992/93, 18, table 2.5.

15. In 1990, the figure for Sambas district was sixty-two people per square kilometer, a 26 percent increase from 1980. See BPS Kabupaten Sambas 2000, 46, table 4.1.1.

16. From 1984 to 1992, Sambas's economy expanded at an average annual rate of 6.3 percent, notable but below the provincial average of 8.7 percent. See *Produk domestik regional bruto propinsi & kabupaten/kotamadya Kalimantan Barat* 1993, 2, table 1.

17. On the shooting death of a notorious local Madurese thug in Sambas district, see *Tempo*, November 12, 1983.

18. BPS Kabupaten Sambas 2000, 58, table 4.2.7. On the link between migration to Sarawak and the state of the province's economy, see Sidney Jones (2000, 35), who notes that the number of *jeruk* farmers migrating to Malaysia rose from 250 in 1989–90 to 6,000 in 1996–97.

19. After the widespread violence erupted, the police made (possibly) seven arrests. Three persons were indicted—Jabak and Hasan's parents. This left many unsatisfied given the large number of attackers. Sentenced to seven years in prison, Jabak was found guilty on three counts: aiding and abetting a crime leading to a fatality (Article 56 of the Indonesian Criminal Code), participating in an attack that endangered a life (Article 358), and illegal possession of a knife (Article 2, Emergency Regulation No. 12/1951).

20. Besides Bujang, they included M. Jamras, Djaili Idris, Sanusi H. Koko, (the late) Haji Rustam Effendi, (the late) Haji Uray Yunadi Nalaprana, Ikhdar Salim, Mansur SH, Uray Amundin, Asyari SH, and Rosita Nengsih.

21. Interview, Singkawang, January 13, 2004.

22. On this, see also Saad 2003, 97.

23. In some sources it is spelled Semparuk.

24. Of the five army platoons (Satuan Setingkat Pleton), two each were stationed in Tebas and Jawai and another in Pemangkat. Meanwhile, the police mobilized six platoons, two in Pemangkat, one in Jawai and three in Tebas (*Akcaya*, March 17, 1999).

25. As for the suspiciously delayed outbreak of violence in Paloh, a local commented, "I don't understand why this incident suddenly rocked Paloh. Here there is nothing that differentiates the Malays and Madurese. They have assimilated well (and) . . . they were not excessively wealthy" (*Suaka*, April 5–8, 1999).

26. On March 23, six companies of anti-riot brigades (sometimes referred to as PPRM-PPHH) arrived from Jakarta. Reportedly, they comprised 459 police personnel and 280 army troops (*Akcaya*, March 24, 1999). Whereas under the New Order the army responded to public demonstrations and violence, in the early post-Soeharto era, the police and army began joint operations.

27. Consonant with UN stipulations, the term most fitting here is internally displaced persons (IDPs). The term refugee connotes the crossing of internationally recognized borders. However, in Indonesia, the word used is *pengungsi*, which is best rendered refugee. To keep closer to Indonesian denotations, I will use the English term refugee.

28. There were two decentralization acts, Law No. 22/1999 on Regional Government and Law No. 25/1999 on Fiscal Balance between the Central Government and the Region. They were passed in 1999 and took effect on January 1, 2001.

29. For a thorough list of troubled *bupati* elections in the early decentralization era, see *Kompas*, September 13, 2000.

30. At the same time, the number of provinces has increased from twenty-six in 1999 to thirty-three in 2006.

31. The new districts include Bengkayang, Landak, Sekadau, and Melawi, while Singkawang's status was upgraded to municipality (*kota*). To this day, there is constant talk of forming new districts and of districts joining forces to form a new province.

32. This is a rough estimate—356, 442 Malays out of a district population of 509,000. It reflects a figure prior to the 1999 violence and the redistricting, and for only the subdistricts that comprise the new Sambas district. Again, the difficulty of verification stems from the fact that the 2000 census was conducted after the Madurese expulsion, and the Madurese were expelled from a district (Sambas) that then was split into two (Sambas and Bengkayang).

33. This statement is a version of a popular rallying cry during Malaya's independence struggle. I thank M. S. B. Yaapar and Tim Barnard for bringing this to my attention.

34. On the importance Malay leaders placed on capturing the bureaucracy, see the illustrative quote in Saad 2003, 86–88.

35. Formally, the PPP and a coalition faction (Fraksi Gabungan) backed Rasyid. One subdistrict head of FKPM said that they supported Rasyid because he had displayed an unyielding loyalty toward FKPM since its inception (interview, Pemangkat, February 27, 2001). For the first few years of the reform era—the time period under consideration in this chapter—*bupati* continued to

be elected by the district DPRD, as they were under the New Order. The principal difference was that the election process was freed from heavy interference from the center. Since 2005, *bupati* have been directly elected.

36. Here the split of the old Sambas district into Sambas and Bengkayang district needs emphasis. The Madurese were expelled from the former. In Bengkayang they were forced toward the coast and placed in camps. As of 2004, Madurese were allowed to return to Bengkayang's towns. For years following the riots in Sambas, Madurese that entered there did so at risk of death. For one incident that happened in 2002, see Purwana 2003, 78.

37. It would have been inconceivable or preposterous for the FKPM leadership to think that it alone could accomplish such a feat. The surprise of their "success," albeit with Dayak aid, was vividly expressed in my interviews with FKPM leaders.

38. Having Dayaks join the fray also would also divert attention from the fact that two Islamic groups were fighting. In my interviews with Islamic leaders in Pontianak, they admitted their embarrassment over this predicament. Interestingly, from a Dayak vantage point, some claimed that they joined (*bergabung*) Sambas Malays to fight the Madurese. Others insisted they fought to defend their honor and uphold *adat* traditions in the face of Amat's death.

39. The cattle population of Sambas was estimated to be 26,700 in 1997. See BPS Propinsi Kalimantan Barat 1998, 161, table 6.3.1.

40. Interviews, Karimuting, Sungai Raya subdistrict, May 6, 2001.

41. Wimpi is the grandson of Mohammad Mulya Ibrahim Syafuddin, who was killed by the Japanese during World War II. On Wimpi's father, see *Kompas,* November 29, 1974.

42. In an interview, Wimpi said he looked to the Malaysian model, where sultans had considerable symbolic prestige (not political power) and access to state resources (interview, Pontianak, January 17, 2004).

Chapter 5. Refugees, a Governor, and an Urban Racket

1. See chapter 3, note 78. The board had since added "Dayak" to its name.

2. Here some complicated terms require elucidation. *Penduduk asli* is often translated as "indigenous people" (or original inhabitants) while *putera daerah* means "native son." They are frequently used interchangeably. There are, however, certain contexts in which they differ. In West Kalimantan, Javanese or Bataks born in the province may argue for *putera daerah* status, but not *penduduk asli* status. Others reserve the *putera daerah* moniker for Malays, Dayaks, and Chinese, although the latter is controversial (see below). As for *penduduk asli,* the debate concerns Dayaks and Malays (see chapters 1 and 4).

3. In mid-1999, the newspaper *Akcaya* changed its name to *Pontianak Post* to distance itself from New Order association and to reflect a commitment to reform.

4. In mid-2005, motions were made in the provincial DPRD calling for the Jawi script (Arabic script adjusted to Malay) be added to street signs in Pontianak and proposing that government buildings and the city's gateway be decorated with Malay cultural trappings (*Pontianak Post,* June 7, 2005).

5. Effendi would later be one of the province's "Malay" provincial representatives in the MPR for the 1999–2004 term (see below).

6. Direct elections of *bupati* by the electorate did not commence until 2005.

7. Malay *bupati*-Dayak vice *bupati* packages won in Kapuas Hulu and Ketapang, and vice versa in Landak and Sintang.

8. This looting occurred amid a string of similar incidents across the country at the time (Van Dijk 2001, 361). The Dayak Customary Board, urged by the local military, called in Dayaks from Darit (Pontianak district) to protect Chinese warehouses. It is believed Chinese businessmen were extorted to pay for this protection.

9. It was headed by Syamsul Rizal, a local contractor close to Aswin.

10. Its former head, Ato' Ismail, admitted that PMKB had done little until the Parit Setia attack galvanized it into action. It then raised money to aid the victims and fund the anti-Madurese mobilizations (interview, Pontianak, August 2, 2001).

11. Syarif Toto Alqadrie, a former Pontianak City DPRD member for Golkar and functionary of the *kraton,* headed Lembayu. On the mosque's dilapidated condition, see *Tempo,* April 11, 1981.

12. In doing so, the Malay champions have simplistically glossed over the Arabic heritage of Kadriah sultanate. In January 2004, the grandnephew of Sultan Hamid II was installed as sultan.

13. Some sources include the word *Islam* in the title, Panglima Melayu Islam Arus Bawah (Islamic Malay War Leader of the Undertow).

14. Interview, Abas Fadhilah, Pontianak, May 14, 2001. Benua Indah was owned by Budiono Tan, Adjianto's rival. Donni Aswin, the governor's son, was one of Kayu Mukti's principal partners.

15. Ali Anafia, then head of Pontianak City's DPRD, was closely associated with Al-Faqar. A Golkar cadre, Anafia once ran the Pontianak branch of Pemuda Pancasila, a national youth organization infamous for its criminality.

16. Isman had been arrested for writing about the 1997 violence (see chapter 3, note 28).

17. On the political interplay between Dayak and Islam identities, see below.

18. For specific accusations of corruption, see *Libas* July 1998; and *Suaka,* June 30–July 2, 1999.

19. Aswin served as the commander of Korem 121 in Sintang (1986–88) and then as vice governor in Bali. When he was appointed governor of West

Kalimantan in 1993, he was a one-star brigadier general. Although he was not native to the area, he was the first non-Javanese governor of West Kalimantan to be appointed during the New Order. He hails from Samarinda in East Kalimantan.

20. Some student groups were loosely aligned in an umbrella organization called Forum Kapuas. These included The Movement of Indonesian Islamic Students (PMII), Association of Indonesian Catholic Students (PMKRI), Movement of Indonesian National Students (GMNI), Union of Muhammadiyah Students (IMM), Association of Chinese Students (HMTI), and the Islamic Students Association (HMI).

21. In the 1999 elections, Golkar won fourteen out of the forty-nine contested seats, followed by PDI-P with eleven.

22. The five dissenting factions accounted for thirty-eight out of fifty-five DPRD members.

23. At that time, Odang was head of the now-defunct Provincial Representatives (*Utusan Daerah*) of the MPR in Jakarta. For more on Odang, see Saptono 2003.

24. Article 45 (subsection 1) of Law No. 22/1999 included the term *accountability* (*pertanggungjawaban*). If the official's report was rejected, according to article 46, the relevant regional executive had thirty days in which to present his or her case. If the report was rejected a second time, the assembly could "recommend impeachment" (*mengusulkan pemberhentinya*) to the president.

25. That numerous DPRDs were plotting to impeach regional heads via the rejection of accountability speeches alarmed officials in the Regional Autonomy Ministry. The revised law on regional government (No. 32/2004) has outlawed the practice of rejecting annual reports as a means of impeaching regional heads.

26. Golkar cadres burned party shirts in protest of Syamsumin's anti-Aswin stance (*Kalbar Pos,* June 26–28, 2000). Anafia's political career faltered in the post-Aswin era. He was removed from the leadership of the Pontianak City DPRD, was forced out of Golkar, and failed to regain a legislative seat in the 2004 elections with the small Reform Star Party (PBR).

27. Whereas police and forensic experts concluded that a blunt object had caused Syafruddin's death, eyewitnesses claimed to have heard sniper fire coming from the direction of the governor's office. The police never explained why no one witnessed Syafruddin's bludgeoning.

28. The vote of no confidence came in the form of a petition (*Pontianak Post,* July 29, 2000). Besides mentioning the five DPRD factions, it invoked local ethnic organizations, student groups, and social organizations such as Muhammadiyah. It charged Aswin with perpetrating a "leadership crisis" (*krisis percayaan*).

29. Legislators choose this extralegal route because Law No. 22/1999 was not to take effect until January 1, 2001. Also it was doubtful whether there were

reasonable grounds on which to reject the report on its contents alone. The legislators never met to discuss its findings, and a few admitted to me that they had never read it.

30. Representatives from rural districts were flown to Jakarta to argue Aswin's case (*Equator*, September 15 and 22, 2000).

31. Congruent with the *kraton* revitalization, this street has since been renamed Sultan Hamid II Avenue.

32. The low number of fatalities was due to the methodical buildup of tensions that allowed most Madurese who work or trade in the area to leave.

33. At this point, they comprised local forces, including two companies of police special forces (Perintis), two companies of city police, and one company of the Mobil Brigade (Brimob). According to field reports, they were aided (*dibantu*) by local army troops. Scores of conspicuous plainclothesmen were also deployed.

34. Before attacking the refugees that night, people gathered at Kayu Mukti where Abas was employed. Donni Aswin was one of Kayu Mukti's principal partners (see note 14).

35. Abas reemerged months later, denying rumors that Aswin had purchased a new house for him (interview, Pontianak, May 14, 2001).

36. Several banners around the city read: "This Is a Conflict-Free Area. We Love Peace"; "An All-Ethnic Peace Zone"; and "We Will Not Be Provoked by Instigators."

37. Although the final standing of Aswin's 2000 report was never resolved, his 2001 report was approved without debate.

38. The increasing violence they experienced off-campus, beyond the realm of demonstrations, took its toll. For one exemplary incident, see *Equator*, November 23, 2000.

39. Moreover, consonant with the New Order evisceration of local leadership, the lack of clear alternatives to Aswin compounded the problem.

40. Because a Dayak (Oeray) had last held the governorship, Malay elites insisted that it was time for a Malay *putera daerah* to occupy the post.

41. Although he is a native son, since 1971, when he was elected to the DPR as an NU representative, Haz has spent his political career in Jakarta.

42. As governor, Djafar had been implicated in a corruption scandal involving some Rp. 328 billion worth of bad credit from his tenure as director of a large media company (Lativi Media Karya) in Jakarta. In June 2006, he was officially named as a suspect.

43. This comes across clearly in interviews with her minister of home affairs, Hari Sabarno. See *Tempo*, September 8, 2001.

44. The majority were from Sambas district. The ten thousand or so from Bengkayang district were housed in dilapidated facilities outside Singkawang. Of the 110 refugees I surveyed, only four identified their home district as Bengkayang. This survey was undertaken with the help of several Madurese assistants whom I would like to thank for their tireless efforts. People in camps were

randomly selected but were largely drawn from Asrama Haji, Sultan Syarif Abdurrahman Stadium, and GOR Pangsuma. Those not in camps were selected based on the personal knowledge of my assistants. The June violence (see below) brought the survey to a close prematurely.

45. The majority were the wives of Madurese men. Based on the survey results, about 10 percent of the refugees in Pontianak were not Madurese.

46. A survey conducted by a Madurese organization in April 1999 found that 60 percent of the refugees wanted to return to Sambas (*Akcaya*, April 23, 1999). Two years on, my survey showed similar results (66 percent). Of the remainder, 31 percent were keen on staying in Pontianak; 2 percent chose relocation to somewhere else; and 1 percent selected Madura as a preferred destination.

47. This information also comes from my survey.

48. Recall Aswin's statement quoted in chapter 4, which squarely blamed the Madurese.

49. Islamic student groups engaged in a Herculean effort to provide necessities to refugees as they arrived in Pontianak but lacked the resources to sustain these efforts.

50. Yet, in time refugees developed identities according to their particular camp while organizations such as neighborhood watch groups (*pos ronda*) were formed.

51. Accusations of Sulaiman's support of Aswin and his putative role in the October riots created a storm in the Madurese community. For allegations of Madurese leaders seeking material gain from the refugee crisis, see Petebang and Sutrisno 2000, 30–31. On Sulaiman's background in the salt trade, see *Nusantara*, No. 73, 1996.

52. For instance, he stalled plans announced by Erna Witoelar, the housing and regional development minister, to give Sambas and Pontianak district governments Rp. 3 billion apiece in construction subsidies. Tellingly, Aswin insisted that the monies be channeled via provincial government conduits (*Pontianak Post*, January 29 and February 5, 2000).

53. This was the conclusion of Madurese students at UNTAN who conducted research on the sites' suitability. Similar allegations were frequent in media accounts.

54. For one such photo, see *Pontianak Post*, July 3, 2001. On the misleading headlines, see *Equator*, February 24 and March 9, 2001. The national daily *Kompas* was not above such commentary either, as suggested by photo captions identifying conditions in these designated locations as "subur" (rich) and "makin membaik" (getting better) (July 13, 2001).

55. After six months or so of living under plastic tarps and cardboard boxes, at their own expense the refugees built hundreds of small wooden shacks on the campgrounds.

56. The Jeruju area and the Dahlia market, sites of violence during the October 2000 riots, were again affected. This time the violence was fleeting.

57. To ease Dayak-Madurese tensions, peace ceremonies were held in Siantan and at the Dayak longhouse in Pontianak (*Equator,* June 29, 2001).

58. Another reason is that substantial Malay interests and property would have been damaged as well.

59. According to Syamsuddin, formerly a well-off businessman from Sambas, a refugee and head of the Victims of Sambas's Social Violence Foundation (Yayasan Korban Kekerasan Sosial Sambas)—the organization that represented the refugees in negotiations—roughly seven thousand families were accounted for in Pontianak (in and out of the camps). Another four thousand in the resettlement sites received less based on the value of the houses they had been given. In total, the central government handed out some Rp. 45 billion. What percentage of the estimated sixty-two thousand recipients of the funds were authentic refugees is not clear (interview, Pontianak, July 18, 2002). On Haz's visit, see *Kalimantan Review,* August 2002.

60. The first government-sponsored meeting among ethnic elites to discuss the idea of return was held on June 13, 2002, in Singkawang. Another followed a year later (Bamba 2004, 405).

61. News reports disingenuously blamed the shortages on drought-induced low rivers (*Kompas,* July 18, 2001).

62. For example, following the al Qaida attacks on New York and Washington, D.C., on September 11, 2001, there were anti-American demonstrations in Pontianak in which both Malays and Madurese participated.

63. This scenario materialized briefly during the October 2000 riots when Dayak and Madurese leaders cooperated to prevent members of FKPM-Sambas from convoying through Singkawang (*Pontianak Post,* October 29, 2000). A leading Dayak activist concurs that Malay-Dayak violence is a possibility (Bamba 2004, 409).

64. During the course of the New Order, the province's most prominent Chinese businessman, the late Adijanto (see below), emphasized this point, referring to it as the price of doing business (interview, Pontianak, November 29, 2000).

65. With Presidential Instruction 4/1999, the Habibie administration removed the legal foundations of the Surat Bukti Kewarganegaraan Republik Indonesia (Letter of Proof of Indonesian Citizenship, or SBKRI), which the New Order had used to discriminate against Indonesians of Chinese descent. Yet, implementation in the field has been devilishly slow. The situation deteriorated to the point where in 2004 Pontianak's mayor was forced to pass a decree locally invalidating the SBKRI (*Kalimantan Review,* December 2004). Reports that authorities continue to demand that the SBKRI be presented when Chinese apply for passports and state identity cards continue to surface (*Pontianak Post,* May 12 and 14, 2005).

66. In 1999, most urban Chinese threw their support behind Megawati's PDI-P, illustrative of the party's general Christian support. It was the leading vote-getter in areas with significant Chinese populations, Pontianak and

Bengkayang, which then included Singkawang, whose population is approximately 40 percent ethnic Chinese. Golkar took the other six (largely rural) districts, although it won a majority in none.

67. This is what happened when officials in Singkawang, according to the city's former head of tourism, sought to make Cap Go Mei a recognized event following Soeharto's resignation. Local non-Chinese elites protested, arguing that recognition would help to revive "PGRS/Paraku" and "communism." Officials went ahead with their plans regardless (interview, M. Zeet Hamdi Assovie, Pontianak, June 1, 2005).

68. For the 1982 elections, Soeharto wanted the process expedited, so in 1980 he issued Presidential Decree 13/1980; Presidential Instruction 2/1980 enacted the decree (*Kompas*, July 3, 1980).

69. Born out of the 1967 violence, Bhakti Suci helped to arrange the overwhelming number of burials. At its outset it was a multiethnic effort, but over time government pressure drove non-Chinese support away. Bhakti Suci eventually became the coordinating body for the city's forty-plus Chinese burial associations and the organization through which Adijanto and his associates appeased predatory interests. Adijanto contributed handsomely to Islamic festivals (*Akcaya*, December 3, 1983) and built the province's lone military high school academy.

70. The rise of Adijanto is emblematic of Pontianak's ever-evolving trading arena. The son of a poor immigrant, he started out by collecting and trading shards of glass. His big break came with *Konfrontasi*, when his connections obtained for him much sought after import-export licenses. When the New Order regime set its sights on the area's rich forest reserves, Adijanto followed suit. By 1990, his Bumi Raya Utama Group was estimated to be Indonesia's seventh-largest timber company (*Warta Ekonomi*, July 23, 1990).

71. In 2004, the Benua Indah Group laid off thousands of workers (*Kalimantan Review*, November 2004) and subsequently declared bankruptcy.

72. Recall the Dayak-Malay *utusan daerah* fiasco surrounding Zainuddin Isman.

73. District-level festivals have been held in at least Sambas and Sanggau districts (Jafar 2000; *Pontianak Post* April 10, 2000).

74. Cynically, one might suggest that the Chinese figure was included in order to attract more Chinese consumers, who overwhelmingly have the most purchasing power in the city. It begs the question why the statue was erected in the first place, however.

75. As of late 2006, Effendi was under investigation for using false academic credentials.

76. For a rare and thoughtful discussion of these themes in relation to the violence, see Schiller and Garang 2002.

77. This is important because other results of the 2000 census became an issue. One field of contention concerns the question who is the province's largest ethnic group, Malays or Dayaks, which the census should have settled if it

were not for several coding problems. While ethnologically accurate, the census contained no singular "Dayak" category, but three sub-Dayak ethnicities: Kendayan/Kenayan (7.8 percent), Darat (7.4), and Peasguan (4.8), which left out major ethnic subgroups, leaving the "Dayak" total at an unfathomable 19 percent. Meanwhile, some 37 percent of the provincial population was classified as "Others." Dayak groups in Pontianak protested the results, which led to the banning of the census results (for ethnicity and religion) from the BPS office and an *adat* fine was levied against the provincial BPS head (see *Kalimantan Review*, July 2003). Tanasaldy (2007) retabulated the figures and arrived at the following: Dayaks 33.1 percent, Malays 32.4, Chinese 9.5, and Madurese 5.5. The Chinese were underreported nationwide (Suryadinata, Arifin, and Ananta 2003, chap. 3) and that the Dayak and Malay figures were nearly a statistical tie seems politically palpable, but perhaps demographically unlikely.

78. Christian (and Jewish) conspiracy theories abound in Indonesia (Van Bruinessen 2002).

79. I return to this point in chapter 6.

80. While discussing this discontent with a Dayak activist in Pontianak, I reminded him that his organization had once vigorously supported the candidacies of the *bupati* in question. He responded: "Yes, but that was then. How were we supposed to know? Things have changed." On the disappointment over Andjioe's tenure in Sanggau, see *Kalimantan Review*, September 2003.

Chapter 6. Collective Violence in West Kalimantan in Comparative Perspective

1. There were accusations that the former separatist movement that sought to establish a Republic of the South Moluccas (RMS)—see below—was behind the violence. While largely exaggerated, this did become an issue once the fighting commenced, and it was used as a justification and solidarity issue for Muslims (HRW 1999).

2. This includes significant lulls and distinct phases of violence.

3. I restrict this to the male population due to the overwhelming participation of men in group violence.

4. I designate the conflict zone to encompass the cities of Pontianak and Singkawang and the districts of Pontianak, Landak, Bengkayang, and Sambas.

5. I consider the conflict zone to include Palangkarya and East Kotawaringin.

6. In the latter half of 1999, the province of Moluccas was divided in two: the Moluccas and the North Moluccas. Notwithstanding the violence in the latter, here the term *Moluccas* will refer largely to the former.

7. The Laskar Jihad arrived in the Moluccas in April, although less organized and more ineffectual groups had preceded them (ICG 2000, 9). Its arrival

compelled Wahid, on June 27, 2000, to declare a state of civil emergency for the Moluccas, a status below that of military emergency and martial law.

8. A strong belief exists that outsiders provoked the Moluccan violence. Accusations center on disavowed military officers with close ties to the former first family who sought to disrupt the then upcoming 1999 elections in order to create conditions favorable to the return of military rule (HRW 1999). In particular, the deportation to Ambon of hundreds of Jakarta-based *preman* of Ambonese descent, following a vicious gang turf war in Ketapang (Jakarta) was seen as a ploy meant to inflame local relations. Although links between *preman* and disaffected officers have been established (Aditjondro 2001; HRW 1999; ISAI 2000), settling the local versus outside provocateur debate here is beyond this chapter's scope.

9. These militias included the Laskar Jihad, Jemmah Islamiyah, Laskar Bulan Sabit Merah, and Mujahidin KOMPAK. According to ICG, militias that originated outside of Poso, though still in Sulawesi, included, among others, the Laskar Jundullah and Laskar Wahdah Islamiyah (ICG 2004; see also Sangaji 2004, 13–23).

10. In Central Kalimantan, the police and army clashed in Sampit's port over the right to "tax" Madurese refugees being ferried out of the province (ICG 2001a, 10).

11. This argument dovetails with Hedman's suggestion that: "greater prominence and strength of the country's religious associations (e.g., NU, Muhammadiyah) as compared to ethnic associations . . . tell us something about why 'inter-ethnic' violence in the country has been predominantly 'inter-religious' in nature" (2005, 143 emphasis in the original).

12. Usop was the former rector of the local state university (1981–88).

13. Regionally, LMMDD-KT gained prominence by hotly contesting the 1994 gubernatorial election, a rare occurrence under the New Order.

14. I thank Harold Crouch for making these sources available to me.

15. The details of the violence have been adequately chronicled elsewhere. See especially ICG 2001a; and Institut Dayakology 2001.

16. This helps to explain why, if there were attempts to turn this tragedy into a interreligious affair—as Aditjondro claims (2002, 48)—it failed utterly.

17. Fearon and Laitin (2000) posit that the primary split resides with strategic elites versus discursive orientations. But, given that the work of Petersen and Posen fall outside this divide, I favor the elite-led/mass-led dualism.

18. This emphasis on extensive periods of time rules out southern Mindanao in the Philippines, for it experienced only a year or two of ethnic riots, which gave way to secessionist warfare.

19. These two groups at one time were considered distinct, and some literature today continues to refer to them separately; other works do not and simply use the term *Hausa*. See Paden 1973, 22.

Conclusion

1. The "trigger," however, had more difficulty initiating the killings here than it did in Central Java, East Java, and Bali (see chapter 2).

2. In a survey I conducted (see chapter 5), it was found that 61 percent of Madurese rejected *adat*-based dispute resolution, while another 33 percent answered "not sure" because of confusion over what *adat* entails. For a further discussion of this issue, see Davidson 2007.

3. The problem with Islamic-oriented Malay-Madurese reconciliation is that it emphasizes similarities rather than underscoring ethnic differences (see chapter 5).

4. As Wilkinson (2004) points out, the level of government that controls local security forces is key. In India, this authority rests with the states. In Indonesia, despite decentralization, it remains in the hands of the central government, not the provinces.

5. Interview, Singkawang, January 13, 2004.

6. A key question under decentralization has been who is responsible for funding such activities: the district, provincial, or central governments?

7. Tanasaldy fails to provide the evidence to convincingly demonstrate that these deals are the overriding cause of the recent lack of riots.

8. Incumbents in the province's first round of direct local elections in 2005 did surprisingly well (Subianto 2005), bucking the national trend. Still, local elites will not be able to guarantee strict ethnic representation in these newly elected posts as they once did.

9. Of course, these problems neither uniformly affect the outer islands, nor are they limited to these places.

10. Some of the points raised in this section are discussed more in depth in Henley and Davidson 2007 and Davidson 2007.

Glossary

adat	customs or customary, tradition(s)
anak buah	underling, subordinate
barongsai	lion dance
becak	pedicab
Bhinneka Tunggal Ika	Unity in Diversity
bupati	district head
carok	stabbing adversary from behind
Chung Hua Tsung Hui	Chinese Central Association
Chung Hwa Kung Hui	Chinese General Association
clurut	sickle
Daya	Dayak (old spelling)
Dewan Adat	Customary Council (district-level)
dukun	shaman, sorcerer
dwifungsi	dual function doctrine
Ganyang Malaysia	Crush Malaysia
hukum adat	customary law
jeruk	an orange
kabupaten	district
Kalimantan Barat	West Kalimantan
Kalimantan Utara	North Kalimantan
kampung	village, neighborhood
kebangkitan	(re-)awakening, revival
kecamatan	subdistrict
kepala desa	village head
kerupuk	rice crackers
Konfrontasi	Confrontation (against Malaysia)
kongsi	common management/gold-mining cooperative
kraton	palace
laskar	militia
Majelis Adat Dayak	Dayak Customary Council (provincial-level)
mangkok merah	red bowl
Melayu	Malay
(me)ngayau	headhunting
otonomi daerah	regional autonomy
panglima	(traditional) war leader, military commander

Pembaharuan	Regeneration (a faction in DPRD)
pemekaran	dividing or merging administrative units (lit. "blossoming")
pemuda	youth
pencak silat	traditional art of self-defense
penduduk asli	indigenous people(s)/original inhabitant(s)
pengungsi	refugee(s)/internally displaced person(s)
preman	thug/hoodlum
pribumi	native, indigenous Indonesian
putera daerah	native son
Reformasi	reform movement
sawah	wet-rice field(s)
sukarelawan	volunteer
surau	small Islamic prayer house
swapraja	autonomous administrative regions
tanah adat	customary/traditional land
Tionghoa	Chinese
tjina/cina	Chinese (derogatory)
tolak bala	ceremony to ward off evil
tariu	shrill war cry
tumenggung/timanggong	a traditional Dayak leader
utusan daerah	provincial representative (to the MPR)
warung	food stall
yayasan	a foundation

Bibliography

Government Publications/Reports (Indonesia)

Analisa perkembangan kependudukan menurut sensus penduduk 1990: Dinamika mobilitas: Kalimantan. Yogyakarta: Kantor Menteri Negara Kependudukan dan Lingkungan Hidup/Pusat Penelitian Kependudukan Universitas Gadjah Mada, 1992/93.

Berita acara lanjutan, Nomor: 86/PID/B/1999 PN.SKW, atas nama terdakwa: Jabak Bin Punel. Singkawang: Pengadilan Negeri Singkawang, July 5, 1999.

Berita acara pemeriksaan (tersangka Muhammad Sidik bin H. Baiduri). Kepolisian Negara Repbulik Indonesia—Daerah KB. Direkorate Reserse, ca. June 1997.

BPS. *Penduduk Kalimantan Barat, hasil sensus penduduk tahun 2000.* Jakarta: BPS, 2000a.

———. *Penduduk Kalimantan Tengah, hasil sensus penduduk tahun 2000.* Jakarta: BPS, 2000b.

———. *Penduduk Maluku, hasil sensus penduduk tahun 2000.* Jakarta: BPS, 2000c.

———. *Penduduk Sulawesi Tengah, hasil sensus penduduk tahun 2000.* Jakarta: BPS, 2000d.

BPS Kabupaten Sambas. *Kabupaten Sambas dalam angka, 1999.* Singkawang: Pemerintah Kabupaten Sambas with BPS Kabupaten Sambas, 2000.

BPS Propinsi Kalimantan Barat. *Kalimantan Barat dalam angka, 1974.* Pontianak: BPS Propinsi Kalimantan Barat, 1975.

———. *Kalimantan Barat dalam angka, 1997.* Pontianak: BPS Propinsi Kalimantan Barat, 1998.

Departemen Transmigrasi dan Pemukiman Perambah Hutan. *Laporan Tahunan, Tahun Anggaran 1998/1999.* Pontianak: Departemen Transmigrasi dan Pemukiman Perambah Hutan, Kantor Wilayah Propinsi Kalimantan Barat, 1999.

Dinas Kehutanan Propinsi Kalimantan Barat. *Laporan kegiatan kehutanan 1973/1974 (1 April 1973 s/d 31 Maret 1974).* Pontianak: Dinas Kehutanan Propinsi Kalimantan Barat, n.d.

Djawatan Penerangan Propinsi Kalimantan. *Republik Indonesia: Kalimantan.* Banjarmasin: Kementerian Penerangan, 1953.

Kadarusno. *Pembangunan daerah perbatasan Kalimantan Barat (Disusun untuk bahan diskusi Untan ilmiah pada Study Club UNTAN)*. Pontianak: n.p., July 1974.

Laporan gubernur kepala daerah tingkat I Kalimantan Barat kepada wakil presiden (dalam rangka kunjungan kerja di Kalimantan Barat, 30 Juli s/d 1 Augustus, 1975). Pontianak: n.p., n.d.

Laporan Kerdja Tahun 1963 Gubernur Kdh. Kal-Barat. Pontianak: n.p., n.d.

Laporan tahunan kejaksaan tinggi Kalimantan Barat tahun 1980. Pontianak: Kejaksaan Tinggi Kalimantan Barat, 1981.

Laporan tahunan kejaksaan tinggi Kalimantan Barat tahun 1985/86. Pontianak: Kejaksaan Tinggi Kalimantan Barat, 1987.

Laporan survey kehidupan rakyat perbatasan, buku I–IV. Pontianak: Kantor Wilayah Departemen Sosial Propinsi Kalimantan Barat, 1976.

Notowardojo, R. M. Subianto, with Cumala Noor. *Kalimantan Barat sepintas lalu: Dilihat dari sudut sosial ekonomi*. Jakarta: Kementrian Perekonomian, 1951.

Pelaksana evaluasi pelita nasional di daerah Kalimantan Barat, 1973/1974–1977/1978. Pontianak: n.p., n.d.

Produk domestik regional bruto propinsi & kabupaten/kotamadya Kalimantan Barat, 1985–1992. Pontianak: Kantor Statistik Kalimantan Barat, 1993.

Progress report, propinsi Kalimantan Barat (disampaikan sebagai bahan kepada Departemen Dalam Negeri dalam rangka kundjungan presiden RI ke Kalimantan Barat). October 17–18, 1968.

Pusat Sejarah dan Tradisi ABRI. *Bahaya laten komunisme di Indonesia: Penumpasan pemberontakan PKI dan sisa-sisanya*, vol. 5. Jakarta: Markas Besar ABRI, 1995.

Semdam XII. *Tanjungpura Berjuang: Sejarah Kodam XII/Tanjungpura*. Pontianak: Yayasan Tanjungpura, 1971.

Select Government Publications/Reports
(Malaysia)

Hardy, Tim. *The danger within: A history of the clandestine communist organization in Sarawak*. Kuching: Sarawak Information Services, 1963.

Indonesian involvement in Eastern Malaysia. Kuala Lumpur: Department of Information, ca. 1965.

Sarawak Government. *The threat of armed communism in Sarawak (white paper)*. Kuala Lumpur: Chetak Kerajaan, 1972.

———. "Sri Aman: Peace restored in Sarawak." Kuching: Government Printing Office, n.d.

The origin and development of the Sarawak Communist Organisation (SCO). Kuching: unpublished document, ca. 1974.

Select Internal Army Documents (Indonesia)

Angkatan Darat Kodam XII. *Buku petundjuk daerah Kalimantan Barat*. Pontianak: Sudam V, 1972.

Ass-2 Kaskodam 12 Tdpr. *Formulir berita*. August 10, 1967.

Badan Koordinasi Intelijen Daerah Kalimantan Barat. *Laporan: Hasil rapat Bakorinda Tk-I Kalbar*. Pontianak: Bakorinda, July 10, 1986.

Ba'dullah, Mayor Inf. M.A. *Laporan tahunan 1969 KODIM 1201/TDPR*. Mempawah: Komando Daerah Militer XII Tandjungpura, Komando Distrik Militer 1201, March 4, 1970.

Chronologis kegiatan PGRS setengah tahun terachir 1967. Pontianak: Angkatan Darat Komando Antar Daerah, Kalimantan, n.d.

Hartono, Brigadir Djenderal TNI Seno. *Laporan khusus: Pelaksanaan operasi penangkapan S. A. Sofyan*. Pontianak: n.p., January 14, 1974.

Komandan Korem 121/ABW. November 6, 1993.

Lampiran C, isi laporan tahun Kodam XII Tandjungpura Tahun 1968. Pontianak: Angkatan Darat Komando Daerah Militer XII Tandjungpura, n.d.

Laporan-chusus tentang perkembangan gerombolan PGRS selama tahun 1967 didaerah Kalbar. Pontianak: Angkatan Darat Komando Antar Daerah Kalimantan, n.d.

Laporan tahunan Korem 121/Tdpr dalam tahun 1967. Pontianak: Komando Daerah Militer XII Tandjungpura Komando Resort Militer 121, December 20, 1967.

Laporan umum Operasi Saberda, tahun 1968. Pontianak: Komando Daerah Militer XII/Tandjungpura, n.d.

Manaf, Let. Kol. Eddy. *Daftar kekawatan operasi angkatan darat bulan Okt/Nopember 1965*. Pontianak: Angkatan Darat Daerah Militer XII/Tandjungpura, n.d.

Moeljono, Majoor CPM. *"Laporan chusus" tentang adanja penjerangan gerombolan PGRS terhadap LANU Singkawang II di SG. Ledo pada tanggal 16-7-1967 Dj. 02.00 wita*. Pontianak: Komando Daerah Militer XII/ Tandjungpura Polisi Militer, n.d.

Pangdam 12 TDPR/Panglak OPS Kalbar. *Formulir berita, TR 770/11/1967*, November 8, 1967.

Pang Handa Kalbar. *Formulir berita*. TR-015/1967, February 20, 1967.

Pelita 1975. Pontianak: Kodam XII/Tanjungpura, 1975.

Penumpasan terhadap geromobolan tjina komunis didearah Kalbar. Manuscript, n.d.

Perkiraan keadaan intell. Pontianak: Angkatan Darat Komando Daerah Militer XII Tandjungpura, February 15, 1969.

PKI gaya baru pimpinan SA Sofyan dan hubunguannya dengan PGRS/Paraku. Manuscript, n.d.

Proses timbulnja PGRS/Paraku: Perkembangan dan tarap-tarap penghantjuranja di daerah Kalimantan Barat. Pontianak: Angkatan Darat Kommando Tandjungpura XII, n.d.

Rencana kerja tahun 1969 Kodam XII/Tanjungpura (rencana pokok). Pontianak: Komando Daerah Militer XII Tandjungpura, n.d.

Rentjana kegiatan bidang personil dan moril. Pontianak: Angkatan Darat Komando Daerah Militer XII Tandjungpura, January 1, 1968.

Rentjana Operasi Sapu Bersih III-Tahun 1969. Pontianak: Laksus Pang Kop Kamtib Daerah Kalimantan Barat, n.d.

Ryacudu, Brig. General. *Laporan pangdam XII TDPR/Panghanda Kalbar tentang pelaksanaan 'Operasi Sapu Bersih' sedjak tgn. 1 April 67 s/d 15 Djuni 1967.* Pontianak: Angkatan Darat/Kodam XII Tandjungpura, June 16, 1967a.

———. *Lampiran risalah serah terima Pangdam XII/Tdpr Handa Kalbar.* Pontianak: Angkatan Darat Komando Daerah Militer XII/Tandjungpura, June 30, 1967b.

———. *Risalah serah terima komando daerah militer XII/Tandjungpura komando pertahanan daerah Kalimantan Barat.* Pontianak: Angkatan Darat Komando Daerah Militer XII Tandjungpura, June 30, 1967c.

———. *Surat keputusan panglima daerah militer XII/Tandjungpura selaku pelaksana chusus pangkokamtib dan panglima operasi wilayah Kalimantan Barat, nomor: Kep—247/11/1967 tentang penempatan Lasjkar Pangsuma dibawah komando Pangdam XII/ Tandjungpura selaku pelaksana chusus pangkokamtib dan panglima operasi wilayah Kalimantan Barat.* Pontianak: Angkatan Darat Komando Daerah Militer XII/Tandjungpura, November 18, 1967d.

Witono, Brigadir Djenderal TNI A. J. *Laporan Pang Dam XII/Tandjungpura tentang gerakan suku Dayak terhadap GTK di Kal-Bar (II).* Pontianak: Angkatan Darat Komando Daerah XII/Tandjungpura, December 4, 1967.

———. *Isi laporan tahunan Kodam XII Tandjungpura, tahun 1968.* Pontianak: Angaktan Darat Komando Daerah Militer XII Tandjungpura, 1968.

———. *Lampiran A: Intelidjen, rentjana Operasi Sapu Bersih III tahun 1969.* Pontianak: Laksus Pang Kop Kamtib Daerah Kalimantan Barat, March 1, 1969.

———. *Rentjana kerjda tahun 1968: Komando daerah militer XII/Tandjungpura (rentjana pokok).* Pontianak: Angkatan Darat Komando Daerah Militer XII/Tandjungpura, n.d.

Select Dutch Colonial Documents

ARA (Alegemeen Rijksarchief Tweede Afdeeling, The Hague). Geheim Mailrapport 1947 no. 533, Algemeen Overzicht, Res. West-Borneo, February 1–15, 1947.

Harmsen, H. J. *West-Borneo: Kalimantan Barat. 12 May 1947.* Pontianak: West-Borneo Raad en R.V.D. Pontianak, 1947.

Select Papers of Oevaang Oeray
(Anon. Personal Collection)

Anggaran dasar: Partai Persatuan Daya, Jakarta: Waktu, 1955.

Donatus, P. *Goeroe-goeroe jang terhorhmat.* Pontianak, May 28, 1946.

"Mandau." *Politiek pendjadjahan feodalisme lebih boeroek daripada pendjadjahan Belanda. Belanda menjokong koeat akan politiek dan kedoedoekan feodalisten.* ca. 1947–50.

Memorandum from the Dayak Affairs Office. Pontianak, November 12, 1946.

Oeray, J. Chrys. Oevaang. *Keadaan dan keloehan Daya sebeloem perang dan toentoetannja dewasa sekarang.* Pontianak, November 15, 1947.

Usaha2 P.D. langsung guna kepentingan anggota2. Sanggau, June 15, 1950.

Newspapers, Magazines, and News Services

Indonesian (West Kalimantan)

Akcaya/Pontianak Post

Berani

Equator

Kalbar Pos

Kalimantan Berdjuang (Banjarmasin)

Kalimantan Review

Keadilan

Libas

Suaka

Indonesian (National)

Angkatan Bersenjata

Antara Weekly Review

Apakabar News Service

Bintang Timur

D&R

detik.com (Web site)

Forum Keadilan

Gatra

Harian Kami

Kabar dari Pijar

Kompas

Media

Merdeka

Nusantara

Republika

Sinar Harapan

Sinar Pagi
Suara Pembaruan
Tempo
Tiras
Ummat
Utama
Warta Berita
Warta Ekonomi

English Language

BBC News
CNN
The Economist
Far Eastern Economic Review
The Herald (Karachi)
Sarawak Tribune

Books and Articles

Abbott, Andrew. "On the concept of turning point." *Comparative Social Research* 16 (1997): 85–105.

Acciaioli, Greg. "Grounds of conflict, idioms of harmony: Custom, religion and nationalism in violence avoidance at the Lindu Plain, Central Sulawesi." *Indonesia* 72 (2001): 81–114.

———. "Re-empowering 'the Art of the Elders': The revitalization of *adat* among the To Lindu people of Central Sulawesi and throughout contemporary Indonesia." In *Beyond Jakarta: Regional autonomy and local societies in Indonesia,* edited by M. Sakai, 217–44. Adelaide: Crawford House, 2002.

Aditjondro, George Junus. "Guns, pamphlets and handie-talkie: How the military exploited local ethno-religious tensions in Maluku to preserve their political and economic privileges." In *Violence in Indonesia,* edited by Ingrid Wessel and Georgia Wimhofer, 100–128. Hamburg: Abera Verlag, 2001.

———. "Suharto has gone, but the regime has not changed: Presidential corruption in the Orde Baru." In *Stealing from the People: 16 Studies on Corruption in Indonesia,* book 1, edited by Richard Holloway, 1–66. Jakarta: Aksara Foundation 2002.

———. "Kerusuhan Poso dan Morowali, Akar Permasalahan dan Jalan Keluarnya." Paper presented at Propatria Seminar on "Application of Military Emergencies in Aceh, Papua and Poso?" Jakarta. January 7, 2004.

Alexander, Garth. *Silent invasion: The Chinese in Southeast Asia.* London: MacDonald & Company, 1973.

Alqadrie, Syarif Ibrahim. "Konflik Etnis di Ambon dan Sambas: Suatu Tinjauan Sosiologis." *Anthropologi Indonesia* 58 (1999): 36–57.

AMAN. *System peradilan adat dan lokal di Indonesia: Peluang dan tantangan.* Jakarta: Aliansi Masyarakat Adat Nusantara and Partnership for Governance Reform, 2003.

Anaya, S. James. *Indigenous peoples in international law.* New York: Oxford University Press, 1996.

Andaya, Barbara Watson. *To live as brothers: Southeast Sumatra in the seventeenth and eighteenth centuries.* Honolulu: University of Hawaii Press, 1993.

Andaya, Leonard Y. "The search for the 'origins' of Melayu." In *Contesting Malayness: Malay identity across boundaries,* edited by Timothy P. Barnard, 56–75. Singapore: Singapore University Press, 2004.

Anderson, Benedict R. O'G. *Imagined communities: Reflections on the origin and spread of nationalism.* 2nd ed. London: Verso, 1991.

———. Introduction to *Violence and the state in Suharto's Indonesia,* edited by Benedict R. O'G. Anderson, 9–19. Ithaca: Southeast Asia Program Publications, Cornell University, 2001.

Appadurai, Arjun. "Dead certainty: Ethnic violence in the era of globalization." *Development and Change* 29 (1998): 905–25.

Aragon, Lorraine V. *Fields of the lord: Animism, Christian minorities, and state development in Indonesia.* Honolulu: University of Hawaii Press, 2000.

———. "Communal violence in Poso, Central Sulawesi: Where people eat fish and fish eat people." *Indonesia* 72 (2001): 45–80.

Aspinall, Edward. *Opposing Suharto: Compromise, resistance, and regime change in Indonesia.* Stanford: Stanford University Press, 2005.

Bachtiar, Harsja W. *Siapa dia? Perwira tinggi Tentara Nasional Indonesia angkatan Darat (TNI-AD).* Jakarta: Penerbit Djambatan, 1988.

Balunus, H. M. Baroamas J. "Kedatangan dan penyebaran agama Katolik di tanah Kalimantan." Unpublished manuscript, n.d.

Bamba, John. "Land, rivers and forests: Dayak solidarity and ecological resilience." In *Indigenous social movements and ecological resilience: Lessons from the Dayak of Indonesia,* edited by Janis B. Alcorn and Antoinette G. Royo, 39–55. Washington, D.C: Biodiversity Support Program, 2000.

———. "Kalimantan: Unity or diversity?" In *Searching for peace in the Asia Pacific: An overview of conflict prevention and peacebuilding activities,* edited by Annelies Heijmans et al., 399–415. Boulder, Colo.: Lynne Rienner Publishers, 2004.

Barlow, Colin, and John Drabble. "Government and the emerging rubber industries in Indonesia and Malaya." In *Indonesian economic history in the Dutch colonial era,* edited by Anne Booth et al., 187–209. New Haven: Yale University, Southeast Asia Studies, 1990.

Bates, Robert H. "Modernization, ethnic competition and the rationality of politics in contemporary Africa." In *State versus ethnic claims: African policy dilemmas,* edited by Donald Rothchild and Victor A. Olorunsola, 152–71. Boulder, Colo.: Westview Press, 1983.

Bell, Gary F. "The new Indonesian laws relating to regional autonomy: Good intentions, confusing laws." *Asian-Pacific Law & Policy Journal* 2, no. 1 (2001): 1–44.

Bello, Alhaji Sir Ahmadu. *My life*. London: Cambridge University Press, 1962.

Benda, Harry J. *The crescent and the rising sun: Indonesian Islam under the Japanese occupation, 1942–1945*. The Hague: W. van Hoeve Ltd., 1958.

Benhabib, Seyla. *The claims of culture: Equality and diversity in the global era*. Princeton: Princeton University Press, 2002.

Bertrand, Jacques. *Nationalism and ethnic conflict in Indonesia*. Cambridge: Cambridge University Press, 2004.

Bevis, William W. *Borneo log: The struggle for Sarawak's forests*. Seattle: University of Washington Press, 1995.

Bigalke, Terance. "Government and mission in the Torajan World of Makale-Rantepao." *Indonesia* 38 (1984): 85–112.

Boelaars, Huub, and Max Boli Sabon. *Gambaran umat Katolik paroki Bengkayang Kalimantan Barat*. Jakarta: Pusat Penelitian Atma Jaya, 1979a.

———. *Gambaran umat Katolik paroki Sambas Kalimantan Barat*. Jakarta: Pusat Penelitian Atma Jaya, 1979b.

Boer, Jan H. *Nigeria's decades of blood, 1980–2002*. Belleville, Ont.: Essence Publishing, 2003.

Bowen, John R. "Should we have a universal concept of 'indigenous peoples' rights? Ethnicity and essentialism in the twenty-first century." *Anthropology Today* 16, no. 4 (2000): 12–16.

Brass, Paul R. *Ethnicity and nationalism: Theory and comparison*. New Delhi: Sage Publications, 1991.

———. *Theft of an idol: Text and context in the representation of collective violence*. Princeton: Princeton University Press, 1997.

———. *The production of Hindu-Muslim violence in contemporary India*. Seattle: University of Washington Press, 2003.

Bräuchler, Birgit. "Cyberidentities at war: Religion, identity, and the Internet in the Moluccan conflict." *Indonesia* 75 (2003): 123–52.

Broomfield, J. H. "The forgotten majority: The Bengal Muslims and September 1918." In *Soundings in modern South Asian history*, edited by D. A. Low, 196–224. Berkeley: University of California Press, 1968.

Brosius, Peter. "Prior transcripts, divergent paths: Resistance and acquiescence to logging in Sarawak, East Malaysia." *Comparative Studies in Society and History* 39 (1997): 468–510.

Brown, Michael E. "The causes of internal conflict: An overview." In *Nationalism and ethnic conflict*, edited by Michael E. Brown et al., 3–25. Rev. ed. Cambridge, Mass.: MIT Press, 2001.

Brubaker, Rogers. "Myths and misconceptions in the study of nationalism." In *The state of the nation: Ernest Gellner and the theory of nationalism*, edited by John A. Hall, 272–306. Cambridge: Cambridge University Press, 1998.

Brubaker, Rogers, and David D. Laitin. "Ethnic and nationalist violence." *Annual Review of Sociology* 24 (1998): 423–52.

Bruinessen, Martin van. "Genealogies of radical Muslims in post-Suharto Indonesia." *South East Asia Research* 10, no. 2 (2002): 117–54.

Budiardjo, Carmel. "The politics of transmigration." *The Ecologist* 16, no. 2/3 (1986): 111–16.

Buku Kenangan: 75 Tahun Persekolahan Katolik Nyarumkop, 1916–1991. Nyarumkop [?]: n.p., ca. 1991.

Bunnell, Fred. "The Kennedy initiatives in Indonesia, 1962–1963." Ph.D dissertation, Cornell University, 1969.

Burns, Peter. "Myth of adat." *Journal of Legal Pluralism* 28 (1989): 1–127.

Castree, Noel. "Differential geographies: Place, indigenous rights and 'local' resources." *Political Geography* 23 (2004): 133–67.

Cator, W. J. *The economic position of the Chinese in the Netherlands Indies.* Chicago: University of Chicago Press, 1936.

Chakrabarty, Dipesh. "Communal riots and labour: Bengal's jute mill-hands in the 1890s." In *Mirrors of violence: Communities, riots and survivors in South Asia,* edited by Veena Das, 146–84. Delhi: Oxford University Press, 1990.

Chan, S. C. "Massive arrest." *Sarawak Tribune.* December 7, 1966.

Chang, William. "Kata pengantar." In Bambang Hendarta Suta Purwana, *Konflik antarkomunitas etnis di Sambas 1999: Suatu tinjauan sosial budaya,* iii–viii. Pontianak: Romeo Grafika, 2003.

Chatterji, Joya. *Bengal divided: Hindu communalism and partition, 1932–1947.* Cambridge: Cambridge University Press, 1994.

Chauvel, R. H. *Nationalists, soldiers, and separatists: The Ambonese Islands from colonialism to revolt, 1880–1950.* Leiden: KITLV Press, 1990.

Clarke, Gerard. "From ethnocide to ethnodevelopment? Ethnic minorities and indigenous peoples in Southeast Asia." *Third World Quarterly* 22, no. 3 (2001): 413–36.

Cohen, Abner. *Custom and politics in urban Africa.* Berkeley: University of California Press, 1969.

Colchester, Marcus. "Unity and diversity: Indonesian policy towards tribal peoples." *The Ecologist* 16, no. 2/3 (1986a): 89–98.

———. "The struggle for land: Tribal peoples in the face of the transmigration programme." *The Ecologist* 16, no. 2/3 (1986b): 99–110.

Collier, David, and James Mahoney. "Insights and pitfalls: Selection bias in qualitative research." *World Politics* 49, no. 1 (1996): 56–91.

Collier, Paul. "Economic causes of civil conflict and their implications for policy." In *Managing global chaos,* edited by C. A. Crocker, F. O. Hampson, and P. Aall, 143–62. Washington, D.C.: U.S. Institute of Peace, 2001.

Collier, Paul, and Nicholas Sambanis. "Understanding civil war: A new research agenda." *Journal of Conflict Resolution* 46, no. 1 (2002): 3–12.

Colombijn, Freek. "A cultural practice of violence in Indonesia: Lessons from history." In *Violent internal conflicts in Asia Pacific: Histories, political economies and policies,* edited by Dewi Fortuna Anwar et al., 245–68. Jakarta: Yayasan Obor, 2005.

Colombijn, Freek, and Thomas Lindblad. Introduction to *Roots of violence: Contemporary violence in historical perspective,* edited by Freek Colombijn and Thomas Lindblad, 1–31. Leiden: KITLV Press, 2002.

Conboy, Ken. *Kopassus: Inside Indonesia's special forces.* Jakarta: Equinox, 2003.

Constable, Sharon A. *Guest people: Hakka identity in China and abroad.* Seattle: University of Washington Press, 1996.

Coppedge, Michael. "Thickening thin concepts and theories: Combining large N and small in comparative politics." *Comparative Politics* 31, no. 4 (1999): 465–76.

Coppel, Charles. *Indonesian Chinese in crisis.* Kuala Lumpur: Oxford University Press, 1983.

Coté, Joost. "Colonising Central Sulawesi: The 'ethical policy' and imperialist expansion." *Itinerario* 20, no. 3 (1996): 87–107.

Cribb, Robert, ed. *The Indonesian killings of 1965–1966.* Victoria: Monash Papers on Southeast Asia No. 21, Centre of Southeast Asia Monash University, 1990.

———. "From total people's defence to massacre: Explaining Indonesian military violence in East Timor." In *Roots of violence in Indonesia: Contemporary violence in historical perspective,* edited by Freek Colombijn and J. Thomas Lindblad, 227–42. Leiden: KITLV Press, 2002.

———. "Legal pluralism, decentralisation and the roots of violence in Indonesia." In *Violent internal conflicts in Asia Pacific: Histories, political economies and policies,* edited by Dewi Fortuna Anwar et al., 41–57. Jakarta: Yayasan Obor, 2005.

Crook, Richard C., and James Manor. *Democracy and decentralisation in South Asia and West Africa: Participation, accountability, and performance.* Cambridge: Cambridge University Press, 1998.

Crouch, Harold. *The army and politics in Indonesia.* Ithaca: Cornell University Press, 1978.

Curtis, Robert. "Malaysia and Indonesia." *New Left Review* 28 (1964): 5–32.

Dalton, John. "On the present state of piracy, amongst these islands, and the best method of its suppression." In *Notices of the Indian archipelago and adjacent countries,* edited by J. H. Moor, 15–29. London: Frank Cass & Co. Ltd, 1968 [orig. 1837].

Daniels, E. Valentine. *Charred lullabies: Chapters in an anthropography of violence.* Princeton: Princeton University Press, 1996.

Darwin, Muhadjir. "Freedom from fear: Social disruption and system of violence in Indonesia." In *The Indonesian crisis: A human development perspective,* edited by Aris Ananta, 105–58. Singapore: ISEAS, 2003.

Das, Suranjan. *Communal riots in Bengal, 1905–1947.* Delhi: Oxford University Press, 1991.

Das, Veena. "Introduction: Communities, riots and survivors." In *Mirrors of violence: Communities, riots and survivors in South Asia,* edited by Veena Das, 1–36. Delhi: Oxford University Press, 1990.

———. "Cultural rights and the definition of the community." In *Dynamics of state formation: India and Europe compared,* edited by Martin Doornbos and Sudipta Kaviraj, 299–332. New Delhi: Sage Publications, 1997.

Davidson, Jamie S. "Culture and rights in ethnic violence." In *The revival of tradition in Indonesian politics: The deployment of adat from colonialism to indigenism,* edited by Jamie S. Davidson and David Henley, 224–46. London: Routledge, 2007.

———. "The rise and fall of the Daya Unity Party." In *Violence and identity in the early Indonesian revolution,* edited by Remco Raben. Singapore: NUS Press, forthcoming.

Davidson, Jamie S., and Douglas Kammen. "Indonesia's unknown war and the lineages of violence in West Kalimantan." *Indonesia* 73 (2002): 53–88.

de Jonge, Huub. "Stereotypes of the Madurese." In *Across Madura Strait: The dynamics of an insular society,* edited by Kees van Dijk, Huub de Jonge, and Elly Touwen-Bouwsma, 7–23. Leiden: KITLV Press, 1995.

Diamond, Larry. *Developing democracy: Toward consolidation.* Baltimore: Johns Hopkins University Press, 1999.

Dick, Howard. "Formation of the nation state, 1930s–1966." In *The emergence of a national economy: An economic history of Indonesia, 1800–2000,* edited by Howard Dick et al., 153–93. Leiden: KITLV Press, 2002.

Dijk, Kees van. *A country in despair: Indonesia between 1997 and 2000.* Leiden: KITLV Press, 2001.

Djuweng, Stephanus, ed. *Manusia Dayak: Orang kecil yang terperangkap modernisasi.* Pontianak: IDRD, 1996.

———. *The dominant paradigm and the cost of development.* Pontianak: IDRD, 1997.

———. "Anatomi konflik di Kalbar." *Kalimantan Review,* May 1999, 18.

Doty, E., and W. L. Pohlman. "Tour in Borneo, from Sambas through Montrado to Pontianak, and the adjacent settlements of Chinese and Dajaks during the autumn of 1838." *Chinese Repository* 8 (1839): 285–310.

Dove, Michael R. "The agroecoloigcal mythology of the Javanese and the political economy of Indonesia." *Indonesia* 39 (1985): 1–36.

———. "Rice-eating rubber and people-eating governments: Peasant versus state critiques of rubber development in colonial Borneo." *Ethnohistory* 43, no. 1 (1996): 33–63.

———. "Dayak anger ignored." *Inside Indonesia* 51 (1997).

Down to Earth. "Dayaks clash with transmigrants." *Down to Earth* 32 (February 1997). http://dte.gn.apc.org/news.htm.

———. "Behind the Central Kalimantan violence." *Down to Earth* 49 (May 2001). http://dte.gn.apc.org/news.htm.

Doyle, Michael, and Nicholas Sambanis. "International peacebuilding: A theoretical and quantitative analysis." *American Political Science Review* 94, no. 4 (2000): 779–801.

Drakard, Jane. *A Malay frontier: Unity and duality in a Sumatran kingdom.* Ithaca: Southeast Asia Program, Cornell University, 1990.

Duncan, Christopher R. "From development to empowerment." In *Civilizing the margins: Southeast Asian government policies for the development of minorities,* edited by Christopher R. Duncan, 86–115. Ithaca: Cornell University Press, 2004.

Easter, David. *Britain and the confrontation with Indonesia, 1960–1966.* London: Tauris, 2004.

Edelman, Marc. *Peasants against globalization: Rural social movements in Costa Rica.* Stanford: Stanford University Press, 1999.

Effendi, Chairil. "Melayu: Apa, siapa dan bagaimana dia?" *Pontianak Post,* December 11, 1999.

———. "Solusi tragedi Sambas." *Forum Keadilan,* April 11, 1999, 38.

Effendy, Marchus. *Sejarah perjuangan Kalimantan Barat.* Pontianak: n.p., 1982.

Eklöf, Stepan. *Indonesian politics in crisis: The long fall of Suharto, 1996–98.* Copenhagen: NIAS, 1999.

Eldridge, Phillip J. *Non-government organizations and democratic participation in Indonesia.* Kuala Lumpur: Oxford University Press, 1995.

Ellis, Andrew, and Etsi Yudhini. "Indonesia's new state institutions: The constitution completed, now for the detail . . . A commentary on the MPR Annual Session, November 2002." Jakarta: National Democratic Institute, November 2002.

Falola, Tonyin. *Violence in Nigeria: The crisis of religious politics and secular ideologies.* Rochester: University of Rochester Press, 1998.

Fasbender, Karl, and Susanne Erbe. *Indonesia's managed mass migration: Transmigration between poverty, economy and ecology.* Hamburg: Verlag Weltarchiv, 1990.

Fearon, James D., and David D. Laitin. "Violence and the social construction of ethnic identity." *International Organization* 54, no. 4 (2000): 845–77.

Feith, Herb. "The 'triangle' takes shape." *Asian Survey* 4, no. 8 (1964): 969–80.

———. "Dayak legacy." *Far Eastern Economic Review,* January 25, 1968, 134–35.

First, Ruth. *Power in Africa.* New York: Pantheon Books, 1970.

Fitrani, Fitria, Bert Hofman, and Kai Kaiser. "Unity in diversity? The creation of new local governments in decentralising Indonesia." *Bulletin of Indonesian Economic Studies* 41, no. 1 (2005): 57–79.

Florus, Paulus, and Edi Petebang. *Panen bencana: Kelapa sawit.* Pontianak: Institut Dayakologi, 1999.

Florus, Paulus, et al., eds. *Kebudayaan Dayak: Akualisasi dan transformasi.* Jakarta: Grasindo, 1994.

Fox, Jonathan. "Editor's introduction." *Journal of Development Studies* 26, no. 4 (1990): 1–18.

―――. "How does civil society thicken? The political construction of social capital in rural Mexico." *World Development* 24, no. 6 (1996): 1089–103.

Fujio, Hara. "The North Kalimantan Communist Party: A preliminary study." In *Borneo 2000: Proceedings of the Sixth Biennial Borneo Research Conference,* edited by Michael Leigh, 197–210. Kuching: Universiti Malaysia Sarawak, 2000.

Gagnon, V. P., Jr. "Ethnic nationalism and international conflict: The case of Serbia." *International Security* 19, no. 3 (1994/95): 130–66.

Galvan, Dennis C. *The state must be our master of fire: How peasants craft culturally sustainable development in Senegal.* Berkeley: University of California Press, 2004.

Gaventa, John. *Power and powerlessness: Quiescence and rebellion in an Appalachian valley.* Urbana: University of Illinois Press, 1980.

Gayo, Iwan, ed. *Buku pintar Nusantara.* Jakarta: Upaya Warga Negara, 1990.

Giring, Richardus. *Madura di mata Dayak: Dari konflik ke rekonsiliasi.* Yogyakarta: Galang Press, 2004.

Gledhill, John. "Liberalism, socio-economic rights and the politics of identity: From moral economy to indigenous rights." In *Human rights, culture and context,* edited by Richard A. Wilson, 70–110. London: Pluto Press, 1997.

Goor, J. van. "Seapower, trade and state-formation: Pontianak and the Dutch." In *Trading companies in Asia, 1600–1830,* edited by J. van Goor, 83–105. Utrecht: H&S Hes Uitgevers, 1986.

Gordon, Bernard K. "The potential for Indonesian expansionism." *Pacific Affairs* 36, no. 1 (1963–64): 378–93.

Government of Australia, Department of Foreign Affairs, and Snowy Mountains Corporation. *Preliminary regional survey for road network identification in Kalimantan Barat-Indonesia,* 7 volumes. Canberra: Government of Australia, Department of Foreign Affairs, December 1973.

Gurr, Ted Robert, ed. *People versus states: Minorities at risk in the new century.* Washington, D.C.: U.S. Institute of Peace Press, 2000.

Hadiz, Vedi. "Power and politics in North Sumatra: The uncompleted Reformasi." In *Local power and politics in Indonesia: Decentralisation and democratization,* edited by Edward Aspinall and Greg Fealy, 119–31. Singapore: ISEAS, 2003.

Hardin, Russell. *One for all: The logic of group conflict.* Princeton: Princeton University Press, 1995.

Hardjono, J. M. *Transmigration in Indonesia.* Kuala Lumpur: Oxford University Press, 1977.

Harnischfeger, Johanes. "The Bakassi boys: Fighting crime in Nigeria." *Journal of African Studies* 41, no. 1 (2003): 23-49.

Harwell, Emily Evans. "The un-natural history of culture: Ethnicity, tradition and territorial conflicts in West Kalimantan, Indonesia, 1800-1997." Ph.D. dissertation, Yale University, 2000.

Hatta, Mohammad. "One Indonesian view of the Malaysia issue." *Asian Survey* 5, no. 2 (1965): 139-43.

Haydu, Jeffrey. "Making use of the past: Time periods as cases to compare and as sequences of problem solving." *American Journal of Sociology* 104, no. 2 (1998): 339-71.

Healey, Christopher. "Tribes and states in 'pre-colonial' Borneo: Structural contradictions and the generation of piracy." *Social Analysis* 18 (1985): 3-39.

Hedman, Eva-Lotta E. "Elections, community, and representation: Notes on theory and method from another shore." In *Violent internal conflicts in Asia Pacific: Histories, political economies and policies,* edited by Dewi Fortuna Anwar et al., 134-50. Jakarta: Yayasan Obor, 2005.

Hefner, Robert W. *Civil Islam: Muslims and democratization in Indonesia.* Princeton: Princeton University Press, 2000.

Heidhues, Mary Somers F. "The first two Sultans of Pontianak." *Archipel* 56 (1998): 273-94.

———. "Kalimantan Barat 1967-1999: Violence on the periphery." In *Violence in Indonesia,* edited by Ingrid Wessel and Georgia Wimhöffer, 139-51. Hamburg: Abera-Verlag, 2001.

———. *Golddiggers, farmers, and traders in Pontianak and the "Chinese districts" of West Kalimantan, Indonesia.* Ithaca: Southeast Asia Publications Program, Cornell University, 2003.

Henley, David, and Jamie S. Davidson. "Introduction: The Protean politics of adat." In *The revival of tradition in Indonesian politics: The deployment of adat from colonialism to indigenism,* edited by Jamie S. Davidson and David Henley, 1-49. London: Routledge, 2007.

Hindley, Donald. "Indonesia's confrontations with Malaysia: A search for motives." *Asian Survey* 4, no. 6 (1964): 904-13.

Hinton, Alexander Laban. "A head for an eye: Revenge in the Cambodian genocide." *American Ethnologist* 25, no. 3 (1998): 352-77.

Hoebel, E. Adamson, and A. Arthur Schiller. Introduction to *Adat law in Indonesia,* edited by B. Ter Haar, 1-43. New York: Institute of Pacific Relations, 1948.

Honna, Jun. *Military politics and democratization in Indonesia.* London: RoutledgeCurzon, 2003.

Hooker, M. B. *Adat law in modern Indonesia.* Kuala Lumpur: Oxford University Press, 1978.

Horowitz, Donald L. *Ethnic groups in conflict.* Berkeley: University of California Press, 1985.

———. *A democratic South Africa? Constitutional engineering in a divided society.* Berkeley: University of California, 1991.

———. *The deadly ethnic riot.* Berkeley: University of California Press, 2001.

Houliston, Sylvia. *Borneo breakthrough.* London: China Inland Mission, 1963.

HRW (Human Rights Watch). *Playing the ethnic card: Communal violence and human rights.* New York: HRW, 1995.

———. "Indonesia: Communal violence in West Kalimantan." *Human Rights Watch* 9, no. 10 (1997).

———. "The violence in Ambon." *Human Rights Watch* 11, no. 1 (1999).

———. "Breakdown: Four years of communal violence in Central Sulawesi." *Human Rights Watch* 14, no. 9 (2002).

———. "Revenge in the name of religion: The cycle of violence in Plateau and Kano States." *Human Rights Watch* 17, no. 8 (2005).

Hulten, Herman Josef van. *Hidupku di antara suku Daya: Catatan soerang misionaris.* Jakarta: PT. Grasindo, 1992 (translated from 1983 original Dutch).

Humble, Arnold Lee. "Conservative Baptists in Kalimantan Barat." M.A. thesis, Fuller Theological Seminary, School of World Mission, 1982.

Hussain, Akmal. "The Karachi riots of December 1986: Crisis of state and civil society in Pakistan." In *Mirrors of violence: Communities, riots and survivors in South Asia,* edited by Veena Das, 185–93. Delhi: Oxford University Press, 1990.

Huxley, Tim. "Disintegrating Indonesia? Implications for regional security." Adelphi Paper, 349. London: Oxford University Press for the International Institute for Strategic Studies, 2002.

ICG (International Crisis Group). "Indonesia: Overcoming murder and chaos in Maluku." Asia Report 10. Jakarta/Brussels: ICG, 2000.

———. "Communal violence in Indonesia: Lessons from Kalimantan." Asia Report 19. Jakarta/Brussels: ICG, 2001a.

———. "Indonesia: Violence and radical Muslims." Indonesia Briefing. Jakarta/Brussels: ICG, 2001b.

———. "Indonesia: Managing decentralisation and conflict in South Sulawesi." ICG Asia Report 60. Jakarta/Brussels: ICG, 2003a.

———. "The perils of private security in Indonesia: Guards and militias on Bali and Lombok." ICG Asia Report 67. Jakarta/Brussels: ICG, 2003b.

———. "Indonesia backgrounder: Jihad in Central Sulawesi." Jakarta/Brussels: ICG, 2004.

IDRD. "The role of adat in the Dayak and Madurese War." *Kalimantan Review,* English ed., 1999, 39–44.

Ikelegbe, Augustine. "The perverse manifestation of civil society: Evidence from Nigeria." *Journal of African Studies* 39, no. 1 (2001): 1–24

"Indonesia." In *Yearbook on international communist affairs 1967,* edited by M. M. Drachkovitch and L. H. Gann, 308–20. Palo Alto, Calif.: Hoover Institute Publications, 1968.

"The Insurrection on Java." In *Notices of the Indian Archipelago and adjacent countries,* edited by J. H. Moor, 147–62. London: Frank Cass & Co. Ltd., 1968 [orig. 1837].

Institut Dayakologi. *Amuk Sampit Palangkaraya.* Pontianak: Institut Dayakologi, 2001.

ISAI. *Maluku luka: Militer terlibat.* Jakarta: ISAI, 2000.

ISAI/IDRD. *Sisi gelap Kalimantan Barat: Perseteruan etnis Dayak-Madura 1997.* Jakarta: ISAI, 1999.

Ismail, Muhammad Gade. "Trade and state and power: Sambas (West Borneo) in the early nineteenth century." In *State and trade in the Indonesian Archipelago,* edited by G. J. Schutte, 141–49. Leiden: KITLV, 1994.

Jackson, James C. *Chinese in the West Borneo goldfields: A study in cultural geography.* Hull: University of Hull Publications, Occasional Papers in Geography, no. 15, 1970.

Jafar, H. Umar. "Gelar akbar budaya Melayu, Dayak dan Tionghoa." *Pontianak Post,* July 26, 2000.

Jatiman, Sardjono. "Dari kampung menjadi desa: Suatu studi pemerintahan desa di kabupaten Sambas Kalimantan Barat." Ph.D. dissertation, University of Indonesia, 1995.

Jenkins, David. "The last headhunt." *Far Eastern Economic Review,* June 30, 1978.

Job, Peter. "The bitter war in Kalimantan's jungles." *The Straits Times,* November 21, 1967.

Jones, Howard Palfrey. *Indonesia: The possible dream.* New York: Harcourt Brace Jovanovich, 1971.

Jones, Matthew. *Conflict and confrontation in South East Asia, 1961–1965: Britain, the United States and the creation of Malaysia.* Cambridge: Cambridge University Press, 2002.

Jones, Sidney. *Making money off migrants: The Indonesian exodus to Malaysia.* Hong Kong: Asia 2000 Ltd, 2000.

Kadir, L. H. "Indonesia merdeka (sejarah perjuangan aktual dan masa depan Kalimantan Barat)." Paper presented at the Lokakarya Dalam Rangka Memperingati 50 Tahun Indonesia Merdeka yang diselenggarakan oleh Keuskupan Sintang, October 3–6, 1995.

Kahin, Audrey R., and George McT. Kahin. *Subversion as foreign policy: The secret Eisenhower and Dulles debacle in Indonesia.* New York: The New Press, 1995.

Kahn, Joel. *Constituting the Minangkabau: Peasants, culture and modernity in colonial Indonesia.* Oxford: Berg, 1993.

Kalyvas, Stathis N. *The logic of violence in civil war.* Cambridge: Cambridge University Press, 2006.

Kapferer, Bruce. *Legends of people, myths of state: Violence, intolerance, and political culture in Sri Lanka and Australia.* Washington, D.C.: Smithsonian Institute, 1988.

Kaufman, Stuart J. *Modern hatreds: The symbolic politics of ethnic war.* Ithaca: Cornell University Press, 2001.

Keith, Michael. *Race, riots and policing: Lore and disorder in a multi-racist society.* London: UCL Press, 1993.

Kessler, Clive S. "Archaism and modernity: Contemporary Malay political culture." In *Fragmented vision: Culture and politics in contemporary Malaysia,* edited by Joel S. Kahn and Francis Loh Kok Wah, 133–57. North Sydney: Allen & Unwin, 1992.

King, Gary, Robert O. Kohane, and Sidney Verba. *Designing social inquiry: Scientific inference in qualitative research.* Princeton: Princeton University Press, 1994.

King, Victor T. *Ethnic classification and ethnic relations: A Borneo case study.* Hull, England: University of Hull, Centre for South-East Asian Studies, 1979.

———. *The Maloh of West Kalimantan.* Dordrecht, Holland: Foris Publications, 1985.

Kingsbury, Benedict. "'Indigenous peoples' as an international legal concept." In *Indigenous peoples of Asia,* edited by R. H. Barnes, Andrew Gray, and Benedict Kingsbury, 13–34. Ann Arbor: Association of Asian Studies, 1995.

Kingsbury, Damien. *Power politics and the Indonesian military.* London: RoutledgeCurzon, 2003.

Kipp, Rita. *Dissociated identities: Ethnicity, religion and class in an Indonesian society.* Ann Arbor: University of Michigan Press, 1993.

Klinken, Gerry van. "The Maluku wars: Bringing society back in." *Indonesia* 71 (2001): 1–26.

———. "Indonesia's new ethnic elites." In *Indonesia in search of transition,* edited by Henk Schulte Nordholt and Irwan Abdullah, 67–105. Yogyakarta: Pustaka Pelajar, 2002.

———. "Dayak ethnogenesis and conservative politics in Indonesia's Outer Islands." In *Indonesia in transition: Rethinking "civil society," "Region," and "Crisis,"* edited by Hanneman Samuel and Henk Schulte Nordholt, 107–28. Yogyakarta: Pustaka Pelajar, 2004.

———. "New actors, new identities: Post-Suharto ethnic violence in Indonesia." In *Violent internal conflicts in Asia Pacific: Histories, political economies and policies,* edited by Dewi Fortuna Anwar et al., 79–100. Jakarta: Yayasan Obor, 2005.

———. "Colonising Borneo: The creation of a Dayak province in Kalimantan." *Indonesia* 81 (2006): 23–50.

———. "Return of the Sultans." In *Revival of tradition in Indonesian politics: The deployment of adat from colonialism to indigenism,* edited by Jamie S. Davidson and David Henley, 149–69. London: Routledge, 2007.

Kristiansen, Stein. "Violent youth groups in Indonesia: The cases of Yogyakarta and Nusa Tenggara Barat." *Sojourn* 18, no. 1 (2003): 110–38.

Kroef, Justus M. van der. "Communism and Chinese communalism in Sarawak." *China Quarterly* 2, no. 20 (1964): 38–66.

———. "Indonesian communism since the 1965 coup." *Pacific Affairs* 43, no. 1 (1970): 34–60.

Kumar, Radha. "The troubled history of partition." *Foreign Affairs* 76 (1997): 22–34.

Laffan, Michael Francis. *Islamic nationhood and colonial Indonesia: The umma below the winds.* New York: Routledge, 2003.

Laitin, David D. *Hegemony and culture: Politics and religious change among the Yoruba.* Chicago: University of Chicago Press, 1986.

———. "National revivals and violence." *Journal of European Sociology* 36 (1995): 3–43.

Leigh, Michael. *The rising moon: Political change in Sarawak.* Sydney: Sydney University Press, 1974.

Lemarchand, René. *Burundi: Ethnocide as discourse and practice.* Washington, D.C.: Woodrow Wilson Center Press; New York, Cambridge University Press, 1994.

Lembaga Sedjarah PKI. *Pemberontakan nasional pertama di Indonesia (1926).* Jakarta: Jajasan Pembaruan, 1961.

Lev, Daniel S. "Indonesia 1965: The year of the coup." *Asian Survey* 6, no. 2 (1966a): 103–10.

———. *Transition to guided democracy: Indonesian politics, 1957–1959.* Ithaca: Cornell Modern Indonesia Project, 1966b.

———. Review of *Van Vollenhoven on Indonesian Adat Law,* edited by J. F. Holleman. *Journal of Legal Pluralism* 28 (1984): 147–55.

———. "Colonial law and the genesis of the Indonesian state." *Indonesia* 40 (1985): 57–74.

Levi, Jerome M., and Bartholomew Dean. Introduction to *At the risk of being heard: Identity, indigenous rights and postcolonial state,* edited by Bartholomew Dean and Jerome M. Levi, 1–44. Ann Arbor: University of Michigan Press, 2003.

Lewis, Peter. "Nigeria: Elections in a fragile regime." *Journal of Democracy* 14, no. 3 (2003): 131–44.

Leyden, Dr. "Sketch of Borneo." In *Notices of the Indian archipelago and adjacent countries,* edited by J. H. Moor, 93a–109a. London: Frank Cass & Co. Ltd., 1968 [orig. 1837].

Li, Tania Murray. "Marginality, power and production: Analysing upland transformation." In *Transforming the Indonesian uplands,* edited by Tania Murray Li, 1–44. Amsterdam: Harwood Academic Publishers, 1999.

———. "Articulating indigenous identities in Indonesia: Resource politics and the tribal slot." *Comparative Studies in Society and History* 42, no. 1 (2000): 149–79.

———. "Ethnic cleansing, recursive knowledge, and the dilemmas of sedantarism." *International Social Science Journal* 173 (2002): 361–71.

Liddle, R. William. *Ethnicity, party and national integration: An Indonesian case study.* New Haven: Yale University Press, 1970.

Liem Soei Liong. "It's the military, stupid!" In *Roots of violence in Indonesia: Contemporary violence in historical perspective,* edited by Freek Colombijn and J. Thomas Lindblad, 197-226. Leiden: KITLV Press, 2002.

Linder, Dianne. "Ethnic conflict in Kalimantan." ICE Case Studies, no. 11, November 1997. http://www.conflictrecovery.org/kalimantan.htm.

LMMDD-KT. *Konflik Etnik Sampit: Kronologi, Kesepakatan, Aspirasi Masyarakat, Analysis, Saran.* 2 vols. Palangkaraya: LMMDD-KT, 2001.

Locher-Scholten, Elsbeth. "Dutch expansion in the Indonesian archipelago around 1900 and the imperialism debate." *Journal of Southeast Asian Studies* 25, no. 1 (1994): 91-111.

Lyon, Margo L. *Bases of conflict in rural Java.* Berkeley: Center for South and Southeast Asia Studies, University of California, 1970.

Mabbett, Hugh, and Ping-ching Mabbett. "The Chinese community in Indonesia." In *The Chinese in Indonesia, the Philippines and Malaysia,* 3-15. London: Minority Rights Group, 1972.

MacDonald, Hamish, et al., eds. *Masters of terror: Indonesia's military and violence in East Timor in 1999.* Canberra: Strategic and Defence Studies Centre, Australian National University, 2002.

Mackie, J. A. C. *Konfrontasi: The Indonesia-Malaysia dispute, 1963-1966.* Kuala Lumpur: Oxford University Press, 1974.

———. "Anti-Chinese outbreaks in Indonesia, 1959-68." In *The Chinese in Indonesia: Five essays,* edited by J. A. C. Mackie, 77-138. Honolulu: University Press of Hawaii, 1976.

Maekawa, Kaori. "The Pontianak incidents and the ethnic Chinese in wartime Western Borneo." In *Southeast Asian minorities in the wartime Japanese empire,* edited by Paul H. Kratoska, 153-69. London: RoutledgeCurzon, 2002.

"Malaysia." In *Yearbook on International Communist Affairs, 1968,* edited by Richard F. Staar, 383-91. Palo Alto, Calif.: Hoover Institute Publications, 1969.

Mamdani, Mahmood. *When victims become killers: Colonialism, nativism and the genocide in Rwanda.* Princeton: Princeton University Press, 2001.

Mann, Michael. *The dark side of democracy: Explaining ethnic cleansing.* Cambridge: Cambridge University Press, 2005.

Matheson, Virginia. "Concepts of Malay ethos in indigenous Malay writings." *Journal of Southeast Asian Studies* 10, no. 2 (1979): 351-71.

McAdam, Doug, Sidney Tarrow, and Charles Tilly. *Dynamics of contention.* Cambridge: University of Cambridge Press, 2001.

McCarthy, John. "Changing to grey: Decentralization and the emergence of volatile socio-legal configurations in Central Kalimantan, Indonesia." *World Development* 32 (2004): 1199-223.

McPherson, Kenneth. *The Muslim microcosm: Calcutta, 1918 to 1935.* Wiesbaden: Franz Steiner Verlag, 1974.

McVey, Ruth T. *The rise of Indonesian communism.* Ithaca: Cornell University Press, 1965.

———. "The post-revolutionary transformation of the Indonesian army." *Indonesia* 11 (1971): 131–76; and 13 (1972): 147–81.

"Memoir of the residency of the north-west coast of Borneo." In *Notices of the Indian archipelago and adjacent countries,* edited by J. H. Moor, 5–12. London: Frank Cass & Co. Ltd, 1968 [orig. 1837].

Migdal, Joel S. *State and society: Studying how states and societies transform and constitute one another.* Cambridge: Cambridge University Press, 2001.

Miles, Douglas. *Cutlass and crescent moon: A case study of social and political change in Outer Indonesia.* Sydney: Centre for Asian Studies, University of Sydney, 1976.

Milner, Anthony C. *Kerajaan: Malay political culture on the eve of colonial rule.* Tucson: University of Arizona Press, 1982.

———. "Islam and the Muslim state." In *Islam in Southeast Asia,* edited by M. B. Hooker, 23–49. Leiden: E.J. Brill, 1983.

Moniaga, Sandra. "From *Bumiputera* to *Masyarakat Adat:* A long and confusing journey." In *Revival of tradition in Indonesian politics: The deployment of adat from colonialism to indigenism,* edited by Jamie S. Davidson and David Henley, 275–94. London: Routledge, 2007.

Mortimer, Rex. "Indonesia: Émigré post-mortems on the PKI." *Australian Outlook* 22, no. 3 (1968): 347–59.

———. *Indonesian communism under Sukarno: Ideology and politics, 1959–1965.* Ithaca: Cornell University Press, 1974.

Mukmin, Hidayat. *TNI dalam politik luar negeri: Studi kasus penyelesaian Konfrontasi Indonesia-Malaysia.* Jakarta: Pustaka Sinar Harapan, 1991.

Naimark, Norman M. *Fires of hatred: Ethnic cleansing in twentieth-century Europe.* Cambridge: Harvard University Press, 2001.

Nasution, General Dr. A. H. *Towards a people's army.* Jakarta: Delegasi, 1964.

Niezen, Ronald. *The origins of indigenism: Human rights and the politics of identity.* Berkeley: University California, 2003.

O'Connell, James. "The anatomy of a pogrom: An outline model with special reference to the Ibo of Northern Nigeria." *Race* 9, no. 1 (1967): 95–100.

O'Donnell, Guillermo. "Why the rule of law matters." *Journal of Democracy* 15, no. 4 (2004): 32–46.

Onghokham. "The inscrutable and the paranoid: An investigation into the sources of the Brotodiningrat affair." In *Southeast Asian transitions: Approaches through social history,* edited by Ruth T. McVey, 112–57. New Haven: Yale University Press, 1978.

O'Rourke, Kevin. *Reformasi: The Struggle for Power in Post-Soeharto Indonesia.* Crows Nest, Australia: Allen & Unwin, 2002.

Paden, John N. "Communal competition, conflict and violence in Kano." In *Nigeria: Modernization and the politics of communalism,* edited by Robert Melson and Howard Wolpe, 113–44. East Lansing: Michigan State University Press, 1971.

————. *Religion and political culture in Kano.* Berkeley: University of California Press, 1973.

Pandey, Gyanendra. *Remembering partition: Violence, nationalism, and history in India.* Cambridge: Cambridge University Press, 2001.

Parengkuan, August. *Kompas* (July–December 1971).

Parry, Richard Lloyd. *In the time of madness.* London: Jonathan Cape, 2005.

Peluso, Nancy Lee. "Fruit trees and family trees in an anthropogenic forest: Ethics of access, property zones, and environmental change in Indonesia." *Comparative Studies in Society and History* 38 (1996): 510–48.

————. "Passing the red bowl: Creating community through violence in West Kalimantan, 1967–1997." In *Violent conflicts in Indonesia: Analysis, representation, resolution,* edited by Charles A. Coppel, 205–45. New York: Routledge, 2006.

Peluso, Nancy Lee, and Emily Harwell. "Territory, custom and the cultural politics of ethnic war in West Kalimantan, Indonesia." In *Violent environments,* edited by Nancy Lee Peluso and Michael Watts, 83–116. Ithaca: Cornell University Press, 2001.

Penders, C. L. M., and Ulf Sundhaussen. *Abdul Haris Nasution: A political biography.* St. Lucia: University of Queensland Press, 1985.

Perry, Elizabeth J. "Collective violence in China, 1880–1980." *Theory and Society* 13, no. 3 (1984): 427–54.

Persadja. *Proces peristiwa Sultan Hamid II.* Jakarta: Fasco, 1955.

Persoon, Gerard. "Isolated groups or indigenous peoples: Indonesia and the international discourse." *Bijdragen tot de Taal-, land-, en Volkenkunde* 154, no. 2 (1998): 281–304.

Petebang, Edi, and Eri Sutrisno. *Konflik etnik di Sambas.* Jakarta: ISAI, 2000.

Petersen, Roger D. *Resistance and rebellion: Lessons from Eastern Europe.* Cambridge: Cambridge University Press, 2001.

————. *Understanding ethnic violence: Fear, hatred, and resentment in twentieth-century Eastern Europe.* Cambridge: Cambridge University, 2003.

Peterson, Robert. *Storm over Borneo.* London: Overseas Missionary Fellowship, 1968.

Pierson, Paul. "Not just what, but *when:* Timing and sequence in political processes." *Studies in American Political Development* 14 (Spring 2000): 72–92.

Plotnicov, Leonard. "An early Nigerian civil disturbance: The 1945 Hausa-Ibo riot in Jos." *The Journal of Modern African Studies* 9, no. 1 (1971): 297–305.

Poerwanto, Hari. *Orang Cina Khek dari Singkawang.* Depok: Komunitas Bambu, 2005.

Porritt, Veron L. *The Rise and fall of communism in Sarawak, 1940–1990.* Clayton: Monash Asia Institute, 2004.

Posen, Barry R. "The security dilemma and ethnic conflict." *Survival* 35 (1993): 27–47.

Posner, Daniel N. "The colonial origins of ethnic cleavages: The case of linguistic divisions in Zambia." *Comparative Politics* 35, no. 2 (2003): 127–46.

Poulgrain, Greg. *The genesis of Konfrontasi: Malaysia, Brunei, Indonesia, 1945–1965.* Bathurst, Australia: Crawford House Publishing, 1998.

Pour, Julius. *Benny Moerdani: Profil prajurit negarawan.* Jakarta: Yayasan Kejuangan Panglima Besar Sudirman, 1993.

Pringle, Robert. *Rajahs and rebels: The Ibans of Sarawak under Brooke Rule, 1841–1941.* Ithaca: Cornell University Press, 1970.

Prior, John Mansford. *Church and marriage in an Indonesian village.* Studies in the Intercultural History of Christianity, no. 55. Frankfurt am Main: Verlag Peter Lang 1988.

Purwana, Bambang Hendarta Suta. *Konflik antarkomunitas etnis di Sambas 1999: Suatu tinjauan sosial budaya.* Pontianak: Romeo Grafika Pontianak, 2003.

Rahman, Tariq. *Language and politics in Pakistan.* 2nd ed. Oxford: Oxford University Press, 1998.

Reeve, David. *Golkar of Indonesia: An alternative to the party system.* Singapore: Oxford University Press, 1985.

Reid, Anthony. *The Indonesian national revolution, 1945–1950.* Hawthorn, Australia: Longman, 1974.

——. "Understanding Melayu (*Malay*) as a source of diverse modern identities." In *Contesting Malayness: Malay identity across boundaries,* edited by Timothy P. Barnard, 1–24. Singapore: Singapore University Press, 2004.

Ricklefs, M. C. *A history of modern Indonesia since c. 1300.* 3rd ed. Basingstoke: Palgrave, 2001.

Riwut, Tjilik. *Kalimantan memanggil.* Djakarta: Endang, 1958.

——. *Kalimantan membangun.* Palangka Raya: n.p. 1979.

Robinson, Geoffrey. *The dark side of paradise: Political violence in Bali.* Ithaca: Cornell University Press, 1995.

Robinson, Kathryn. "History, houses and regional identities." *Australian Journal of Anthropology* 8, no. 1 (1997): 71–88.

Rokaerts, Mill. *Tanah Diri: Land rights of tribals.* Belgium: Pro Mundi Vita, 1985.

Roldán, Mary. *Blood and fire: La Violencia in Antioquia, Colombia, 1946–1953.* Durham: Duke University Press, 2002.

Roosa, John. *Pretext for mass murder: The September 30th Movement and Suharto's coup d'état in Indonesia.* Madison: University of Wisconsin Press, 2006.

Ross, Michael L. *Timber booms and institutional breakdown in Southeast Asia.* Cambridge: Cambridge University Press, 2001.

Rothchild, Donald, and Alexander J. Groth. "Pathological dimensions of domestic and international ethnicity." *Political Science Quarterly* 110, no. 1 (1995): 69–82.

Rousseau, Jerome. *Central Borneo: Ethnic identity and social life in a stratified society.* Oxford: Clarendon Press, 1990.

Rozhany, Masdan. "K'mantan Barat bicara dg bahasa pembangunan." *Utama,* March 3, 1973.

———. "Singkawang akan berkembang menjadi kota pariwisata di Kalimantan Barat?" *Utama,* April 4, 1973.

———. "Th. 1972 sebanyak 1,9 juta m3 kayu Kalbar diexport lewat pelabuhan Telok Air." *Utama,* April 5, 1973.

Rule, James. *Theories of civil violence.* Berkeley: University of California Press, 1988.

Ryter, Loren. "Medan gets a new mayor." *Inside Indonesia* 63 (2000).

Saad, Munawar M. *Sejarah konflik antar suku di kabupaten Sambas.* Pontianak: Kalimantan Persada Press, 2003.

Salim, Hairus, and Andi Achdian. *Amuk Banjarmasin.* Jakarta: YLBHI, 1997.

Sambanis, Nicholas. "A review of the recent advances and future directions in the quantitative literature on civil war." *Defence and Peace Economies* 13, no. 3 (2002): 215–43.

Samydorai, Sinapan. "Indonesia: The killing fields of West Kalimantan." Hong Kong, Human Rights Solidarity, Asian Human Rights Commission, 7, 2 (1997). http://www.hrsolidarity.net/mainfile.php/1997v0107n002.

Sangaji, Arianto. "TNI, Polri, milisi bersenjata dan kekerasan di Poso." Paper presented at KITLV Workshop, Leiden, August 4, 2004.

Saptono, Irawan. "Mass leaders and local bosses: The profiles of four actors." In *Indonesia's post-Soeharto democracy movement,* edited by Stanley Adi Prasetyo et al., 603–41. Jakarta: Demos, 2003.

Sarkar, Sumit. *Modern India, 1885–1947.* Delhi: Macmillan India Ltd., 1983.

Sarkar, Tanika. *Bengal 1928-1934: The politics of protest.* Delhi: Oxford University Press, 1987.

Schiller, A. Arthur. *The formation of federal Indonesia, 1945-1949.* The Hague: W. Van Hoeve, 1955.

Schiller, Anne, and Bambang Garang. "Religion and inter-ethnic violence in Indonesia." *Journal of Contemporary Asia* 32, no. 2 (2002): 244–54.

Schrauwers, Albert. *Colonial "reformation" in the highlands of Central Sulawesi, Indonesia, 1892–1995.* Toronto: Toronto University Press, 2000.

Schulte Nordholt, Henk. "A genealogy of violence." In *Roots of violence in Indonesia: Contemporary violence in historical perspective,* edited by Freek Colombijn and J. Thomas Lindblad, 33–62. Leiden: KITVL Press, 2000.

———. "Renegotiating boundaries: Access, agency, and identity in post-Soeharto Indonesia." *Bijdragen tot de Taal-, land-, en Volkenkunde* 159, no. 4 (2003): 550–89.

Schulte Nordholt, Nico G. "Violence and the anarchy of the modern Indonesian state." In *Violence and vengeance: Discontent and conflict in New Order*

Indonesia, edited by Frans Hüsken and Huub de Jonge, 52–70. Saarbrücken: Verlag für Entwicklungspolitik Saarbrücken GmbH, 2002.

Schumacher, Peter. "Soemadi's net thins out guerrillas." (*Weekly*) *Guardian,* August 21, 1971.

Sellato, Bernard. *Nomads of the Borneo rainforest: The economics, politics and ideology of settling down.* Translated by Stephanie Morgan. Honolulu: University of Hawaii Press, 1994 (org. ed. 1989).

Sewell, William H., Jr. "Three temporalities: Toward an eventful sociology." In *The historic turn in the human sciences,* edited by Terrence J. McDonald, 245–80. Ann Arbor: University of Michigan Press, 1996a.

——. "Historical events as transformations of structures: Inventing revolution at the Bastille." *Theory and Society* 25 (1996b): 841–81.

Shaheed, Farida. "The Pathan-Muhajir conflicts, 1985–6: A national perspective." In *Mirrors of violence: Communities, riots and survivors in South Asia,* edited by Veena Das, 194–214. Delhi: Oxford University Press, 1990.

Siahaan, Harlem. "Golongan Tionghoa di Kalimantan Barat." Jakarta: Leknas-LIPI, 1974.

——. "Konflik dan perlawanan kongsi Cina di Kalimantan Barat, 1770–1854." Ph.D. dissertation, University of Gadjah Mada, Yogyakarta, 1994.

Sidel, John T. "Macet Total: Logics of circulation and accumulation in the demise of Indonesia's New Order." *Indonesia* 66 (1998): 159–94.

——. "Riots, church burnings, conspiracies." In *Violence in Indonesia,* edited by Ingrid Wessel and Georgia Wimhofer, 49–63. Hamburg: Abera Verlag, 2001.

Sihbudi, Riza, and Moch. Murhasim, eds. *Kerusuhan sosial di Indonesia: Studi kasus Kupang, Mataram dan Sambas.* Jakarta: Grasindo, 2001.

Slater, Dan. "Indonesia's accountability trap: Party cartels and presidential power after democratic transition." *Indonesia* 78 (2004): 61–92.

Smith, Claire Q. "The roots of violence and prospects for reconciliation: A case study of ethnic conflict in Central Kalimantan, Indonesia." Social Development Papers, Conflict Prevention and Reconstruction, 23. Jakarta: World Bank, February 2005.

Smith, Glenn. "Carok violence in Madura: From historical conditions to contemporary manifestations." *Folk* 39 (1997): 57–76.

Snyder, Jack. *From voting to violence: Democratization and nationalist conflict.* New York: W. W. Norton & Company, 2000.

Snyder, Richard. "Scaling down: The subnational comparative method." *Studies in Comparative International Development* 36, no. 1 (2001): 93–110.

Soeharso, Asmarani, et al. "Jual beli di bawah tanah yang dilakukan oleh warga transmigrasi atas tahan pekarangan dan tanah pertanian di desa Pinang Luar, kecamatan Kubu Kabupaten daerah tingkat II Pontianak." Pontianak: University of Tanjung Pura, Law Faculty, 1992.

Soemadi. *Peranan Kalimantan Barat dalam menghadapi subversi komunis Asia Tenggara.* Pontianak: Yayasan Tanjungpura, 1974.

Soetrisno, Loekman, et al. *Laporan ahkir: Perilaku kekerasan kolektif: Kondisi dan pemicu.* Yogyakarta: Pusat Penelitian Pembangunan Pedesaan dan Kawasan, Universitas Gadjah Mada, and Departemen Agama Republik Indonesia, 1998.

"Speech of Baron Vander Capellen, on Resigning the Government of Netherland's India." In *Notices of the Indian archipelago and adjacent countries,* edited by J. H. Moor, 138–44. London: Frank Cass & Co. Ltd, 1968 [orig. 1837].

Spyer, Patricia. "Fire without smoke and other phantoms of Ambon's violence: Media effects, agency, and the work of imagination." *Indonesia* 74 (2002): 21–36.

Suara Independen. "Ordered out." *Inside Indonesia,* April–June 1997, 23.

Subianto, Benny. "Ethnic politics and the rise of the Dayak bureaucrats in local elections: Pilkada in six kabupatens in West Kalimantan." Paper presented at the "Workshop on PILKADA: The Local District Elections, Indonesia 2005," organized by the Indonesia Study Group, Asia Research Institute, National University of Singapore, May 17–18, 2006.

Subritzky, John. *Confronting Sukarno: British, American, Australian and New Zealand diplomacy in the Malaysian-Indonesian confrontation, 1961–65.* New York: St. Martin's Press, 1999.

Sudagung, Hendro Suroyo. *Mengurai pertikaian etnis: Migrasi swakarsa etnis Madura ke Kalimantan Barat.* Jakarta: ISAI, 2001.

Sukma, Rizal. "Ethnic conflict in Indonesia: Causes and the quest for solution." In *Ethnic conflicts in Southeast Asia,* edited by Kusuma Snitwongse and W. Scott Thompson, 1–41. Bangkok/Singapore: ISIS and ISEAS, 2005.

Suparlan, Parsudi. "Orang Madura dan Orang Dayak." *Tempo,* March 11, 2001.

———. *Hubungan Antar-Sukubangsa.* Jakarta: Yayasan Pengembangan Kajian Ilmu Kepolisian, 2004.

Surodjo, Benedicta A., and J. M. V. Soeparno. *TUHAN, pergunakanlah hati, pikiran dan tanganku: Pledoi Omar Dani.* Jakarta: PT Media Lintas Inti Nusantara untuk ISAI, 2001.

Suryadinata, Leo, Evi Nurvidya Arifin, and Aris Ananta. *Indonesia's population: Ethnicity and religion in a changing political landscape.* Singapore: ISEAS, 2003.

Tagliacozzo, Eric. "Kettle on a slow boil: Batavia's threat perceptions in the Indies' outer islands, 1870–1910." *Journal of Southeast Asian Studies* 31, no. 1 (2000): 70–100.

———. *Secret trades, porous borders: Smuggling and states along a Southeast Asian frontier, 1865–1915.* New Haven: Yale University Press, 2005.

Tajima, Yuhki. *Mobilizing for violence: The escalation and limitation of identity conflicts, the case of Lampung, Indonesia.* Jakarta: The World Bank, August 2004.

Tambiah, Stanley J. *Sri Lanka: Ethnic fratricide and the dismantling of democracy.* Chicago: University of Chicago Press, 1986.

———. *Leveling crowds: Ethnonationalist conflicts and collective violence in South Asia.* Berkeley: University of California Press, 1996.

Tanasaldy, Taufiq. "Ethnic identity politics in West Kalimantan." In *Renegotiating boundaries: Local politics in Post-Suharto Indonesia,* edited by Henk Schulte Nordholt and Gerry van Klinken, 349–72. Leiden: KITLV Press, 2007.

Tangdililing, Andreas Barung. "Perkawinan antar suku bangsa sebagai salah satu wahana pembauran bangsa: Studi kasus perkawinan antara orang Daya dengan keturuan Cina di kecamatan Samalantan, kabupaten Sambas, Kalimantan Barat." Ph.D. dissertation, University of Indonesia, 1993.

Tanter, Richard. "East Timor and the crisis of the Indonesian intelligence state." *Bulletin of Concerned Asian Scholars* 32, nos. 1 and 2 (2000): 73–82.

Tham, David. "The Brunei revolt." *Borneo 2000: Proceedings of the Sixth Biennial Borneo Research Conference,* edited by Michael Leigh, 135–47. Kuching: Universiti Malaysia Sarawak, 2000.

Thelen, Kathleen. "Historical institutionalism in comparative politics." *Annual Review of Political Science* 2 (1999): 369–404.

The Siauw Giap. "Rural unrest in West Kalimantan: The Chinese uprising in 1914." In *Leyden studies in Sinology,* edited by W. L. Idema, 138–52. Leiden: E. J. Brill, 1981.

Thomas, K. D., and J. Panglaykim. "The Chinese in the South Sumatran rubber industry: A case study in economic nationalism." In *The Chinese in Indonesia: Five essays,* edited by J. A. C. Mackie, 139–98. Honolulu: The University of Hawaii Press, 1976.

Tilly, Charles. *The politics of collective violence.* Cambridge: Cambridge University Press, 2003.

Tobing, K. *Kalimantan Barat.* Bandung: NV Masa Baru, ca. 1953.

Toer, Pramoedya Ananta. *This earth of mankind.* Translated by Max Lane. New York: Penguin Books, 1992 (orig. ed. 1980).

Touwen, Jeroen. *Extremes in the archipelago: Trade and economic development in the outer islands of Indonesia, 1900–1942.* Leiden: KITLV Press, 2001.

Ukiwo, Uhoka. "Politics and ethno-religious conflicts and democratic consolidation in Nigeria." *Journal of Modern African Studies* 41, no. 3 (2003): 115–38.

Ukur, Fridolin. *Tantang-djawab suku Dajak: Suatu penyelidikan tentang unsur2 jang menjekitari penolakan dan penerimaan Indjil dikalangan suku-Dajak dalam rangka sedjarah geredja di Kalimantan: 1835–1945.* Jakarta: BPK Gunung Mulia, 1971.

Usman, Syafaruddin. *Peristiwa Mandor: Sebuah tragedi dan misteri sejarah.* Pontianak: Romeo Grafika, 2000.

Usop, KMA M. *Pakat Dayak: Sejarah integrasi dan jatidiri masyarakat Dayak & daerah Kalimantan Tengah.* Palangkaraya: Yayasan Pendidikan dan Kebudayaan Batang Garing, 1994.

Utrecht, Ernest. "The Communist Party of Indonesia (PKI) since 1966." In *Ten years' military terror in Indonesia*, edited by Malcolm Caldwell, 275–95. Nottingham, England: Spokesman Books, 1975.

Varshney, Ashutosh. *Ethnic conflict and civic life: Hindus and Muslims in India*. New Haven: Yale University Press, 2002.

Verkaaik, Oskar. *Migrants and militants: Fun and urban violence in Pakistan*. Princeton: Princeton University Press, 2004.

Vickers, Adrian. "The new order: Keeping up appearances." In *Indonesia today: Challenges of history*, edited by Grayson Lloyd and Shannon Smith, 72–84. Singapore: ISEAS, 2001.

Wadley, Reed L. "Trouble on the frontier: Dutch-Brooke relations and Iban rebellion in the West Borneo Borderlands (1841–1886)." *Modern Asian Studies* 35, no. 3 (2001): 623–44.

———. "Lines in the forest: Internal territorialization and local accommodation in West Kalimantan, Indonesia (1865–1979)." *South East Asia Research* 11, no. 1 (2003): 91–112.

———. "Punitive expeditions and divine revenge: Oral and colonial histories of rebellion and pacification in Western Borneo, 1886–1902." *Ethnohistory* 51, no. 3 (2004): 609–36.

Wadley, Reed L., and F. Andrew Smith. "Dayak kings, Malay sultan, oral histories, and colonial archives: A comment on Djuweng (1999) and Sellato (1999)." *Borneo Research Bulletin* 32 (2001): 57–67.

Walhi Kalbar and Down to Earth. "Manis Mata dispute: The dispute between the indigenous community and PT Harapan Sawit Lestari Oil Palm Plantation Manis Mata, Ketapang District—West Kalimantan." Jakarta: Walhi National, 2000.

Walker, J. H. *Power and prowess: The origins of Brooke kingship in Sarawak*. Crows Nest, Australia: Allen & Unwin, 2002.

Walter, Barbara F. "Does conflict beget conflict? Explaining recurring civil war." *Journal of Peace Research* 41, no. 3 (2004): 371–88.

Wang Tai Peng. *The origins of Chinese kongsi*. Selangor Darul Ehsan, Malaysia: Pelanduk Publications, 1994.

Ward, Ken. *The 1971 election in Indonesia: An East Java case study*. Melbourne: Centre of Southeast Asian Studies, Monash University, 1974.

Ward, Marion W., and R. Gerard Ward. "An economic survey of West Kalimantan." *Bulletin of Indonesian Economic Studies* 10, no. 3 (1974): 26–53.

Wardoyo, Emanuel Lalang. "Local community empowerment: Experiences of the YPR and YPK." In *Indonesia's post-Soeharto democracy movement*, edited by Stanley Adi Prasetyo et al., 287–306. Jakarta: Demos, 2003.

Weingast, Barry R. "Constructing trust: The political and economic roots of ethnic and regional conflict." In *Institutions and social order*, edited by Karol Soltan et al., 163–200. Ann Arbor: University of Michigan Press, 1998.

Weinstein, Franklin B. *Indonesia abandons confrontation: An inquiry into the functions of Indonesian foreign policy.* Ithaca: Cornell Modern Indonesia Project, 1969.

Wessel, Ingrid. "The politics of violence in New Order Indonesia in the last decade of the 20th century." In *Violence in Indonesia,* edited by Ingrid Wessel and Georgia Wimhofer, 64–81. Hamburg: Abera Verlag, 2001.

Wiessner, S. "Rights and status of indigenous peoples: A global comparative and international legal analysis." *Harvard Human Rights Journal* 12 (1999): 57–128.

Wilkinson, Steven I. *Votes and violence: Electoral competition and ethnic riots in India.* Cambridge: Cambridge University Press, 2004.

Williams, Ada, and Lionel Rosenblatt. "Few options for Madurese IDPs in West Kalimantan." *Refugees International,* March 29, 2002.

Williams, Jeff. "Where the innocent are also victims." *The Straits Times,* November 21, 1967.

Wilmer, Franke. *The indigenous voice in world politics: Since time immemorial.* New Park: Sage Publications, 1993.

Wilson, Ian. "Continuity and change: The changing contours of organized violence in post–New Order Indonesia." *Critical Asian Studies* 38, no. 1 (2006): 265–97.

Wiyata, A. Latief. *Carok: Konflik kekerasan dan harga diri orang Madura.* Yogyakarta: LKIS, 2002.

Wood, Elisabeth Jean. *Insurgent collective action and civil war in El Salvador.* Cambridge: Cambridge University Press, 2003.

World Bank. *Village justice in Indonesia: Case studies on access to justice, village democracy and governance.* Jakarta: World Bank, 2004.

Yanis, M. *Kapal terbang sembilan: Kisah pendudukan Jepang di Kalimantan Barat.* Pontianak: Yayasan Perguruan Panca Bhakti, 1983.

———. *Djampea: Novel sejarah perjuangan rakyat Kalimantan Barat.* Pontianak: Dewan Kesenian Kalimantan Barat, Badan Penerbit Universitas Tanjungpura, 1998.

Yashar, Deborah. "Democracy, indigenous movements, and the postliberal challenge in Latin America." *World Politics* 52, no. 1 (1999): 76–104.

Yuan Bingling. *Chinese democracies: A study of the Kongsis of West Borneo (1776–1884).* Leiden: University of Leiden, 2000.

Index

NEW PERSPECTIVES IN
SOUTHEAST ASIAN STUDIES

From Rebellion to Riots: Collective Violence on Indonesian Borneo
Jamie S. Davidson

Pretext for Mass Murder: The September 30th Movement and
Suharto's Coup d'État in Indonesia
John Roosa

Việt Nam: Borderless Histories
Edited by Nhung Tuyet Tran and Anthony Reid